RECORDS OF CIVILIZATION

SOURCES AND STUDIES

EDITED UNDER THE AUSPICES OF THE

DEPARTMENT OF HISTORY, COLUMBIA UNIVERSITY

NUMBER XXVI

SEVEN BOOKS OF HISTORY AGAINST THE PAGANS

SEVEN BOOKS OF HISTORY
AGAINST THE PAGANS

The Apology of Paulus Orosius

Translated with Introduction
and Notes by

IRVING WOODWORTH RAYMOND

ASSISTANT PROFESSOR OF HISTORY
COLUMBIA UNIVERSITY

NEW YORK : MORNINGSIDE HEIGHTS
COLUMBIA UNIVERSITY PRESS
M·CM·XXXVI

FOREIGN AGENTS

OXFORD UNIVERSITY PRESS
HUMPHREY MILFORD, AMEN HOUSE
LONDON, E.C.4, ENGLAND

KWANG HSUEH PUBLISHING HOUSE
140 PEKING ROAD
SHANGHAI, CHINA

MARUZEN COMPANY, LTD.
6 NIHONBASHI, TORI-NICHOME
TOKYO, JAPAN

OXFORD UNIVERSITY PRESS
B. I. BUILDING, NICOL ROAD
BOMBAY, INDIA

PRINTED IN THE UNITED STATES OF AMERICA

To My Mother and Father
MARION WOODWORTH RAYMOND
WILLIAM WISE RAYMOND
WITH LOVE AND GRATITUDE

PREFACE

 OROSIUS belonged to an age of controversy. Paganism, severely wounded when Constantine and his house adopted Christianity as the religion of the court and state, was by no means dead. Large numbers still refused to follow the new Christ and clung, more perhaps with sentiment than conviction, to the old gods. In their hatred of the new faith, leading pagans appealed to the emotions and credulity of the Roman people and tried to persuade them that their misfortunes and calamities were due to the abandonment of the ancient gods and rites. The stark misery and violence of the age gave strong support to this outcry. The Visigoths had captured Rome, the barbarians were ravaging the provinces, and the Romans were slaughtering one another in civil wars. These ills seemed to follow directly upon the apostasy of the emperors. The Christians could not refuse to answer so serious a charge. St. Augustine labored long years to produce a refutation in his *De civitate Dei*. But he did not feel that the philosophical arguments advanced in the eleven books he had already written sufficiently met the crisis nor that he should wait to complete the remaining books of his apology before more adequately answering the challenge of his adversaries. He thereupon requested his friend Orosius to prepare with the least possible delay an apology offering a factual demonstration of his thesis. In little more than a year Orosius completed a work of more than three hundred pages. He drew examples from the entire history of the world to prove the falsity of the pagan accusation and the truth of St. Augustine's position. So was born his work, the *Seven Books of History against the Pagans*.

This "apologia" later became a standard history. Its fame

and importance lie less in its own merits than in the influence it exerted upon later generations. As the first continuous history of the world written from a Christian point of view, medieval students preferred it to world histories written by pagans. To study history was to read Orosius. For a thousand years his facts and prejudices informed and shaped the medieval mind. The popularity of the work, attested in hundreds of manuscripts, survived the decline of the Middle Ages and the advent of printing. In fact, the text was one of the earliest histories printed in a vernacular language. New and improved texts in Latin appeared repeatedly. Other philosophies of history, however, finally won support, and the *Seven Books* lost their popularity. But the work had achieved for itself a secure place in the history of history. Whenever anyone studies that subject, Orosius lives again, trying to persuade the reader to view history as he saw it.

In the preparation of this translation—the first and only complete translation in any language—I have been blessed with kind friends. Dr. C. S. Ogden, who many years ago began a translation for the *Records of Civilization,* has with great generosity placed at my disposal his rendering of the seventh book. I have made free use of his excellent translation. Professor Jacob Hammer of Hunter College kindly reviewed the greater part of my first draft. His suggestions for improvement have been invaluable. My colleagues in Columbia, Professors Clinton W. Keyes and Dino Bigongiari, Doctor Moses Hadas, and Miss Margaret Bancroft have cleared up for me many obscure passages of the text. I am much indebted to Professor J. B. Brebner, Dr. Jacques Barzun, and Mr. June Mussey for suggestions as to style and wording. My brother, Carrington Raymond, has read the entire translation and given me the benefit of his scholarly criticism. Miss Theresia Miller has graciously allowed me to reprint the map from the volumes of maps published by her uncle, the late Professor Konrad Miller. To Professor

Austin P. Evans goes my sincere gratitude, not only for inviting me to make the translation but also for his painstaking
care in editing the manuscript.

IRVING WOODWORTH RAYMOND

COLUMBIA UNIVERSITY
January 30, 1936

CONTENTS

INTRODUCTION

OROSIUS, although a prominent person in his day, received scant written notice from his contemporaries.[1] Nor did he tell much about himself in his own writings. It is therefore possible to piece together from fragmentary materials only the barest outline of his life. He was born in the eighties of the fourth century after Christ, perhaps about 385.[2] The place of his birth has long been in dispute.[3] Some critics have thought that his native city was Tarraco, for Orosius says "throughout various provinces there exist today poor and insignificant settlements situated in the ruins of great cities, which still bear evidences of their names and tokens of their misfortunes. *Our* own city of Tarraco in Spain is one of these and we can point to it to comfort ourselves over our recent misery." [4] Since it is true that Orosius frequently used an editorial "we" for "I," these authorities would read "*my* Tarraco" for "*our* Tarraco" and thus they consider Tarraco his birthplace. Yet if this passage is seen in relation to its whole

---

[1] His surname, Paulus, was first mentioned by Jordanes in his *Getica* according to M. Schanz, *Geschichte der römischen Litteratur,* VIII, Pt. iv, 2 (Munich, 1920), 483, footnote 1; but H. Sauvage, *De Orosio* (Paris, 1874), p. 6, maintains that the name gained circulation first in the thirteenth century. T. Mörner, *De Orosii vita eiusque historiarum libris septem adversus paganos* (Berlin, 1844), p. 17, footnote 1, takes the same position; Spaniards to this day frequently have only one name. Cf. P. B. Gams, *Die Kirchengeschichte von Spanien* (Regensburg, 1864), II, Pt. 1, 399.

[2] J. A. Davids, *De Orosio et Sancto Augustino Priscillianistarum adversariis, commentatio historica et philologica* (Rotterdam, 1930), p. 11. This estimate is based on the fact that St. Augustine, who was sixty in the spring of A.D. 415, when he wrote to St. Jerome, speaks of Orosius as "iuvenem, qui filius suus esse posset."

[3] Mörner, *op. cit.,* p. 17, footnote 2, mentions many of these authorities. No source definitely states where Orosius was born.

[4] Orosius vii. 22. 8. "Exstant adhuc per diversas provincias in magnarum urbium ruinis parvae et pauperes sedes, signa miseriarum et nominum indicia servantes, ex quibus nos quoque in Hispania Tarraconem nostram ad consolationem miseriae recentis ostendimus."

context, another interpretation is possible and indeed prefer-
able. The patriotic Orosius was here telling the people of the
entire Roman world that this Spain, too, had its devastated
towns and districts. Naturally Tarraco came to his mind both
because it had recently been ravaged by barbarians and because
as a provincial capital it was one of the leading cities of Hispania.[5] He might just as well have selected any other plundered city of his native land to illustrate his remark. Certainly
this single passage (and this is the only evidence) is insufficient
to warrant any assertion that Tarraco was the birthplace of
Orosius.

Indeed there is far stronger evidence to support the
claim of Bracara.[6] It was from this city of western Hispania
that Orosius set out for the shores of Africa where he met
St. Augustine.[7] Then, too, when Avitus, a citizen of Bracara,
met Orosius in Palestine, he spoke of him "as my beloved son
and fellow presbyter" and also gave him certain relics of the
protomartyr St. Stephen to deliver to Palchonius, the bishop
of Bracara.[8] Furthermore, Braulio (A.D. 631–651), the archbishop of Caesaraugusta, mentioned Orosius as one of the
illustrious men of Gallaecia, the division of Hispania Tarraconensis in which Bracara was located.[9] Such evidence, though

[5] Davids, op. cit., p. 12.

[6] The controversy with regard to his birthplace involves national pride.
Bracara is in Portugal and Tarraco in Spain.

[7] "Nam inde ad nos usque ab oceani littore properavit." St. Augustine Ep.
166 in J. P. Migne, Patrologiae cursus completus, Series Latina (Paris, 1841),
XXXIII, 721. "Qui ad nos ab ultima Hispania, id est, ab oceani littore . . .
advenit." St. Augustine Ep. 169 in Migne, PL, XXXIII, 748. "The shore of the
ocean" is used in the sense in which an Easterner speaks of a city "on the Pacific
coast." The city may be inland as Bracara was.

[8] "Primum ut dilectissimus filius et compresbyter meus Orosius usque ad has
partes ab Africanis episcopis mitteretur, cuius mihi charitas et consolatio ves-
tram omnium praesentiam reddidit." Letter of Avitus to Palchonius, Migne, PL,
XLI, 806. There is some dispute whether these words were spoken by the same
Avitus who had left Bracara to join St. Jerome in Palestine. Davids is convinced that they were, and not by some other Avitus. Cf. Davids, op. cit., p.
14; see also Gams, Kirchengeschichte, II, Pt. 1, 399–400. For delivery of relics,
see Migne, PL, XI, 809.

[9] Migne, PL, LXXX, 698–99: "ex ea [sc. provincia quam incolitis] ortos
fuisse recordamini elegantissimos et doctissimos viros . . . Orosius presbyterum . . ."

it is not conclusive, leads one to believe that Bracara probably was his birthplace.

Only a few definite statements can be made about Orosius's early life in Hispania. He became a presbyter,[10] a title which in this instance seems to signify "parish priest." He also took prominent part in the heated controversies then raging in the peninsula over the teachings of the Priscillianists and Origenists. His own writings and other sources show clearly that he was well educated in both pagan and Christian culture. He had made a thorough study of the classical authors of Rome —Vergil, Horace, and Cicero—and had undergone sound training in the rhetorical schools. He had also attained a strong grasp of Christian principles and had won a general reputation as one well grounded in the faith.

When Orosius was nearly thirty years old, he left his native country.[11] Barbarian invaders, the Alans and Vandals, were ravaging the land and compelled him to flee for safety.[12] Probably his forced departure only hastened his purpose to seek elsewhere for counsel and instruction to help him in the struggles against the heresies that he was fighting so zealously. Orosius himself would have it believed that he took ship for an unknown destination under no compulsion at all, but that his ship was overtaken by a storm and driven under the guidance of Providence to the shores of Africa near Hippo, where St. Augustine was then living.[13] These hospitable shores, as well as their greatest citizen, welcomed him as a fellow Roman and Christian.[14]

[10] Mörner, op. cit., p. 19.

[11] Idem, p. 19.

[12] Orosius iii. 20. 6, 7. "Si quando de me ipso refero, ut ignotos primum barbaros viderim . . . ," a vivid description apparently told in the language of an eye witness.

[13] Orosius, Consultatio sive commonitorium Orosii ad Augustinum de errore Priscillianistarum et Origenistarum. "Ad te per Deum missus sum; de te per eum spero, dum considero qualiter actum est, quod huc venirem. Agnosco cur venerim; sine voluntate, sine necessitate, sine consensu de patria egressus sum, occulta quadam vi actus, donec in istius terrae littus allatus sum." Migne, PL, XLII, 666.

[14] Orosius v. 2. 2. "Nunc me Africa tam libenter excepit quam confidenter accessi . . ."

St. Augustine regarded his coming as providential. His own words give a clear picture of the impression that Orosius made upon him.

Behold, a religious young man has come to me, by name Orosius, who is in the bond of the Catholic peace a brother, in the point of age a son, and in honor a fellow presbyter—a man of quick understanding, ready speech, and burning zeal, desiring to be in the Lord's house a vessel rendering useful service in refuting those false and pernicious doctrines, through which the souls of men in Spain have suffered much more grievous wounds than have been inflicted on their bodies by the sword of the barbarians. For from the remote western coast of Spain he has come with eager haste to us, having been prompted to do this by the report that from me he could learn whatever he wished on the subjects concerning which he desired information.[15]

At St. Augustine's request for a statement of what the heretics were preaching, Orosius soon after his arrival composed the treatise, *Consultatio sive commonitorium de errore Priscillianistarum et Origenistarum,* and presented it to him. St. Augustine at once replied in his *Librum ad Orosium contra Priscillianistas et Origenistas.*[16] Orosius appears to have tarried about a year at the side of his master, who at that time was hard at work composing his great apologetic masterpiece, *De civitate Dei,* of which he had already finished the first five books. Orosius, now highly regarded by St. Augustine, undertook to deliver to St. Jerome various treatises and letters.[17] The great fathers had not always agreed in controversial matters, and St. Augustine now decided that this was a rare opportunity to consult the master scholar and, incidentally, by soothing the exceedingly sensitive Jerome with some flattering words to secure his support in the controversies raging at the time. No doubt there were also verbal messages of a personal nature and much to report on the general situation in Africa. The Pelagian controversy was at that time troubling Africa as well as other parts of the Empire, and the

[15] St. Augustine *Ep.* 166. 1. 2 in Migne, *PL,* XXXIII, 720–21. This translation has been taken from *A Select Library of the Nicene and Post-Nicene Fathers of the Christian Church* (New York, 1907), First Series, I, 523.
[16] Davids, *op. cit.,* p. 17. [17] *Ibid.,* pp. 17–24.

African bishops wanted to keep St. Jerome informed as to what was happening.[18] St. Augustine also wished to warn St. Jerome that certain false friends were attacking him behind his back. Orosius, furthermore, knowing of St. Jerome's mastery of the problem of the origin of the human soul (Orosius had not been satisfied by St. Augustine on this point), desired to consult him in order to set his own mind at rest. St. Augustine wrote of Orosius when the latter was about to leave:

I have taught him all that I could, and as for the things which I could not teach him, I have told him from whom he may learn them and have exhorted him to go on to you. As he received this counsel, or rather injunction, of mine with pleasure and with the intention of complying with it, I asked him to visit us on his way home to his own country when he comes from you.[19]

In the spring of 415, Orosius journeyed to Palestine by way of Egypt.[20] After performing his devotions in the sacred shrines of Christianity, he went to Bethlehem, where he met St. Jerome, who speaks of him as "that honorable man, my brother and your Excellency's son, the presbyter Orosius [whom] I have, both on his account and in obedience to your request, made welcome . . ."[21] The learned doctor was then so busy with the Pelagian controversy and with his quarrel with John, the bishop of Jerusalem, that he could not find the time to consider the difficulties propounded by St. Augustine.[22] Orosius at once threw himself heart and soul into these controversies, particularly the one raging over the teachings of Pelagius. Upon invitation of the bishops, he attended a council at Jerusalem and there set forth what St. Augustine and St. Jerome had written about Pelagianism. He

---

[18] Davids, *op. cit.*, p. 23.

[19] St. Augustine *Ep.* 166. 1. 2. The translation is taken from Schaff's edition, p. 523.

[20] Orosius vi. 15. 32 speaks of the chests of books he saw there.

[21] St. Augustine *Ep.* 122 in Migne, *PL*, XXXIII, 752. "Virum honorabilem fratrem meum, filium Dignationis tuae, Orosium presbyterum, et sui merito, et te jubente suscepi."

[22] F. Cavallera, *Saint Jérôme, sa vie et son œuvre* (Paris, 1922), I, Pt. 1, pp. 323–27. This volume belongs to the series, "Spicilegium sacrum Lovaniense, Études et documents," fascicule 1.

became involved in a quarrel with John, the presiding bishop
and a friend of Pelagius, over what had been said in an
address. John charged him with blasphemy. What John had
heard was not what had actually been said, but what the inter-
preter thought had been said. In his book, *Liber apologeticus,*
Orosius has described these controversies at length.[23] He did
not attend the Council of Diospolis in December of that
year [24] but wrote the above apology to defend and justify
his own conduct and at the same time to set forth all the
teachings of St. Augustine and St. Jerome on the matter in
dispute.

Early in 416, Orosius set out on his homeward voyage.
He had various commissions to execute. He had a short letter from St. Jerome and his treatise against the Pelagians to
deliver to St. Augustine; there were some of the relics of St.
Stephen, together with an explanatory letter that gave a
Latin version of their discovery by Lucian, to be placed in the
safekeeping of Palchonius, the bishop of Bracara; there was
a letter of his fellow citizen Avitus to that same bishop; and
lastly there were the letters of Heros of Arles and Lazarus
of Aix, which later were read to the bishops assembled at
the Council of Carthage.[25] It is uncertain whether Orosius
went directly to Africa or first to the island of Minorca and
then to Africa. Because of St. Augustine's urgent request, he
probably went to Africa first. After delivering his letters and
messages, he sailed for home by way of Minorca, which
boasted one of the finest harbors in the Mediterranean, Mago,
the present Port Mahon. After he had stayed there some time,
he made ready to depart for Spain, but when he learned
from reports that barbarians were overrunning that land, he
was forced to change his plans.[26] He left his relics in care of
a church on the island and sailed back to Africa,[27] where he

---

[23] *Liber apologeticus contra Pelagium,* in C. Zangemeister's edition of Orosius
in *Corpus scriptorum ecclesiasticorum Latinorum* (Vienna, 1882), V, 603–64.
[24] Davids, *op. cit.,* p. 26.   [25] Schanz, *op. cit.,* p. 484.
[26] Davids, *op. cit.,* pp. 26–27.
[27] Severus *Epistola ad omnem ecclesiam* 3, in Migne, *PL,* XLI, 823. The relics
soon became famous for their power in working miracles, one of which, the

rejoined St. Augustine. At the latter's request, he began his famous treatise against the pagans. After he had finished this work in 418, Orosius disappeared from view.[28]

Gams vividly describes this:

The zealous, pious, energetic, and brilliant youth, who as a mature man under favorable circumstances might have attained the fame of a Jerome and an Augustine, had flashed by like a meteor. We seek further traces of him and it grieves us not to discover them. But even so we may call him happy. He hurried by as in flight, and yet his memory remains blessed for all time.[29]

The lasting reputation of Orosius rests chiefly upon his famous *Seven Books of History against the Pagans.* His own words well describe the purpose of this apology and the circumstances in which he undertook it.

You [St. Augustine] bade me reply to the empty chatter and perverseness of those who, aliens to the City of God, are called "pagans" *(pagani)* because they come from the countryside *(ex pagis)* and crossroads of the rural districts, or "heathen" *(gentiles)* because of their wisdom in earthly matters. Although these people do not seek out the future and moreover either forget or know nothing of the past, nevertheless they charge that the present times are unusually beset with calamities for the sole reason that men believe in Christ and worship God while idols are increasingly neglected. You bade me, therefore, discover from all the available data of histories and annals whatever instances past ages have afforded of the burdens of war, the ravages of disease, the horrors of famine, of terrible earthquakes, extraordinary floods, dreadful eruptions of fire, thunderbolts and hailstorms, and also instances of the cruel miseries caused by parricides and disgusting crimes.[30]

Such also was the theme of the third book of the *City of God,* in which, after discussing the moral and spiritual evils that the gods of the pagans had not checked but rather had caused, St. Augustine described those bodily and material afflictions that alone the pagan world regarded as serious— famine, pestilence, war, pillage, captivity, massacre, and like calamities. Not satisfied with the series of examples that he

---

conversion of many Jews, is mentioned. Gams, *Kirchengeschichte,* II, Pt. 1, 406–7, discusses the whole question. [28] Davids, *op. cit.,* p. 28. [29] *Kirchengeschichte,* II, Pt. 1, 411. [30] Dedication, p. 30.

had drawn wholly from Roman history, from its Trojan origin to the birth of Christ, he requested Orosius to prove the thesis by citing examples from the entire history of the world and, so far as Rome was concerned, to carry the story from the birth of Christ to his own day. He himself was too busy at work on his great treatise, of which eleven books had already appeared, to undertake the preparation of this more complete proof.[31] His request was also seconded by one Julian of Carthage.[32]

Orosius set to work upon his apology in a spirit of humility. He was conscious of his own lack of historical training and was somewhat overwhelmed at the confidence that his beloved father in Christ had reposed in him. The basic principles upon which he founded his philosophy of history were those which he held in common with his guide and friend St. Augustine. Orosius did not develop intricate and closely reasoned arguments to support these beliefs; on the contrary he was usually content either to state his principles as truths convincing in themselves or to give simple and direct arguments to win his stubborn adversaries. For materials to illustrate his thesis, he drew upon the whole record of human acts, thoughts, and feelings from the time of Adam to his own day. The Christian Revelation in its earlier unfolding in Hebrew history and in its later development in the Church was the focus of his philosophy of history. History for Orosius, as for Augustine, was "the whole course of social happenings in time, in relation to a timeless Deity." [33]

As a man of religion, Orosius was deeply aware of the existence of God and of His presence in His creation. The reasons why God should create a world and man in it were not stated by Orosius. The will of God was unsearchable. It could only be stated that God had created this world and in it had placed man without sin. Adam and his generation, however, had fallen into sin and thus estranged the relations

---

[31] Dedication, p. 6.   [32] Ibid., p. 30.

[33] J. N. Figgis, The Political Aspects of S. Augustine's "City of God" (London, 1921), p. 39.

between God and the human society that He had created.[34] The consequences of man's fall were twofold: (1) man thenceforth inherited original sin with its tendency to induce acts contrary to Divine standards of conduct; (2) God was compelled to restrain and discipline man by punishments intended for his good. Whatever evils there were in the world were therefore either the open sins of man or the hidden punishments of God.

Since mankind everywhere was tainted with original sin, it followed that the disasters and evils that afflicted the human race were world-wide. Orosius, therefore, felt compelled to describe the geography of the whole world in order to furnish the proper setting for his drama. The meaning of this drama was the attempt of God to win the soul of a corrupt human being who had been given the power to accept or to reject God's help. The devil also was an actor in this drama, but apparently his influence was less powerful in shaping conduct than those strong desires of man's unregenerate nature. God was no mere spectator in this struggle. Though His grant of free will to man somewhat limited His action, yet to accomplish some purpose He frequently intervened in the mundane order. He was a God of mercy as well as of justice.

Just as God provided for the physical side of man by fashioning and adorning the world with plant and animal life that must share the fortunes of man, so too He took measures to insure the development of his social nature. Governments were established to regulate his activities, and laws were enacted to guide his conduct. Four great empires which furnished the background of the drama of salvation had been supreme in separate ages—the Babylonian, the Macedonian, the African, and the Roman. The first and last of these, that is, the Babylonian and the Roman, were the greatest; the other two served only as guardians and trustees for them. The first three empires came to an end at an appointed time after they had played their historic rôles. The number seven

[34] Compare, p. 48.

apparently had a distinct effect upon their destiny. The future lay with the Church, which would make life livable so long as the Roman Empire survived.

In these successive settings man worked out his earthly lot. Original sin made his entire history prior to the Incarnation inevitably a record of disaster and of suffering. Human nature was dominated by its less noble traits. Man was fickle, obstinate, intemperate, heedless, superstitious, lustful, proud, cruel, greedy, and pugnacious. These traits caused the specific ills that made human life so hideous and horrible throughout the course of history. Balancing these bad traits were those of moderation, peacefulness, modesty, humility, honor, courage, and reverence. These traits, however, were none too common. In the past man was bad from deliberate choice. He was not stupid but stubborn; he knew the good but refused to admit or to follow it. God in His mercy, therefore, had to chastise him as He would chastise a child in order to make him mend his ways and thereby to restore him to his former heritage of sonship and grace.

Unlike the modern philosopher who sees that "history is of blood and tears, of helpless blundering, of wild revolt, of stupid acquiescence, of empty aspirations" with nothing but darkness in the end,[35] Orosius saw in the long record of human failure and human misery a prelude to better times and to a future life of peace. God had not abandoned His creation, but rather had guided its development toward a definite end. The three earlier empires, begun in warfare and bloodshed, culminated in the Roman Empire, which furnished a perfect setting for God's manifestation in Christ to the world. This took place at the most auspicious time, that is, in the reign of Caesar Augustus, when peace reigned over all the earth and the Roman Empire covered most of the regions of the world.

The coming of Christ ushered in a new era of world history. The noble traits of human nature received reinforce-

[35] A. Balfour, *Foundations of Belief* (New York, 1902), pp. 29-31.

ments in their battle for supremacy over the ignoble. The Christian now had both an ideal of conduct and the means in sacramental grace to enable him to reach that ideal. The pagans now strove mightily to crush the followers of the Christ. They directed ten persecutions against the Christians. In retaliation God sent nine punishments upon the pagans, reserving the tenth for a later time. The presence of Christians among the pagans mitigated God's wrath and His punishments. Indeed Christian times were better in contrast to those of the past; the vividness of present suffering alone warped judgment in these matters. In truth, by comparison past ages were the more wretched the further they were removed from the balm of true religion. The Christian faith alone saved the Empire from a worse fate at the hands of the barbarians, who at times acted as scourges of God. At the close of his apology, Orosius summed up his belief in the salutary rôle of Christianity:

My description, I think, has shown not more by words than by my guiding finger, that countless wars have been stilled, many usurpers destroyed, and most savage tribes checked, confined, incorporated, or annihilated with little bloodshed, with no real struggle, and almost without loss. It remains for our detractors to repent of their endeavors, to blush on seeing the truth, and to believe, to fear, to love, and to follow the one true God, Who can do all things and all of Whose acts (even those which they think evil) they have found to be good.[36]

The whole course of history now is seen to have been and is proved to have been providential. God had guided its course through a succession of empires to its culmination in the Roman Empire and now, with the gradual decline of that Empire, had come the triumph of the Church.

Though St. Augustine's *De civitate Dei* furnished the inspiration and philosophic basis of the *Seven Books of History against the Pagans,* Orosius did not use this treatise very extensively. To have done so would have defeated the very purpose of writing his apology, namely, to prepare a supplement giving more extended proof of the main thesis of St.

[36] Orosius vii. 43. 17-19.

Augustine's third book. Orosius, to be sure, took his data for Roman history from many of the books which his preceptor had used, that is, from Livy, Florus, and Eutropius;[37] the use of these common authorities produced some similarity in the two apologies, but Orosius used these sources directly and not through the medium of St. Augustine's work.

When faced with the task of writing a history of the world from its origin to his own day, Orosius did what a modern historian usually does in similar circumstances: he first consulted other world histories in contemporary use, and, when these were too brief or inadequate, turned for further material to the standard histories of particular countries. He divided his history into seven books. The first extends from the creation of the world to the founding of Rome, the second to the conquest of Rome by the Gauls and to the battle of Cunaxa, the third ends with the wars of the Diadochi, the fourth treats of the Pyrrhic wars as far as the destruction of Carthage, the fifth extends to the Slave War, the sixth covers the period to Augustus and the birth of Christ, and the seventh describes the history from then to his own day. For the period before the rise of the great empires of the Near East, Orosius did not have any of the elaborate and scientific studies such as anthropologists have placed at the disposal of modern historians. Indeed he complained that most historians either had neglected or had not known the history of the period which extends from the time of Adam to that of Ninus, a period during which 3,184 years elapsed.[38] He raised high hopes that he himself would write a satisfactory account of this period, but instead he presented a few general statements taken from Justin and some data from the *Chronicle* of Eusebius-Jerome. For his description of the geography of the

---

[37] S. Angus, *Sources of the First Ten Books of Augustine's De civitate Dei* (Princeton, 1906), pp. 26–35, 42–50. The relation of the lost epitome of Livy to these sources is discussed by H. A. Saunders in "The Lost Epitome of Livy," a treatise included in *University of Michigan Studies, Humanistic Series: Roman Historical Sources and Institutions* (N. Y. 1904), I, 149–260.

[38] Orosius i. 1. 5.

world, Orosius relied upon a second-century work based upon the geography of Agrippa.[39] He supplemented this account by using other sources and by introducing materials drawn from his own experience and thus produced a geographical description of the world that was more complete and original than others current in his age. As sources for the history of ancient empires of the Near East and of the Greeks, Orosius drew heavily upon Justin.[40] The sources for Roman history down to the time of Augustus he found in Eutropius (Orosius used almost the entire work of this epitomizer), Livy, Florus, and Caesar. For the history of Rome from Augustus down to his own day he relied upon Suetonius and Eutropius mainly, taking data occasionally from Tacitus and from Eusebius-Jerome. Throughout his account of all periods he interspersed a few quotations from Vergil and from the Old and New Testaments, besides taking some material from Sallust, Lucan, Rufinus, Julius Obsequens(?), and St. Augustine.[41] He also mentioned many other historians by name.[42] Though he described ten persecutions of the Christians, he nowhere gave an account of the history of the Christian Church, probably thinking that Eusebius's famous history of the Church adequately treated this topic. It is disappointing that Orosius, having a wealth of historical writing of the highest rank at his command, based so much of his work upon second-rate manuals. Still it must be remembered that in the fifth cen-

[39] J. Partsch, *Die Darstellung Europa's in der geographischen Werke des Agrippa* (Breslau, 1875), p. 11; also F. Braun, "Die Entwicklung der spanischen Provinzialgrenzen in römischer Zeit" in *Quellen und Forschungen zur alten Geschichte und Geographie,* 17 (Berlin, 1909), 19. Compare also D. Detlefsen, "Ursprung, Einrichtung und Bedeutung der Erdkarte Agrippas" in *Quellen und Forschungen zur alten Geschichte und Geographie,* 13 (Berlin, 1906), 19, where the relation of Orosius to Aethicus is discussed. The map in the text is taken from K. Miller, *Die ältesten Weltkarten.* Mappaemundi VI, Rekonstruierte Karten (Stuttgart, 1898), Table 3. Further references in Schanz, *op. cit.,* p. 488.

[40] C. Zangemeister, *CSEL,* V, 681–707, lists all authors mentioned and used and gives exact references.

[41] Mörner, *op. cit.,* pp. 49–157; also Schanz, *op. cit.,* p. 488. Though Orosius tried to give the impression that he used many authorities, it is very evident that he used only a few.

[42] Zangemeister, *op. cit.,* pp. 681–83, where these are listed.

tury such works were in high favor and that in relying so much upon them he was only following the popular fashion in that day.

The method, or lack of method, used by Orosius was prescribed by his purpose in writing. His work was essentially apologetic. He was primarily interested in proving a thesis, and wherever he found materials fitted to his purpose he borrowed them. The stronger of two examples, no matter how exaggerated, was selected if it seemed better to illustrate his point. Just as the orators of that day overstated their cases to produce a stronger impression, so too did the writers of apologies. Such exaggeration was expected and allowance was made for it. The technique of composition may be guessed from a study of the text. Orosius probably had the main sources before his eyes. He used one for a while, then turned to another for further illustrations, and finally returned to his first source or to some other. He copied sentences, paraphrased ideas, and even made his own order of topics follow that of his sources. Plagiarism did not trouble his conscience any more than it did other writers of his time. If names would lend weight to the words quoted, he mentioned authorities like Moses, Tacitus, and Justin. In many cases he drew upon several sources and out of them patched together an account of his own. He worked very rapidly and completed the three hundred pages of the text in little more than a year.

The speed and the manner of composition permitted little time for the critical sifting of evidence and for the exclusion of contradictory statements. In a few instances, to be sure, Orosius did hesitate and weigh the evidence with some care before giving judgment, but on the whole such procedure was rare. He usually reproduced the errors of the original sources, and these errors, together with those introduced by his own imagination and policy of exaggeration, went to produce that strange mixture of truth and error—his apology.

The chronological structure of the work was based upon the four great empires of Babylon, Macedon, Carthage, and

Rome. For general and specific dates Orosius relied mainly upon those given in the *Chronicle* of Eusebius-Jerome.[43] From this work he copied dates directly or else computed his own from dates given there. He also borrowed dates freely from Justin, Livy, Eutropius, Suetonius, and other sources. He did not produce from these materials any accurate and consistent chronological system but was satisfied to compose a rough scheme more or less true in its larger sweep. He frequently made errors when he had to state dates precisely and fully. When exact computations were needed to prove a point, he did not hesitate to force his figures to conform to his wishes.[44] For instance, Babylon and Rome both suffered invasion after 1,164 years; Babylon succumbed to the power of the Medes at the same time that Procas began to rule among the Latins.[45]

Orosius employed both definite and relative dates. The former consisted of generally accurate dates expressed in terms of exact reference to the event; the latter were expressed in round numbers of years—the reigns of emperors, consulships, general computations, and more or less accurate comparisons. There were also indefinite references to time such as "in the Middle Ages." The dates expressed in consulships were, before the birth of Christ (75 A.U.C.), generally set a few years in advance of the dates of the Calendar of the Capitol, the greatest variance being four to six years. Following the birth of Christ, the dates were computed from the year in which the reigns of emperors began and were usually set a few years later, the variance here being two or three years; there are, however, a few instances of wider discrepancy. These practices were at times reversed, but such

[43] The *Chronicle* is composed of two parts, the *Chronographia* and the *Chronological Canons*. The former, an epitome of universal history, has been lost. The latter, a chronological table with marginal notes, was translated into latin by Jerome and brought down to A.D. 375. Cf. J. T. Shotwell, *An Introduction to the History of History* (New York, 1922), pp. 304–5; M. L. W. Laistner, *Thought and Letters in Western Europe: A.D. 500 to 900* (New York, 1931), p. 52. A recent edition of Eusebius-Jerome is J. K. Fotheringham, *Eusebii Pamphili chronici canones, Latine vertit, adauxit, ad sua tempora produxit S. Eusebius Hieronymus* (London, 1923).

[44] Note careful treatment of Orosian chronology in Mörner, *op. cit.*, pp. 67–83. I have based my discussion upon it. [45] Orosius ii. 2. 2–3.

cases are rare and occur more often in dates before than in those after the birth of Christ.[46]

For events which took place before the founding of Rome, Orosius borrowed from Eusebius the reckoning based on the era of Abraham. Since 2,015 years elapsed from Abraham to the birth of Christ (752 A.U.C.), the date for the founding of Rome in this system was 1264.[47] Orosius computed the dates of his early history on this basis. He usually cited dates of events that he considered worth recalling—wars, floods, famines, and all the ills that afflicted a fallen mankind. He did not follow Eusebius exactly but computed dates generally to the nearest tenth year for the earliest events and to the nearest fifth year for the later.[48]

For events which took place after the founding of Rome, Orosius relied almost exclusively upon Eusebius and Eutropius. His *ab urbe condita* (A.U.C.) reckonings at times show strange inconsistencies. His treatment of the chronology of the Punic wars is a case in point. He set the beginning of the Second Punic War in 534 A.U.C.[49] Nevertheless, shortly thereafter, he asserted that in 546 A.U.C. the Second Punic War, which had been waged for seventeen years, was brought to an end.[50] From Roman sources this would be a period of thirteen years; yet Orosius said that it was seventeen. He also stated that Carthage was destroyed 606 A.U.C., fifty years after the Second Punic War.[51] Since 546 A.U.C. is his own date for the close of the Second Punic War, the interval would surely be sixty rather than fifty years. A third error was made when he said that Carthage (1336 A.U.C.), founded seventy-two years before Rome (1264 A.U.C.), endured for seven hundred years.[52] The date for the destruction of Carthage ought therefore to have been 636 A.U.C. instead of 606 A.U.C. as he stated it.

The use of so many sources and the presence of both defi-

---

[46] Compare tables in Mörner, *op. cit.*, pp. 78 and 79. The dates furnished by other historians may be studied in E. W. Fischer, *Römische Zeittafeln* (Altona, 1846).   [47] Mörner, *op. cit.*, p. 69.

[48] Mörner, *op. cit.*, p. 70. Consult table.   [49] Orosius iv. 14. 1.

[50] *Ibid.*, iv. 20. 1.   [51] *Ibid.*, iv. 23. 1.   [52] *Ibid.*, iv. 6. 1; iv. 23. 6.

nite and relative dates produced many inaccuracies and contradictory statements. To make the situation worse, Orosius
was careless in his arithmetic and disinclined to take the
trouble to eliminate obvious inconsistencies. One example will
suffice. He assigned a reign of three years to Vespasian and
yet stated that the latter died in the ninth year of his reign.[53]
Evidently three years fitted perfectly into the chronological
calendar that he had established for the reigns of emperors.
The nine years he copied from Eutropius. This discrepancy,
however, may have been an error that crept into the text
through some mistake of a copyist. It is more likely, nevertheless, since such mistakes occur frequently, that Orosius
himself was responsible. Orosius also reproduced the error
of Eusebius in placing the first consuls five years in advance
of the usual date for the institution of the consulship.[54] The
dates of Orosius, therefore, vary by that amount from the
dates usually given. Orosius tried to reduce all Eusebius's dates
after 244 A.U.C. to those of the A.U.C. system, but here he
never consistently chose between the A.U.C. date of Cato, 752
B.C. (following Eusebius), and that of Varro, 753 B.C., and
thereby introduced a variation of one year.[55]

Despite inaccuracies in chronology and distortions of fact,
the *Seven Books* possess some historical merit.[56] Though they
do not furnish much new historical data, they at least confirm
information already at hand and at times even add materials
not mentioned in other sources. Then, too, his approach to
history placed the facts in a new light. Usually the histories
of the ancient world were patriotic in spirit, moral in purpose,
and restricted in sweep. They were written for average citizens of the day and had their interests and prejudices in mind.
The *Seven Books,* however, form a sharp contrast. They are
Christian in spirit, apologetic in purpose, and universal in
sweep. The great civilizations of Babylon, Macedon, Carthage, and Rome, stand before a bar where judgment is

[53] Orosius vii. 9. 12.   [54] Mörner, *op. cit.,* p. 79.   [55] *Ibid.,* p. 80.
[56] The number "seven" has a mystical significance. Schanz, *op. cit.,* p. 488,
commentary.

rendered according to the universal standards of Christian principles. The imperialism of Rome is no longer described in glowing terms of praise. Conquered as well as conquerors must be considered. All peoples are God's children. Indeed, Orosius seems to tear aside the veil behind which the patriotic historians concealed the ugly spots that marred the features of the history of their countries and to reveal the less pleasing aspects of ancient civilizations in their true light.

As to the value of the *Seven Books* for the history of his own day, it must be admitted that they contribute little not found elsewhere. In fact, Orosius reviews almost the same topics discussed by the other histories of that age—the division of the Empire between Arcadius and Honorius, the rebellion of Gildo, the supremacy of Stilicho, the raid of Radagaisus, the repeated invasions of Alaric, the capture of Rome, the rise of usurpers, the inroads of barbarians into Gaul and Spain, and the plan of Athaulf to establish a Gothic empire.[57] He weakened his treatment of these topics by allowing his apologetic purpose too free play. These days, he says, were really not so unhappy as the pagans thought them. The fire at Rome was not so devastating as had been the earlier fire in the time of Nero; the barbarians were not then ravaging Spain so severely as had the Romans ravaged it in the past.[58] Indeed only the presence of Christians among the blaspheming Romans saved them from experiencing the full force of the blows dealt by barbarian and by usurper. They should see the hand of God directing the course of events by repeated interventions. That alone accounted for the mild character of their sufferings. At any rate, the deaths must not be regarded as calamities. To Christians death meant only an earlier reception into a blessed future, and to pagans it was of no importance in any case since their faith had no meaning.[59]

[57] General surveys of the period may be found in J. B. Bury, *History of the Later Roman Empire* (London, 1923), Vol. I, chaps. 5 and 6, and also in E. F. Humphrey, *Politics and Religion in the Days of Augustine* (New York, 1912).　[58] Orosius vii. 39. 16; vii. 41. 2.　[59] *Ibid.*, vii. 41. 9.

Orosius clearly reveals the strong feelings engendered by the religious controversies of the day and also many of the popular beliefs and prejudices of his contemporaries. He was especially bitter against the Arian heresy. As a patriotic Spaniard he was very proud of his country's heroic resistance to Roman aggression. As a loyal Roman he hated Stilicho. To the ambition and treachery of this great Vandal general, he attributed most of Rome's disasters. If only Stilicho had crushed Alaric in any one of the opportunities presented, Rome would have weathered the storms of invasion. Yet Orosius did not feel with many of his contemporaries that the barbarians were a standing menace to Roman civilization. Rome indeed was becoming accustomed to their presence in her midst. The barbarians, particularly the Christians, were really a source of strength. In fact the leaders of these barbarians saw that their duty lay in maintaining the Empire and in being its servants rather than in establishing a barbarian empire to succeed it.[60] Orosius did not perceive in contemporary events the rapidly approaching destruction of the Empire. Indeed his pages and those of Salvian (written some time between 439 and 450) reflect different ages.[61] It was the belief of Orosius that the barbarians would in time be assimilated and become good Romans and Christians. To Salvian, however, it appeared that moral rottenness was destroying the vitals of the Empire and that its life was doomed to a quick ending.[62]

During the gloomy days that marked the dismemberment of the Empire in the West, Orosius did not share the fate of many of his fellow authors and become lost to the coming generations of the new society that was forming on the ruins of the western provinces. Perhaps the fame and commanding position of his master St. Augustine saved him from oblivion, for in the popular mind he was usually linked with his great

[60] Orosius vii. 43. 5–7.
[61] G. Bossier, *La Fin du paganisme* (7e éd., Paris, 1913), I, 410.
[62] Salvian, *On the Government of God* (translated by E. M. Sanford: New York, 1930), pp. 84 ff., 119 ff., 189 ff., 223 ff.

preceptor.[63] At any rate, he survived the debacle, and at the close of the fifth century a bull of Pope Gelasius (494) gave its unqualified approval to the *Seven Books*, spoke of its author as "most learned" and as one who had written a "most indispensable work against the calumnies of the pagans, woven together with admirable brevity," and thus established his position in the Church, which from this time largely controlled education and learning.

With regard to the subsequent use and influence of the *Seven Books*[64] during the Middle Ages, it is difficult to speak with much certainty.[65] The continuous citation of the text throughout the medieval centuries shows that it was extremely well known. How intimate and profound was the knowledge of it is impossible to determine. Citation of passages does not, of course, prove that the entire work was read; at times the passages from Orosius clearly were quoted from other works. The apology, however, enjoyed great favor as a textbook of history, though in more selective circles it had to yield place to St. Augustine's *De civitate Dei*. Despite competition with this masterpiece and with other world histories, the *Seven Books* was one of the principal work through which medieval scholars studied ancient history.

Though most authors quoted only a few passages, some borrowed freely from certain sections of the work, and a still smaller number used the entire work.[66] In the last group were Isidore of Seville and Otto of Freising.[67] The sections most

[63] Schanz, *op. cit.*, p. 482, Zeugnisse A, quoting Gennadius, Cassiodorus, and Venantius Fortunatus.

[64] The *Seven Books* are frequently known as "Orosius." The titles "Hormista," "Ormesta," and "Ormesia" also occur. What these names mean and how they originated are matters of dispute. Consult Gamble, *op. cit.*, p. 61, and Mörner, *op. cit.*, pp. 178–81.

[65] There are more than two hundred extant manuscripts.

[66] The indices of the various volumes of M. Manutius, *Geschichte der lateinischen Litteratur des Mittelalters* (second edition; Munich, 1914–) furnish a long list of authors. Schanz, *op. cit.*, p. 490, gives a brief survey of authors who used the text and also mentions an Arabic translation made for Abdurrahman III, caliph at Cordova, at the request of the Byzantine emperor Romanus II. Zangemeister, in *CSEL*, V, has also listed the authors, up to the ninth century, who used Orosius.

[67] For Isidore, G. F. Hertzberg, *Die Historien und die Chroniken des Isidorus*

popular with later writers were the one describing the geography of the world and the one continuing the narrative from the conclusion of the Eusebius-Jerome *Chronicle* to the year 417, when Orosius ended his history.

Among those who made direct use of the whole text Alfred the Great must be especially mentioned. He is usually said to have made a translation of Orosius's history.[68] It would be more accurate to say that he made a loose paraphrase which is perhaps two-thirds as long as the original. Alfred omitted many of the introductory and closing paragraphs that contained Orosius's philosophic digressions upon the facts presented, added new materials of his own, especially in the section on geography, and made numerous corrections in the text. So different are the texts that the reader must recognize them as two distinct books.

Dante was also influenced by Orosius.[69] But from Dante on through the so-called Italian Renaissance, the Augustinian tradition of writing history weakened. The text, however, continued to enjoy widespread popularity. It was printed in revised versions in Latin in the sixteenth century, and also rendered into modern vernaculars.[70] The best known of the latter translations are the German version of Hieronymus Boner and the Italian version of B. Giamboni. Like the so-called translation of Alfred the Great, these vernacular texts are abridged and loose paraphrases of the original. Since the sixteenth century, there has been a number of editions of the

---

von Sevilla (Göttingen, 1874), and H. Philipp, "Die historisch-geographischen Quellen in den Etymologiae des Isidorus von Sevilla" in *Quellen und Forschungen zur alten Geschichte und Geographie*, 25 (Berlin, 1912); for Otto, the translation of C. C. Mierow, *The Two Cities: a Chronicle of Universal History to the Year 1146 A. D.* (New York, 1928).

[68] J. Bosworth, *King Alfred's Anglo-Saxon Version of the Compendious History of the World by Orosius* (London, 1859); G. F. Browne, *King Alfred's Book* (New York, 1920), edition of H. Sweet in "Early English Text Society" (Oxford, 1885), and of B. Thorpe in "Bohn Library" (London, 1859).

[69] R. Klussmann, *Bibliotheca scriptorum classicorum, et Graecorum et Latinorum* (Leipzig, 1913), II, 2, 37–38, cities literature.

[70] W. Potthast, *Wegweiser durch die Geschichtswerke des europäischer Mittelalters* (2d ed., Berlin, 1896), II, 882–83.

Latin text.[71] The most famous of these is that of Sigebertus Havercampus. This version was widely used and later included by Migne in his famous *Patrologia Latina*.[72] In 1882 Zangemeister published a thoroughly revised text based upon a careful study of superior manuscripts. This edition was included in the *Corpus scriptorum ecclesiasticorum Latinorum* [73] published in Vienna. The preface contains a survey of the manuscripts; the supplement provides detailed references to the sources used by Orosius and the authors who later used Orosius as a source, and the footnotes give the authorities studied by Orosius and also the variant readings of manuscripts collated. In 1889 Zangemeister issued a revised text in the Teubner series. This is now considered the standard text and is the one used in preparing the present translation.[74]

The style of the *Seven Books* was largely determined by the content.[75] The long and dreary recital of human woes and trials from the time of Adam to his own day was not a theme that inspired Orosius to great literary efforts. For the most part the story was written in a matter-of-fact style, and in many places there was a reproduction of the style of the authors he had used as sources. Only when his impersonal descriptions give way to personal reflections does he reveal the vivid style that ancients praised so much.[76] In these sections the slow and heavy pace quickens to one that fairly races as he plunges with enthusiasm and energy into the argu-

[71] Schanz, *op. cit.,* p. 491, lists the principal editions.

[72] Volume XXXI, 635–1174. There are several editions. Elaborate notes accompany the text.

[73] The full title is *Pauli Orosii historiarum adversum paganos libri VII; accedit eiusdem Liber apologeticus* (Vienna, 1882). For a review of the text, see A. Goldbacher in *Zeitschrift für die österreichischen Gymnasien* XXXIV (1883), 104.

[74] *Pauli Orosii historiarum adversum paganos libri VII* (Bibliotheca Teubneriana: Leipzig, 1889).

[75] A recent study of the uses of words and constructions in Orosius is that of J. Svennung, *Orosiana: syntaktische, semasiologische, und kritische Studien zu Orosius.* Inaugural dissertation (Uppsala, 1922). Uppsala Universitets Årsskrift, 1922: Filosofi, språkvetenskap och historika vetenskaper, 5. Svenning also lists a good bibliography. An earlier work is that of C. Paucker, *Vorarbeiten zur lateinischen Sprachgeschichte,* Kleine Studien, 3, hrsg. von H. Rönsch (Berlin, 1884), pp. 24–64. Mörner, *op. cit.,* pp. 174–78, has some remarks on his style.

[76] The *Liber apologeticus* furnishes the best material for a study of his style.

ments that he is supporting. His cosmic sweep, somber ideas, and austere approach reveal the true Spaniard. But as a whole the writing fails to achieve clarity and interest. Lack of organization is everywhere apparent, and digressions are carried to unwarranted lengths. A poor sense of proportion permitted the author in some places to pile up too much evidence and in others to give too little. Verboseness and terseness alternate. The vocabulary is rich; at times it is vivid and forceful, but it lacks precision. In fact it is a medley assembled from all ages of Latin literature. Metaphors, often arresting by their strength and aptness, too frequently become mixed and involved. As a rule the sentences are too long and diffuse and their parts badly related. The meaning of many passages is obscure, and they can only be understood in the light of their sources, since the words themselves merely suggest the true sense. Orosius, indeed, preferred to leave a sentence vague rather than sacrifice some fancied rhetorical effect. Furthermore, excessive superlatives spoil much of the writing. The marked unevenness in writing may be due to the fact that he composed the work at different times and did not attempt to revise it after completion. The presence of errors it would have been impossible to overlook in any careful revision makes this very probable.

Peculiarities of style, of course, cannot be reflected in a translation. Every language has its own patterns of thought and modes of expression. Any attempt to transfer them to another tongue invariably results in a hybrid language that has no excuse for existence. I have attempted to avoid this pitfall and have tried to translate as accurately and simply as possible the thought of the original. In places, for the sake of clarity and order, I have made new paragraphs where in the text there was one long paragraph. In transliterating names of places and of persons, I have usually given the commonly accepted forms and not those in the text where errors in copying may have introduced variations. On account of the length of the work, I have purposely limited explanatory notes to the minimum necessary to clarify obscure points and to indicate correct dates.

SEVEN BOOKS OF HISTORY
AGAINST THE PAGANS

DEDICATION

I HAVE obeyed your instructions, blessed Augustine, and may my achievement match my good intentions. I am not at all certain, however, that I have done the work well. You, indeed, have already assumed the burden of judging whether I was capable of doing what you requested, but I am content with the evidence of obedience alone, if I have really done justice to that obedience by my will and my effort. So on a great and spacious family estate many different animals are able to help in the work of the estate, yet the care of the dogs is a particular concern.[1] For these animals alone are so endowed by nature that they are driven on instinctively to do the things in which they are trained; through some inborn spirit of obedience they are held in check only by their fear of certain punishment, until the time when they are given permission, by word or sign, to do as they please. Indeed they have qualities peculiarly their own, so superior to those of brutes that they approach those of human beings, that is, they distinguish, they love, and they serve. When they distinguish between masters and strangers they do not really hate the strangers whom they attack but rather are zealous for their masters whom they love; in their attachment to their master and home they keep watch, not because they are so disposed naturally, but because they are inspired by a love filled with anxiety. Hence, according to the mystic revelation in the Gospels, the woman of Canaan was not ashamed to mention, nor did our Lord disdain to hear, that little dogs were eating the crumbs under their master's table.[2] Nor did the blessed Tobias, following the guidance of an angel, scorn to have a

---

[1] Vergil *Georgics* iii. 404.

[2] Matthew 15: 27. The lowly position of the dog in eastern thought increases the force of the comparison.

dog as his companion.[3] Therefore, since the love that all have for you is in my case united with a special love, I have willingly obeyed your wish. My humble self owes all that I have accomplished to your fatherly advice, and my entire work is yours, because it proceeds from you and returns to you, so that my only contribution must be that I did it gladly.

You bade me reply to the empty chatter and perversity of those who, aliens to the City of God, are called "pagans" (*pagani*) because they come from the countryside (*ex pagis*) and the crossroads of the rural districts, or "heathen" (*gentiles*) because of their wisdom in earthly matters. Although these people do not seek out the future and moreover either forget or know nothing of the past, nevertheless they charge that the present times are unusually beset with calamities for the sole reason that men believe in Christ and worship God while idols are increasingly neglected. You bade me, therefore, discover from all the available data of histories and annals whatever instances past ages have afforded of the burdens of war, the ravages of disease, the horrors of famine, of terrible earthquakes, extraordinary floods, dreadful eruptions of fire, thunderbolts and hailstorms, and also instances of the cruel miseries caused by parricides and disgusting crimes.[4] I was to set these forth systematically and briefly in the course of my book. It certainly is not right for your reverence to be bothered with so trifling a treatise as this while you are intent on completing the eleventh book of your work against these same pagans. When your ten previous books appeared, they, like a beacon from the watchtower of your high position in the Church, at once flashed their shining rays over all the world. Also your holy son, Julian of Carthage, a servant of God, strongly urged me to carry out his request in this matter in such a way that I might justify his confidence in asking me.

I started to work and at first went astray, for as I repeatedly turned over these matters in my mind the disasters of my

[3] Tobit 6: 1.
[4] *Flagitiis,* that is, crimes against oneself, e.g., drunkenness.

own times seemed to have boiled over and exceeded all usual limits. But now I have discovered that the days of the past were not only as oppressive as those of the present but that they were the more terribly wretched the further they were removed from the consolation of true religion. My investigation has shown, as was proper it should, that death and a thirst for bloodshed prevailed during the time in which the religion that forbids bloodshed was unknown; that as the new faith dawned, the old grew faint; that while the old neared its end, the new was already victorious; that the old beliefs will be dead and gone when the new religion shall reign alone. We must, of course, make an exception of those last, remote days at the end of the world when Antichrist shall appear and when judgment shall be pronounced, for in these days there shall be distress such as there never was before, as the Lord Christ by His own testimony predicted in the Holy Scriptures.[5] At that time, according to that very standard which now is and ever shall be—yes, by a clearer and more searching discrimination—the saints shall be rewarded for the unbearable sufferings of those days and the wicked shall be destroyed.

[5] Matthew 24 and Mark 13.

THE FIRST BOOK

1. NEARLY all writers of history (Greek as well as Latin) who have perpetuated in their various works the deeds of kings and peoples for the sake of forming an enduring record have commenced their histories with Ninus, the son of Belus and king of the Assyrians. Indeed, these historians with their very limited insight would have us believe that the origin of the world and the creation of man was without beginning. Yet they definitely state that kingdoms and wars began with Ninus, as if forsooth the human race had existed up to that time in the manner of beasts and then, as though shaken and aroused, it awoke for the first time to a wisdom previously unknown to it. For my part, however, I have determined to date the beginning of man's misery from the beginning of his sin, touching only a few points and these but briefly.

From Adam, the first man, to Ninus, whom they call "The Great" and in whose time Abraham was born, 3,184 years elapsed, a period that all historians have either disregarded or have not known. But from Ninus, or from Abraham, to Caesar Augustus, that is, to the birth of Christ, which took place in the forty-second year of Caesar's rule, when, on the conclusion of peace with the Parthians, the gates of Janus [1] were closed and wars ceased over all the world, there were 2,015 years. During this later period, whether one considers the men of action or the historians, the labors of all of them, both literary and active, were lavishly expended. My subject, therefore, requires a brief mention of at least a few facts from those books which, in their account of the origin of the world, have gained credence by the accuracy with which

---

[1] A two-faced statue of Janus stood in a passageway near the Roman Forum. In times of peace the gates were barred to keep the god within the city; in war they were open to permit him to accompany the troops.

their prophecies were later fulfilled. I used these books not because I purpose to press their authority upon anyone, but because it is worth while to repeat the common opinions that we ourselves all share.

In the first place, we hold that if the world and man are directed by a Divine Providence that is as good as it is just, and if man is both weak and stubborn on account of the changeableness of his nature and his freedom of choice, then it is necessary for man to be guided in the spirit of filial affection when he has need of help; but when he abuses his freedom, he must be reproved in a spirit of strict justice. Everyone who sees mankind reflected through himself and in himself perceives that this world has been disciplined since the creation of man by alternating periods of good and bad times. Next we are taught that sin and its punishment began with the very first man. Furthermore, even our opponents, who begin with the middle period and make no mention of the ages preceding, have described nothing but wars and calamities. What else are these wars but evils which befall one side or the other? Those evils which existed then, as to a certain extent they exist now, were doubtless either palpable sins or the hidden punishments for sin. What, then, prevents us from unfolding the beginning of this story, the main body of which has been set forth by others, and from showing, if in briefest outline, that the earlier period, which, we have pointed out, covered far more centuries than the latter, underwent the same kind of miseries?

I shall, therefore, speak of the period from the creation of the world to the founding of the City, and then of the period extending to the principate of Caesar and the birth of Christ, from which time dominion over the world has remained in the hands of the City down to the present day. So far as I can recall them, viewing them as if from a watchtower, I shall present the conflicts of the human race and shall speak about the different parts of the world which, set on fire by the torch of greed, now blaze forth with evils. With this in mind, I

believe I must describe first the world itself, which the human
race inhabits, how it was divided by our ancestors into three
parts, and what regions and provinces compose its divisions.
In this way when the theaters of war and the ravages of diseases shall be described, whoever wishes to do so may the
more easily obtain a knowledge not only of the events and
their dates but of their geography as well.

2. OUR elders made a threefold division of the world,[2]
which is surrounded on its periphery by the Ocean. Its three
parts they named Asia, Europe, and Africa. Some authorities, however, have considered them to be two, that is, Asia,
and Africa and Europe, grouping the last two as one continent.

Asia, surrounded on three sides by the Ocean, stretches
across the whole East. Toward the west, on its right, it
touches the border of Europe near the North Pole, but on its
left it extends as far as Africa, except that near Egypt and
Syria it is bounded by Mare Nostrum,[3] which we commonly
call the Great Sea.

Europe begins, as I have said, in the north at the Tanaïs
River,[4] where the Riphaean Mountains, standing back from
the Sarmatian Sea, pour forth the Tanaïs flood. The Tanaïs,
sweeping past the altars [5] and boundaries of Alexander the
Great to the territories of the Rhobasci, swells the Palus
Maeotis,[6] whose immense overflow spreads afar into the

2 Since the knowledge of geography in the time of Orosius was so different
from that of our generation, it is necessary to consult a map showing the old
conceptions in order to follow with any understanding the account of Orosius.
Consult the map facing this page.

3 The allusion is of course to the Mediterranean Sea. The origin of the
names of this sea and its divisions is discussed in V. Burr, *Mare Nostrum*
(Stuttgart, 1932).

4 The traditional boundary between Europe and Asia. The Tanaïs is now
called the Don. Orosius wrongly ascribed its source to the Riphaean Mountains
instead of to Lake Ivan Ozero.

5 Ancient conquerors frequently marked the limits of their conquests by erect-
ing monuments. The soldiers of Alexander had mistakenly said that the altars
were erected on the Tanaïs. Their true location was in Central Asia on the
Jaxartes River. A recent discussion of Alexander's Gate is that of A. R.
Anderson, *Alexander's Gate, Gog and Magog, and the Inclosed Nations* (Cam-
bridge, Mass., 1932). 6 The Sea of Azof.

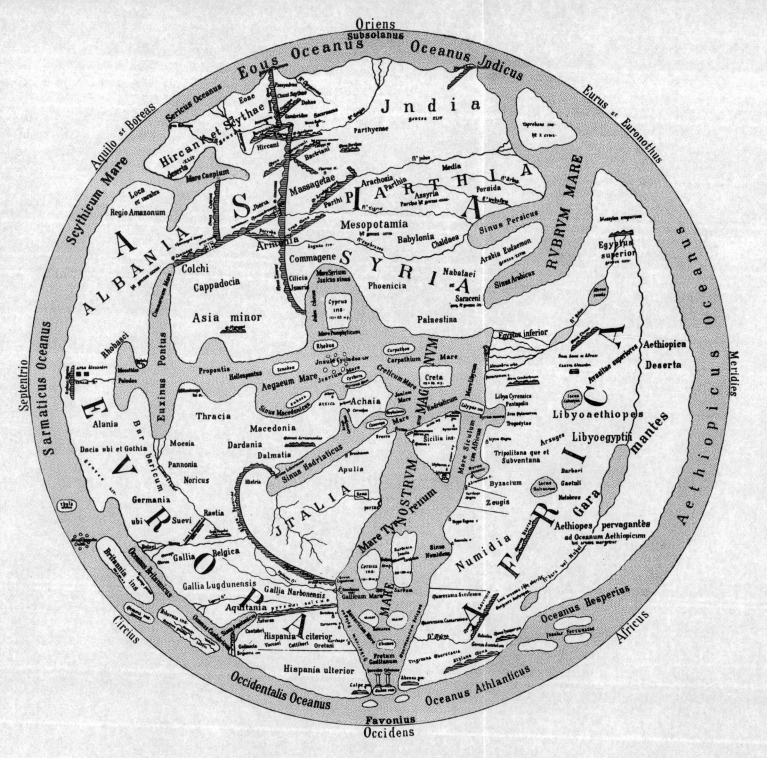

MAP OF THE WORLD ACCORDING TO OROSIUS

From *Die ältesten Weltkarten*, by Konrad Miller

MAP OF THE WORLD ACCORDING TO HECATÆUS

Euxine Sea near Theodosia. From the Euxine near Constantinople a long narrow body of water leads to the sea which we call Mare Nostrum. The Western Ocean forms the boundary of Europe in Spain at the very point where the Pillars of Hercules stand near the Gades Islands and where the Ocean tide comes into the straits of the Tyrrhenian Sea.

Africa begins with the land of Egypt and the city of Alexandria. On the shore of that Great Sea,[7] the waters of which touch all the continents and the lands in the center of the earth, we find the city of Paraetonium.[8] From there the boundaries of Africa lead through districts which the inhabitants call Catabathmon,[9] not far from the camp of Alexander the Great above Lake Chalearzus, whence they pass near the lands of the Upper Avasitae and across the deserts of Ethiopia to reach the Southern Ocean. The western boundary of Africa is the same as that of Europe, that is, the entrance of the Strait of Gades; its furthest boundaries are the Atlas Range and the islands which people call Fortunate.[10]

Now that I have given briefly the three great continents of the world, I shall also take pains, as I promised, to point out the divisions of the continents themselves.

Asia has at the center of its eastern boundary on the Eastern Ocean the mouths of the Ganges River; to the left we find the Promontory of Caligardamana, to the southeast of which lies the island of Taprobane.[11] From this point the Ocean is called the Indian Ocean. To the right of the Imavian Mountains, where the Caucasian Chain [12] ends, we find the Promontory of Samara, northeast of which lie the mouths of the Ottorogorra River. From this point the Ocean is called the Serian Ocean.

In this region lies India, the western boundary of which

---

[7] Orosius is referring to the Mediterranean. [8] The present Marsa Labeit.

[9] Akabah.

[10] The fabulous islands of the Western Ocean, the abodes of the blessed; some consider them the Canary Islands. [11] Ceylon.

[12] Orosius used the term "Caucasus" to denote the whole chain of mountains stretching from the Black Sea to the Pacific Ocean as well as the shorter range which we usually associate with that name.

is the Indus River, which empties into the Red Sea, and the
northern boundary of which is formed by the Caucasian
Range; the other sides, as I have said, are bounded by the
Eastern and the Indian oceans. This land has forty-four
peoples, not including either those who dwell on the island
of Taprobane, which has ten cities, or those who live on the
many other densely populated islands.

Between the Indus River on the east and the Tigris River,
which lies to the west, are the following territories: Ara-
chosia, Parthia, Assyria, Persida, and Media, by nature rough
and mountainous lands. On the north they are bounded by
the Caucasian Range, on the south by the Red Sea and the
Persian Gulf, while in the center flow their principal rivers,
the Hydaspes and the Arbis. In these regions are twenty-three
tribes. It is all commonly spoken of as Parthia, although the
Sacred Scriptures often call the whole area Media.

Between the Tigris and Euphrates rivers is Mesopotamia,
beginning in the north between the Taurian and Caucasian
ranges. To the south we meet in order, first Babylonia, then
Chaldaea, and lastly Arabia Eudaemon, a narrow strip of
land facing east and lying between the Persian and Arabian
gulfs. Twenty-eight peoples live in these lands.

Syria is the name generally given to the land that extends
from the Euphrates River on the east to Mare Nostrum on
the west, from the city of Dagusa on the boundary between
Cappadocia and Armenia near the place where the Euphrates
rises on the north, as far south as Egypt and the end of the
Arabian Gulf. This gulf extends southward in a long and
narrow furrow which abounds with rocks and islands; from
the Red Sea, that is, from the Ocean, it stretches in a westerly
direction. The largest provinces of Syria are Commagene,
Phoenicia, and Palestine, not including the lands of the Sara-
ceni and the Nabathaei, whose tribes number twelve.

At the head of Syria is Cappadocia, which is bounded on
the east by Armenia, on the west by Asia,[13] on the northeast

---

[13] That is, Asia Minor.

by the Themiscyrian Plains and the Cimmerian Sea, and on the south by the Taurian Mountains. Below these mountains lie Cilicia and Isauria extending as far as the Cilician Gulf, which faces toward the island of Cyprus.

Asia Regio, or, to speak more correctly, Asia Minor,[14] exclusive of the eastern part where it touches Cappadocia and Syria, is surrounded on all sides by water; on the north by the Euxine, on the west by the Propontis and Hellespont, and on the south by Mare Nostrum. Here towers Mount Olympus.

Lower Egypt is bounded by Syria and Palestine on the east, by Libya on the west, by Mare Nostrum on the north, and by the mountain called Climax, Upper Egypt, and the Nile on the south. This river seems to rise from the shore where the Red Sea begins at the place called Mossylon Emporium. Thence it flows west for a long distance, forming in its midst the island called Meroe;[15] finally, bending to the north, swollen by seasonal floods, it waters the plains of Egypt. Some authors say that it rises not far from Mount Atlas and gradually disappears in the sands, from which, after a short interval, it flows out into a vast lake and then glides eastward through the Ethiopian Desert toward the Ocean, and finally, turning to the left, flows down to Egypt. Of a truth there is a great river of this kind which has such an origin and such a course and which truly begets all the monsters of the Nile. The barbarians near its source call it the Dara, but by the other inhabitants it is called the Nuhul. This river, however, is swallowed up in a huge lake in the land of the people called Libyo-Egyptians, not far from the other river which, as we have said, rushes forth from the shore of the Red Sea, unless, as may be the case, it pours from a subterranean channel into the bed of that river which flows down from the east.

Upper Egypt stretches far to the east. On the north is the Arabian Gulf, on the south the Ocean. On the west its bounda-

[14] Archbishop Richard Trench in his *On the Study of Words* (New York, 1858), p. 111, cites Orosius as the first writer to use the term "Asia Minor."
[15] Sometimes written "Merve." I follow the use of the Permanent Committee on Geographic Names for British Official Use in *First List of Names in Anglo-Egyptian Sudan* (London, 1927), p. 8.

ries begin at Lower Egypt, and on the east it is bounded by
the Red Sea. In this region are twenty-four peoples.

Now that I have described the southern part of all Asia,[16]
it remains for me to take up the remaining lands, working
from east to north.

The Caucasian Range [17] rises first in the territories of the
Colchi, who dwell above the Cimmerian Sea, and in the lands
of the Albani, who live near the Caspian. Indeed, as far as
its eastern extremity it seems to be one range, though it has
many names. Some wish to consider these mountains part of
the Taurian Range, because as a matter of fact the Parcoha-
tras Range of Armenia, lying between the Taurian and Caucasian, is believed to form an unbroken chain with the other
two ranges. The Euphrates River, however, proves that this
is not the case, for, springing from the foot of the Parcoha-
tras Mountains, it bends its course southward, veering constantly to the left, but keeping the Taurian Range on the
right. The Caucasus in the territories of the Colchi and the
Albani, where there are also passes, are called the Caucasian
Mountains. From the Caspian passes to the Armenian Gates
or to the source of the Tigris River, between Armenia and
Iberia, they are called the Acroceraunian. From the source
of the Tigris to the city of Carrhae between the Massagetae
and the Parthi they are named the Ariobarzanes. From the
city of Carrhae to the town of Cathippus, between the Hyrcani and the Bactriani, they are called the Memarmalian.
There amomum [18] grows in abundance. The nearest range to
the Memarmalian is called the Parthau. From the town of
Cathippus to the village of Saphri in the intervening lands
of the Dahae, Sacaraucae, and the Parthyenae are the peaks
of the Oscobares. There the Ganges River rises and asa-
fœtida grows.[19] From the source of the Ganges River to the

---

[16] In this description Orosius has also included parts of Africa.

[17] The detailed picture of the chain of mountains in Asia can be clearly
followed only by consulting the map facing page 34.

[18] An aromatic herb from which the Romans prepared a costly, fragrant
balsam.

[19] A gum resin taken from the root of the herb *ferula foedita* and used as
a drug in Greek medicine.

sources of the Ottorogorra River on the north, where lie the Paropamisadae Mountains, we find the Taurian Range. From the sources of the Ottorogorra to the city of Ottorogorra between the Chuni Scythians and the Gandaridae are the Caucasian Mountains. The farthest range is the Imavus between the Eoae and the Passyadrae, where the Chrysorhoas River and the Promontory of Samara meet the Eastern Ocean. In the lands that extend from the Imavus Mountains (that is, from the eastern tip of the Caucasian Range) and from the right division of the East where the Serian Ocean lies as far as the Promontory of Boreum and the Boreum River, and thence to the Scythian Sea on the north, to the Caspian Sea on the west, and to the wide range of the Caucasus on the south, there are the forty-two tribes of the Hyrcanians and Scythians, who, on account of the barrenness of the extensive lands of the country, wander far and wide.

The Caspian Sea rises from the Ocean in the northeast. The shores and the lands on both sides of it in the vicinity of the Ocean are considered to be desert and uncultivated. Thence, toward the south, the sea extends through a long channel, until, spreading out over a great area, it ends at the foothills of the Caucasian Mountains. In the lands from the Caspian Sea on the east, along the edge of the Northern Ocean as far as the Tanaïs River and the Palus Maeotis on the west, to the shores of the Cimmerian Sea on the southwest, and to the heights and passes of the Caucasus on the south, there are thirty-four tribes. The nearest region is usually called Albania, while the more distant territory near the sea and the Caspian Mountains is called the land of the Amazons.

The boundaries of Asia have been described as briefly as possible. Now I shall let my pen wander through Europe as far as it is known to man.

Europe begins at the Riphaean Mountains, the Tanaïs River, and the Palus Maeotis, all of which lie toward the east. Its territories extend along the shores of the Northern Ocean to Gallia Belgica and the Rhine River, which flows in from the west, and thence to the Danube. This last river is also called the Hister; it starts from the south, and, flowing to the east, empties into the Pontus. The lands of Europe in the East are first, Alania; in the middle, Dacia (there we also find Gothia); and finally, Germania, the main part of which is held by the Suebi. In all there are fifty-four tribes.

Now I shall describe the lands between Mare Nostrum and the Danube, a river which separates these lands from the territories of the barbarians.

The boundaries of Moesia are on the east the mouth of the Danube River, on the southeast Thrace, on the south Macedonia, on the southwest Dalmatia, on the west Histria, on the northwest Pannonia, and on the north the Danube again.

Thrace is bounded on the east by the Gulf of Propontis and the city of Constantinople, which was formerly called Byzantium, on the north by part of Dalmatia and a gulf of the Euxine Sea,[20] on the west and southwest by Macedonia, and on the south by the Aegean Sea.

The boundary of Macedonia on the east is the Aegean Sea, on the northeast Thrace, on the southeast Euboea and the Macedonian Gulf, on the south Achaia, on the west the Acroceraunian Mountains, lying on the narrows of the Adriatic Gulf opposite Apulia and Brundisium; to the west is Dalmatia, to the northwest Dardania, and to the north Moesia.

Achaia is almost entirely surrounded by water; its boundaries are the Myrtoan Sea on the east, the Cretan Sea on the southeast, the Ionian Sea on the south, the islands of Cephalenia and Cassiopa on the southwest and west, the Corinthian Gulf on the north. On the northeast a narrow ridge of land joins it to Macedonia, or rather to Attica. This place is called the Isthmus and on it is Corinth, which is not far distant from the city of Athens to the north.

Dalmatia is bounded on the east by Macedonia, on the northeast by Dardania, on the north by Moesia, on the west

[20] Orosius presents a confused description. Dalmatia is southwest of Thrace.

by Histria, the Liburnian Gulf, and the Liburnian Islands, and on the south by the Adriatic Gulf.

The boundaries of Pannonia, Noricum, and Raetia are on the east Moesia, on the south Histria, on the southwest the Poenean Alps, on the west Gallia Belgica, on the northwest the source of the Danube and the boundary that separates Germany from Gaul between the Danube and Gaul, and on the north the Danube and Germany.

The territory of Italy extends from the northwest to the southeast, having on the southwest the Tyrrhenian Sea, on the northeast the Adriatic Gulf. That part of Italy which borders on and forms one mass with the continent is walled in by the barriers of the Alps which rise from the Gallic Sea above the Ligurian Gulf. The Alps limit first the territories of the Narbonese and then Gaul and Raetia, until they sink in the Liburnian Gulf.

Gallia Belgica has as its eastern boundaries the Rhine River and Germany; as its southeastern, the Poenean Alps; as its southern, the province of Narbo; as its western, the province of Lugdunum; as its northwestern, the Britannic Ocean; and as its northern boundary the island of Britain.

Gallia Lugdunensis, very long but extremely narrow, half surrounds the province of Aquitania. On the east it is bounded by Belgica and on the south by part of the province of Narbo, where the city of Arles is situated and the Rhone River empties into the Gallic Sea.

The province of Narbo, a part of the Gauls, is bounded on the east by the Cottian Alps, on the west by Spain, on the northwest by Aquitania, on the north by Lugdunum, on the northeast by Belgica Gallia, and on the south by the Gallic Sea, which lies between Sardinia and the Balearic Islands. The Stoechades Islands [21] lie in front of the southern coast-line of this province, where the Rhone River empties into the sea.

The province of Aquitania is formed into a circle by the

[21] Isles d'Hyères.

slanting course of the Liger River,[22] which for almost its entire length serves as a boundary of the province. On the northwest the province touches that ocean which is called the Aquitanian Gulf; to the west it borders on Spain, to the north and east on Lugdunum, and to its southeast and south lies Narbo.

Spain, taken as a unit, is formed by its natural contour into a triangle and is almost an island owing to the fact that it is surrounded by the Ocean and the Tyrrhenian Sea. Its first corner, facing east, is walled in on the right by the province of Aquitania and on the left by the Balearic Sea, and is wedged in next to the territories of the Narbonese. The second corner extends toward the northwest. There in Gallaecia is situated the city of Brigantia, which raises its towering lighthouse, one of the few notable structures in the world, toward the watchtower of Britain. Its third corner is at the Gades Islands, which face to the southwest and look toward the Atlas Mountains across the intervening gulf of the ocean.

The Saltus Pyrenaei [23] forms the boundary of Hither Spain, beginning on the east and extending on the northern side as far as the territory of the Cantabri and the Astures; from this point on through the territory of the Vaccaei and Oretani, which lies to the west, Carthage, which is situated on the coast of Mare Nostrum, determines the boundary.

Further Spain has on the east the Vaccaei, Celtiberi, and Oretani; on the north and west the Ocean; and on the south the Strait of Gades. This strait belongs to the Ocean, and through it Mare Nostrum, which is called the Tyrrhenian Sea, enters.

Inasmuch as there are in the Ocean islands called Britain and Ireland, which are situated opposite the Gauls in the direction of Spain, they will be briefly described.

Britain, an island in the Ocean, extends a long distance to the north; to its south are the Gauls. The city called Portus

[22] The Loire.
[23] A *saltus* is a mountainous and wooded district commonly used for pasturage, not for agriculture.

Rutupi [24] affords the nearest landing place for those who cross the water. From this point Britain faces directly the territories of the Menapi and Batavi, which are located not far from the land of the Morini in the south. This island is eight hundred miles long and two hundred miles wide.

In the limitless ocean which stretches behind Britain are the Orcades Islands,[25] of which twenty are deserted and thirteen inhabited.

Next comes the island of Thule,[26] which is separated from the others by a great space and is situated in the middle of the Ocean toward the northwest; it is known to only a few.

Ireland, an island situated between Britain and Spain, is of greater length from south to north. Its nearer coasts, which border on the Cantabrian Ocean, look out over the broad expanse in a southwesterly direction toward far-off Brigantia, a city of Gallaecia, which lies opposite to it and which faces to the northwest. This city is most clearly visible from that promontory where the mouth of the Scena River is found and where the Velabri and the Luceni are settled. Ireland is quite close to Britain and is smaller in area. It is, however, richer on account of the favorable character of its climate and soil. It is inhabitated by tribes of the Scotti.

The island of Mevania,[27] its next door neighbor, is itself fair sized and possesses a rich soil. It, too, is inhabited by tribes of the Scotti.

These are the boundaries of all the countries of Europe.

As I have said earlier, when our ancestors stated that Africa must be considered the third part of the world,[28] they did not consider the comparative sizes of the continents but followed their actual divisions. Indeed this Great Sea, which originates in the Western Ocean, by inclining more to the south has limited the area of Africa and made the conti-

[24] Richborough in Kent. [25] The Orkneys.

[26] Some identify this island as Iceland, others, as Mainland, the largest of the Shetlands.

[27] The Isle of Man. This island has borne eight different names in the course of thirteen hundred years. Cf. J. J. Kneen, *Place-Names of the Isle of Man* (Manx Society, Douglas, 1925), I, xxii. [28] Orosius i. 2. 1.

nent narrower between its own waters and those of the Ocean. Hence there are even some who, although they think that Africa is equal in length to Europe, yet at the same time considering her to be much narrower, believe it inappropriate to call this continent the third part. They have preferred, therefore, by allotting Africa to Europe, to call the continent a part of the latter. Furthermore, much more land remains uncultivated and unexplored in Africa because of the heat of the sun than in Europe because of the intensity of the cold, for certainly almost all animals and plants adapt themselves more readily and easily to great cold than to great heat. There is an obvious reason why Africa, so far as contour and population are concerned, appears smaller in every respect; owing to her natural location the continent has less space and owing to the bad climate she has more deserted land. The provinces and peoples of Africa may be described as follows:

After Egypt, the next province of Africa that I shall describe is Libya Cyrenaica and Pentapolis. This region begins at the city of Paraetonium and the Catabathmon Mountains, from which, following the sea, it extends as far as the Altars of the Philaeni.[29] The territory behind it, which reaches to the Southern Ocean, is inhabited by the Libyo-Ethiopian and Garamantian peoples. Egypt is on the east, the Libyan Sea on the north, the Greater Syrtis[30] and the country of the Troglodytes on the west (opposite the Troglodytes is the island of Calypso), and the Ethiopian Ocean on the south.

The province of Tripolis is also called Subventana or the country of the Arzuges, as these people are generally called throughout the length and breadth of Africa. In this province the city of Leptis Magna is situated. Tripolis is bounded on the east by the Altars of the Philaeni which are between the Greater Syrtis and the country of the Troglodytes, on the

---

[29] The altars are situated on the eastern frontier of Carthage toward Cyrene. An improbable story tells that they were named for two Carthaginian brothers, who, out of love for their country, allowed themselves to be buried alive there.

[30] The Greater Syrtis is a broad and deep gulf near Cyrenaica and is now called the Gulf of Sidra.

north by the Sicilian Sea, or rather by the Adriatic, and the Lesser Syrtis,[31] on the west by Byzacium as far as the Lake of Salinae, on the south by the lands of the barbaric Gaetuli, Nathabres, and Garamantes, whose territories stretch as far as the Ethiopian Ocean.

Next are the provinces of Byzacium, Zeugis, and Numidia. To begin, Zeugis is not the name of one *conventus,* but we find that it was the general name of a whole province. Byzacium, then, with the city of Hadrumetum, Zeugis with Magna Carthago, Numidia with the cities of Hippo Regius and Rusiccada, are bounded on the east by the Smaller Syrtis and the Lake of Salinae, and on the north by Mare Nostrum, which faces toward the islands of Sicily and Sardinia. These provinces are bounded on the west by Mauretania Sitifensis and on the south by the Uzarae Mountains behind which the Ethiopian peoples wander about as far as the Ethiopian Ocean.

Mauretania Sitifensis and Mauretania Caesariensis border to the east on Numidia, to the north on Mare Nostrum, to the west on the Malva River,[32] to the south on Mount Astrixis, which separates the fertile soil from the sands that stretch as far as the Ocean. In this desert the Gangines Ethiopes roam.

Mauretania Tingitana is the last part of Africa. This region is bounded on the east by the Malva River, on the north by Mare Nostrum as far as the Strait of Gades which is confined between the two opposite promontories of Abyla and Calpe, on the west by the Atlas Range and the Atlantic Ocean, on the southwest by the Hesperian Mountains, on the south by the territory belonging to the tribes of the Autololes, who are now called Galaules and who inhabit the lands which extend as far as the Western Ocean.

This is the boundary line of the whole of Africa. Now I shall set forth the locations, names, and sizes of the islands which are in Mare Nostrum.

---

[31] The Lesser Syrtis is located near Byzacene and is now the Gulf of Cabes. Both Syrtes were very dangerous to navigate on account of their shoals and rocks.   [32] Sometimes called the Mulucha, or Μαλούα.

The island of Cyprus is surrounded on the east by the Syrian Sea which people call the Gulf of Issus, on the west by the Sea of Pamphylia, on the north by Aulon of Cilicia, and on the south by the Syrian and Phoenician seas. In extent it is one hundred and seventy-five miles in length and one hundred and twenty-five miles in width.

The island of Crete is bounded on the east by the Carpathian Sea, on the west and north by the Cretan Sea, on the south by the Libyan Sea, which people also call the Adriatic. It is one hundred and seventy-two miles long and fifty miles wide.

The islands of the Cyclades are these: the first, on the east, is Rhodes, then on the north Tenedos, on the south Carpathus, and finally on the west Cythera. These islands are bounded on the east by the shores of Asia, on the west by the Icarian Sea, on the north by the Aegean Sea, and on the south by the Carpathian Sea. The entire number of the Cyclades is fifty-four. These islands extend from north to south five hundred miles, from east to west two hundred miles.

The island of Sicily has three promontories: the first, called Pelorus, faces toward the northeast, and its nearest city is Messana; the second, called Pachynum, on which is the city of Syracuse, faces toward the southeast; the third, called Lilybaeum, is inclined to the west and on it is a city of the same name. The distance from Pelorus to Pachynum is one hundred and fifty-eight miles, and that from Pachynum to Lilybaeum one hundred and eighty-seven miles. Sicily is bounded on the east by the Adriatic Sea and on the south by the African Sea, which is opposite the land of the Subventani and the Lesser Syrtis. On the west and on the north it is bounded by the Tyrrhenian Sea, which extends on the north as far as the eastern strait of the Adriatic Sea. This strait divides the lands of the Tauromenitani in Sicily from those of the Bruttii in Italy.

The islands of Sardinia and Corsica are divided by a small strait twenty miles in width. The southern part of Sardinia, which faces Numidia, is inhabited by the Caralitani; its northern part, which faces the island of Corsica, by the Ulbienses. Sardinia is two hundred and thirty miles long and eighty miles wide. To the east and northeast of the island is the Tyrrhenian Sea, which faces toward the harbor of the city of Rome, to the west the Sardinian Sea, to the southwest the Balearic Islands situated far away, to the south the Numidian Gulf, and to the north, as I have said, Corsica.

The island of Corsica has many corners because of its numerous promontories. This island, bounded on the east by the Tyrrhenian Sea and harbor of the City, on the south by Sardinia, on the west by the Balearic Islands, and on the northwest and north by the Ligurian Gulf, is one hundred and ten miles long and twenty-six miles wide.

There are two Balearic Islands, the larger and the smaller. On each of these are two towns. The larger island, toward the north, faces the city of Tarraco in Spain; the smaller, the city of Barcelona. The island of Ebusus lies near the greater. On the east these islands face Sardinia, on the northeast the Gallic Sea, on the south and the southwest the Mauretanian Sea, and on the west the Iberian Sea.

These then are the islands situated in the waters of the entire Great Sea from the Hellespont to the Ocean, which because of their culture and history, are considered more famous.

I have completed my survey of the provinces and islands of the whole world as briefly as I could. Now, so far as I am able to give them, I shall make known the local disasters of individual nations as they arose in an unending stream from the beginning, and I shall discuss their nature and their origin as well.

3. AFTER the fashioning and adornment of this world, man, whom God had made upright and immaculate, became defiled by sin. As a consequence, the human race, because it had become depraved by its lusts, was also corrupted. A just pun-

ishment then followed directly upon man's unlawful use of his liberty. This sentence of God, Creator and Judge, delivered against man because of his sin and against the earth because of man, and lasting as long as the human race shall inhabit this earth, we all, even though unwilling, affirm by our very denials and sustain by our admissions. And even those who would reject its truth because they are unwilling to hearken to the words of faith confirm it by that weakness which is born of their obstinacy. Subsequently, as the truthful writers of the Scripture declare, the sea overflowed the land, a flood covering the entire earth was let loose, only sky and sea remained, and the whole human race was destroyed. Only a few, because of their faith, were saved in the Ark so that they might be the founders of a new race. Other writers, too, have testified to this truth. Though ignorant of the past and even of the very Creator of the ages, they have nevertheless learned about the flood by drawing logical inferences from the evidence offered by stones which, encrusted with shells and often corroded by water, we are accustomed to see on far-away mountains. Although I could bring forward other arguments of this sort, which are worthy of mention and accurate in point of truth, let these two principal ones suffice concerning the trangression of the first man and the condemnation of his offspring and his life, and thereafter concerning the destruction of the whole human race. I shall make this reservation: if pagan historians have discussed these subjects, we shall extend our account to cover their treatment.

4. ONE thousand three hundred years before the founding of the City, Ninus, the first king of the Assyrians, as my opponents wish him to be considered, was led on by his lust for dominion to wage wars abroad.[33] For fifty years he maintained a reign of bloodshed throughout all Asia. Start-

[33] In reality Ninus was the third king according to Berosus, but Diodorus ranks him first because of his preëminence. Other historians have followed this custom. Earlier kings had fought wars for the glory of their people, but Ninus engaged in war in order to win new territories to govern.

ing from the south and from the Red Sea, he laid waste and subjugated the territory in the extreme north along the Euxine Sea. He taught barbaric Scythia, hitherto an unwarlike and inoffensive country, to quicken into action her dormant spirit of ferocity, to become conscious of her strength, to drink not as heretofore the milk of domestic animals but the blood of men, and in the end to conquer even as she was being conquered. Finally he engaged in battle with Zoroaster,[34] the king of the Bactrians, and after defeating him slew him. This was the same man who they say invented the art of magic.[35] Later Ninus himself, while storming a rebellious city, was struck by an arrow and died.

His wife Semiramis [36] succeeded him on the throne. She had the will of a man and went about dressed like her son.[37] For forty-two years she kept her own people, lusting for blood from their previous taste of it, engaged in the slaughter of foreign tribes. Not satisfied with the boundaries that she had inherited from her husband, who was the only king of that age to be warlike and who had acquired these lands in the course of fifty years, the woman added to her empire Ethiopia, which had been sorely oppressed by war and drenched with blood. She also declared war upon the people of India,[38] a land which nobody ever had penetrated excepting herself and Alexander the Great. To persecute and slaughter peoples living in peace was at that time an even more cruel and serious matter than it is today; for in those days neither the incentive for conquest abroad nor the temptation for the exercise of cupidity at home was so strong.

Burning with lust and thirsty for blood, Semiramis in the course of continuous adulteries and homicides caused the death of all those whom she had delighted to hold in her adulterous

[34] Berosus says that Ninyas, the son of Ninus, killed him.

[35] St. Augustine *De civitate Dei* xxi, 14.

[36] Orosius employs the ancient Assyrian form Samiramis rather than the Greek transliteration.

[37] Dissembling her sex, she pretended to be the son of Ninus, and dressed like him, for their features and voices were very similar.

[38] She failed to conquer this land.

embrace and whom she had summoned to her by royal command for that purpose. She finally most shamelessly conceived a son, godlessly abandoned the child, later had incestuous relations with him, and then covered her private disgrace by a public crime. For she prescribed that between parents and children no reverence for nature in the conjugal act was to be observed, but that each should be free to do as he pleased.

5. TACITUS, too, among others, mentions that one thousand one hundred and sixty years before the founding of the City the region which bordered on Arabia and which at that time was called Pentapolis was burnt, even below its surface, by a fire from heaven. This is what he says: "Not far from there lie the plains, which, they say, were once fertile and were the sites of great cities, but which later were burnt by lightning. It is said that traces of this disaster still remain, but that the earth itself, which looks fruitful, has lost its powers of fertility." [39] Although at this point, as if he were unaware of it, he said nothing about cities having been burnt because of the sins of mankind, yet a little later, as if he had forgotten his purpose, he adds this statement: "For my own part, although I am willing to admit that those famous cities of old were destroyed by fire from heaven, yet I still hold the opinion that it was the exhalations from the lake that infected and poisoned the land." [40] By this statement he has admitted, although loath to do so, that he had known and agreed with me about the burnt cities, which undoubtedly were destroyed by fire as a punishment for their sins. Thus he has openly proved that he did not lack a trustworthy source of knowledge but merely a willingness to express his belief. I will now explain this more fully.

On the border of Arabia and Palestine, where the mountains, as they disappear on each side, merge into the fields which lie below them, were five cities—Sodom, Gomorrah,

---

[39] Tacitus *Histories* v. 7. Tacitus writes *torridam* for *solidam* and *et* for *sed*.
[40] *Ibid.,* v. 7. To *terram* Tacitus adds *superfusum spiritum*.

Adama, Soboim, and Segor. Of these, Segor was small, whereas the others were large and spacious. For the soil near these cities was fertile, and the Jordan River, spreading out through the plains and dividing them into convenient sections, served to increase the productivity of the land. But this very abundance of resources brought evils upon the entire region because the inhabitants misused their blessings. For out of abundance grew luxury, and out of luxury came such shameful passions that men rushed to commit vile practices upon their own sex without even taking into consideration place, condition, or age. Therefore God in His anger rained fire and brimstone upon this land, and by burning its inhabitants and cities pronounced upon the entire region a sentence of eternal ruin to serve as a witness of His judgment for future generations.[41] Thus, although the contour of the region is even now visible, it is found covered with ashes. The sea has flowed over and at the present time covers the middle of the valley that the Jordan once watered. So great was God's displeasure, aroused by matters which the inhabitants had held to be petty, that, because the people had misused their blessings and turned the fruits of His mercy to the nourishment of their passions, the very land itself, on which these cities were built, was first burnt by fires, later overwhelmed by waters, and finally vanished from the sight of men into eternal condemnation.

6. THEREFORE, if it be now agreeable, let those who spit as much as they can upon Christ, Whom we ourselves have shown to be the Judge of the centuries, distinguish between the cases of Sodom and Rome and let them compare their punishments. To these matters I must not again give special consideration, since they are known to all. And yet how gladly would I accept their opinions if only these people would faithfully acknowledge what they really feel. Although they murmur now and then about Christian times (and this only in

[41] Genesis 19: 24, 25.

out-of-the-way places) I do not think that this ought to be taken too seriously, since the feelings and general views of the entire Roman people may be learned from the expression of their unanimous judgment. The Roman people, indeed, have unmistakably borne witness that the disturbance which for a short time interrupted their customary pleasures was of but slight importance, for they freely cried out, "If we are given our circus back again, we have suffered nothing." That is to say, the swords of the Goths had accomplished nothing at Rome if the Romans might still be allowed to be spectators at the circus games. Yet possibly the explanation is, as many in our age believe, that those who have long been freed from care regard even the slightest anxiety as an intolerable burden; they are the type of people who consider those gentle admonitions, by which we all from time to time are reproved, still more severe than the punishments exacted in other times about which they have only heard or read. At any rate, I remind them of the fate of the inhabitants of Sodom and Gomorrah, so that they may learn and understand in what way God has punished sinners, in what way He can punish them, and in what way He will punish them.

7.   ONE thousand and seventy years before the founding of the City, the Telchines and Caryatii fought a stubborn battle against Phoroneus,[42] king of the Argives, and against the Parrhasians.[43] The course of the struggle fluctuated, and the battle ended without decision. In a battle shortly afterward, these Telchines were defeated and fled from their native land; ignorant of the true state of affairs they seized the island of Rhodes, which was earlier called Ophiussa, in the belief that it was a place of safety and that they were cutting themselves off completely from contact with the whole civilized world.

One thousand and forty years before the founding of the City, a raging flood brought great destruction upon almost all the province of Achaia. Inasmuch as this flood took place

[42] A legendary king who is said to have been the first to use fire and to unite his people.   [43] A poetic name for the Arcadians.

in the days of Ogygius, who was the founder and king of
Eleusis at this time, it was he who gave the name to the place
and to the era.

8. THE historian Pompeius,[44] through Justin who made an
epitome of his work, informs us that one thousand and eight
years before the founding of the City, Egypt experienced first
a period of unusual harvests, so rich as to excite disgust, and
then a continuous period of unbearable famine, which Joseph,
a just and wise man, relieved by divine foresight. Among
other things Justin states:

Joseph was the youngest of his brothers who, fearing his superior
ability, kidnapped him and sold him to foreign merchants. After being
brought by them to Egypt he there became a master of the arts of magic
by reason of his exceptional native ability, and in a short time was a
favorite of the king himself. Joseph was also skilled in prodigies and
was the first to establish the science of interpreting dreams; no branch
of divine or human law seems to have been unknown to him. So true
was this that when he foresaw a future barrenness of the land many
years before it actually came to pass, he had the produce of the fields
stored up. So remarkable were the instances of his skill that his words
of advice seemed to come from God rather than from man. His son
was Moses who, besides inheriting his father's knowledge, was also
graced with a comely appearance. But the Egyptians, who were suffering from scabies and tetter, when warned by an oracle, drove Moses
out of the land and also the others who were affected by the disease,
lest the pestilence should gradually spread among a greater number.[45]

Such then is Justin's statement.

Now this same Moses, who according to the testimony of
these historians was a man of wisdom and understanding,
wrote quite fully and accurately about these events, as he
naturally would about happenings in which he and his people
were participants. Therefore we must first supplement the
want of knowledge on the part of these men by his trustworthiness and authority, which even they recognize; secondly,

[44] Pompeius Trogus, a historian living in the age of Augustus. He wrote
Historiae Philippicae, a history of Macedon, which in reality was a universal
history. Justin probably lived in the fourth century A.D.
[45] Justin *Histories* xxxvi. 2.

we must confute the deceit and malice of the Egyptian priests, who by cunning (and this is perfectly evident) attempted to bury in oblivion the memory of the manifest wrath and mercy of the true God. To be specific, these priests told a confused story in order not to cast reproach upon their own idols. For by telling the truth they would have proved that they should worship that God, Who by His counsel had foretold their disasters and Who by His help had enabled them to escape them. Perhaps we might give a kindlier interpretation and say that they had forgotten the truth. For through the foresight of that Joseph of ours, who was a servant of the true God and who was dutifully and zealously concerned about the welfare of his Master's people, they themselves as priests had plenty of produce; but because they were false priests, they did not suffer when the rest were hungry. In truth, "Whoever is satisfied, forgets; whoever suffers, remembers." [46]

Although the histories and registers are silent, nevertheless the land of Egypt itself is a witness which offers evidence of that age. In those days the country was brought under the king's power and was restored to its own cultivators; from that time to the present day, it has regularly paid a tax of a fifth part of its entire produce. It was during the reign of the king Diopolita, whose name was Amasis, that the great famine came to Egypt. This was also the time that Baleus was ruling over the Assyrians and Apis over the Argives. The seven years of famine, however, were preceded by seven years of plenty. Exercising his usual shrewdness, our Joseph collected and stored the surplus of these years. This surplus ordinarily would have perished through neglect in proportion to the bountifulness of the crop. He thus saved all Egypt. He amassed all the money for Pharaoh and all the glory for God, rendering, by his just stewardship, "tribute to whom tribute was due and honor to whom honor." [47] He acquired the flocks, lands, and wealth of all, in accordance with a fixed

[46] Cicero *Pro Murena* xx. 42.   [47] Romans 13:7.

agreement with them; and in return for a fifth of their property he released those who had sold both themselves and their lands in exchange for a grant of [grain]. Who would believe that this Joseph, whom God had placed over the Egyptians as the author of their deliverance, should have been so quickly forgotten that a little while later the Egyptians would condemn his sons and entire kinship to slavery, would inflict hardships upon them, and would crush them by massacres? Hence we must not be astonished if there are some men in our own age who, though they would remove the sword hanging over their necks by pretending to be Christians, either never mention or else defame the very name of Christ, through Whom alone they are saved, and maintain that they are sorely oppressed in Christian times. In reality they are made free by the benefits which these times confer upon them.

9.   EIGHT hundred and ten years before the founding of the City, Amphictyon,[48] the third king after Cecrops,[49] reigned at Athens. In his time a flood carried away most of the population of Thessaly, although some were saved by taking refuge on the mountains, especially on Mount Parnassus, whose environs were then ruled over by Deucalion. Because he supported and fed the refugees who came to him on rafts and who were resting upon the twin ridges of Parnassus, Deucalion is said to have saved the human race. Plato is a witness that in those days numerous plagues and terrible diseases afflicted Ethiopia and reduced the population almost to a state of desolation. And, lest perchance anyone should think that there was any interval between the time of God's wrath and the visitation of war's fury, let it be known that Father Liber[50] drenched with blood an India which had already been reduced to subjection. He filled this land with slaughter and polluted it with lusts, and all of this despite the fact that

48 Amphictyon is said to have named the city.
49 Cecrops, a legendary king, of whom many fables are told.
50 Later identified with the Greek "Bacchus."

the people of India never offended others and wished only to live the quiet lives of slaves.

10. POMPEIUS and Cornelius [51] bear witness to the fact that in the eight hundred and fifth year before the founding of the City the Egyptians were oppressed by unspeakable evils and intolerable plagues. The disagreement in the testimony of these historians disturbed me somewhat, though both declared that the following facts relating to the Jews should be recorded. For Pompeius—or possibly Justin—has this to say:

When the Egyptians were suffering from scabies and tetter, they took warning from an oracle and drove Moses and all those diseased from the boundaries of Egypt, so that the pestilence might not gradually spread among a greater number of people. After he had become leader of the exiles, Moses stealthily carried off the sacred vessels of the Egyptians, who, when they tried to recover them by force of arms, were compelled by storms to return home.[52]

Cornelius, however, speaks about the same events as follows:

Most authors agree that when leprosy, which horribly disfigures the bodies of its victims, had broken out throughout Egypt, King Bocchoris consulted the oracle of Ammon[53] and, upon asking for a remedy, was ordered to cleanse his kingdom and to drive away to other lands this race of men because it was hateful to the gods. So the Jewish people were sought out in their dwellings and gathered together. Afterward, when they were abandoned in the desert and all of the exiles, except Moses, were downcast and weeping, it was he who warned them not to look for any assistance from the gods or from men but to place their trust in themselves under the guidance of the heaven-sent leader. By his aid they would first cast off the burden of their present miseries.[54]

Thus Cornelius tells us that the Jews were forcibly driven into the desert by the Egyptians; but later, when evidently off his guard, he adds that in Egypt they had cast off the burden of their miseries with the help of their leader Moses. Therefore it is clear that certain prompt measures taken by Moses have been concealed. Justin likewise asserts that when Moses was driven out with the rest of the people he took

[51] That is, Pompeius Trogus and Cornelius Tacitus.
[52] Justin *Histories* xxxvi. 2.   [53] Zeus Ammon.
[54] Tacitus *Histories* v. 3. The meaning of the entire passage is in dispute.

away by stealth the sacred vessels of the Egyptians and that
when the Egyptians strove to recover these by force of arms
they were compelled by storms to stop and to return home.
Justin then has recorded something more, though not all of
the story, which Cornelius has concealed. Since both, therefore, have given testimony to the greatness of Moses as a
leader, his deeds and words should be taken on his own testimony just as he has related them.

The Egyptians then began to torture the people of God,
that is, the race of that Joseph by whose efforts they had
been preserved. Previously they had oppressed and forced
this people to do the work of slaves. When by a cruel edict
the Egyptians also compelled them to slay their own children,
God, through Moses as His spokesman, commanded that His
people be set free so that they might serve Him. God then
inflicted harsh punishments on the Egyptians for their contempt and stubbornness. Overburdened and worn out at last
by ten plagues, the Egyptians now compelled the Jews, whom
they had been unwilling to let go earlier, to hasten their departure. After waters turned into blood had brought to the
Egyptians, parched as they were from thirst, relief from suffering far worse than the suffering itself; after creeping frogs
had spread horrid filth over everything clean or unclean;
after the whole air had become alive with glowing sciniphes [55]
from which no one could escape; after dog-flies had run about
the interior parts of their bodies, moving in a loathsome manner and bringing sharp pains as severe as they were disgusting; after all the flocks and cattle had been suddenly destroyed
in a general murrain; after running sores and festering ulcers,
or, as they themselves preferred to say "scabies and tetter,"
had broken out all over their bodies; after hail (and there
was fire mingled with the hail) had beaten down man, beast,
and tree; after swarms of locusts had devoured everything
and had attacked even the very roots and seeds of the plants;
after a darkness had come that was dreadful with its appari-
tions, so dense that it could be felt, and so lasting that it

[55] A kind of stinging insect. The Latin form is usually *cinifes*.

brought death; and finally, after the first-born had been
slaughtered throughout all Egypt and all the people were
passing through a common period of mourning, those who
had not yielded before to God when He commanded, yielded
now when He punished.[56] But their repentance was insincere.
Soon afterward they dared to pursue the exiles and paid with
their lives for their impious obstinacy. For the king of the
Egyptians led his entire army, which included chariots and
horsemen, against the wanderers. The size of the army may
be inferred from this evidence, or at least chiefly therefrom,
that once six hundred thousand men fled in terror before it.
But the God who protects the oppressed and chastises the
stubborn suddenly divided the waters of the Red Sea. On
each side of the path opened, He formed the waters into motionless walls like unto mountains. He held these walls in
position so that the good, encouraged by the hope that their
journey was nearing its end, might enter unharmed upon the
path leading to safety of which they had despaired, while the
wicked should enter a pitfall where they would unexpectedly
meet their death. After the Hebrews had thus passed in
safety over the dry passage, the masses of stationary water
collapsed behind them, overwhelming and destroying the
whole host of Egypt together with its king.[57] The entire province, which had previously been afflicted with plagues, was
emptied by this final slaughter. Even at the present day there
remain unmistakable evidences of these events. For the tracks
left by the chariots and the ruts made by the wheels are visible not only on the shore but also in the deep as far as the
eye can see; and if by chance these marks are at times disturbed, accidentally or purposely, Divine Providence at once
restores them to their former appearance with the help of
the wind and waves. Thus if a man be not taught the fear of
God by the study of revealed religion, that fear may be borne
in upon him by this example of God's wrath.

In those days also the heat was so continuous, oppressive,
and intense, that it is said that the sun, after passing through

[56] *Exodus* 1–14.   [57] Exodus 14.

the regions of the heavens outside of its regular course, did not visit the earth with its warmth but scorched it with fire. Neither the Ethiopians, who were more used to heat than other peoples, nor the Scythians, who were unaccustomed to it, could endure this raging heat beating down upon them. In accounting for this phenomenon, some people would not concede to God His own ineffable power, but sought worthless, petty explanations and invented the absurd story of Phaethon.

11. DURING the seven hundred and seventy-fifth year before the founding of the City, in the course of the quarrel between Danaus and his brother Aegyptus, the daughters of the former murdered the fifty sons of the latter.[58] Later Danaus himself, the instigator of these many crimes, was driven from the kingdom which he had won by many shameful deeds. He then betook himself to Argos and there persuaded the Argives to help him in a despicable act: for he drove Sthenelas from his kingdom and made himself king, even though Sthenelas had welcomed him when he was an exile and in need.

The hospitality extended by the bloody tyrant Busiris in Egypt was barbarous and his religion was still more barbarous; it was his custom to drink to the health of his gods, who were partners in his crimes,[59] with the blood of his innocent guests. I wonder whether this practice seemed as detestable to the gods themselves as it undoubtedly seemed to men. In those days, too, a parricide was added to the incest involving Tereus, Procne, and Philomela. More detestable than either of these crimes was the meal embellished with a dish too horrible to mention: for in avenging her sister Philomela, whose honor Tereus had violated and whose tongue he had torn out, Procne killed her own little son and Tereus, his father, ate him. In those same times Perseus

---

[58] Actually there were only forty-nine murders, since one of the brides, Hypermnestra, spared her husband Lyncaeus. For her disobedience to her father's orders, she was kept in close confinement, but she was later forgiven and permitted to rejoin her husband.

[59] On the advice of Phrasius, a soothsayer from Cyprus, Busiris sacrificed foreigners to Zeus in order to free the land of continued famine.

traveled from Greece to Asia where, after a long and difficult campaign, he subdued some barbarian tribes. Now a conqueror, Perseus gave his own name to one of the conquered tribes, and henceforth these people were called Persians.

12.   But I am forced to confess that in the interest of anticipating the end of my book, I have left out many details concerning the evil conditions of the age and have abbreviated everything, since in no way could I have ever passed through so thick a forest of evils unless I had hastened my journey by frequent leaps. Inasmuch as the Assyrian kingdom was governed by about fifty kings and was hardly ever at peace during the one thousand one hundred and sixty years that elapsed before the reign of Sardanapalus (offensive and defensive wars were always being waged) what purpose will be served if I attempt to recall these events by enumerating them, to say nothing of describing them? This is especially so since I must discuss the deeds of the Greeks, and above all I must survey those of the Romans. Neither is there any need for me to recount the disgraceful deeds of Tantalus and Pelops, which are even more disgraceful when told. You will recall how the Phrygian king Tantalus most scandalously seized Ganymedes, the son of Tros, king of the Dardanians, and how he took him into his disgusting embrace. The poet Phanocles [60] confirms the story and also mentions the fact that a great war arose on this account. Perhaps Phanocles tells this story because he wished this same Tantalus to appear as the servant of the gods when he corrupted the stolen boy in his own home in order to prepare him for the lust of Jove. Tantalus, indeed, did not hesitate to employ at Jove's banquets even his own son Pelops.   .

Likewise one grows weary of referring to the struggles, however great they may have been, of this Pelops against Dardanus and the Trojans. We are accustomed to hear them repeated so often in stories that no one pays much attention

[60] A Greek elegiac poet, living in the age of Philip and Alexander the Great, who wrote of the manner and spirit of old Greek life.

to them. I am also omitting those stories about Perseus, Cadmus, the Thebans, and the Spartans, which Palaephatus [61] describes as he follows their winding course through mazes of successive evils. I am silent about the disgraceful crime of the Lemnian women.[62] I pass over the lamentable flight of Pandion, the king of the Athenians. I conceal the hatreds, debaucheries, and parricides of Atreus and Thyestes, which even the gods detested. I omit Oedipus, the slayer of his father, the husband of his mother, the brother of their children, his own stepfather. I prefer to be silent about how the brothers Eteocles and Polynices attacked each other, each one striving to be the murderer of the other. Nor do I wish to call to mind Medea, "smitten by a savage love," who rejoiced in the slaughter of her little children, or anything else that was done in those days. One may guess how much men then suffered from the fact that even the stars are said to have fled.

13. IN THE five hundred and sixtieth year before the founding of the City, the Cretans and Athenians engaged in a bitter struggle in which both sides suffered disastrous losses. The Cretans were victorious and made their triumph even bloodier by cruelty, handing over some children of noble Athenian parentage to be devoured by the Minotaur. I do not know whether it would be more accurate to describe this creature as a man with the qualities of a wild beast or as a beast with the qualities of a human being. But the Cretans fattened this misshapen monster on these noble children who had been torn away from their native land. In those same days the Lapithae and Thessalians struggled in contests no less famous. In his first book, "Concerning Incredible Tales," Palaephatus relates that the Lapithae believed and asserted that the Thessalians were themselves centaurs because, when

---

[61] Palaephatus cannot be identified. He wrote, probably in the Alexandrian Age, a book called "Concerning Incredible Tales," in which he reëxamines old Greek myths and then presents what he considers reasonable versions of these tales.   [62] In one night all slew their husbands.

their horsemen rushed here and there in battle, horse and man appeared to be one body.

14. FOUR hundred and eighty years before the founding of the City, Vesozes,[63] the king of Egypt, eager to engage in war with the South and the North (regions separated by almost the whole heaven and the whole sea) or to annex them to his kingdom, first declared war upon the Scythians. He had previously sent ambassadors to bid them obey his laws. In answer, the Scythians told the ambassadors that Vesozes, who was already an extremely wealthy king, had stupidly undertaken war against a poor people and that he himself ought to fear this war more than they, because it was clear that the uncertain issues of the struggle promised only losses instead of rewards. They further declared that they would not await his attack, but would on their own initiative go forward to plunder his army.

There was no delay, for deeds followed these words. First the Scythians forced Vesozes himself to flee back in terror to Egypt. Then they attacked his army, which was now without a leader, and captured all of its war equipment. If they had not been prevented by the swamps from entering Egypt, they would have ravaged that entire country. Returning at once they exacted tribute from Asia, whose people had been the victims of repeated slaughter and massacre and which was now in a state of complete subjection. They remained at war in Asia for fifteen years until they were recalled by the demand of their wives, who threatened to allow their neighbors to become the fathers of their children unless their husbands returned.

15. MEANWHILE among the Scythians, two young men of the royal family, Plynos and Scolopetius, were driven from their home by a faction of the nobility.[64] They took with them

---

[63] One would expect "Sesostris" to be the name, since Justin so gives it in *Histories* ii. 3.

[64] This chapter is almost wholly taken from Justin *Histories* ii. 4; and the

a large band of young men and founded a settlement on the
coast of Cappadocia Pontica near the Thermodon River and
close to the Themiscyrian Plains. From that base they plundered the nearby lands for a long time, until their neighbors
finally united for common action, led them into ambush, and
slaughtered them. Violently agitated by their own exile and by
the loss of their husbands, their wives took up arms and
killed the men who survived so that the common lot of widowhood might unite all of them in one purpose. Enraged against
the enemy, these women then destroyed their neighbors and
at the cost of their own blood exacted vengeance for their
dead husbands. Later they obtained peace by force of arms
and entered into marital relations with foreigners. They put
their sons to death as soon as they were born, but brought up
their daughters carefully. They burned off the right breasts
of these girls so that they might discharge arrows without hindrance. For this reason these women were called
Amazons.[65]

The two queens of these Amazons, Marpesia and Lampeto,
divided the army into two parts and drew lots to decide which
should carry on war and which should guard the homeland.
When the Amazons had subdued most of Europe and had
captured some cities of Asia as well—they themselves became founders of Ephesus and other cities [66]—the principal
part of their army, laden with rich booty, was then recalled
home. The rest of the army, which had remained with Queen
Marpesia to protect their empire in Asia, was cut to pieces
in battle with the enemy.

Sinope, the daughter of Marpesia, took her place. As a
crowning achievement to her matchless reputation for courage,
she remained a virgin to the end of her life. So great was the
admiration and fear spread by her fame among peoples al-

---

meaning must be supplemented in the light of this text, since Orosius is often
vague in his wording.

[65] A word which Justin takes as ἀ-μαζός, "without breast," but the real deri-
vation of the word is unknown.

[66] Smyrna, Cyme, and Myrine. Compare Strabo *Geography* xi. 5. 4.

ready alarmed that even Hercules, when he was ordered by his master to bring the weapons of the queen, certain that he would have to face inevitable peril, gathered together the pick of the noble youth of all Greece and prepared nine vessels of war. After estimating his forces, he was still not satisfied and preferred to proceed against the queens suddenly and to surround them when they had no suspicion of attack.

Two sisters, Antiope and Orithyia, were ruling the kingdom at this time. Arriving by sea, Hercules overcame them when they were off their guard, unarmed, and indolent from the care-free existence of peaceful times. Among the large number slaughtered or captured were the two sisters of Antiope, of whom Hercules kept Melanippe while Theseus took Hippolyte. Theseus married Hippolyte, but Hercules returned Melanippe to her sister Antiope and received as the price of her ranson the weapons of the queen. After the reign of Orithyia, Penthesilea became ruler of the kingdom, and the accounts of her courage exhibited among men during the Trojan War have come down to us.

16. O GRIEF! The shame of human error! Women, fleeing from their native land, entered, overran, and destroyed Europe and Asia, the largest and most powerful sections of the world. For almost a hundred years they kept control of these lands by overthrowing many cities and founding others. The blame for the oppression of the times was nevertheless not to be imputed to the utter worthlessness of men. On the contrary, recently these Getae, who are at present also called Goths (Alexander publicly said that they must be shunned, Pyrrhus dreaded them, and even Caesar avoided them), after stripping their homes bare and abandoning them, united their forces in one body and invaded the Roman provinces. By proving themselves to be a menace over a long period of time, these barbarians hoped upon their request to obtain an alliance with Rome—an alliance which they could have won by force of arms. They asked only enough land for a small settlement, not a location which they themselves

might choose, but one which we should grant them. These
barbarians who were free to take for themselves as much as
they wanted, since the whole world was subdued and lay
open to them, these barbarians, I say, requested this favor.
They who alone were feared by unconquered kingdoms offered now their services to protect the Roman Empire.

Since in their blindness the pagans do not see that these
things were brought to pass by Roman virtue, and won
through the faith [Christian] of the Romans, they do not
believe and are unwilling to acknowledge, though they realize it, that it was through the mediation of the Christian
religion, which, unites all peoples in the recognition of a common faith, that those barbarians became subject to the Romans without a conflict—those men whose wives had destroyed the greater part of the earth with measureless
slaughter.

17. But four hundred and thirty years before the founding
of the City, the abduction of Helen, the covenant of the
Greeks, the assembly of a thousand ships, then the ten years'
siege, and lastly the celebrated destruction of Troy, is well
known to all. That war was waged for ten years with the
utmost cruelty. The most renowned poet Homer in his glorious song has clearly shown what nations and how many peoples were caught in the path of that hurricane and destroyed.
It is not our concern to unfold again the story in sequence,
since that would take a long time and besides it is well known
to everybody. If there is really any justification for my critics
being displeased with the present state of affairs, whatever
their condition, let those who have learned about the length
of that siege, the savagery and massacre accompanying the
overthrow of the city, and the state of bondage that followed,
consider the enemies of Rome. For although these enemies
might have pursued the Romans through all lands with troops
prepared to attack, they were led by the hidden mercy of
God to follow these same Romans over all seas and even to
offer hostages in order to obtain peace. And lest people think

that their actions were motivated only by love of a quiet life,
behold them offering to risk their lives against other tribes to
maintain the Roman peace.

18. MOREOVER, in the next few years came the events that
followed the arrival of Aeneas in Italy after he had fled from
Troy,[67] that is, the strifes he aroused, the kinds of wars he
provoked over a period of three years, and the number of
peoples he involved in hatred and ruthlessly overthrew. All
these have been imprinted upon our memories by the instruction received in our elementary schools. And interspersed
with these events were the exiles and shipwrecks of the Greeks,
the disasters of the Peloponnesians at the time when Codrus
died, the uprisings of the barbarian Thracians in new wars,
and the general disorders throughout all Greece and Asia.

19. IN THE sixty-fourth year before the founding of the
City, Sardanapalus reigned over the Assyrians. He was their
last king and a man more corrupt than a woman. Arbatus, who
was his prefect at that time and in authority over the Medes,
cursed his king when he saw him dressed in the garb of a
woman spinning purple cloth in the midst of a flock of harlots.
Soon afterward the Median people rose in revolt and forced
Sardanapalus to go to war. When he was defeated, he threw
himself upon a burning pyre. The kingdom of the Assyrians
then gave way to that of the Medes. After many wars had
broken out on all sides (to discuss them in due order does not
seem to me to be at all appropriate) the sovereignty passed
through various stages in a cycle first to the Scythians, next to
the Chaldeans, and finally back again to the Medes. We ought
to treat briefly the number of disasters and massacres of
peoples that occurred and also the many wars that arose in
the course of which over and over again many great monar-
chies changed hands.

After these events, Phraortes ruled over the Medes. He
consumed twenty-two years of his reign in continual warfare

[67] Vergil *Aeneid* i. 1 ff.

with the Assyrians and the Persians. His successor was Diocles, a man expert in arms and constantly engaged in war. On the death of Diocles, Astyages received a greatly enlarged empire. Lacking a male heir, he adopted his nephew Cyrus, who was a Persian by birth. As soon as Cyrus grew into manhood, he gathered together a band of Persians and declared war upon his adopted father. Furthermore, Astyages had forgotten the crime which a short while before he had committed against Harpagus.[68] He had killed the latter's only little son and had served him to his father at a banquet; and in order that none of a father's great sorrow over the loss of his child might be lessened through happy ignorance, he tauntingly emphasized the gruesome character of the banquet by displaying the hands and head of the child to his father. Forgetting what he had done, Astyages entrusted the highest command of the war to this same Harpagus who, upon receiving command of the army, at once betrayed him and turned over the army to Cyrus.

When Astyages learned of this, he assembled his troops and marched against the Persians. He began a battle which was the more fiercely contested because he announced to his men that whoever became afraid and attempted to withdraw from battle would be put to the sword. When the battle line of the Persians was compelled to yield ground gradually under the attack of the Medes who, because of this threat, were fighting furiously, the mothers and wives of the Persians blocked their path and begged them to return to the battle. The women exposed their nakedness to all, lifting up their dresses and asking whether the men wished to take refuge in the wombs of their mothers or of their wives. Shamed by this action, the men returned to battle, made an attack, and forced their pursuers to flee. In this engagement Astyages was taken prisoner. Cyrus deprived him of his kingdom only and put him in charge of the powerful nation of the Hyrcani. Astyages indeed had no wish to return to the Medes. This

[68] This episode and the rest of the story are told with greater detail in Justin *Histories* i. 4–7.

was the end of the Median Empire. The states that paid tribute to the Medes, however, revolted from Cyrus; and this was the cause and source of many wars against him.

20. AT THAT time Phalaris [69] the Sicilian set up a tyranny and began to plunder the people of Agrigentum. He was cruel in his designs and even more cruel in their execution; he perpetrated all kinds of outrages upon innocent people. At length, though unjust himself, he discovered a man whom he punished justly. For a certain Perillus, a worker in bronze, who professed friendship for the tyrant, conceived a work befitting the latter's cruelty. He constructed a brazen bull in whose side he ingeniously fashioned a door that would allow those condemned to be thrust inside the animal. Thus, when the imprisoned victim was roasted by a fire placed underneath, the vacuum of the hollow bronze would magnify his tortured cries and would send forth a sound corresponding, in its funereal tone, to that of its namesake. This abominable wonder made the cries seem like the bellowing of cattle, not the groans of men. Phalaris was delighted with the contrivance, but detested its inventor. It furnished the opportunity for both vengeance and cruelty, for he punished the maker in his own invention.

There was also among the Latins in a somewhat earlier age a king named Aremulus who prospered by a career of crime and impiety over a period of eighteen years. But by divine judgment he was struck by a bolt of lightning and paid at an early age a penalty long overdue.

Let the Latins and Sicilians now choose whether they would prefer to have lived in the days of Aremulus and Phalaris or in these Christian times. In the former times these tyrants tortured to death innocent people; in the latter, the Roman emperors, who were among the first to be converted to the Christian religion, did not demand punishment even for the injuries committed by the tyrants themselves, after their overthrow had brought good to the Republic.

[69] The ruler of Agrigentum in Sicily about 570 B.C.

21. THIRTY years before the founding of the City, the Peloponnesians and the Athenians waged a great war into which both peoples entered with their full strength and enthusiasm. Each side was finally forced by mutual destruction to withdraw from combat and to terminate the war, as if both had been defeated. At this time a tribe of Amazons, accompanied by the Cimmerians, made a sudden incursion into Asia and wrought severe, prolonged, and widespread devastation and carnage.

Twenty years before the founding of the City, the Lacedaemonians involved in ruin the entire resources of Greece by waging a war of untiring fury against the Messenians, because the latter had outraged their virgins during the offering of a solemn sacrifice. The Lacedaemonians had bound themselves by great curses and had pledged themselves by solemn vows never to return home until they had captured Messena. Nevertheless they were recalled home when they had become weary from the siege which, though lasting ten years, had brought them none of the fruits of victory. They were also moved by the complaints of their wives who drew attention to their long widowhood and the danger of their becoming sterile. After deliberating on the matter, they became fearful that with no possibility of begetting children their own perseverance would promote their ruin even more than the Messenian War. They therefore sent back to Sparta those selected soldiers who, after taking the oath of allegiance, had come to the army as reinforcements. These soldiers were allowed to have promiscuous relations with all the women, a license infamous enough and not of any real use. But the Lacedaemonians persevered in their plan, captured the Messenians by fraud, and reduced them to slavery. When they had suffered cruel domination, scourgings, and chains for a long while, the Messenians shook off the yoke, took up arms, and renewed hostilities.

The Lacedaemonians chose the Athenian poet Tyrtaeus to be their leader in this war. After being routed in three battles, they made good their losses by adding to their army a band of slaves who had been granted their freedom. Even then they thought that they ought to give up the struggle because of threatening danger, but they were again inflamed by a poem composed by their poet and leader Tyrtaeus. When he recited the poem before the assembly of the people, they at once rushed again into the struggle. Their feelings were so greatly stirred when they attacked that hardly ever has a bloodier battle raged. Although the Lacedaemonians finally won the victory, the Messenians renewed the struggle a third time. Neither did the Lacedaemonians delay. Each side brought many troops to supplement its own forces. The Athenians prepared to attack the Lacedaemonians in a new quarter while the latter were engaged elsewhere. But the Lacedaemonians did not remain passive. Though they themselves were embroiled with the Messenians, they dispatched Peloponnesian troops to engage the Athenians in battle. The Athenians, who had sent a small fleet to Egypt, could not match the enemy's strength and were easily defeated in a naval engagement. Later when this fleet had returned and the Athenian forces had also been strengthened by the flower of their troops, they challenged the victors to battle.

Abandoning the campaign against the Messenians, the Lacedaemonians turned their arms against the Athenians. A long and severe war followed in which there was a succession of victories and defeats, and it was uncertain which side would be victorious; finally, while the issue was still hanging in the balance, both withdrew from the fray. (It must be most clearly understood that it was Sparta herself that was given the title of the Lacedaemonian state and hence the Lacedaemonians are called Spartans.) When the Lacedaemonians were later recalled to the Messenian War, they made an agreement with the Thebans, in order that the Athenians might not have any rest in the interim. They promised to restore to the Thebans the rule over the Boeotians, which the latter had lost in the days of the Persian War, on the condition that the Thebans would undertake a war against the Athenians in their behalf. So great a fury possessed the Spartans that, even though they were already engaged in two wars, they would not refuse to undertake a third, provided they could obtain new allies against their enemies.

Alarmed by such a storm of wars, the Athenians chose two leaders: Pericles, a man of proven courage, and Sophocles, a writer of tragedies. Dividing their forces, the Athenians, ravaged far and wide the territories of the Spartans and added many cities of Asia to the Athenian Empire. From this beginning the struggles continued for fifty years on land and sea with victory ever doubtful, until the Spartans, with their wealth dissipated and their confidence completely shattered, were regarded as disgraced even by their own allies.

But we think of little moment those afflictions which lay so heavily upon Greece. What we at present find difficult to bear is any interference whatsoever in our pleasures or any restraint placed upon our passions, even for a moment. There is this difference, however, between men of that age and of this: the men of that age endured with patience those unbearable burdens because they were born and raised amid them and knew no better times, whereas men of our age, accustomed to perpetual peace in a life of tranquillity and pleasure, are disturbed by every little cloud of anxiety that envelops them. If only they would pray to Him who can end this period of unrest, trifling though it be, and to Whom they owe this continued peace which was unknown to other ages!

Remembering that I promised (even though I limit the order of my narrative by some sort of division) to tell the history of the world from the creation to the foundation of the City, let me here bring to an end this book, which has set forth the story from the foundation of the world. My following book then may begin from the foundation of the City. It will contain the account of the evils of those days, which became more closely intertwined, forasmuch as men indeed grew more versed and skilled in wickedness.

THE SECOND BOOK

1. THERE is no person living today, I think, who does not acknowledge that God created man in this world. Hence, whenever man sins, the world also becomes subject to censure, and owing to our failure to control the passions that we ought to restrain, this earth on which we live is punished by having its animal life die out and its crops fail. It follows, too, that if we are the creation of God, we are also properly the object of His concern. For who loves us more than He who made us? Who orders our existence better than, He who has created and loves us? Who can order and control our actions more wisely or more firmly than He who foresaw what must be done and then brought to pass what He had foreseen? Hence those who have not read, feel, and those who have read, recognize, that all power and all government come from God. But if powers are the gift of God, all the more so are the kingdoms from which all other powers proceed. If the kingdoms, however, are rivals, it is better that some one kingdom be supreme, to which all the other kingdoms are subject. Thus, for instance, in the beginning there was the Babylonian kingdom, then the Macedonian, later the African, and finally the Roman, which endures even unto our own day. By the same inscrutable plan, four main kingdoms were preëminent in successive stages at the four cardinal points of the world, to wit, the Babylonian kingdom in the East, the Carthaginian in the South, the Macedonian in the North, and the Roman in the West. Between the first and the last, that is, between the Babylonian and the Roman, bridging as it were the space of years between an aged father and his little son, there intervened the brief period of supremacy of the African and Macedonian empires, circumstances rather than the law of inheritance determining their rôle as guardians and trustees. I shall

now try to explain as clearly as possible whether this is really
the truth.

2.   AMONG the Assyrians, Ninus was the first king who
achieved preëminence. After his death, his wife Semiramis,
the queen of all Asia, restored the city of Babylon and made
it the capital of the Assyrian kingdom. For a long time the
power of the Assyrian kingdom remained unshaken. But when
Arbatus, otherwise called Arbaces, the prefect of the Medes
and himself born a Mede, had killed his king Sardanapalus
at Babylon, he transferred the title and supreme power of the
kingdom to the Medes. In this way the kingdom of Ninus
and of Babylon was turned over to the Medes the same year
in which Procas, the father of Amulus and of Numitor and
the grandfather of Rhea Silvia, who was the mother of Romulus, began to rule among the Latins. Moreover, I will prove
beyond question that all these events were arranged according
to the inscrutable, mysterious, and unfathomable judgments
of God and that they were not brought to pass either by
human agencies or by mere chance. Now, all histories of ancient times begin with Ninus, and all histories of Rome begin
with Procas. There was an interval of sixty-four years from
the first year of the reign of Ninus to the time when Semiramis began to restore Babylon, and from the first year of
the reign of Procas to the founding of the city of Romulus
there was a like interval of sixty-four years. Thus in the reign
of Procas the seed of future Rome was sown, although as
yet the shoot had not appeared. In the same year of the reign
of this Procas, the kingdom of Babylon came to an end, though
Babylon herself has survived to our own day. But when Arbatus withdrew to the Medes, the Chaldeans successfully maintained their right to Babylon in opposition to the Medes and
continued to hold part of the kingdom. In this way the Medes
legally ruled Babylon, but the Chaldeans were in actual possession. The latter, however, on account of the ancient dignity
of the royal city, preferred not to name the city after themselves, but rather to take their own name from it. Hence it

happens that although Nebuchadrezzar [1] and his successors down to Cyrus are considered powerful because of the strength of the Chaldeans and famous because of the Babylonian name, nevertheless they are not included in the number and line of illustrious kings.

To resume my argument, Babylon under her prefect Arbatus was dishonored in the very year when during the reign of King Procas, to speak accurately, the seeds of future Rome were sown. Babylon was finally overthrown by Cyrus at the time when Rome first freed herself from the despotism of the Tarquin kings. Indeed, it was as if the one fell and the other arose at the same instant: while Babylon endured foreign rule, Rome for the first time began to resent the arrogance of her own princes; Babylon, like a person awaiting death, bequeathed an inheritance, for which Rome, though still a minor, presented herself as the heir; and as the rule of the East fell, the rule of the West arose.

And now without further delay I commit myself to the teeth of madmen, to be freed by the assistance of truth alone.

3. NINUS reigned for fifty-two years and, as I have said, was succeeded by his wife Semiramis. In the middle of her reign after ruling forty-two years, she established Babylon as her capital. Babylon thus had almost reached the one thousand one hundred and sixty-fourth year from her foundation, when she was robbed of her wealth and deprived of both king and kingdom by the Medes under Arbatus, the king of the Medes and the prefect of Babylon as well. The city herself, however, flourished for some time afterward. In like manner, after an equal number of years, that is, almost one thousand one hundred and sixty-four years after her foundation, Rome, too, was invaded, but in this case by the Goths under Alaric, king of the Goths and count of Rome. The city was despoiled of her wealth but was not deprived of her sovereignty. She abides even unto our own day and exercises her

---

[1] Orosius writes "Nabuchodnossor." The name is popularly written "Nebuchadnezzar," but accurately it is "Nebuchadrezzar."

rule unimpaired. Indeed the hidden decrees of God have preserved to so great an extent the parallelism between the histories of the two cities that at Babylon, Arbatus, the prefect of
that city, usurped the rule, while at Rome, Attalus, the prefect
of Rome, attempted to seize control of the government; yet
the impious attempt was frustrated at Rome alone and then
only by the aid of a Christian emperor.

Therefore I have believed that these matters should be
especially mentioned, so that by a partial exposition of the
inscrutable judgments of God, those who grumble (foolishly,
to be sure) about our Christian times may know that one God
has directed the course of history, in the beginning for the
Babylonians and in the end for the Romans; and that they
may also know that it is only because of His mercy that we
live at all, and that if we live in misery it is because of our
own uncontrolled passions. Mark well how similar were Babylon and Rome in their origin, how similar in power, in size,
in age, how similar in good and in evil. Yet how different
were their decline and fall. For while Babylon lost her rule,
Rome retains her rule; the one was left desolate by the murder
of her king, the other is secure with her emperor unharmed.
And why is this? Because in Babylon the punishment for the
shameless passions of her people was visited upon the king,
whereas in Rome the serene, even temper of the Christian
faith was preserved in the person of the king; in Babylon
wanton folly, lacking all reverence for religion, satisfied to
the full its thirst for pleasure, whereas here in Rome there
have been Christians who were merciful and Christians to
whom mercy was shown, and Christians on account of whose
memory and in whose memory mercy was shown. So let these
grumblers stop railing at religion and provoking the patience
of God, who will surely grant them forgiveness if at any time
in the future they cease abusing Him. By all means let them
reflect with me upon the times of their ancestors, which were
so disturbed by wars, accursed with crimes, rank with dissensions, and unending in miseries. They then can properly
shudder to think that such times existed, and they cannot help

but pray that they may never return. They will pray to Him as the one God, Who by His inscrutable justice permitted such days to exist in the past, and who by His manifest mercy is now responsible that they are no longer here. I will now set forth these matters more fully by unfolding my history in due order from the very beginning of the City.

4.   FOUR hundred and fourteen years after the overthrow of Troy, in the sixth Olympiad (at the beginning of the fifth year to be exact), which was wont to be celebrated with contests and games at the city of Elis in Greece, the city of Rome in Italy was founded by the twins Romulus and Remus. Romulus at once ruined the reputation of his reign by murdering his brother and immediately followed this crime by another of equal cruelty. He gave as a dowry to the Sabine women, who had been seized and bound in shameless wedlock to the Romans, the blood of their husbands and parents. After killing first his grandfather Numitor and next his brother Remus, Romulus seized the sovereign power and founded the city. With blood he dedicated the kingdom of his grandfather, the walls of his brother, and the temple of his father-in-law; and he assembled a band of criminals by promising them exemption from punishment. His first battlefield was the Forum of the City, a fact signifying that foreign and civil wars, always interrelated, would never cease. His action in holding the Sabine women, whom he had enticed by offering them a treaty and by inviting them to a celebration of games, was as wicked as was his dishonesty in seizing them in the beginning. As soon as he had received Titus Tatius into an alliance, he killed this old man, who had always pursued the cause of honor and piety and whose forces had long been repelled by Roman arms. He provoked a war with the Veientes, hitherto of little importance, but now a very powerful people. The town of the Caeninenses was captured and destroyed. Once the Romans took up arms, there was no more rest, since they were fearful of the abject poverty and dreadful famine which threatened them at home if they should ever become peaceful.

From this point on, I shall touch as briefly as possible upon the struggles that went on without interruption, the seriousness of which may be gauged by the number of men involved.

I shall tell how Tullus Hostilius, the founder of the military system, with full confidence in his well-trained army, declared war on the Albans, and how, although the issue was for a long time in doubt, disaster to both sides was inevitable; how the short conflict of the triplets finally put an end to this destructive and indecisive struggle;[2] how when peace was again broken, Mettus Fufetius, during the war with the Fidenates, planned to betray his country but was prevented and paid the penalty of his double-dealing by having his body torn in two by chariots moving in opposite directions; how the Latins, who had always fought under the leadership of Ancus Marcius, were at last defeated; how Tarquinius Priscus in repeated conflicts destroyed all the powerful, neighboring peoples of Tuscany, at that time twelve in number; how the Veientes were conquered but not crushed by the persistent attacks of Servius Tullius; how Tarquinius Superbus gained control of the state by murdering his father-in-law, how he held on to it by his brutal attacks on citizens, and finally how he lost it by his disgraceful defilement of Lucretia. Along with his vices at home I may also mention his brilliant achievements abroad, namely, his capture of the powerful towns of Ardea, Oricolum, and Suessa Pometia in Latium, and his exploits against the city of Gabii, accomplished either by his own trickery, or by the executions carried out by his son, or by the strength of the Roman forces.[3]

The expulsion of one king, together with the abandonment of the very name and office of king, shows what continuous misfortunes the Romans had suffered for two hundred and

[2] Three brothers belonging to the Roman army fought against three brothers who were members of the Alban army. The Roman Horatius alone survived the contest and brought victory to the Roman arms.

[3] Tarquinius deceived the people of Gabii by pretending to be at odds with his own son Sextus. The latter fled to Gabii to escape his father's cruelty and wrath. There he won the confidence of the people and soon became their leader. Acting upon the advice of his father, he systematically slew the leading men of the city and thus made its capture easy.

forty-three years under the despotism of their rulers. For if only the arrogance of a single king had been at fault, he alone would have necessarily been expelled, and the royal prerogative would have been reserved for better men. Accordingly, after the kings had been expelled, the Romans thought that they ought to look after their own affairs rather than to allow any other person to restrain their liberty, and they therefore created consuls. As the Republic grew older and more mature, it entered upon harder enterprises under the direction of the consuls.

5. Two hundred and forty-four years after the founding of the City, Brutus, the first Roman consul,[4] desired not only to equal but to surpass the number of parricides committed by the founder and first king of Rome. He dragged before the assembly his own two young sons and the two youthful Vitellii (his wife's brothers) on the charge that they had been plotting to recall the kings to the City; and he had them beaten with rods and beheaded. Later, in the war with the Veientes and the Tarquinienses, Brutus himself fell in an encounter in which Arruns, the son of Superbus, also lost his life. Porsena, king of the Etruscans and a strong supporter of royal prerogative, attempted to restore Tarquinius to his throne by force and for three whole years harassed, encompassed, and besieged the terrified city. Mucius made a profound impression upon the enemy by the heroic fortitude that he displayed in burning his own hand and the virgin Cloelia made a like impression by the admirable bravery that she showed in crossing the river. But for them,[5] the Romans would surely have been

---

[4] L. Junius Brutus, 509 B.C. Beginning at this point I have given in footnotes the full names of the consuls and the year as found in E. M. Fischer, *Römische Zeittafeln* (Altona, 1846). Many of the early dates are unreliable and cannot be verified.

[5] Gaius Mucius, a noble youth, indignant at the helplessness shown by the Romans in combatting the Etruscans, offered to settle the issue alone. He planned to murder the Etruscan king, Porsinna, and thus end the struggle. After making his way to the camp of the enemy, he made his attempt, but he mistook the secretary of that king for the king himself and was captured. To show the contempt he had for his body, he put his hand into a dish of hot coals and allowed it to be burned. This brave deed made so great an im-

forced to suffer captivity after defeat at the hands of an unrelenting enemy or else slavery by becoming the subjects of
Tarquinius, who would once more be their king.

After this, the Sabines gathered together every available
soldier and with a great army hastened towards Rome.
Alarmed by the danger which threatened, the Romans elected
a dictator whose authority and power exceeded that of a
consul. At this juncture of the war, this move was of the
greatest advantage. Then followed the secession of the
plebeians from the patricians. The people, aroused by divers
wrongs, took up arms and occupied the Sacred Mount[6] at
the time when the dictator M. Valerius was making a levy of
soldiers. What could have been more dreadful than the ruin
that resulted when the body, severed from its head, planned
the destruction of that which gave it life? Had not a hasty
reconciliation taken place before the separation had made
itself felt, the Roman nation would have been destroyed by
internal disaster. For an insidious disease through its malig-
nant growth spreads and threatens destruction as surely as
do the visible disasters of war. And in the consulships of T.
Gesonius and P. Minucius[7] the two evils most abhorred by the
human race, famine and pestilence, swept the wearied city.
There was some respite from battles, but there was none from
deaths.

The Veientes and the Etruscans, both dangerous enemies,
reinforced by the troops of their neighbors, took arms and
were met by the consuls M. Fabius and Cn. Manlius.[8] The
Romans then took an oath pledging themselves not to return

---

pression upon the king that he offered terms of peace. To prove that a maiden
could equal the audacity of a man, Cloelia, a hostage in the Etruscan camp,
gathered together a band of her fellow hostages and swam the Tiber, despite
the showers of arrows discharged by the enemy. The king, admiring her
bravery, though at first incensed, finally regarded her action as no violation
of the peace treaty. Rather he allowed her to return to his camp and take
half the remaining hostages with her. The details of these stories are found in
Livy *Histories* ii. 12–14.

[6] An isolated hill in the country of the Sabines, on the right bank of the
Anis and west of the Via Nomentana, three miles from Rome.

[7] T. Geganius Macerinus and P. Minucius Augurinus, 492 B.C.

[8] M. Fabius Vibulanus II and Cn. Manlius Cincinnatus, 480 B.C.

to camp unless victorious. So fierce a struggle ensued, bringing disaster to conquered and conqueror alike, that the greater part of the Roman army was lost. Manlius, the consul, and Quintus Fabius, a man of consular rank, were killed in the battle. The consul M. Fabius, however, refused to accept the triumph granted him by the Senate on the ground that the Republic should rather mourn such great losses.

The family of the Fabii, greatly renowned for its size and power, was chosen by lot for the conflict with the Veientes. The death of its members caused the Republic so great sorrow that even today the evil names given both to the river in which they were drowned and to the gate through which they set out remain as witnesses.[9] Three hundred and six of the Fabii, the brightest lights of the Roman state, sought permission to carry on alone the war against the Veientes. They were strengthened in their hope of victory by the initial successes of the expedition they had so rashly undertaken. Afterward they were drawn into ambush and surrounded by the enemy. All were killed on the spot. Only one man was spared to report the news of the great disaster, so that his country might experience even greater misery when it learned of the losses which it had suffered.[10] Not only were these calamities taking place in Rome, but in addition each province was aflame from its own fires; and what the poet has particularly described in one city, I myself shall apply to the whole world:

Bitter mourning everywhere, everywhere fear, and many a shadow of
     death.[11]

6.   AT THAT time, Cyrus, king of the Persians (I have mentioned him earlier in the course of my history when he was ravaging Asia, Scythia, and the whole East, at the time when Tarquinius Superbus, king or traitor as you will, was oppress-

[9] Livy *Histories* ii, 49–51, tells the story in detail. The river is the Cremera. The right arch of the Porta Carmentalis was called the Unlucky Way.
[10] Livy and Dionysius of Halicarnassus, though they give entirely different stories, agree that all the Fabii were killed and that the one member of the family to remain alive was a young man who was too young to join the expedition and therefore stayed home. [11] Vergil *Aeneid* ii. 368–69.

ing Rome either by reducing her people to slavery or by making war upon them) Cyrus, as I said, after subduing all his adversaries, attacked the Assyrians and Babylon, a people and a city at that time richer than all others. But the Gyndes River, the second in size after the Euphrates, blocked his attack. Now one of the royal horses, remarkable for its glossy coat and its beauty, and very confident of its ability to cross the river at a ford where the dashing waves were lifted high by the rapid current, was carried away by the force of the current, cast headlong, and drowned. In his anger the king decided to punish the river, declaring that this river which had just now devoured his splendid horse should be made so shallow that women would scarcely have to wet their knees in crossing. In order not to waste a whole year there with his entire army, Cyrus diminished the volume of the water in the Gyndes River by cutting canals through it and drawing off its water through four hundred and sixty streams. After he had shown the trench diggers how to do this work, he also drew off the water of the Euphrates, which flowed through the middle of Babylonia and which was by far the mightiest of rivers. Cyrus was thus able, without getting wet, to make his way by means of the passable fords—now that parts of the river bed lay exposed—and captured a city that men scarcely believed either that human labor could have constructed or human strength have destroyed.

Many, indeed, have told how Babylon was founded by Nebrot the Giant, and how she was restored later by Ninus or by Semiramis. This city, surrounded by level country and delightfully situated, was arranged like a camp, with her four surrounding walls formed into a square. The report of the strength and size of these walls hardly seems credible; they were fifty cubits wide and four times as high. The wall, constructed of burnt brick with bitumen used as mortar, was surrounded on the outside by a very wide moat in place of a stream. In the circuit of the walls were a hundred bronze gates. Small stations for defenders, facing one another, were placed at regular intervals along the edges of the two sides of the wall and between them there was sufficient room for a four-horse chariot to pass. The houses within the city were of eight stories and were remarkable for their imposing height. Yet that great Babylon, the first city founded after the reëstablishment of the human race, was now almost immediately conquered, captured, and overthrown. At this time Croesus, a Lydian king famous for his wealth, came to bring relief to the Babylonians. He was defeated and fled back in alarm to his own kingdom. After Cyrus had attacked Babylon as an enemy, had overthrown it as a conqueror, and had set it in order as a king, he transferred the war to Lydia. There he had no trouble in defeating an army already demoralized by the previous battle. He also captured Croesus himself but granted him both his life and a patrimony.

It is unnecessary to add here further instances of the unstable conditions that have followed the changing events of history; for whatever has been built up by the hand of man falls and comes to an end through the passage of time. This truth is illustrated by the capture of Babylon. Her empire began to decline just as it had reached the height of its power, so that, in accordance with a certain law of succession which runs through the ages, posterity might receive the inheritance due to it—posterity which was fated to hand on the inheritance according to the same law. Thus great Babylon and vast Lydia fell at the first attacks that Cyrus made after his arrival. The mightiest arms of the East and also the head [12] succumbed in a campaign of a single battle; and now we ourselves, as we anxiously watch the structure of the once powerful Roman Republic, debate whether it is trembling more from the weakness common to old age or from the blows struck by foreign invaders.

7. WITH the approach of the next season, this same Cyrus declared war on the Scythians. Though Queen Thamyris,[13] who was then ruling over this people, could have prevented

---

[12] The metaphor is taken from the human body. Babylon is the head and the members of its empire are the arms. [13] The Tomyris mentioned by Herodotus.

Cyrus from crossing the Araxes River,[14] she permitted it: first because she had full confidence in her own abilities, and secondly because she would be able to hem in her enemy by using the river to block his retreat. Cyrus then advanced into Scythia and pitched his camp at some distance from the river that he had crossed. After preparing wine and food, he craftily abandoned the camp and fled back as if terrified. On learning of this, the Queen sent a third of her forces under her young son to pursue Cyrus. The barbarians, as if guests at a banquet, were overcome by drunkenness, and when Cyrus shortly thereafter returned, all, including the young man, were cut down. After the loss of her army and her son, Thamyris prepared to wash away her sorrow—that of a mother or of a queen as you will—with the blood of the enemy rather than with tears. She feigned anxiety and despair over the disaster that she had suffered and retreated gradually, drawing the over-confident enemy into ambush. By placing ambuscades among the mountains, she destroyed two hundred thousand Persians together with their king; beyond all else, her delight at this success was increased by the fact that not even one man survived to carry news of the disaster. The Queen had the head of Cyrus cut off and thrown into a leather bottle full of human blood, mocking him in unwomanly fashion: "I satisfy you," she said, "with the blood for which you thirsted, and of which for thirty years you have never had your fill." [15]

8. IN THE two hundred and forty-fifth year of the City, some time after Cyrus had lost his life among the Scythians, Darius obtained possession of the kingdom by a stroke of luck. The ruler of the kingdom in the interval between the reigns of Cyrus and Darius was Cambyses, the son of Cyrus. After conquering Egypt, Cambyses abolished its sacred ceremonies and destroyed its temples because he abominated the whole religion of the country. After his death, the magi, using the

[14] A river in eastern Scythia, not to be confused with the large river of the same name in Armenia.

[15] This entire episode is taken from Justin *Histories* i. 8.

name of the Smerdis [16] whom they had murdered, attempted
to foist an impostor upon the kingdom, but they were soon
found out and overcome. Darius, one of those who had put
down the insolent magi by the sword, was then unanimously
closen king. After Darius had reconquered the Assyrians and
Babylon, which had broken away from the Persian kingdom,
he declared war on Idanthyrsus, king of the Scythians. The
real reason for this action was his failure to obtain the king's
daughter whom he had sought in marriage. Undoubtedly an
urgent reason for exposing seven hundred thousand men to
death—the lust of one man! Taking with him incredible quantities of war material and accompanied by seven hundred
thousand armed men, he invaded Scythia to war against an
enemy who gave him no opportunity for a regular battle, but
who tore his rear guard to pieces by their sudden attacks.
Fearing that his retreat would be blocked by the destruction
of the bridge over the Hister, Darius fled back in alarm after
losing eighty thousand of his troops. He did not, however,
reckon the number of slain among his losses; [17] indeed that
famous king did not even feel a loss, which involved numbers
that few other kings would have dared to surround with an
army.

Darius then attacked Asia and Macedonia and completely
subdued them. After a sharp naval struggle he also conquered the Ionians. Next he directed his arms in an attack
against the Athenians on the ground that they had lent assistance to the Ionians. The Athenians, when they learned that
Darius was advancing, requested aid of the Lacedaemonians.
But when they found out that the Persians would be delayed
by a religious holiday lasting four days, [18] they grew confident
as a result of this favorable opportunity. Drawing up ten thousand citizens and a thousand Plataean allies in battle array, they

[16] The magi murdered the lawful heir to the throne whose name was Smerdis.
They then ruled the kingdom by controlling a puppet king whom they called
Smerdis to deceive the people and to conceal their crime.

[17] The number was small in comparison with the size of his army.

[18] Orosius has confused the original story; it was the Lacedaemonians who
were delayed by a religious holiday.

rushed forth against six hundred thousand on the fields of
Marathon. On that day Miltiades was in command of the
battle. Relying more on speed than on courage, he engaged
the enemy at close quarters, making a well-timed and swift
attack before the enemy could repulse his charge by a shower
of arrows. So great was the contrast between the two modes
of fighting that it gave the impression that on the one side
there were men prepared to slay, whereas on the other the
men were like cattle ready to be led to slaughter. Two hundred thousand Persians fell on the field of Marathon that
day. Darius really felt that loss and, beaten and routed, he
fled back to Persia in the vessels which he had seized. While
he was on the point of renewing the war and striving his utmost to take revenge upon the victors, he died in the midst of
his preparations. This was in the seventy-fourth Olympiad,
that is, in the two hundred and seventy-fifth year after the
founding of the City, at the time when Popilia, a Vestal
Virgin, was buried alive at Rome because she had violated
her chastity.

9.   XERXES, who succeeded his father Darius on the throne,
took fifteen years to make preparations for the continuation
of the war which his father had begun against Greece. De-
maratus, the Lacedaemonian, who at that time happened to
be an exile at the court of Xerxes, imparted this information
to his countrymen by writing upon tablets and then covering
the writing with wax. Xerxes' forces are said to have numbered seven hundred thousand soldiers from his own kingdom
and three hundred thousand from allied states; he also had
one thousand and two hundred beaked ships and three thousand transports. Thus it has been recorded, and not without
reason, that there were scarcely enough rivers to drink from,
scarcely enough lands to invade, and scarcely enough seas to
traverse for an army so unprecedented in size and for a fleet
so huge.
   This army, so incredibly large from the point of view of our
times—it is more difficult to count its numbers now than it was

to conquer it then—was met in the passes of Thermopylae by the Spartan king Leonidas and his four thousand men. Contemptuous of the small numbers of his opponents, Xerxes ordered battle started at once and to be fought at close quarters. Those Persians whose relatives and comrades-in-arms had fallen on the field of Marathon were at the forefront of the struggle and the slaughter. Following on their heels was a larger and more sluggish group that was neither free to advance, ready to fight, nor prepared to flee, because its members were standing on the bodies of the dead. The battle, which lasted three days, was not a battle of two peoples but the slaughter of one.

On the fourth day, however, Leonidas saw that the enemy had surrounded him on all sides. He urged his auxiliary allies to withdraw from the battle and to escape to the summit of the mountain, so that they might save themselves for better times; but for himself and his Spartans another fate was in store: they owed a greater duty to their native land than to life itself. After dismissing the allies, Leonidas warned the Spartans that they had much to hope from glory, but nothing from life; that they should not wait for either the enemy or daybreak, but, taking advantage of the night, must break into the camp, attack in hand-in-hand conflict, and throw the lines of battle into confusion. Where could victors perish more honorably than in the camp of the enemy? Persuaded, therefore, to prefer death, they armed themselves to avenge their approaching death as if both making sure and taking vengeance for their own destruction. Remarkable as it may seem, six hundred men burst into a camp of six hundred thousand. An uproar arose throughout the camp. The Persians themselves lent aid to the Spartans by killing one another. The Spartans, seeking the king and not finding him, cut down and overthrew everything. As they overran the whole camp, they were barely able to pursue the fleeing men on account of the dense piles of bodies. Without doubt they would have been victors had they not chosen to die.[19] The battle continued

[19] Here again Orosius follows Justin closely. Compare Justin *Histories* ii. 11.

from nightfall through the greater part of the next day; and then each man, worn out at last by his efforts to conquer and with his limbs now failing him, seemingly satisfied that he had avenged his own death, sank down in exhaustion and died amid the tangle of dead bodies, in fields palpitating with thick and half-congealed blood.

10. XERXES, twice defeated on land, prepared for war on the sea. Themistocles, the Athenian general, now learned that the Ionians were sending a fleet, ready for action, to assist Xerxes. He decided to win them over to his side and to detach them from the enemy. As a matter of fact he had turned the attack of the Persians against himself by furnishing aid to these Ionians in an earlier war. Since there was no opportunity for a conference, he ordered signs to be displayed and fastened on rocks in those places toward which the Ionian ships were believed to be heading. By these signs he fittingly rebuked and blamed his former allies and comrades in peril, who through inactivity were now failing to do their duty. By means of a religious exhortation he persuaded them to respect the oaths of their old treaties and especially urged them, when battle had begun, to stop rowing instead of advancing and then to withdraw wholly from the battle.

The king kept part of the fleet nearby and stayed on shore as a spectator of the fight. On the other hand, Artemidora, queen of Halicarnassus, who had come to the aid of Xerxes, joined very fiercely in the fray among the foremost leaders. Thus the actual characteristics of the sexes were reversed; feminine caution was seen in a man and manly boldness in a woman.

While the issue of the battle [20] was still in doubt, the Ionians, complying with Themistocles's request, gradually began to withdraw from the battle. Their defection persuaded the Persians, who were already contemplating flight, to flee openly. In this panic many ships were sunk and many were

[20] The engagement was fought in the Strait of Salamis that lies between the eastern end of the island and the coast of Attica.

captured; but the greater part of the fleet, fearing the rage of the king no less than the cruelty of the enemy, slipped away and set sail for home. Mardonius came to Xerxes, now a prey to anxiety because of his many misfortunes, and told him that he must return to his kingdom before the news of defeat stirred up revolution at home and that he, provided that the remaining troops were entrusted to him, would wreak vengeance upon the enemy and avert disgrace from the royal family. But if the reverses of war should continue, he would indeed yield to the enemy, but yet without bringing dishonor upon his king. Xerxes approved the plan and entrusted the army to Mardonius.

The king set out with a few men for Abydos, where, as though he were conqueror of the sea, he had built a bridge. But when he found that the bridge had been shattered by winter storms, he crossed over in a fishing skiff in fear and trembling. What a sight for men to look upon and grieve over as they measured the fickleness of fate by this great reversal of fortune! He before whom the very sea had lain concealed and had borne as the yoke of its captivity the bridge that joined its shores was content to hide in a tiny boat; he to whose power nature herself had yielded as he leveled mountains, filled valleys, and emptied rivers, lacked even the humble service of a single slave. The foot soldiers also, who had generals assigned to them, became exhausted by toil, hunger, and fear. As disease spread and grew worse, a great and deadly stench arose from the dying and the roads were filled with corpses. Horrible birds of prey and scavenging beasts, attracted by the lure of food, followed the dying army.

11. MARDONIUS, however, whom Xerxes had appointed to finish the war, first enjoyed a brief period of success but soon was reduced to sore straits. He took Olynthus, a Greek city, by storm. He then tried by various inducements to win over the Athenians to a peaceful settlement, but when he saw their indomitable spirit of independence he set fire to part of the city and shifted the entire field of operations to Boeotia.

Thither a hundred thousand Greeks pursued him and at once engaged him in battle. After destroying his forces,[21] the Greeks compelled Mardonius to flee with a few men, destitute, as if he had been shipwrecked. They captured a camp filled with royal treasure, but this wealth greatly weakened their former industry, because after the division of this booty Persian gold at once began to corrupt the virtue of the Greeks. Complete ruin followed hard upon these wretched beginnings. For it happened that on the same day that the forces of Mardonius were destroyed in Boeotia, part of the Persian army in Asia was engaged in a naval battle under Mount Mycale.[22] There a report suddenly spread among each of the fleets and people to the effect that the forces of Mardonius had been wiped out and that the Greeks had been victorious. A wonderful ordering of divine judgment this, that the report of a battle joined in Boeotia at sunrise reached Asia at noon of the same day, even though so great a stretch of sea and land lay between! This report agreed well with the fact because when the Persians heard of the destruction of their allies they were overcome first with grief and then with despair, so that they were neither ready to fight nor swift to flee. Thus strengthened by continued good fortune, the Greek army attacked the enemy while they were still overwhelmed by their defeat and utterly demoralized. Xerxes, despicable in the eyes of his own subjects on account of his unsuccessful campaigns in Greece, was deceived by his prefect Artabanus and assassinated in the royal palace.

Surely such times are ideal and worthy of commemoration! Oh those days of uninterrupted serenity that are laid before us to be recalled as though we were in darkness! In a short time three wars with three neighboring kings carried away nine million men from the bowels of one kingdom, not to mention the wretched condition of Greece at that time, where the deaths by war exceeded even this number, the very thought of which makes us grow faint. Leonidas, the most famous

[21] The battle of Plataea, 479 B.C.
[22] In Lydia. The battle was fought both on the water and on land.

of the Lacedaemonians in this war against Xerxes, realizing that the moment of his own death and that of the enemy was at hand, spoke to his own six hundred these famous words of encouragement: "Eat your breakfast as if you were about to eat among the dead." But he mercifully persuaded his auxiliaries, whom he ordered to withdraw from the battle, to save themselves for better times. Take note that whereas Leonidas promised better times in the future, our contemporaries insist that the better times were in the past. What else can be deduced, when both berate their own times, but that the times either have always been good though unappreciated, or that they will never be better in the future?

12. IT IS my purpose now to return to Rome and to that period from which I have digressed. The fact is, I am not forced by any cessation of calamities to pass over to other peoples. But since in former times evils were everywhere rampant, intermingled in their actual occurrences, it is perfectly proper to report them in this manner. Indeed it is my aim to compare the periods of history, not to scoff at the trials of any particular age.

In Rome, then, during a short interval of peace, two hundred and ninety years after the founding of the City, a severe plague raged violently throughout the city. This plague was like those that had so often disturbed the rare periods of truce or forced such truces to be made. Just as the omen had foretold, the heavens themselves seemed to be aflame when the mistress of the nations burned with the fires of this disease. In that year the plague killed both consuls, Aebutius and Servilius,[23] and carried away most of the military forces. Its horrible contagion led to the death of many nobles, but even more of the plebeians, whose numbers had already been depleted by a plague forty years earlier.

In the next year the exiled citizens and fugitive slaves under Herbonius, a Sabine, invaded and burned the Capitol. There

[23] L. Aebutius Elva and P. Servilius Priscus Structus, 463 B.C.

the young men, led by the consul Valerius,[24] opposed them with the utmost bravery; but so savage and desperate was the battle that the consul Valerius himself was killed and by his own death diminished the glory of his victory, ignominious at best since it was gained in a battle against slaves.

The following year a consul was besieged after the defeat of his army. The Aequi and the Volsci had met and overcome the consul Minucius [25] in battle. After he had taken refuge on the Algidus,[26] they surrounded his army and began to reduce it by famine and sword. It would have turned out badly for the consul had not the renowned dictator Quintius Cincinnatus raised this close siege by defeating the enemy. While he was working in the fields, Quintius was summoned from the plough to high office and, after assuming command and marshaling his army, he soon conquered and imposed the cattle yoke upon the Aequi. Holding victory in his hands as he had held the handle of the plough, he was the first to drive his enemies before him like oxen under the yoke.

13. IN THE two hundred and ninety-ninth year of the City, while the Romans were waiting for the return of the legates whom they had sent to the Athenians to copy the laws of Solon, they were restrained from further warfare by famine and pestilence. But in the three hundredth year, that is, in the ninety-fifth Olympiad, the *potestas* [27] of the consuls was entrusted to the decemvirate in order to establish the laws of

[24] P. Valerius Publicola, 460 B.C., second consulship.

[25] L. Minucius Esquilinus Augurinus, 458 B.C.

[26] A mountain in Latium, but the name is generally applied to the northeastern section of the Alban Hills. A plain of high elevation in this region was frequently the scene of battles.

[27] "The *imperium* represents the supreme authority of the community in its dealings with the individual. It is not strictly opposed to *potestas,* which is a generic term to indicate the power with which a magistrate was vested for the discharge of his duties. Under the Republic the exercise of the *imperium* within the city was limited, especially by the right of appeal. It was still enjoyed by the magistrate abroad, however, and the term was practically restricted in its application to the absolute power exercised by him." See F. F. Abbott, *A History and Description of Roman Political Institutions* (Boston, 1901), p. 153.

Attica. This brought great disaster to the Republic. For one of the decemvirate, Appius Claudius, continued to hold the *imperium* after the others had retired from office. Immediately there followed a conspiracy of the others. All of them contemptuously disregarded the custom which reserved the distinction of the *imperium* to one officer alone, while it awarded the *potestas* to all alike, and each one, pursuing his own evil inclinations, helped to throw everything into confusion. Among other actions they all had the insolence and presumption to appear unexpectedly in public with the twelve fasces and with the other symbols of authority. When this new and evil régime had begun and the consuls had abandoned all sense of duty, there sprang up a line of tyrants who added two tables of laws to the previous ten. Acting always in a most overbearing and arrogant manner they appeared in public with these same symbols of authority on the day when it was customary to lay down their official powers. Likewise the lust of Appius Claudius aroused the greatest hatred. In order that he might dishonor Verginia, he first accused her of being a slave. For this reason, her father Verginius was driven to commit a righteous murder out of his anxiety for her liberty and by his shame at her disgrace. As the people looked on, he killed his daughter, whom Appius had already reduced to slavery. The people, thoroughly aroused by this necessary atrocity and warned by the danger threatening their liberty, took up arms and occupied Mount Aventine.

In the one hundred and third and one hundred and fifth Olympiads, frequent earthquakes shook Italy throughout the entire year. They were so severe that Rome was constantly disturbed by reports of innumerable tremors and of the destruction of villas and towns. A drought came later. It was so parching and lasted so long that hope was then and there abandoned of raising crops on the land during that or the succeeding year. At this time the Fidenates, terrible enemies and supported by great auxiliary forces, were threatening the Roman defenses. But Aemilius, dictator for the third time, captured the city of Fidenae with great difficulty and thereby

rid the state of a great burden of evil and restored it to
health. These evils which they had suffered and the excited
state of their minds created such a tension in the Romans that
the wars which spread far and wide abroad caused them to
forget the disasters at home. On the other hand, following
the losses of war, various plagues raged in heaven and on
earth and by their increasing malignity caused the breaking
of the truces which previously had been observed.

14.   IN THE earliest times Sicily was the land of the Cyclopes
and since that time has ever been the nurse of tyrants. Much
of the time, moreover, Sicily found herself under the rule of
slaves.[28] These Cyclopes were gratified by the flesh of men,
the tyrants by the torture of men, and the slaves by the death
of men. This was her fate except that in foreign wars she was
wont to be considered an object of spoil or booty. To put it
briefly, the island has never known any respite from misfortune until now; nay rather, as her changing fortunes show, in
times past this island alone of all countries has always suffered from both internal and external revolutions, but now
she alone is free from them. Indeed, to make no mention
either of the long period of suffering and misfortune that the
island has undergone or of the peace that she now enjoys, Etna,
which in former days used to boil over from frequent eruptions that brought ruin upon cities and fields, at present only
smokes harmlessly as if to prove that it has been active in
the past.

For the time being I shall omit the history of the tyrants,
which records how one tyrant took vengeance upon his predecessor and then succeeded him, and I shall resume my narrative with the middle period, that is, from the three hundred
and thirty-fifth year after the founding of the City. The
people of Rhegium, a city near Sicily, were suffering at this
time from internal discord, and the city was divided into two

[28] The allusion is probably to Micythus. He was a slave of Rhegium, who
exercised the regency for the young sons of the king, 476 B.C. His rule was wise
and vigorous. When the sons came of age, he retired to private life.

factions by dissensions. One party called to its assistance veterans from Himera, a city of Sicily. After these soldiers had driven from the city the citizens whom they had been asked to fight, they proceeded to kill those whom they had come to assist. They seized the city as well as the wives and children of their allies, thus daring to commit a crime more extreme than that of any tyrant. Surely it would have been better for the inhabitants of Rhegium to suffer anything at the hands of their fellow citizens rather than to call in of their own accord strangers who would take as booty from them their native land, wives, children, and Penates after they themselves had been driven into exile.

Similarly, when the inhabitants of Catana [29] were suffering harsh treatment at the hands of the hostile Syracusans, they asked help from the Athenians. The latter equipped and at once dispatched a fleet to Sicily. But they did this in their own interest rather than in that of their allies. For they were striving to extend their own power and were afraid that the Syracusan fleet, which had been recently equipped, would increase the strength of the Lacedaemonians. Seeing that the first detachment of their troops had made an auspicious beginning, cutting the enemy to pieces, the Athenians again sent an expedition to Sicily, but this time with more supplies and a stronger army under the command of Laches and Chariades. Wearied by the long war, the people of Catana concluded a treaty with the Syracusans and later spurned the assistance of the Athenians. But when the Syracusans, wishing to expand their power, transgressed the terms of peace, the people of Catana again sent envoys to Athens to beg for assistance. They came clad in mourning, with hair and beard unshorn, trying to excite sympathy by their manner of dress and speech.

A large fleet was then fitted out and placed under the

[29] Orosius writes "Catina." This city is located on the eastern coast of Sicily about midway between Tauromenium and Syracuse, and almost at the foot of Mt. Etna. Orosius records the story almost word for word from Justin *Histories* iv. 3, as he did the preceding episode. He reproduces many errors which he could have avoided by a more careful handling of the subject.

command of Nicias and Lamachus, who set sail once more for Sicily with so large a force that even the people of Catana, who had summoned them, became frightened at the consequences of their own decision. The Athenians fought two successful infantry battles and shut up the exhausted enemy in the city. As a result of the blockade by the fleet, the enemy were now surrounded on both land and sea. The Syracusans, after their resources had been dissipated and they themselves had become exhausted, begged assistance from the Lacedaemonians. The latter at once sent Gylippus. He was alone, but his personal value was greater than that of many troops. Hearing on his arrival that the course of the war was going adversely, he gathered auxiliaries, partly from Greece and partly from Sicily, and then seized strategic positions. Defeated in two battles, he was undismayed. In the third encounter he killed Lamachus, put the enemy to flight, and freed his allies from the siege.

After this defeat on land, the Athenians undertook to try their fortunes on the sea and prepared to engage in a naval struggle. On learning of this, Gylippus summoned the fleet which the Lacedaemonians had been fitting out. Thereupon the Athenians sent reinforcements under Demosthenes and Eurymedon, two generals who were to take the place of their lost leader. The Peloponnesians, too, acting in accordance with a decree approved by many cities, sent large reinforcements to the Syracusans. Thus, under the guise of waging a war in behalf of their confederates, both sides carried on their domestic quarrels and, as if by an official order, transferred the struggle from Greece to Sicily. In this way the war was prosecuted by both sides with the utmost vigor.

In the first engagement the Athenians were conquered and lost their camp with all its wealth, both that belonging to the state and that owned by private citizens. They also lost the entire equipment which had been prepared for a long campaign. Their resources were now destroyed and they were in a critical position. In these circumstances Demosthenes advised them, while all was not yet lost, however much they seemed to be afflicted, to leave Sicily and to return home. Nicias, however, more desperate than the others because he was conscious of his own bad management from the beginning, begged earnestly to remain. The Athenians renewed the naval battle and soon, through lack of skill, were enticed into the straits of the Syracusan Sea and caught in the trap prepared by the enemy. Their commander Eurylochus [30] was among the first killed, and eleven of their ships were burnt. Demosthenes and Nicias abandoned the fleet, thinking that it would be safer to make their escape by a land expedition. Gylippus first took possession of one hundred and thirty of their abandoned ships and then set out to pursue the fugitives themselves, of whom he captured and killed as many as he could. Demosthenes escaped the disgrace of slavery by taking his own life, but Nicias crowned his discreditable and shameful career with a dishonorable captivity.

15. THE Athenians, after being harassed in Sicily for two years (during this time the Lacedaemonians also were not without losses) were then encompassed by other disasters at home.[31] Alcibiades, who earlier had been appointed general in the war against the Syracusans, was shortly afterward summoned to stand trial in answer to an accusation. He went into voluntary exile in Lacedaemon. There he urged the Spartans to concentrate their efforts once more upon a new war against the Athenians and not to allow them any breathing spell while they were sore pressed. All the Greek states agreed to carry out this undertaking. It was as if they had planned, for the public good, to assemble their forces to extinguish a general conflagration. Moreover, the Persian king Darius, remembering his father's and grandfather's hatred of Athens, employed Tissaphernes, the prefect of Lydia, to act for him and instructed the latter to conclude a treaty with the Lacedaemonians, promising to send them troops and money to defray the costs of the war. Strange to relate, the

[30] Undoubtedly the Eurymedon mentioned above.
[31] Chapters 15 to 19 follow closely the narrative of Justin.

wealth of the Athenians at that time was so great that, though
the forces of Greece, Asia, and the entire East were launched
against them, that is, against a single city, yet by constantly
fighting and never yielding, they seem to have been worn
down rather than conquered.

First of all, Alcibiades forced all the Athenian allies to
desert to the Lacedaemonians, but when the latter in their
envy plotted against him he fled (to Media) and took refuge
at the court of Tissaphernes. By his genius in adapting himself easily to circumstances and through his ability to speak
with eloquence and tact, Alcibiades soon came to be quite intimate with his host. He persuaded him not to assist the
Lacedaemonians with such lavish support, but rather to play
the rôle of an arbiter and spectator of the struggle and to
maintain intact the forces of Lydia against the victor. For
this reason Tissaphernes ordered only part of the fleet to sail
to Lacedaemonia. It was manned by a considerable force, so
that the Lacedaemonians, supported by just enough reinforcements, should have to fight and yet not be entirely safe from
danger at the hands of the enemy; but these were large
enough so that they should not feel ill supported and therefore give up the struggle which they had begun.

16. THE Athenians, long disturbed by domestic discord,
when threatened by actual danger transferred the highest
authority, by will of the people, to the Senate. For discords
are nourished by idleness, but when necessity presses, people
normally put aside private contentions and hates and take
counsel together. In the case of the Athenians, however, this
move would have ended in disaster, because they had an innate pride in their race and were enslaved by their lusts.
Alcibiades, therefore, was finally recalled from exile by the
army and put in charge of the fleet. When this became known,
the nobles first tried to betray the city to the Spartans, but
when they had come to the conclusion that this would be
useless they voluntarily went into exile. After freeing his native land, Alcibiades directed the fleet against the enemy.

The Athenians were victorious in the battle that followed. What is more, the greater part of the Spartan army was slain, almost all their leaders killed, and eighty of their ships captured, that is, all those ships which had not been either burnt or sunk in the battle.[32]

When the war was transferred to the land, the Spartans were equally unfortunate. Broken by these disasters, they sued for peace but were unable to obtain it. Moreover, the Syracusan troops were recalled to Sicily upon receiving news that Carthage was threatening war. Taking advantage of the situation, Alcibiades and his victorious fleet sailed up and down the entire coast of Asia, ravaging and destroying the country by warfare, fire, and sword. He captured and regained as many as possible of the cities that had withdrawn from their alliance not long before. Having thus gained a great reputation, Alcibiades came as conqueror to Athens where everyone received him with admiration and joy. Shortly afterward he strengthened his forces, increased the size of the army and fleet, and once more attacked Asia.

Thereupon the Lacedaemonians put Lysander in charge of their fleet and the direction of the war. Cyrus, the brother of Darius, who had been placed at the head of the government of Ionia and of Lydia to succeed Tissaphernes, also strengthened the forces of the Spartans with large supplies and reinforcements. Lysander then suddenly attacked and crushed the army of Alcibiades while it was intent upon booty and for that reason was scattered far and wide. Lysander was able, therefore, to gain the victory without any real conflict and to slaughter the soldiers while they were running away. The Athenians suffered a great disaster in this battle [33] and received a much more serious blow than any that they themselves had previously inflicted. When the Athenians learned of this disaster, they thought that Alcibiades had made it his concern to avenge himself upon them by becoming a traitor because he was still resentful over his former exile. They therefore appointed Conon in his place and en-

[32] The battle of Cyzicus, 410 B.C.   [33] The battle of Notium, 406 B.C.

trusted to him the remaining forces and the highest command
of the war.

In his desire to increase the number of his depleted forces,
Conon gathered together old men and boys and enrolled them
into an army. But a force of this kind could not prolong the
war, since a war is usually decided by the strength of an
army, not by its numbers. This unwarlike band was immediately captured or slain. The losses in that battle were so
great that not only the empire but even the Athenian state
seemed to have been destroyed. These desperate conditions
led the Athenians to give the freedom of their city to foreigners. Thus those who a little while before had dominated
the whole province of Asia were now reduced to the position
of safeguarding their own walls and liberty with the help of
this last line of defense. Though they did not judge themselves strong enough to protect their homes and liberty even
behind their own walls, yet they prepared to try their fortune in a second naval battle. Madness divorced from reason
thinks anger bravery; and rashness promises the fulfillment
of what wrath contemplates. Consequently all were either
captured or killed. There was nothing left for the survivors
to do.[34] Conon was the sole general to survive the fighting,
and he, fearing the vindictiveness of the citizens, withdrew
to the court of king Cyrus.[35] Evacoras, leader of the Lacedaemonians, deprived the Athenians of all their (subject)
cities, leaving them naught save a spiritless city. And even
this was not left them for long, because he afterward blockaded Athens herself. Famine, desolation, and disease harassed
the besieged Athenians. After suffering frightful miseries too
horrible to relate and seeing that there was nothing to look
forward to except death, they sued for peace. 65768

17. AT THIS point an important conference between the
Spartans and their allies was held. Most of the allies voted

---

[34] The disaster of Aegospotami, 405 B.C.
[35] Conon withdrew to Cyprus to enter the service of Evagoras. The text is in
error here.

to raze the restless city of Athens to her foundations and to blot out her troublesome people together with her very name; but the Spartans said that they would not permit one of the two eyes of Greece to be torn out. Furthermore the Spartans promised peace, provided that the fortifications of the harbor of Piraeus, which led to the city, be dismantled, that the remaining ships be voluntarily surrendered, and finally that the Athenians be willing to accept the thirty rulers chosen for them. The Athenians agreed and submitted to these terms. The Lacedaemonians then appointed Lysander to frame the laws that the city was to obey.

This year was noteworthy for the capture of Athens, the death of the Persian king Darius, and the exile of Dionysius, the tyrant of Sicily.

The thirty rulers who had been set over the Athenians became thirty tyrants. Their first action was to surround themselves with three thousand bodyguards and soon afterward they summoned to their side seven hundred soldiers from their victorious army. They then began an indiscriminate slaughter of all the citizens, after first murdering Alcibiades who, as he fled, was cornered in a bedroom and there burned alive. After his death, the tyrants, no longer dreading his vengeance, proceeded to deplete the ranks of the wretched survivors in the city by murdering them and confiscating their property. They also put to death Theramenes, one of their own number who, they felt, did not approve of their actions, making his fate an example to inspire fear among the others.

All the people left the city, fleeing in every direction; but since throughout all Greece exiles were denied hospitality by an interdict of the Lacedaemonians, they betook themselves to Argos and to Thebes.[36] There they were so heartened by their cordial reception that they not only succeeded in mastering their grief over the loss of their country, but even came to consider the possibility of recovering it. Among the exiles was Thrasybulus, a man of action and distinguished among

[36] These cities had refused to obey the edict.

the people because of his noble birth. He originated a daring project in behalf of his native Athens. The exiles gathered their forces into one body and captured the fortress of Phyle on the Attic border. Strengthened by the assistance offered by many states, they grew more powerful. To help the city that had been the universal home of eloquence, Lysias, the Syracusan orator, sent them five hundred soldiers and the money with which to pay their wages.

The battle that followed was fiercely fought. One party was struggling for the liberty of its native country, the other to uphold the rule of a foreign power. The battle itself reflected well the spirit and causes of both sides. After suffering defeat the tyrants fled back into the city and relieved from their posts all those Athenians whom they had earlier chosen as guards of the city, but whom they now suspected of treason. They even dared to tempt Thrasybulus himself with a bribe; but when this hope failed, they summoned reinforcements from Lacedaemonia and again rushed into battle. In this engagement the two tyrants who were by far the most cruel of them all were killed. Thrasybulus, realizing that the others who had been defeated and put to flight were for the most part Athenians, shouted and ran after them. He halted their flight by a speech and held them fast by the force of his entreaties. He pointed out clearly to them "the kind of people from whom they wished to flee, and the kind of people to whom they wished to flee for refuge." He also stressed the fact "that his party had undertaken war against the thirty tyrants, not against unfortunate citizens; nay, rather that all who remembered that they were Athenians ought to join those who were exacting vengeance in the name of Athenian liberty." This exhortation proved so convincing that they turned back immediately to the city and forced the tyrants to withdraw from the citadel and to emigrate to Eleusis.

Those citizens who only recently had been exiles and who had been welcomed and restored to full citizenship by Thrasybulus and his party now stirred up jealousy and strife among the tyrants, who saw in the freedom of others slavery for themselves. Soon after the declaration of war, the tyrants assembled as if to take part in a conference.[37] They were surrounded by ambuscades and butchered like the sacrificial victims in times of peace.

Thus restored to unity, the Athenians shed copious tears to express their great joy and built the foundations of their new-born liberty on the binding force of a solemn oath: to consign past discords and animosities to perpetual oblivion and unending silence. This kind of agreement, forming, as it were, a new structure of society and a new basis for happiness, they called an amnesty, that is, a complete abolition of existing differences. This was a very wise provision of the Athenians, especially after so many examples of misery; if the pact had been honored, human affairs would have prospered as a result of the harmony which prevailed when it was originally made, but this decree was vitiated to such an extent by its very wording that hardly two years had elapsed before Socrates, the most renowned of philosophers, was driven by the evil conditions of his time to take his own life by drinking poison. When almost forty years had passed (I shall say nothing about other matters) the Athenians themselves completely lost their liberty and became subjects of Philip, king of the Macedonians. What is more, being wiser than the rest, they now banished their domestic hatreds and brought their foreign wars to an end. They were well convinced by their own misfortunes that even the smallest affairs prosper as a result of harmony but that the greatest fail as a result of discord and that all actions, whether advantageous or harmful, which had been performed abroad, had been sown and had sprouted from roots at home. Their descendants were left an example of ruin and a plan for recovery, if indeed, after making allowance for the vacillation of the human mind, we concede that man remembers in prosperity what he heeded in adversity.

[37] Apparently they expected to enter into agreements that would enable them to recover their power.

18. ABOUT this time a civil war was waged among the Persians. Indeed it was even more than a civil war, for it ended only after a fratricide. Following the death of their father Darius, Artaxerxes and Cyrus contended for the throne. After both sides had made great preparations, they finally began a struggle that brought ruin to provinces and inhabitants alike. In this conflict, fortune set the two brothers charging against one another. Artaxerxes [38] was the first to be wounded by his brother, but he was saved from death by the swiftness of his horse. Cyrus, on the other hand, was soon overwhelmed by the royal cohort. So the struggle was brought to an end. Artaxerxes, gaining possession of his brother's army and its booty, strengthened his power over the kingdom by killing his brother. Thus all the peoples of Asia and Europe, now one against the other, now among themselves, were from time to time involved in murders and infamous deeds.

Notice that though I have discussed in so small a book and in so few words such a great number of events affecting many provinces, peoples, and cities, I have set forth no deeds that did not also involve a great number of misfortunes. Who could describe the desolation of that age, who could find words to tell of its deaths or who could weep sufficient tears for its sorrows? [39] Yet these very misfortunes, because they have grown dim with the passing of centuries, have afforded us exercise for our talents and interesting subjects for our stories. Let any one really apply himself wholeheartedly to an investigation of wars and their causes, and, standing as if on the top of a watchtower, let him compare the conditions of both ages. I am sure that he will then say that these unhappy and disturbed times could not have come about except through the will of an estranged and angry God. Nor can the present times become quiet again unless He becomes gracious and merciful.

[38] Artaxerxes II. The battle was fought at Cunaxa, 401 B.C.
[39] Vergil *Aeneid* ii. 361 ff.

Later Sicily was shaken by an exceedingly severe earthquake and was devastated by erupting fires and hot ashes from Mount Etna. These greatly damaged the fields and villages. At that time, too, the city of Atalante, adjoining the territory of Locris, was suddenly cut off by an inundation of the sea and was left an island. Also a plague attacked the wretched remnant of the Athenians and ravaged them for a long time.

19. THREE hundred and fifty-five years after the founding of the City, the siege of Veii, which lasted ten continuous years, destroyed the besiegers rather than the besieged. The Romans lost large numbers through sudden sallies made by the enemy. Moreover, they were driven to carry on war from winter quarters and to pass the winter under furs. In the end they even had to endure hunger and cold within sight of the enemy. Though they failed to show any signs of true Roman courage, they finally took the city by surprise, employing mines and a concealed attack. A retreat followed this advantageous rather than famous victory, which Camillus, dictator for the first time, had won over the Veientes. Then came the invasion of the Gauls and the burning of Rome. Let any one dare, if he can, compare any disturbances of this age with that disaster; he must, however, overcome a natural tendency that refuses to attach equal importance to a story of a past disaster and a calamity suffered in the present.

The Senonian Gauls had become angry on account of an outrage. They had received the legates whom the Romans had sent to conclude a peace. But when a well-equipped and strong Gallic army under Brennus was besieging Clusium, now called Tuscia, they saw these legates fighting against them in the opposing battle line. They at once raised the siege of Clusium and hurried with all their forces towards Rome. The consul Fabius [40] and his army overtook them as they were pushing on towards Rome, but did not succeed in halting them; on the contrary, the attack of the enemy overthrew, cut down,

[40] Quintus Fabius Ambustus. Military Tribune, 390 B.C.

and passed over the army of Fabius as if it were a ripe corn-field. The Allia River [41] commemorates the disaster of Fabius as the Cremera did that of the Fabii. It would not be easy to recall a similar disaster to a Roman army, even if in addi-tion Rome herself had not been destroyed by fire.

The Gauls poured into the defenseless city and slew the senators who sat as rigid as statues in their chairs. They set fire to the houses, the flames cremating the bodies and the falling roofs burying them. They then besieged and sur-rounded the entire group of the survivors, reckoned at that time to be barely a thousand young men, who were concealed in the citadel on the Capitoline Hill. There the Gauls first wore them down through hunger, plague, desperation, and fear. They then subdued them and imposed a ransom on the unhappy survivors. As the price of their departure the Gauls bargained for a thousand pounds of gold, not because they held Rome in small esteem, but because they had already so depleted the city that it could not bear a higher price. When the Gauls had departed, only offensive heaps of shapeless ruins remained within the circuit of the former city. Every-where the echo of the voices of those who wandered amid the obstructions, ignorant where their own property was, re-sounded and kept the ears alert. Horror shook men's cour-age. The very silence was terrifying; for loneliness in the open is in itself a cause of fear. On this account, the Romans considered, accepted, and attempted a plan of changing their home, settling in another town, and calling themselves by a new name.

Behold the times in comparison with which our present age is judged! Behold the times for which memory breathes a sigh! Behold the times which demand penitence on the part of the religion that has been elected, nay rather on the part of the religion that has been neglected! For truly these cap-tivities are similar and comparable with one another. The one raged for six months; the other ran its course in three days. The Gauls, after wiping out the populace and destroy-

[41] A small river which flows into the Tiber about eleven miles north of Rome.

ing the city, continued to persecute the very name of Rome even when the city lay in ashes. The Goths, relinquishing their intention of plundering, drove the bewildered crowds to a safe refuge, that is, to the sacred precincts. During the Gallic invasion scarcely a senator could be found who had escaped death even by flight; in this Gothic invasion there was scarcely a senator missing who chanced to meet his death while hiding. I could make the correct and sound comparison that the number surviving in one case was the same as the number lost in the other. It must be freely admitted, as the fact is clear, that in the present calamity God has been more angry and men less so, because by performing what they could not have accomplished He has proved why He sent the Goths. Certainly it was beyond human strength to set fire to bronze beams and to destroy great and massive structures. The Forum with its vain images, which by a wretched superstition gave God a human shape, was smitten by lightning bolts; all those abominations, which the fire let loose by the enemy did not reach, Heaven-sent fire destroyed.

Since the descriptive material is very rich and can in no case be exhausted in this book, I shall bring to an end the present volume, so that we may pursue the subject further in subsequent books.

THE THIRD BOOK

PREFACE. In an earlier book I began my argument and now, in accordance with your instructions, I must resume the story of the struggles of bygone ages.[1] I cannot here relate in full detail everything that has happened and how it came to pass, since many authors have already written at great length about innumerable matters of importance. These historians, however, came to no agreement in their interpretations despite the fact that they had at their disposal the same materials; for they were describing wars, whereas I for my part am more concerned with the miseries caused by wars. Moreover, the very abundance of the subject matter—and I do lament this —is in itself the cause of a dilemma, and I am limited by the rather knotty problem which it presents. If I strive to be brief and omit some things, people will think either that I do not have the materials at hand or else that the events never took place. But if I strive to include everything without describing it, restricting myself to a treatment entirely too brief, I shall not then make matters sufficiently clear. Many people will say that I have hardly touched upon events, especially since from my point of view I am concerned with preserving for posterity the meaning of events rather than their description. But brevity and obscurity, or rather brevity, as it is ever obscure, though aiding one to grasp easily the picture of occurrences, does prevent a genuine comprehension of their meaning. Since I know that both of these faults should be avoided, I shall attempt so to deal with my subject that the one may be somewhat tempered by the other. In this way I shall appear neither to have omitted too much nor to have been unduly brief in my treatment.

[1] Compare *Dedication* above p. 29. "I have obeyed your instructions, blessed Augustine."

1. THE three hundred and sixty-fourth year of the City was a year which Rome felt to be just as disastrous as Greece considered it glorious; for Rome was in a state of bondage which she had never before experienced, whereas Greece was enjoying an unaccustomed period of peace. At this time the Gauls held and sold the city of Rome, which they had captured and burned. This was also the time when the Persian king Artaxerxes sent envoys to warn all Greece to lay arms aside and be at peace, proclaiming that he himself would make war upon anyone who broke the peace. The Greeks could have been as firm in defying his orders as they had often been brave in winning victories over him, but they gladly seized any opportunity, whatever its source, to attain the peace they had been so eagerly desiring. In this way they showed how weakly and wretchedly they had hitherto been carrying on wars which now they ended so readily and on such discreditable terms. For what can be so base as for free and brave men to lay down their arms and to remain in peace at the command of a king who is far away, who has been frequently defeated, who has hitherto been an enemy, and who even now continues to threaten them? The Greeks could not have acted as they did, had not all inclination for war melted away in their hearts. Indeed they were already weary of war when they first heard the proclamation of peace, which brought them an unexpected respite from war and gave them a taste of peace while they were still bewildered and stupefied after their hardships and long vigils. So great, in fact, was their war-weariness that they proceeded to enjoy the peace even before formal deliberation could bring about this respite. I shall now set forth as briefly as possible the origin of this great lassitude which oppressed the minds and bodies of all peoples throughout Greece and which persuaded their fierce spirits to accept an inactivity hitherto unknown to them.

The Lacedaemonians exhibited an attitude characteristic of mankind in general and of the Greeks in particular: the more they had, the more they coveted. When they had become masters of the Athenians, they turned their eyes greedily on Asia in the hope of acquiring dominion over all that country. After stirring up war in the entire East, they chose Dercyllidas as leader for this campaign. When Dercyllidas saw that he would have to fight against Pharnabazus and Tissaphernes, two of the most powerful satraps of Artaxerxes, the Persian king, he took counsel for the moment to consider how he might avoid the consequences of fighting against two men at the same time. He declared war and attacked one of them, but held the other off by making a treaty with him. Pharnabazus brought Tissaphernes before Artaxerxes, to whom at that time they both owed allegiance, and accused him of being a traitor, charging him specifically with negotiating a treaty in time of war. Pharnabazus then urged the king to appoint in the traitor's place, as chief of naval operations, Conon, an Athenian citizen who happened at that time to be living as an exile in Cyprus. Pharnabazus then summoned Conon to appear, gave him five hundred silver talents, and put him in command of the fleet.

When the Lacedaemonians learned of this, they themselves sent envoys to seek assistance from the Egyptian king Hercynio [2] for the prosecution of the naval war; they received from him one hundred fully equipped triremes and six hundred thousand *modii of* grain.[3] From every side they likewise gathered together huge auxiliary forces which were contributed by their allies. By common agreement they decreed that Agesilaus was to be their general in this campaign; he was lame, but in such a crisis as this they preferred that their king, rather than their kingdom, should limp.

Rarely if ever have generals in the same war been so nearly equal in every activity. Exhausted in turn by bitter conflicts and covered with blood, they parted as if each were undefeated. Conon, upon receiving a second payment from the

[2] Called "Psammitichus" by Diodorus Siculus in his *Library of History* xiv. 35.

[3] A Roman measure that was one-sixth of the Greek *medimnus* or one-third of an *amphora*, and about equal to two English gallons. It contained about twenty pounds of Gallic wheat.

Great King, returned to the fleet, invaded the territory of the enemy, took citadels, fortresses, and other defenses by storm, and like a cloudburst laid low everything he struck. Beset by troubles at home, the Lacedaemonians now ceased to concern themselves with foreign affairs and, when threatened by an uprising of their slaves, they gave up the hope of expansion. Agesilaus, whom they had sent with an army into the province of Asia, was recalled to the defense of his native land.

In the meantime Pisander, who had been left in command at Sparta by King Agesilaus, had equipped a great and powerful fleet. Desiring to emulate the courageous example of Agesilaus, who at that time was engaged in an infantry expedition, he on his part sailed about making naval raids along the sea coast. After undertaking the campaign, Conon, who owed obligations to his allies as well as loyalty to his own country, began to weigh his twofold responsibility: how he might show himself true to the latter and how he might furnish an example of his industry to the former. In this instance, he was more inclined to be on the side of his fellow citizens, because it was to insure their peace and liberty that he was about to imperil the blood of foreigners and to contend against most arrogant enemies. In this war the king would bear all the risks, but the advantages would accrue to his own native land.[4] A naval encounter then took place. The Persians were led by Conon and the Spartans by Pisander. Soldiers, rowers, and even generals themselves were one and all seized with the same desire to kill. The position of the Lacedaemonians, growing weaker as it did from this time on, reveals how great and how severe that war was. Thereafter the hopes of the Spartans seemed to ebb and, backward stealing, receded[5] until Sparta, finally exhausted by a great effort to rise again and by a second wretched collapse, lost both power and reputation. Indeed for the Athenians this battle

[4] By helping the Persians to conquer, Conon would weaken the Lacedaemonians and thereby aid Athens to reëstablish herself.

[5] Vergil *Aeneid* ii. 169–70.

marked the beginning of the restoration of power, just as for the Lacedaemonians it had signified the loss of power.

The Thebans were the first to take advantage of this situation. Relying upon the support of the Athenians and filled with confidence because of the courage and energy of their general Epaminondas, under whose leadership they thought they could easily win dominion over all Greece, they advanced against the Spartans. The latter were still suffering from the blow of their earlier defeat and consequently were demoralized. A land battle took place, which the Thebans won without great difficulty. In this engagement [6] Lysander was defeated and killed. Pausanias, the other Lacedaemonian leader, was accused of treason and driven into exile.

After winning this victory the Thebans collected their entire army and hastened to Sparta, thinking that they could easily enter a city devoid of defenders. For they had already destroyed almost all the Spartan forces together with their king, and they saw, too, that the Spartans had been deserted by their allies. The Lacedaemonians became alarmed by the danger threatening their city and after making a levy of untrained troops from whatever sources available, they advanced to meet the enemy. When these levies had once been defeated, the Spartans then had neither the courage nor the spirit to offer further resistance to the victors. The slaughter was almost wholly confined to one side. But suddenly and unexpectedly King Agesilaus, who had been summoned from the province of Asia, appeared on the field of battle. He at once attacked the Thebans who had now become rather overconfident and careless as the result of their double victory. He therefore had no trouble at all in defeating them, especially since he had kept the strength of his own forces unimpaired up to this time. Agesilaus himself, however, was seriously wounded.

Learning that the Lacedaemonians were encouraged by their

---

[6] A battle fought in 395 B.C. in the neighborhood of Haliartus, a Boeotian town near the southern side of Lake Copais, and situated between the mountain and the lake.

unexpected victory, the Athenians became much alarmed; for they feared that they themselves might return to their former state of servitude, from the effects of which they had only just begun to recover. They therefore assembled their own army and united it as an auxiliary force to that of the Boeotians. The army was entrusted to the leadership of Iphicrates, who, though a very young man (he was not quite twenty years old), possessed a mature mind which compensated for the instability characteristic of youth.

Conon, an Athenian but also the leader of the Persian army, upon hearing of the return of Agesilaus, turned back to lay waste the territory of the Lacedaemonians. The Spartans, shut up within their own walls and terrified by the clamor that the enemy was raising on all sides, became utterly despondent. When Conon grew weary of the campaign of devastation that he had visited far and wide upon the enemy's soil, he proceeded to Athens where he was joyfully acclaimed by the citizens; but he himself became sad when he saw the city, once most famous for her people and her culture, now reduced to a state of misery, squalor, ruin, and desolation. As a great testimonial of his affection and pity, he undertook the work of restoring the city. He used spoils taken from the Lacedaemonians to replace what the Lacedaemonians had plundered; and he employed Persian artisans to rebuild what Persian incendiaries had reduced to ashes.

In the meantime the Persian king Artaxerxes, as has been mentioned above, sent envoys to command all the peoples of Greece to lay down their arms and to remain at peace. He did so not because he was aroused by pity for their state of exhaustion, but in order that no invasion of his own kingdom might be attempted while he was engaged in carrying on war in Egypt.

2.   THE peace which the Greeks had so earnestly desired now made them weak, and leisure at home led to sluggishness. Taking advantage of this, the Lacedaemonians, who were restless rather than strenuous, and irresistible through their

impetuosity rather than their courage, embarked upon the stratagems of war after they had apparently given up war. When they observed that the Arcadians were away, they made a sudden attack upon their citadel and broke into it. Aroused by this unlawful act, the Arcadians, with the assistance of the Thebans who had joined them, sought to regain by arms what had been lost through this sly maneuver on the part of the Lacedaemonians. In the battle that followed [7] Archidamus, the leader of the Lacedaemonians, was wounded. Seeing that his men were defeated and were beginning to be slaughtered, he sent a herald to ask permission to bury the bodies of the dead. Among the Greeks this action is wont to be considered as an acknowledgment of defeat. Content with this admission, the Thebans gave the signal to cease fighting and thus brought the struggle to an end.

After a few intervening days of armistice, the Lacedae-monians turned their attention to other wars. The Thebans, under the leadership of Epaminondas, then placed their reli-ance in an attack upon Sparta during a time, as they thought, it was quiet and deserted. Silently and in the dead of night they came to the city, but they did not find it as much off guard and as defenseless as they had expected. The old men and those who were too young to fight, having armed them-selves in anticipation of the arrival of the enemy, had stationed themselves in the very entrances of the gates. Although barely one hundred strong, the old men, despite the feebleness due to their years, rushed forth against fifteen thousand soldiers. While they were bearing the brunt of the fighting, the young men arrived on the scene and decided without delay to engage the Thebans in the open. Defeat faced the Lacedaemonians when suddenly the Theban general Epaminondas was wounded while exposing himself recklessly in the fight.[8] The Thebans were at once filled with anxiety as a result of their grievous loss, but the Spartans were overcome with joy. Both sides

[7] The battle was fought in the neighborhood of Cromnus, to which Archi-damus was leading troops in order to raise the siege, 365 B.C.
[8] Epaminondas was wounded at Mantinea, 362 B.C. The account is confused.

then withdrew from battle as if by common consent. When Epaminondas, who was seriously wounded, received the news that his men had been victorious, he kissed his shield. Then removing his hand with which he had closed up the wound, he opened wide a passage for the flow of his blood and an avenue leading to death. The ruin of the Thebans themselves followed so closely upon his death that they seemed not only to have lost their leader but to have perished with him.

I have woven together strands of unrelated events into a historical wickerwork that cannot be unraveled, and following the evidence closely, I have worked in a description of the uncertain cycles of wars waged here and there with uncontrolled fury. I could do this because, as I see it, the more I retained the order of events, the more was my account without order. Who can arrange either by number, chronology, or logic the disturbances springing from every kind of hatred, and the numerous causes of strife which the Lacedaemonians's wicked lust for conquest has brought to numerous and important peoples, cities, and provinces? The Lacedaemonians, it is true, are reported to have been afflicted by the disorders arising out of wars no less than by the wars themselves. Indeed when this war had lasted several years without interruption, the Athenians, Lacedaemonians, Arcadians, Boeotians, Thebans, and finally, Greece, Asia, Persia, Egypt together with Libya, and the largest islands, all became involved in an endless series of conflicts on land and sea. Even if I enumerated the wars, I could not record the thousands of slaughters suffered by mankind.

But now let those rail at our times and extol the past who do not know that all the inhabitants of those cities and provinces mentioned are at the present time wasting their declining strength attending the games and theaters as their sole occupation, just as in former days they exhausted their energies for the most part in camps and battles. That very flourishing Lacedaemonian state, which in those times was striving for the mastery of the whole East, could muster barely one hundred old men. Beset as she was by unending troubles, she miserably expended the lives of her youth. And at the present time we hear the complaints of men whose cities, filled with children and old men, are growing rich as their young men travel safely in foreign lands and acquire from peaceful pursuits the funds for their pleasures at home! Or possibly the explanation is—according to the fickle human habit of holding all present achievements of no account—that even life itself has become boring to those who itch to do and to hear new things.

3.   IN THE three hundredth year of the City, a violent earthquake shook all Achaia; two cities, Ebora and Helice, were swallowed up by fissures rent in the ground.

But I myself could tell of similar happenings in our own day at Constantinople, now as then the first city of the world —happenings, it is true, predicted and under way, but not completed. After a terrible intimation and a prophetic consciousness of its own misfortune, the earth below trembled and was shaken to its depths. Above, a flame, spreading from the sky, was suspended until God, moved by the prayers of the emperor Arcadius and the Christian population, averted the imminent catastrophe, proving that He alone was the preserver of the meek as well as the punisher of the wicked. But I should admit (a concession to modesty) that I have merely mentioned these events rather than set them forth at any length, so that whoever knows them may recall them and whoever does not know them may investigate them further.

In the meantime, the Romans, who had been held in subjection for seventy years by the city of the Volsci and by the cities of the Falisci, Aequi, and Sutrini, and who had been worn down by constant warfare, were exhausted. Despite this, however, during the period mentioned above, under the leadership of Camillus,[9] they finally captured these cities and put an end to the struggle when it had broken out anew. In a battle at the Allia River, under the leadership of T. Quintius,

[9] M. Furius Camillus was consular tribune (several times), interrex, and dictator. These wars took place from 401 to 381 B.C.

they defeated the Praenestini who, fighting and slaughtering as they went, had come to the very gates of Rome.

4.   IN THE three hundred and eighty-fourth year of the City, during the consulship of L. Genucius and Q. Servilius,[10] a great plague gripped the entire city of Rome. Instead of the usual variations that differ more or less from the norm of the seasons, that is, untimely dryness in winter, sudden heat in spring, unseasonable moisture in summer, and the varied seductions of a fruitful autumn, a breeze laden with destruction swept in from the pastures of Calabria, carrying in its wake a violent epidemic that spread rapidly through the land. Unlike a common plague, it was severe, of long duration, and had no regard for either sex or age. For two years without interruption it destroyed everything, so that even those whose lives it did not take were left exhausted, despondent, and horribly emaciated.

Those who disparage the Christian era would complain at this point, I believe, were I to pass over in silence the ceremonies with which the Romans at that time sought to placate their gods and to allay the epidemic. When the plague grew worse day by day, it was decided, upon the advice of the pontifices, to give dramatic plays in honor of the gods who coveted such rites. In order to purge their bodies of a plague that was only temporary, the Romans summoned to their souls a disease that was eternal. I have now indeed a rich opportunity of expressing my grief and reproach, but where your reverence [11] has already exercised your zeal for wisdom and truth, it is not proper for me to venture further. Let it suffice that I have reminded the reader and have turned his attention from any other object to your complete account.

5.   IN THE next year, a very ill-boding prodigy followed this wretched plague and its even more wretched expiation. Suddenly in the middle of the City the earth shook and a chasm

---

[10] L. Genucius Aventinensis and Q. Servilius Ahala, 365 B.C.
[11] That is, St. Augustine.

opened and exposed the lower regions of the earth. This impudent chasm with its open abyss long remained a spectacle and an object of terror to all. According to the interpreters of the gods, it demanded that a man be buried alive—an abominable rite. M. Curtius, a mounted knight in armor, satiated its wicked jaws by throwing himself in headlong and thus gave satisfaction to the cruel earth, which was not content to receive in graves those who had died from the effects of the great plague, but must also swallow the living in its open chasm.

6. IN THE three hundred and eighty-eighth year of the City, the Gauls again overflowed the land in a terrible invasion and encamped by the side of the Anio River at the fourth milestone from the City. Without doubt the Gauls would have easily overwhelmed the City, which was thrown into a panic by their great numbers and by their reputation for courage, had they not become sluggish as a result of ease and inactivity. Manlius Torquatus [12] began the very fierce struggle by engaging in single combat. The dictator T. Quintus brought it to an end only after a battle that caused much blood to flow.[13] Many of the Gauls who had been put to flight in this battle later renewed the struggle after they had rested. They rushed into battle but were overcome by the dictator Sulpicius.[14] After a short time there followed the battle fought under C. Marcius [15] against the Tuscans. I leave you to imagine how many men were killed when eight thousand of the Tuscans were captured.

For the third time during these days the Gauls, in order to obtain booty, overran the maritime regions and the fields that lay beneath the Alban Mountains. After a new levy had been held and ten legions had been conscripted, sixty thousand

[12] T. Manlius engaged in combat with a Gallic champion and slew him. He took one chain from the neck of the vanquished and so earned the name Torquatus.

[13] The battle was fought not far from the Colline Gate. The dictator was T. Quintus Pennus.

[14] After long delaying battle, the dictator C. Sulpicius Peticus finally crushed the Gauls near Pedum, a city of Latium.

[15] C. Marcius Rutilius.

Romans advanced against them. The Latins refused to come to the aid of the Romans. M. Valerius ended this battle with the aid of a crow and for that reason was later called Corvinus.[16] The Gallic challenger was killed; the enemy scattered and fled in terror, sustaining heavy losses.

7. AMONG other evils I think I should also count the treaty made with the Carthaginians—it was the first ever made with them—especially since so serious troubles followed its conclusion that they seem to have had their origin in it. In the four hundred and second year after the founding of the City, ambassadors sent by Carthage to Rome concluded the treaty. The trustworthy accounts of historians, the ill-omened character of the places, and the horror of the days in which these things happened all testify that the entrance of the Carthaginians into Italy was destined to be followed by a hailstorm of evils and perpetual night of uninterrupted ills. At that time, moreover, night seemed to last into more than half of the next day and a storm, raining stones instead of hail, came down from the clouds and lashed the earth. Also there was born in those days Alexander the Great, a veritable whirlpool of evils and a hurricane that swept the whole East in its fury.

At that time, too, Ochus,[17] who was also called Artaxerxes, after completing a long and severe war in Egypt, forced many of the Jews to migrate and ordered them to make their home in Hyrcania near the Caspian Sea. They have remained there even to the present day and have greatly increased their numbers. It is the common belief that some day they will be forced to leave because of the pressure caused by overpopulation. At the time of this war, Ochus, as he was passing through the land, also destroyed Sidon, the richest city of the province of Phoenicia and, despite an earlier defeat, now brought Egypt

---

[16] This crow lighted on the helmet of M. Valerius when he advanced to meet the Gallic challenger. During the conflict the crow attacked the Gaul with its beak and talons. The Gaul was so disturbed by this prodigy that he succumbed to the attack of the Roman soldier. The story is graphically told in Livy *Histories* vii. 26.

[17] Artaxerxes III. His reign extended from 362 to 339 B.C.

under his control, a land previously subdued and crushed by
the sword of the Persians.

8. IMMEDIATELY after this, the Romans, in behalf of the
Campanians and Sidicinians, began a war against the Samnites,
a people mighty in arms and rich in resources. The conduct
of the Samnite War, which so far had been waged with indecisive results, was taken over by Pyrrhus, the bitterest enemy
of the Roman people. The Punic War followed close upon
the war fought against Pyrrhus. Indeed the ever-open gates
of Janus indicate that never after the time of Numa's death
had there been any cessation of the disasters of war; but from
that time on misfortune pressed upon the Romans with the
same intensity as the glowing heat that is kindled in the whole
vault of heaven by the noonday sun. Furthermore, after the
Punic War had once begun, let anyone who thinks Christian
times should be decried, inquire, discover, and proclaim in
public whether wars, massacres, destruction, and all kinds of
horrible deaths ever ceased except during the reign of Caesar
Augustus. With the exception of that one year during the
Punic wars, which passed as swiftly as a bird's flight, the
Romans were but once deluded by the briefest indication of
peace and then only by the closing of the gates of Janus during
a period when fevers and diseases raged in the republic. The
situation reminds one how a sick person, by taking a sip of
cold water, merely increases his fever and makes his suffering
more violent and more difficult to bear.

It is settled beyond dispute, however, that it was under
Augustus Caesar and after peace had been made with the
Parthians that the whole world first laid down arms and
brought to an end the causes of dissension. The world was
then in a state of universal peace and quiet hitherto unknown.
It rendered obedience to the Roman laws, preferred Roman
justice to its own arms, and chose Roman judges in place of its
despised leaders. There also existed a single will to preserve
peace by the zealous exercise of a free and honest spirit, and
to plan for the common welfare of all nations, entire prov-

inces, innumerable cities and countless peoples—in fact of the whole world. This was a condition that not even one city nor any group of citizens, nay, what is more, not one household of brothers, had previously ever been able to enjoy in common. If we agree that all these things came to pass during the reign of Caesar, it is then most clearly proved and evident that the birth of our Lord Jesus Christ had begun to illuminate the world in his reign. Men, though prompted to blasphemy by hatred, are unwillingly forced to recognize and to concede that this quiet, serenity, and peace throughout the entire world has come not from the greatness of Caesar, but by the power of the Son of God, Who appeared in the time of Caesar; also that they have obeyed, according to general knowledge, not the ruler of one city but the Creator of the whole universe itself, a Creator who, like the rising sun which bathes the day with light, mercifully clothed the world in prolonged peace at His advent. How this came to be will be discussed more fully in the proper place when the Lord wills it.

9.   IN THE four hundred and ninth year after the founding of the City, during the consulship of Manlius Torquatus and Decius Mus,[18] the Romans declared war against the Latins who were in rebellion. In this war one consul was killed while the other survived by committing a parricide. For Manlius Torquatus killed his own son, who was a young man, a conqueror, and the slayer of Maecius Tusculanus, a well-known member of the equestrian order and an especially provoking and abusive enemy. The second consul, Decius Mus, when the conflict had been renewed, upon seeing that the wing which he commanded was being slaughtered and overwhelmed, went forth alone into the dense ranks of the enemy and was killed. Although Manlius was the victor, nevertheless, triumphing as he did by committing a parricide, he did not receive the welcome that the noble youths of Rome customarily tendered to conquerors in accordance with the provisions of the law.

In the following year Minucia, a Vestal Virgin, confessed

[18] T. Manlius Imperiossus Torquatus III and P. Decius Mus, 340 B.C.

that she had committed incest. She was condemned and buried alive in the field which is now called "Polluted."

10.   AND truly do I shudder when I refer to what happened a few years later. In the consulship of Claudius Marcellus and Valerius Flaccus,[19] some Roman matrons were frenzied by an incredible madness and a love of crime. It was that same horrible year of the plague when everywhere corpses were heaped up in piles and carted away. At first it was the general belief that the pestilence came from poisoned air. Later, however, a certain maidservant turned informer and proved beyond doubt what had really happened. Many matrons were compelled to drink the poisons that they themselves had mixed for others; and as soon as they had drunk the potions, they died. So great was the number of the matrons involved in these crimes that three hundred and seventy of them, according to report, were condemned at one time.

11.   IN THE four hundred and twenty-second year of the City, Alexander, the king of the Epirots and the maternal uncle of Alexander the Great, transported his forces to Italy and made preparations for war against the Romans. In his eagerness for war he tried his best to strengthen his own army and auxiliaries either by bringing the cities near Rome over to his own side or by detaching them from the enemy. In a great battle in Lucania, however, he was defeated and killed by the Samnites who were bringing assistance to a Lucanian tribe.

I have indeed progressed somewhat on my course by reviewing the disasters which befell the Romans, but since I am particularly moved by the mention of this Alexander, I shall bring together in the smallest possible space, by retracing a few years, the great events which took place under Philip. He was that Macedonian king who had married Olympias, the sister of Alexander of Epirus and the mother of Alexander the Great.

[19] M. Claudius Marcellus and C. Valerius Potitus Flaccus, 331 B.C.

12. IN THE four hundredth year of the City, Philip, the son of Amyntas and the father of Alexander, obtained possession of the Macedonian crown and held it for twenty-five years. During this period he was responsible for the storing up of much bitterness and for a great number of wicked deeds. Philip first was sent by his brother Alexander as a hostage to the Thebans among whom for three years he was educated in the company of Epaminondas, an extraordinarily vigorous commander-in-chief and also a most distinguished philosopher. Alexander subsequently was murdered by his mother Eurydice who, although she had already committed adultery, previously killed another son, and made a widow of her daughter, contracted a marriage with her cousin upon the death of her husband. The people now forced Philip to accept the throne for which he had been acting as regent in behalf of the little son of his murdered brother.

Philip was harassed abroad by the attacks of enemies who rose up on all sides, while at home he was troubled by the fear of plots which, however, he usually detected. In the midst of all this, he waged his first war against the Athenians.[20] When he had defeated them, he directed his arms against the Illyrians and, after killing thousands of the enemy, captured the celebrated city of Larissa. He next invaded Thessaly, not so much because he loved conquest as because he wanted to obtain the Thessalian cavalry, the strength of which he might add to his own army. He took the Thessalians by surprise and brought them under his control. By incorporating the strongest divisions and forces of their cavalry and infantry he formed an almost invincible army. When the Athenians had been defeated and the Thessalians subjugated, he married Olympias, the sister of Arubas,[21] who was king of the Molossians. This Arubas supposed that he could enlarge his own empire because he was contracting a Macedonian alliance

---

[20] They had sent a fleet to help seat a rival of Philip on the Macedonian throne. Philip, however, displayed considerable generosity when he had defeated them and offered them most favorable terms of peace.

[21] The name appears in several different forms. The common Greek form was Ἀρύββας.

through his new relationship to the king. He was deceived in this expectation, however, and having failed in his attempt, passed his declining years as a private citizen in exile.[22] Later, while storming the city of Methone,[23] Philip was struck by an arrow and lost an eye. Nevertheless he quickly took the city by assault.

Although his designs had been anticipated, Philip and his forces subdued almost all Greece. In fact, while each one of the Greek states was eager to extend its own control over other states, all lost their empire; and while they were recklessly rushing to a common ruin, they realized, only after they had been defeated and enslaved, that what each one had lost individually was lost to them all. Philip, looking, as it were, from a watchtower and observing their foolish attempts to save themselves, always brought assistance to the weaker side. An adroit contriver of trickery, he fostered disputes, the kindling wood of war, and reduced to his rule conquered and conquerors alike.

But the unbridled rule of the Thebans gave Philip an opportunity to obtain political control over all Greece. The Thebans had defeated the Lacedaemonians and Phoceans, who had been completely exhausted by repeated slaughter and plundering. Then at the common council of Greece they burdened them with more debt than they could possibly pay and thus forced them to take up arms. The Phoceans were led by Philomelus and were reinforced by Lacedaemonian and Athenian auxiliaries. They joined battle with the Thebans, put them to flight, and captured their camp. In a later battle, amid heavy casualties on both sides, Philomelus was slain. In his place the Phoceans elected Onomarchus as their leader.

Without holding any election by their citizens, the Thebans and Thessalians willingly invited Philip, the Macedonian king, to be their leader. This was the king whom earlier they had striven hard to repel as an enemy. Battle was joined and the

[22] Philip deprived him of his crown.
[23] Methone, a town of Pieria in Macedonia, is situated on the Thermaic Gulf. The text has "Mothona."

Phoceans were butchered almost to the last man. Philip gained
the victory. When the Athenians learned the outcome of this
battle, they occupied the passes of Thermopylae in order to
prevent him from entering Greece. In so doing they were
motivated by the same reason as that which they had acted
upon in the past when the Persians were drawing near.[24]

When Philip saw that his entrance into Greece would be
barred at Thermopylae, which had now been rendered impassable, he directed the war intended for the enemy against his
own allies. His armies attacked and cruelly plundered states
of which but a short time before he had been the leader and
which were now ready to receive him with open arms and to
give him a hearty welcome. Completely putting aside all sense
of honor in regard to his alliance with them, he sold their
wives and children into slavery and destroyed and plundered
all their temples. And as if the gods showed no resentment at
his actions, never once in twenty-five years did he suffer defeat.

After these deeds, Philip crossed into Cappadocia, where
he waged war with equal perfidy. By employing deception he
captured the neighboring kings and put them to death; thus
he brought all Cappadocia under Macedonian rule. After
visiting slaughter, conflagration, and robbery upon the cities
of his allies, he turned to parricide. Fearing his brothers as
co-heirs of the kingdom, since they were children of his father
and his stepmother, he attempted to kill them. When he had
slain one of them, the other two fled for refuge to Olynthus.
Philip at once made a hostile attack upon this ancient and
flourishing city, overwhelming it with blood and slaughter,
and emptying it of its wealth and men. He carried off his
brothers, tortured them, and put them to death.

Elated by the destruction of his allies and by the murder
of his brothers, Philip then began to think that it was lawful
for him to do everything that he had planned. He seized the
gold mines in Thessaly and the silver mines in Thrace. In
order not to allow any law, human or divine, to remain unbroken, he seized control of the sea, dispatched his boats in

[24] Justin *Histories* viii. 2 says that they were motivated by other reasons.

different directions, and began to engage in piracy. Furthermore, when two brothers, who were kings in Thrace, agreed
to appoint him as arbiter in their dispute over the boundaries
of the kingdom, he acted with his customary genius. Advancing to the court of justice with an army drawn up as for war,
he deprived the unsuspecting young men of their lives and
their kingdom.

Despite all these acts, the Athenians, who had earlier
blocked the advance of Philip by fortifying Thermopylae,
now of their own free will sought peace with him and impressed upon the mind of their very deceitful enemy the careless character of their watch over the pass. Other Greek
states also, in order to devote themselves more fully to civil
wars, voluntarily subjected themselves to the control of a
foreign power in the form of a treaty of peace and an alliance.
Their principal reason for doing this at that time was that the
Thessalians and Boeotians were asking Philip to present and
acknowledge himself as their leader in the war which they
had undertaken against the Phoceans, who, supported by the
Athenians and Lacedaemonians, were trying by bribery and
entreaties either to defer or to avert the war.

Philip secretly made different promises to both sides. To
the Phoceans he gave assurance under oath that he would
grant them peace and forgiveness, but at the same time he
solemnly promised the Thessalians that he would soon appear
with his army. Having forbidden both sides to prepare for
war, he then drew up his own forces and entered the passes
of Thermopylae in perfect safety. He fortified these passes
by stationing garrisons at intervals. At this moment not only
the Phoceans but also all the peoples of Greece for the first
time saw that they had been deceived. Philip, contrary to his
pledge and in defiance of his oath, inflicted a terrible massacre
upon the foremost Thebans. He then ravaged all their cities
and territories and made his bloody presence so dreaded that
he was feared even when he was absent.

When Philip had returned to his own kingdom, following
the custom of the shepherds who lead their flocks now to

summer and now to winter pasture, he transplanted, according
to his capricious whims, cities and populations to other districts as he deemed it necessary to people them or leave them
desolate. Everywhere Greece presented a pitiable sight, and
people suffered from the most dreadful forms of misery—
destruction without hostile invasion, captivity without war,
exile without punishment, and political domination without
victory. Fear spread abroad and oppressed a wretched people
already tortured by the wrongs they had endured. Their distress was increased by its very concealment and the more it increased the less were the terrified people able to express their
feelings, lest their very tears be taken as an indication of stubborn resistance. Philip tore some populations from their
homesteads and settled them in hostile territory; he placed
others at the extreme frontiers of the kingdom; and still
others, because he was jealous of their strength, he distributed
among the deserted cities in order to increase the population
there. Thus that magnificent structure of Greece, once so
prosperous, crumbled when its liberty disappeared into many
mutilated fragments.

13. WHEN Philip had carried out these measures in a large
number of Greek cities and was striking fear into the hearts
of them all, he began to calculate the wealth of all the cities
on the basis of the booty taken from a few. He decided that
if he were to be successful in bringing equal devastation upon
all alike it was necessary to control a maritime city. He concluded that the famous city of Byzantium would prove a
suitable base for operations on land as well as on sea. When
the city resisted him, he immediately surrounded and besieged
it. Now this was the same Byzantium which was founded by
Pausanias in days gone by, but which was later enlarged by
Constantine, the Christian emperor, and renamed Constantinople. At present it is the capital of our most glorious empire
and the leading city of the entire East.

The siege was long and fruitless. Philip finally turned
pirate and sought by plundering to regain the wealth that he

had exhausted in the siege. He sold a hundred and seventy captured ships loaded with merchandise and thus relieved a little of his pressing poverty. In order to obtain booty and at the same time conduct the siege, he divided his army. Setting out in person with the bravest of his men, he captured many cities of the Chersonese,[25] crushed the inhabitants, and carried off their wealth. He and his son Alexander also crossed to Scythia with the intention of plundering that country. Atheas was then reigning over the Scythians. When he was hard pressed in his war with the Istriani, he had sought assistance from Philip through the people of Apollonia; but as soon as the king of the Istriani had died, feeling free from any threat of war and need of assistance, he broke the treaty of alliance he had made with Philip. Philip at once abandoned the siege of Byzantium, marshalled all his forces, and began war against the Scythians. When battle was joined, the Scythians, though they outnumbered him and exhibited greater courage, were defeated by trickery. In that battle twenty thousand Scythian women and children were captured, a great number of cattle were carried off, but no gold or silver was discovered. Twenty thousand fine mares were sent to Macedonia to improve the breed. When Philip was returning, the Triballi barred his way and made war upon him. During the fighting Philip was wounded in the thigh in such a way that the horse on which he was riding was killed by the weapon which had passed through his own body. Thinking that Philip had been killed, everyone turned to flight and abandoned the booty.

For a short time, while convalescing from his wound, Philip remained at peace, but as soon as he had recovered he declared war against the Athenians, who, when faced with this great crisis, accepted the Lacedaemonians, their former enemies, as allies. The Athenians wearied all the cities of Greece by sending embassies to induce them to attack the common enemy with united forces. Several cities did ally themselves with the Athenians, but the dread of war led others to go over to

[25] Cherronesus (Chersonesus) Thracica. The region is now known as the peninsula of Gallipoli.

Philip. When battle was joined,[26] the Athenians, although
superior in numbers, were defeated by the Macedonians,
whose courage had been steeled by unceasing warfare. The
consequence of this battle proved it to have been far severer
than any of those preceding. For this day brought to an end
the renowned empire and the glorious and ancient liberty of
all Greece.

14.   LATER Philip completed his triumph over the Thebans
and Lacedaemonians by cruel and bloody measures. He beheaded some of the leading men of these peoples, drove others
into exile, and deprived all of their property. He restored to
their native land those who had recently been banished by the
citizens and appointed three hundred of these exiles as judges
and officials. These men, in order to heal their old resentment
through an exercise of their new authority, would not allow
the unhappy and oppressed people to entertain the hope of
regaining their liberty. Besides this, Philip also made a great
levy of soldiers from all parts of Greece to support his campaign. Just before departing for his Persian expedition
against Asia he drew up in battle array two hundred thousand
foot soldiers and fifteen thousand cavalry of the Macedonian
army, together with a countless number of barbarian tribes.
He selected three leaders, Parmenio, Amyntas, and Attalus,
with the intention of sending them to Persia in advance of
the main army.

While these forces were assembling from Greece, Philip
decided to marry his daughter Cleopatra to Alexander.[27]
This Alexander was the brother of Philip's wife Olympias,
and he later was overthrown by the Sabines in Lucania.[28]
Philip had earlier made him king of Epirus in redress for the
disgraceful indignities he had inflicted upon him.[29] When

[26] The battle was fought at Chaeronia in Boeotia, 338 B.C.

[27] Alexander I, king of Epirus.

[28] He had been warned by an oracle to avoid Pandosia. He knew of a Pandosia in Greece on the banks of the Acheron, but the Italian town, near which
he was defeated, was unknown to him.

[29] As a youth Alexander had gone to the court of Philip who used him to
gratify his lust.

some one asked Philip on the day before he was killed what
end was most to be desired by man, he is said to have answered
that the happiest lot which could befall a brave man was to
reign in peace, enjoying a lifelong reputation for virtue, and
then to die by a sudden stroke of the sword, without suffering
any bodily illness and without having any mark of dishonor
on his soul. This soon turned out to be his own fate. Nor
could the angry gods whom he had always held in low esteem,
and whose altars, temples, and shrines he had destroyed, prevent him from meeting his death in the way that seemed to him
most desirable. For, on the day set for the wedding, as he
was walking unattended by guards between the two Alex-
anders, his son and his son-in-law, on his way to the games
that had been prepared on a magnificent scale, he was entrapped in a narrow passageway and slain by Pausanias, a
young Macedonian noble.

My adversaries may now assert and loudly proclaim that
these were glorious deeds and successful achievements of
brave men. Indeed the bitterest calamities of others become
pleasant tales to these opponents of mine so long as they themselves are not tormented from time to time by injuries which
they must needs relate with sadness and bitter tears. But if
my adversaries are willing, when their troubles are reported to
others, to receive sympathy only from those who have suffered
from the same events, first let them compare, not the past with
the present, but events with events, and let judges decide both
cases as if they were listening to strangers. During twenty-
five years a single king's knavery, brutality, and tyranny
brought about the burning of cities, the ruin of war, enslave-
ment of provinces, slaughter of men, plundering of wealth,
pillage of flocks, robbery of the dead, and slavery of the living.

15.   These deeds of Philip, which have made an impression
upon our minds, would suffice as examples of calamities even
if Alexander had not succeeded him on the throne.   But for
the time being I shall omit Alexander's wars, or rather the
evils that afflicted the world following his wars, in order to

keep the proper sequence of events, and I shall bring forward at this point a discussion of the Roman wars.

In the four hundred and twenty-sixth year of the City, the Romans suffered a signal disgrace that made the Caudine Forks [30] not only celebrated but notorious. In a previous war twenty thousand of the Samnites fell in a cavalry battle in which Fabius, master of the horse, had engaged them. The Samnites, more cautious and better equipped, then established themselves at the Caudine Forks where their armed forces blocked the passes and shut in the consuls Veturius and Postumius [31] and all the Roman troops. Their leader Pontius was so certain of victory that he thought he ought to consult his father Herennius whether he should slay those whom he had surrounded or should spare them after he had subdued them. He decided to grant the survivors their lives but to dishonor them. The Romans in the past had very frequently been defeated and slaughtered, but never could they be captured or compelled to surrender. When the Samnites had gained a victory, they therefore ordered the entire Roman army—it had ignominiously surrendered and had been stripped of its arms and even of its clothing so that individuals had not the wherewithal to cover their nakedness—to be sent under the yoke, to be reduced to slavery, and to take their places at the head of the long line in the public procession. The Samnites took six hundred Roman knights as hostages and sent back the consuls empty-handed and utterly disgraced.

Why should I, who would have preferred to remain silent, struggle to find words to enlarge upon the stigma of this most disgraceful treaty? The Romans today either would not exist at all or else would be slaves under Samnite domination, if, after their defeat at the hands of the Samnites, they had honestly upheld the sanctity of a treaty, a policy which they now wish to be observed by those whom they themselves have conquered.

[30] A pass consisting of two narrow defiles situated near the road from Beneventum to Capua, about twenty-one miles from the former. The Romans were forced by hunger to surrender.

[31] T. Veturius Calvinus II and Sp. Postumius Albinus II, 321 B.C.

In the following year, the Romans broke the pact which they had made with the Samnites and drove them into a war. This war, begun at the insistence of the consul Papirius,[32] caused great disasters to both peoples. The combatants on one side were angered by their recent disgrace while the others were spurred on by the glory of their last victory. The Romans, however, finally conquered by their determination to fight to the death.[33] They continued to slay and be slain until, after defeating the Samnites and capturing their leader, they at last replaced the yoke. Papirius then stormed Satricum,[34] expelled its Samnite garrison, and captured the city. Papirius enjoyed at that time a great reputation among the Romans for valor and energy in war; so much so that when Alexander the Great was reported to be arranging an expedition from the East to occupy Africa and thence to cross to Italy, the Romans considered Papirius the best fitted of all generals in the Republic to withstand his attack.

16.   IN THE four hundred and twenty-sixth year of the City, Alexander succeeded his father Philip on the throne. He gave the first proof of his spirit and courage by quickly supressing the rebellions of the Greeks. Under the leadership of the orator Demosthenes, who had been bribed by Persian gold, the Greeks had revolted in order to free themselves from Macedonian rule. In response to the entreaties of the Athenians, Alexander gave up his war against them and thereby relieved them of their anxiety. He then wiped out the Thebans after uprooting their city; he sold the survivors into slavery and made other cities of Achaia and Thessaly pay tribute to him. Shortly thereafter he transferred the war from this territory and conquered both the Illyrians and the Thracians. Then, just as he was about to start out for the Persian War,

[32] L. Papirius Mugillanus Cursor. He was elected consul several times, but there is doubt as to the dates of his consulships.

[33] The battle was fought at Luceria in Apulia.

[34] After the disaster of Caudine Forks, the people of Satricum had declared in favor of the Samnites. Satricum was situated on the frontier of Volscian territory between the Alban Hills and the sea.

he killed all his relatives and next of kin. In his army there were thirty-two thousand infantry, four thousand five hundred cavalry, and in addition he had one hundred and eighty ships. With so small a force as this it is uncertain whether Alexander is more to be admired for conquering the whole world or for daring to begin his expedition.

When he first encountered King Darius there were six hundred thousand Persians in battle array.[35] Their defeat and flight was as much due to the strategy of Alexander as to the courage of the Macedonians. This was indeed a great disaster for the Persians. In the army of Alexander one hundred and twenty cavalrymen and only nine infantrymen were lost. Alexander next blockaded, stormed, captured, and gave over to pillage the Phrygian city of Gordie, which is now called Sardis.[36] There he was informed of the arrival of Darius accompanied by a great body of troops. Fearing the narrowness of the passes through which he had entered, Alexander crossed the Taurus Range with remarkable speed, covering five hundred stadia within one day,[37] and came to Tarsus. There, while overheated, he plunged into the icy waters of the Cydnus. He was seized with cramps and nearly died.

In the meantime Darius with three hundred thousand infantry and a hundred thousand cavalry advanced to battle. The vast numbers of the enemy alarmed even Alexander, principally because his forces were so limited. Earlier, however, when he had defeated six hundred thousand of the enemy with just as small a number, he had declared that not only did he not fear battle but even hoped for victory. The armies took their stand within spear range and tensely awaited the signal for battle. Both generals went rapidly to and fro, arousing their hosts by promising all sorts of advantages. Thus both sides began the conflict in high spirits.

The two kings, Alexander and Darius, were both wounded

---

[35] This battle is generally known as the battle of Granicus, 334 B.C.
[36] Probably Gordium. Its association with Sardis is perhaps an error of an annotator of the text. [37] About fifty-seven and one half miles.

in this battle.[38] The issue of the battle long hung in the balance until Darius fled. The slaughter of the Persians then followed. Eighty thousand infantry and ten thousand cavalry were slain; forty thousand were captured. The losses of the Macedonians amounted to one hundred and thirty infantry and one hundred and fifty cavalry. In the camp of the Persians much gold and other rich booty were discovered; and among the captives taken were the mother of Darius, his wife, who was also his sister, and two of his daughters. Though he offered one-half of his kingdom, Darius could not obtain their ransom. He therefore assembled all the Persian forces and the auxiliaries of his allies and renewed the war for the third time.

While Darius was thus engaged, Alexander sent Parmenio with troops to attack the Persian fleet. He himself went to Syria, where many kings, wearing fillets on their heads, came voluntarily to meet him. Some he accepted as allies, some he removed from their thrones, and others he had put to death. Then he overpowered and captured the ancient and flourishing city of Tyre which, trusting in the support of its kinsmen the Carthaginians, opposed him. Next he visited his unrelenting fury upon Cilicia, Rhodes, and Egypt. From there he proceeded to the Temple of Jupiter Ammon, where, in order to blot out the ignominy of his uncertain paternity and the infamy arising from the adultery of his mother, he fabricated a falsehood appropriate to the occasion. For the historians who speak of these events tell us that Alexander summoned the high priest of the sanctuary to his side and secretly instructed him what answers he wished to have made when he consulted him. Thus Alexander was certain, and he has handed his opinion down to us (since the gods themselves are both deaf and dumb), that either the high priest had the power to frame what answer he wished or else the petitioner might will to hear what answer he desired. While he was returning from Ammon to the Third Persian War, Alexander founded Alexandria in Egypt.

[38] The battle was fought at Issus, 333 B.C.

17. AFTER Darius had given up all hope of peace, he offered battle at Tarsus to Alexander who was on his way back from Egypt. Darius had four hundred thousand infantry and one hundred thousand cavalry. The battle began quickly and everyone, blinded by fury, rushed to the sword.[39] The Macedonians were undaunted in the presence of an enemy whom they had time and again defeated, while the Persians preferred death to defeat. Rarely in any battle was so much blood spilled. When Darius saw that his men were being defeated, he himself was prepared to die while fighting, but his men prevailed over him and compelled him to flee. As a result of this battle, the military forces and the kingdoms of Asia declined in power and the entire East came under the control of Macedon. The morale of the Persians was so completely shattered that thereafter none dared to rebel. And they who had enjoyed supremacy for so many years now patiently accepted the yoke of servitude.

Alexander spent thirty-four consecutive days counting the booty of the camp. He then attacked Persepolis, the capital of the Persian kingdom and the most renowned and opulent city in the whole world. But when he learned that Darius was being held by his own relatives and had been bound in golden fetters, he decided to hasten to the king's side. Accordingly, after giving orders for his army to follow, he himself set out with six thousand cavalry and came upon Darius, who had been deserted and abandoned by the roadside. Darius, who had been wounded many times, was now breathing his last as the result of his injuries. In a spirit of specious pity, Alexander ordered the corpse to be carried back and buried in the sepulchre of the Persian kings. Alexander held in cruel captivity not only the mother and wife of Darius but even his little daughters.

To speak the truth in the midst of so vast a number of evils is most difficult. In three battles in as many years five million

---

[39] This may mean "to arms" or perhaps "against the enemy who had their swords raised for action." The battle was fought in 331 B.C. near Gaugamela, a village eighteen miles northeast of Mosul.

infantry and cavalry were destroyed; and this loss was inflicted
upon the same kingdom and upon those same armies of whom
more than one million, nine hundred thousand are said to have
been destroyed a few years earlier. In addition to these disasters and during these same three years the greatest states
of Asia were crushed, Syria was completely devastated, Tyre
uprooted, Cilicia exhausted, Cappadocia subdued, and Egypt
enslaved; the island of Rhodes voluntarily submitted, fearful
of slavery; and a great number of provinces that lie near
the Taurus, and the Taurian Range itself, were subdued,
conquered, and forced to accept the yoke that they had so
long refused.

18.   LET no one by chance think at this point that the East,
which had been subdued by the forces of Alexander, or Italy,
which had been worn out by the ruthlessness of Rome, were
the only sufferers. For at that time war was in progress in
Greece with Agis, the king of the Spartans, in Lucania with
Alexander, the king of Epirus, and in Scythia with Zopyrion,
the prefect. Agis, the Lacedaemonian, aroused all Greece to
join him in a rebellion. He then encountered the bravest
troops of Antipater. He lost his own life amid the general
slaughter wrought upon both armies.[40] In Italy, Alexander,
who was striving after the rule of the West and vying with
Alexander the Great, was overcome and killed by the Bruttians and Lucanians after he had fought many severe battles
in those lands. His body was redeemed for burial. Zopyrion,
the prefect of Pontus, assembled an army of thirty thousand
and was so foolhardy as to declare war upon the Scythians.
His whole army was slaughtered almost to the last man and
it disappeared from the scene along with its leader.

After the death of Darius, Alexander the Great brought
the Hyrcani and the Mardi into subjection. While he was in
their lands as eager for war as ever, the bold Amazon Thales-
tris, or Minothea, with three hundred women in her train,
came to meet him because she was desirous of conceiving

[40] At Megalopolis, the capital of Arcadia, 331 B.C.

offspring by him. Afterward Alexander entered into battle with the Parthians whom, despite a protracted resistance, he destroyed almost as soon as he had defeated them. Then he subdued the Drangae, Evergetae, Parimae, Paropamisadae, Adaspii, and other peoples living at the foot of the Caucasus, and established, on the banks of the Tanaïs River, the city of Alexandria.

His cruelty to his friends was no less intense than his insane rage against his enemies. The story is that he slew his cousin Amyntas, put to death his stepmother and her brothers, and murdered Parmenio and Philotas. Attalus, Eurylochus, Pausanius, and many leading men of Macedonia also lost their lives at his hands. Cleitus, too, heavy with years and enjoying a friendship of long standing, was heinously done to death at a banquet when, trusting to his friendship with the king, he defended the reputation of Philip against Alexander, who was claiming that his own deeds surpassed those of his father. The king, angry without adequate cause, pierced him with his hunting spear. As he died, the blood of Cleitus stained the entire banquet hall. Alexander, insatiable as he was for human blood, whether of his enemies or of his own allies, was always thirsty for fresh slaughter. He rushed forward to battle and after a hard-driven attack received the surrender of the Chorasmi and of the Dahae heretofore never vanquished. He also put to death Callisthenes, a philosopher, who was a fellow student under Aristotle, because Callisthenes would not honor him as a god with the prescribed salutation. Likewise he killed a great many other leading men.

19. NEXT Alexander attacked India so that his empire might be bounded by the Ocean and the extreme parts of the East. He led his troops against the city of Nysa and then extended his sway over the Daedalian Mountains and the realms of Queen Cleophidis, who surrendered and redeemed her kingdom by becoming his concubine. After he had entered and made himself master of India, Alexander came to a rocky eminence of remarkably uneven formation and height to which many people had fled for refuge. He learned that Hercules

had been prevented by an earthquake from capturing it. Moved by a spirit of rivalry to surpass the exploits of Hercules, Alexander, after great exertion and danger, made himself master of the rock and received the surrender of all the local tribes. He fought a very bloody battle with Porus, the most powerful king of the Indians. In this battle Alexander encountered Porus himself in personal combat. Alexander was hurled from his dead horse but escaped death for the moment by the rallying of his bodyguard about him. Porus was wounded many times and captured. As a testimonial to his courage, Alexander restored Porus to his kingdom and then founded the two cities of Nicaea and Bucephale. The latter city he ordered to be so named after his horse.

The Macedonians then cut to pieces the armies of the Adrestae,[41] Catheni, Praesidae, and Gangaridae, and subdued them. On arriving at Cofides,[42] they joined battle with two hundred thousand of the enemy's cavalry. Worn out by the heat as they now were, their spirits depressed, and their strength exhausted, they barely managed to win the victory. As a memorial they founded a camp of more than usual magnificence.

From there Alexander proceeded to the Acesines River,[43] on which he took ship to the Ocean; he overcame the Gesonae and Sibi, who are mentioned by Hercules. Thence he sailed to the land of the Mandri [44] and Subagrae, where the tribes rose up in arms and attacked him with eighty thousand infantry and sixty thousand cavalry. The battle was bloody and the issue was long in doubt, but it finally ended in a victory for Alexander. This victory, however, proved almost disastrous. For, after scattering the troops of the enemy, Alexander led his army against a city. There he was the first to scale the wall and, thinking that the city was deserted, he leaped down inside alone. The fierce enemy surrounded him on every side. Incredible as it may seem, he was not at all terrified by the number of the enemy, by the great show of

---

[41] The battle of the Hydaspes (Thelum), 326 B.C.
[42] Corrupted from "Sopithis" or "Sopithes."
[43] Chenab River.   [44] The "Andri" of the text.

weapons, or by the loud shouting of his assailants, for alone
in the past he had killed and put to flight many thousands.
When he saw, however, that he was being overwhelmed by
the sheer weight of the numbers that surrounded him, he defended himself in a corner with his back to the wall. There he
held his assailants quite easily in check until his entire army
entered the city through a breach in the wall. This action endangered Alexander and at the same time caused the enemy
to shout with dismay. During the fighting, Alexander was
struck in the chest by an arrow, but resting on one knee he
fought on until he had killed the man who had wounded him.
He next embarked and sailed along the shores of the Ocean
until he came to a certain city over which Ambira ruled as
king. In storming the city he lost a large number of his army
who were struck by poisoned arrows. But he and others were
cured by drinking herbs, a remedy which had been revealed to
him in a dream. He later carried the city by storm and captured it.

20.   AFTERWARD, when, as it were, he had driven his chariot
around the turning post,[45] Alexander entered the Indus River
from the Ocean and quickly returned to Babylon,[46] where ambassadors from the terror-stricken provinces of the whole
world awaited him. There were ambassadors from the Carthaginians, from all the states of Africa, also from the Spanish provinces, the Gallic provinces, Sicily, Sardinia, and from
the greater part of Italy. So great a fear of the acknowledged
leader of the most distant East had gripped the peoples of
the farthest West that legations were present from countries
that one would hardly believe could even have heard of Alexander's name. But Alexander, ever thirsty for blood, was
poisoned and died at Babylon. Thus was his wicked appetite
punished by the treachery of a servant.

O callous soul of man, and heart ever inhuman! Did not

[45] Orosius is using a metaphor taken from the chariot racing in the Circus.
[46] Alexander himself returned by land from Barce, a city he built on the
Indus River.

my eyes fill with tears as I reviewed the past in order to prove that calamities have recurred in cycles throughout all ages; did I not weep as I spoke of evils so great that the entire world trembled from death itself or from fear of death? Was not my heart torn with grief? As I pondered over all this, did I not make the terrible experiences of my ancestors my own, seeing in them the common lot of man? And yet, if I may speak of my own story, how for the first time I saw the strange barbarians, how I avoided my enemies and flattered those in authority, how I guarded myself against the pagans, fled from those who lay in wait for me, and how finally, enveloped by a sudden mist, I slipped through the clutches of those who with stones and spears pursued me over the sea, I would that I could move all my audience to tears. I would grieve in silence for those who were unmoved, attributing their apathy to the callousness of men who, never having undergone suffering themselves, were insensible to the suffering of others.

The Spaniards and Morini voluntarily went to Babylon to humble themselves before Alexander. That he might not regard them as enemies, these ambassadors sought the bloody over-lord throughout Assyria and India, visiting the ends of the earth and to their misfortune becoming acquainted with both oceans. Yet the memory of their sad plight either has become dim with age or has passed into oblivion. Can we really imagine for a moment that some thief will win ever-lasting fame because he has despoiled a single corner of the world, leaving the greater part of it untouched? It is as if peace were sought from the Goths and the Suebi by an Indian or an Assyrian, to say nothing of the reverse, and even by the Spaniard himself, who is now being attacked. Let judgment be passed whether the days of Alexander should be praised on account of his valor in conquering the world or be accursed because of the ruin he brought upon mankind. Many people will be found today who think the present good because they themselves have overcome obstacles and because they consider the miseries of others their own good fortune. Yet some-one may say: "the Goths are enemies of the Roman world."

We shall reply: "the whole East in those days thought the same of Alexander, and so, too, have the Romans appeared to others when they attacked distant and harmless peoples." The destruction wrought by an enemy is one thing, the reputation of a conqueror another. The Romans and Alexander formerly harried with wars peoples whom they later received into their empires and ruled by their laws. The Goths as enemies are now throwing into disorder lands which, if they should ever succeed in mastering (which God forbid) they would attempt to govern by their own code. Posterity will call mighty kings those whom we now regard as our most savage enemies. By whatever names such deeds as these are known, whether as sufferings or acts of bravery, when compared with former times, both are less numerous in our own age. In either case comparison with the times of Alexander and the Persians points to our advantage. If "bravery" is the proper word, the valor of the enemy is less marked; if "suffering" is the word to use, the distress of the Roman is less acute.

21.   IN THE four hundred and fiftieth year of the City, during the consulship of Fabius Maximus (consul for the fifth time) and Decius Mus (consul for the fourth time),[47] four of the strongest and most flourishing peoples of Italy made an alliance and formed one army. For the Etruscans, Umbrians, Samnites, and Gauls conspired together and attempted to destroy the Romans. The latter were in a state of fear and trembling at the prospect of this war, and their confidence in themselves was severely shaken. They did not dare to rely fully upon their troops, but separated the enemy by strategy, thinking it safer to engage in many small battles than in a few great ones. By sending some troops in advance into Umbria and Etruria to ravage hostile territories, the Romans compelled the army of the Umbrians and Etruscans to return in order to protect their own lands. The Romans then hastened

[47] Q. Fabius Maximus Rullianus V and P. Decius Mus IV, 295 B.C.

to start a war against the Samnites and Gauls. In this war [48] the Romans were hard pressed by an attack of the Gauls, and the consul Decius was killed. Fabius, however, finally won the battle despite the wholesale slaughter of the Decian division. In that battle forty thousand Samnites and Gauls lost their lives, but the Romans are reported to have lost only seven thousand, and these from the division of the slain Decius. Livy, however, states that, excluding the Etruscans and Umbrians whom the Romans had craftily diverted from this campaign, the losses of the Gauls and Samnites amounted to 140,330 infantry and 47,000 cavalry, and that a thousand armored chariots opposed the Roman line of battle.

It has often been said that the domestic peace of the Romans was always being interrupted by foreign wars and that their foreign ventures were made more difficult by internal disorders. This was so true that their colossal arrogance was completely held in check from all sides. A pestilence in the city in this case climaxed their bloody and tragic victory. Funeral corteges met and violated the sanctity of the triumphal processions. There was no rejoicing over the triumph, for the entire state was grieving for the sick and the dead.

22. A YEAR followed in which, after the resumption of the Samnite War, the Romans were defeated and fled to their camp. Later the Samnites, assuming a new garb and new spirit (they had covered their arms and clothing with silver and had prepared their minds for death if they did not conquer), dedicated themselves to the war. The consul Papirius [49] was sent against them with an army. Although forbidden to advance by the *Augures Pullarii* who predicted adverse results, he laughed at them and ended the war as successfully as he had resolutely undertaken it. In this battle [50] twelve thousand of the enemy were slain and three thousand are reported to

[48] Battle of Sentinum, 295 B.C.   [49] L. Papirius Cursor, 293 B.C.
[50] Near Aquilonia in the heart of Samnium.

have been captured. But disease suddenly broke out and ruined his truly praiseworthy victory, a victory which false auspices had not been able to prevent. So great and so unbearable a pestilence then swept the City, for the sake of allaying it by any means whatsoever, the Romans thought that they should consult the Sibylline Books.[51] They even brought in the famous and dreadful Epidaurian snake and the very statue of Aesculapius,[52] as if, in truth, pestilence had never died out in the past and would not spring up again in the future.

During the following year the consul Fabius Gurges[53] fought without success against the Samnites. He was defeated, lost his army, and, fled back to the city. While the Senate was deliberating whether to remove him from office, his father Fabius Maximus, although detesting the ignoble behavior of his son, offered to go as his legate provided his son were given an opportunity of wiping out the disgrace and of renewing the war. His request was granted and battle was joined. The pious old man suddenly saw his son, the consul, hard pressed in combat with the Samnite leader Pontius and surrounded by the enemy's spears poised for the throw. He at once rode his horse into the middle of the line of battle. Inspired by this deed, the Romans stood fast along the entire battle front. After they had destroyed the army of the enemy, they finally captured its leader Pontius, who had been defeated and utterly crushed. In that battle twenty thousand Samnites were slain, and four thousand, including their king, were captured. Thus the Samnite War, which had been carried on for forty-nine years with much disaster to the Romans, was at last ended by the capture of the Samnite leader.

The next year the consul Curius [54] waged a war against the Sabines. In this war the consul himself tells us how many thousand men were killed and captured. When in the Senate

[51] These books were consulted only at times of great anxiety in order to learn what interpretation and advice the books could give in the circumstances.

[52] The snake was supposed to have the power to find curative herbs. In this instance the snake voluntarily came aboard ship. It left the ship during the trip up the Tiber and where it landed the Romans built a temple to Aesculapius.

[53] Q. Fabius Maximus Gurges, 292 B.C.   [54] M. Curius Dentatus, 290 B.C.

he wished to report the amount of the land acquired from the Sabines and the number of their inhabitants captured, he was not able to give exact figures.

In the four hundred and sixty-third year of the City and during the consulship of Dolabella and Domitius,[55] the Lucanians, Bruttians, and Samnites made an alliance with the Etruscans and Senonian Gauls, who were attempting to renew war against the Romans. The Romans sent ambassadors to dissuade the Gauls from joining this alliance, but the Gauls killed the envoys. The praetor Caecilius was sent with an army to avenge their murder and to crush the uprising of the enemy. He was, however, overwhelmed by the Etruscans and Gauls, and perished. Seven military tribunes were also slain in that battle,[56] many nobles were killed, and thirty thousand soldiers likewise met their death.

Thus just as often as the Gauls became inflamed, the entire wealth of Rome was reduced. During the present invasion of the Goths we should therefore do well to remember the Gauls.

23. I SHALL turn back now to relate the wars which the Macedonian leaders waged among themselves and recall how each of the generals upon the death of Alexander obtained certain provinces by lot and how they then destroyed one another in wars. These events occurred at the same time that the Romans were enduring the disasters mentioned above. I seem to see this tumultuous age as if looking from a watchtower out into the night upon an immense camp where I can distinguish nothing in the great expanse of the field except innumerable campfires. Thus throughout the kingdom of Macedonia, that is, throughout all Asia, the greater part of Europe and most of Libya, the terrible fires of war suddenly burst into flame. The fires laid waste those places in which they had flared up and the news of these conflagrations, spreading like a cloud of smoke, terrified and threw into confusion

[55] P. Cornelius Dolabella Maximus and Cn. Domitius Calvinus Maximus, 283 B.C.   [56] At Lake Vadimo in Etruria.

all other lands. But I shall not set forth the wars and defeats of these great kings and kingdoms until I have first discussed the kingdoms themselves and their rulers.

For twelve years Alexander oppressed with the sword a world which trembled beneath him. His generals rent it asunder for fourteen years more. Just as whelps greedily tear to pieces a rich prize brought to earth by a full-grown lion, these generals, stirred to rivalry by the prize, threw themselves upon one another. By the first lot, Egypt, Africa, and part of Arabia fell to Ptolemy. Laomedon of Mytilene was allotted Syria, which bordered on Ptolemy's province: Philotas received Cilicia; Philo, the Illyrians; and Atropates was put in command of Greater Media. The father-in-law of Perdiccas was given Lesser Media. The people of Susiana were assigned to Scynus, and Greater Phrygia to Antigonus, the son of Philip. Nearchus drew Lycia and Pamphylia; Cassander, Caria; and Menander, Lydia. Leonnatus received Lesser Phrygia; Thrace and the regions bordering on the Pontic Sea fell by lot to Lysimachus; and Cappadocia, together with Paphlagonia, was assigned to Eumenes. The chief command of the camp fell by lot to Seleucus, the son of Antiochus; and Cassander, the son of Antipater, was placed in command of the Bodyguards and Companions of the King. In Further Bactriana and the regions of India, the former prefects, who had taken office under Alexander, kept their posts. Taxiles received the Seres who were settled between the Hydaspes and Indus rivers. Peithon, the son of Agenor, was sent to the colonies in India. Oxyartes was assigned to the Paropamisadae at the foot of the Caucasus Mountains. The Arachossi and Cedrosi were awarded to Sibyrtius. Stasander obtained the inhabitants of Drangiana and of Aria; Amyntas was allotted the Bactriani; Scythaeus, the Sogdiani; Stasanor, the Parthi; Philip, the Hyrcani; Phrataphernes, the Armenii; Tlepolemus, the Persians; Peucestas, the Babylonians; Archon, inhabitants of Pella; and Archelaus, Mesopotamia.

Now the immediate cause of the wars was the letter of

King Alexander in which he ordered all exiles to be restored to freedom in their native lands. The powerful cities of Greece, apprehensive lest these exiles revenge themselves after they had recovered their freedom, revolted against Macedonian rule. The foremost Athenians assembled an army of thirty thousand men and two hundred ships and made war upon Antipater, to whom Greece had fallen by lot. With the aid of Demosthenes, an orator like his namesake, they allied themselves with Sicyon, Argos, Corinth, and other states. They then surrounded and besieged Antipater. Their leader Leosthenes was pierced by a spear hurled from the walls and was killed. The Athenians then encountered Leonnatus, who was bringing help to Antipater, and after overwhelming his forces, put him to death.

Perdiccas, on the other hand, declared war against Ariarathes, the king of the Cappadocians,[57] and conquered him. Nothing came of that victory except wounds and dangers. For before the assault on their city all the citizens had set fire to their homes and to all their possessions and had perished with them.[58]

After these events, war arose between Antigonus and Perdiccas. These generals most severely ravaged many provinces and islands regardless of whether the inhabitants refused or agreed to furnish auxiliary troops. It was long in doubt whether they would transfer the war to Macedonia or carry it on in Asia. Perdiccas himself finally led a huge army against Egypt. Macedonia, with its leaders separated into two parties, was thus armed against itself. Ptolemy, supported by the forces of Egypt and by the Cyrenean troops, prepared to wage war against Perdiccas. While these events were taking place, Neoptolemus and Eumenes contended fiercely against each other in a most bloody battle. Neoptolemus was defeated and,

---

[57] Cappadocia, which had been neglected by Alexander the Great, remained in virtual independence under its satrap Ariarathes.

[58] Orosius has confused two separate incidents. Some time after this battle which took place in the spring of 322 B.C., Perdiccas invaded Pisidia and there attacked the city of Isaura, the inhabitants of which died in the manner Orosius has described.

fleeing to Antipater, urged him to make a surprise attack upon Eumenes. The latter, however, anticipated this move and overcame the plotters by the use of a stratagem. In that battle Polyperchon was killed while Neoptolemus and Eumenes suffered wounds which they had inflicted upon each other; Neoptolemus, indeed, died, but Eumenes, who had been victorious, escaped. Perdiccas now engaged in a very bitter war with Ptolemy, lost his forces, and was himself killed. Eumenes, Peithon, Illyrius, and Alcetas, the brother of Perdiccas, were publicly proclaimed enemies by the Macedonians, and the conduct of the war against them was assigned to Antigonus.

After each had assembled mighty armies, Eumenes and Antigonus met on the field of battle.[59] Eumenes was defeated and fled to a certain strongly fortified citadel.[60] From here he sent legates to beg assistance from Antipater who was at this time very powerful. But not even then did Eumenes feel absolutely confident and assured of his own safety. Therefore as a final measure he summoned to his assistance the Silver Shields,[61] that is, the soldiers who fought under Alexander and who were so named from their arms which were covered with silver. They were disdainful of following the plans which their leader had made for the battle and as a result were defeated by Antigonus.[62] They were deprived of their camp and lost their wives and children as well as everything they had gained under Alexander. Later, through legates, they most shamefully requested their conqueror to return what they had lost. Antigonus promised that he would do so but only on the condition that they should hand over to him Eumenes bound in chains. Won over by the inducement of recovering their property and most shamefully betraying the

[59] The engagement took place on the plains of Orcynium in Cappadocia.

[60] This fortress was situated at Nora on the borders of Lycaonia and Cappadocia.

[61] The Argyraspids. They were regarded as invincible.

[62] A series of battles were fought in the neighborhood of Gabiene, one of the eparchies into which Elymais, a province near Susa, was divided. As a matter of fact the engagement was indecisive, but the camp of the Silver Shields happened to be plundered during the course of the battle.

leader under whose standards they had served a little while before, they led him forth in chains as a prisoner. These soldiers, now completely humiliated and disgraced, were at once distributed among the army of Antigonus.[63]

In the meantime Eurydice, the wife of the Macedonian king Arridaeus,[64] acting in the name of her husband, committed many crimes. She was helped by Cassander with whom she had formed a most shameful alliance and whom she had advanced through all the grades of honor to the highest rank. Out of his lust for a woman, Cassander harassed many states of Greece. Olympias, the mother of King Alexander, was at this time coming from Epirus to Macedonia with the Molossian king [65] Aeacides attending her. Eurydice barred her from the territories. Acting on the advice of Polyperchon, Olympias ordered the execution of King Arridaeus and Eurydice. The Macedonians supported her in this demand. Nevertheless, she herself immediately suffered a just punishment for her cruelty; for even as she was causing the slaughter of many nobles, acting with the foolhardiness characteristic of women, she heard of the approach of Cassander. As the Macedonians distrusted her, she withdrew to the city of Pydna with her daughter-in-law Roxane and her grandson Hercules: there she was soon captured and killed by Cassander. The son of Alexander the Great was sent with his mother to the citadel of Amphipolis for safe keeping.

With the slaughter of Perdiccas, Alcetas, Polyperchon, and a number of other generals of the opposing party too many to mention, the wars among the successors of Alexander seemed about to come to an end. But Antigonus, inflamed with the desire to be lord and master, pretended that it was necessary to resort to war in order to free Hercules, the son of the king, from his imprisonment. When his activities became known, Ptolemy and Cassander entered into an alliance

[63] They were sent to frontier districts where the constant fighting would kill them off.

[64] Philip Arridaeus, the half-brother of Alexander. He was feeble-minded.

[65] The Molossians were a tribe of Epirots who gave their name to the dynasty at this time ruling.

with Lysimachus and Seleucus and prepared strenuously for war on land and sea. In this war Antigonus and his son Demetrius were defeated.

When Cassander, whom Ptolemy had made a partner in the victory, was returning to Apollonia, he came upon the Avieniatae. They had left the land of their forefathers and emigrated from their ancient habitations because they could not bear the enormous number of frogs and mice, and they were seeking to find new homes while peace prevailed. But Cassander, knowing the reputation of this people for courage and numbers, received them into an alliance and settled them on the farthest boundaries of Macedonia. He was afraid that under the pressure of necessity they would invade Macedonia and ruin the land by warfare. When Hercules, the son of Alexander, had reached his fourteenth year, Cassander, fearing that everyone would prefer Hercules as the legitimate king, took care to have him and his wife secretly put to death.

Ptolemy engaged in a second battle with Demetrius, a naval battle in which he lost almost his entire fleet and army.[66] After his defeat he fled to Egypt. Antigonus, elated by this victory, ordered that both he and his son Demetrius be called king. The other generals followed this example, each assuming the name and authority of king. When Ptolemy and Cassander saw that Antigonus was deceiving the leaders of the other faction one by one, they communicated with one another by letters, agreed upon a time and place for meeting, and prepared their common forces to war against him. Cassander, who was involved in war with his neighbors, sent Lysimachus, the most renowned of all his generals, with a huge force to assist his allies in his stead. Seleucus, arriving from Greater Asia, added a new enemy to those who were hostile to Antigonus. Indeed, this Seleucus took part in most of the great wars throughout the East among the allies of the Macedonian kingdom. At the beginning of the war, he stormed and captured Babylon. He then subdued the Bactriani who

---

[66] This battle, one of the greatest sea fights in antiquity, took place in 306 B.C. off the harbor of Salamis, a city on the east coast of the island of Cyprus.

had risen in new revolts. Next he made a journey to India, whose people, after the death of Alexander, had killed his prefects. Rising in revolt and seeking to win their freedom under the leadership of a certain Sandrocottus,[67] they had thrown off his yoke from their necks. Later Sandrocottus, acting with great cruelty toward the citizens whom he had saved from foreign domination, oppressed them with slavery. Seleucus, although he had waged bitter wars against Sandrocottus, finally withdrew from the country after concluding a pact with him and arranging the terms by which the latter should hold the kingdom.

As soon as the forces of Ptolemy and his allies united, battle began. Here was an instance in which the mightier the armaments, the more disastrous was the slaughter; for at that time the forces of almost the whole Macedonia kingdom fell in battle.[68] Antigonus was slain. But the end of this war was only the beginning of another. The victors could not agree about the booty and again split into two factions, Seleucus joining forces with Demetrius and Ptolemy with Lysimachus. After the death of Cassander, Philip succeeded to the throne. New wars, as if taking a fresh start, arose to trouble Macedonia.

Although Thessalonice, his own mother and the wife of Cassander, pleaded pitifully for her life, Antipater pierced her with his own sword. His brother Alexander, while preparing for war against him to avenge his mother, was surrounded and slain by Demetrius, whose assistance he had sought. Lysimachus, hard pressed in an extremely dangerous war with Dromichaetes, king of the Thracians, was not able to fight against Demetrius. Elated by the conquest of Greece and all Macedonia, Demetrius now prepared to cross into Asia. Ptolemy, Seleucus, and Lysimachus, however, having learned from experience in the earlier struggle how much strength there was in union, once more formed an alliance, united

[67] The text has "Androcottus." His Indian name was Chandragupta.

[68] The engagement was fought in 301 B.C. on the plains of Ipsus, a small town of Phrygia.

their armies, and transferred to Asia the war against Demetrius. Pyrrhus, the king of Epirus, joined them as their companion and ally, hoping to drive Demetrius out of Macedonia.
Nor was this hope in vain; for after Demetrius had been
abandoned by his army and forced to flee, Pyrrhus invaded
the kingdom of Macedonia. Lysimachus killed his son-in-law
Antipater, claiming that the latter was plotting against him;
he then slew his own son Agathocles, whom he hated with a
hate unnatural to man.

In these days a most terrible earthquake overthrew the city
of Lysimachia; its population was destroyed and the city became a cruel tomb. Moreover, all the allies of Lysimachus
deserted him because he was staining himself with blood by his
repeated murders. They joined Seleucus, a king already engaged in the struggle for the crown, and encouraged him to
declare war against Lysimachus. It was a shameful spectacle.
The two kings (Lysimachus was seventy-four years old and
Seleucus seventy-seven), standing in battle line and bearing
arms, were striving to deprive each other of the kingdom. To
be sure this was the last war among Alexander's companions,
but it was one which has been reserved as an example of human
misery. Even when they alone held the world, after the destruction of the thirty-four generals of Alexander, they took
no thought of the approaching end of their lives, now so nearly
finished. Rather they continued to regard the ends of the entire world as too-narrow boundaries for their empire. In that
battle Lysimachus was the last to be killed.[69] His fifteen children either had been sent away or killed before this battle had
begun. Thus the death of Lysimachus proved to be the end
of the Macedonian War. But Seleucus did not rejoice with im-
punity; for he himself did not enjoy a natural and peaceful
death after seventy-seven years of life. Rather he died before
his time in circumstances which were most unhappy. While he
was resisting the attack of Ptolemy, whose sister had married

[69] The engagement took place in 281 B.C. on the plains of Corus.

Lysimachus, he was treacherously assassinated.[70]

Such are the ties of blood and fellowship between parents, sons, brothers, and friends. Such is the importance they attach to heavenly and earthly bonds. Let the people of this generation blush with shame over the recollection of these past events. They now realize that it is only by the intervention of the Christian faith and by means of the sworn oath that they live at all with their enemies and suffer no injury. This proves beyond question that now barbarians and Romans, no longer after the ancient manner, when "with the sacrifice of a sow they made a treaty," [71] but calling their Creator and Lord to witness, assure one another such loyalty by the oath taken on the Gospels, as nature was unable in those days to ensure even between fathers and sons.

Now let this book conclude with the end of the Macedonian War, especially since the wars of Pyrrhus begin just at this point and the Punic wars follow directly.

[70] Ptolemy Ceraunus, the eldest son of Ptolemy Lagus, stabbed him as he stepped out of a boat.
[71] Vergil *Aeneid* viii. 641.

THE FOURTH BOOK

PREFACE. Vergil relates that when Aeneas was having a hard time consoling the few companions he had left after their common dangers and the shipwreck of their fellows, he spoke these words:

Perchance some day it will be a joy to recollect even this.[1]

This sentiment, so aptly expressed, always carries a meaning that may be interpreted in three different ways. The more trying past events were in actual experience, the more pleasing, it is held, they are to relate. Future events, which become desirable because of our feeling of disgust for the present, we always believe will be better. But so far as present events are concerned, we can make no just comparison of miseries; for no matter how insignificant present evils may be, they cause much more trouble than either those which have taken place in the past or those which will come in the future. Furthermore, even if we speak of past and future evils as great, they do not exist for us at the present moment.

A man who is annoyed by fleas at night and unable to sleep may happen to recall other wakeful hours that he once endured from burning fevers. Without doubt he will bear far less patiently the restlessness of these hours than the recollection of his earlier experience. Everyone on the basis of his own experience can testify that the time element does introduce a new consideration here. But will anyone come forth and assert, whatever his pain, that fleas cause greater suffering than do fevers? Or will anyone maintain that it is more unpleasant to be kept awake while in sound health than to be unable to sleep when at the point of death? Since this is so, I am quite willing to allow those dandies and my other critics

[1] Vergil *Aeneid* i. 203.

to consider severe the evils confronting them (evils which occasionally reprove us for our benefit), yet I do not approve their making them more severe, by comparison, than they actually are.

It is as if a man should have left his soft bed and comfortable chamber early in the morning and should see in the distance that the surfaces of the ponds had become frozen from the chill of the night and that the plants had become white with hoarfrost. Prompted by the unexpected sight, he might say, "We have winter weather today." I should not consider that this man should in any way be censured, for in his description he employed the terms in their common usage and in their proper sense. But let us suppose that in a state of alarm he should rush back into his bedchamber and pull the covers over himself, completely hiding himself from view, and then should shout that there never had been such cold in the Apennines, no, not even at the time when Hannibal, overcome and buried by a heavy snowstorm, lost his elephants, horses, and most of his army. Then not only could I not bear a man talking in this way and uttering such childish nonsense, but I would also drag him out from under those covers, the witnesses of his idle life, and expose him before the people in a public place. Once I had led him out of doors, I should show him the children who were playing there, taking delight in the cold and yet perspiring in spite of it. Thus I would teach this man, so full of verbose nonsense and corrupted by his luxurious upbringing, that his discomfort was due not to the severity of the weather but to sluggishness in himself. By comparison and careful examination of the actual conditions, I would also prove to him that his ancestors bore really great burdens but that he himself is not even strong enough to bear little ones.

I shall prove this more clearly by turning over in my memory the disasters of the past in due order. Among the first, I shall discuss the Pyrrhic War. Its causes and origin were as follows.

1. FOUR hundred and sixty-four years after the founding of

the City, some Tarentines, who were seated in a theater, saw in the distance a Roman fleet that happened to be sailing by. They proceeded to attack this fleet, and only five boats managed to escape. The rest they dragged into the harbor and destroyed. They killed the captains of the ships and slew all men of any use in war; the remainder they sold into slavery. The Romans at once sent envoys to Tarentum to complain about the outrage that they had suffered. The Tarentines, however, beat these ambassadors, who then brought back the story of this still greater outrage. From these causes a great war arose.

After the Romans had made a careful survey to discover the identity and the number of the enemies who on all sides were raising a clamor, they were forced as a final measure to arm the proletariat and enroll them in the army. This proletariat was composed of those in the city who had always been free to devote themselves to raising children. As a matter of fact, any careful provision with regard to children was useless unless measures were taken to deal with present emergency. Therefore a Roman army under the consul Aemilius[2] invaded all the territories of the Tarentines, laid waste everything with fire and sword, captured many towns, and exacted a cruel vengeance to expiate those outrages inflicted contrary to all custom.

The numbers of the Tarentines, who were supported by large contingents of their neighbors, were greatly increased by Pyrrhus, who, because of the magnitude of the forces and plans involved, took over the command and gave his name to the war. In order to free Tarentum, a city founded by the Lacedaemonians and thus related by blood to Greece, Pyrrhus brought the entire forces of Epirus, Thessaly, and Macedonia to Italy. Here he was the first to introduce elephants, which the Romans had never before seen. Pyrrhus would

---

[2] Q. Aemilius Papus, 282 B.C. During this consulship he was engaged in wars in northern Italy. In 278 B.C. he was consul for a second time; and with the other consul, C. Fabricius Luscinus, he so firmly resisted Pyrrhus that the latter was forced to leave Italy. He was granted a triumph by his grateful countrymen because of his military victories.

have inspired terror on land and sea on account of his men, horses, arms, and beasts, and especially on account of his own energy and skill in trickery, but he was deceived by the ambiguous response of the Delphian God, that most boastful and lying scoundrel whom they called a great prophet. Consequently he met the same end as one would have met who had not consulted the oracle.

The first battle between King Pyrrhus and the consul Laevinus [3] was fought near the Liris River [4] and Heraclea, a city of Campania. The terrible struggle lasted the whole day. On both sides every man expected death and did not know the meaning of retreat. When the Romans saw elephants, savage in appearance, strong in odor, and terrifying in their huge bulk, entering between the clashing lines of battle, they fled in all directions. In meeting this new kind of warfare they became terror-stricken, while the horses trembled greatly from fear. But Minucius, the first *hastatus* of the fourth legion, used his sword to cut off an elephant's trunk and forced the beast, now distracted by the pain of his wound, to leave the battle and to vent his rage upon the army to which he belonged. Pyrrhus's army began to be thrown into disorder and confusion by the wild charge of the beast. Darkness finally put an end to the battle.

The disgraceful flight showed that the Romans had been defeated. Their losses at that time were as follows: 14,880 of the infantry dead and 1,310 captured; 246 of the cavalry slain and 802 taken prisoner. Twenty-two standards were lost. Tradition does not tell us if as great a number of Pyrrhus's allies were destroyed on the opposite side. For it is certainly not the custom of writers of olden times to preserve for posterity the number of the victor's dead, lest his losses tarnish the glory of his victory, unless by chance so few fall that the number lost enhances the admiration for and the fear of the victor's courage. This was the case with Alexander the

---

[3] P. Valerius Laevinus, 280 B.C.

[4] The river is the Siris in Lucania, where Heraclea is also located. Orosius and Florus both make the same error.

Great in the first battle of the Persian War. It is reported that
his army lost only nine infantrymen, whereas the enemy's
losses numbered almost four thousand. Pyrrhus, however,
bore witness before gods and men to the frightfulness of the
disaster that he had suffered in that battle, when he wrote
these words, adding them to the inscription in the temple of
Jove at Tarentum:

> Those men who were earlier unconquered, blessed father Olympus,
> I myself have defeated in battle and have been defeated by them.

When rebuked by his allies for saying that though a conqueror
he had been defeated, Pyrrhus is said to have replied: "If I
win another victory of the same kind, I shall return to Epirus
without one soldier."

In the meantime the Roman army, which had been defeated
and had fled secretly from its camp, saw plainly that the miserable disaster suffered in battle had been greatly increased and
aggravated by still more troublesome portents. As if aiding
the enemy, a terrific thunderstorm arose and by the fire of its
dreadful lightning bolts destroyed some foragers who had
gone out from camp and had been overtaken by the storm.

In fact that hurricane laid low thirty-four of the party,
twenty-two were left half alive, and many of the baggage animals were driven mad and died: so that it is rightly said that
this happened not as foreshadowing a disaster but was a
disaster in itself.

A second battle was fought between Pyrrhus and the Roman consuls on the borders of Apulia.[5] Both generals suffered severe losses, especially Pyrrhus. The victory, however,
fell to the Romans. For a long time and with all their strength
both armies hurled themselves against each other to their
common destruction. While the outcome of the battle still
hung in the balance, Pyrrhus was wounded by a thrust in his
arm and was the first to withdraw from the battle. The legate
Fabricius was also wounded at that time. In the first battle
it had been discovered that elephants, if wounded, could be

---

[5] The battle was fought near Asculum, a city of Apulia.

forced to flee; that they could then be enraged by imbedding
fiery brands in their hind-quarters and tender parts; and that
the beasts, maddened by rage as they carried burning scaf-
folding on their backs, would bring destruction to their own
army. In that battle five thousand Romans lost their lives,
whereas Pyrrhus's army lost twenty thousand. The latter
army lost also fifty-three royal standards, while the Romans
lost only eleven.

Shattered by this battle, Pyrrhus betook himself to Syracuse, whither he had been summoned to the rule of Sicily on
the death of Agathocles, the Syracusan king.

2. THE misery of the Romans, however, did not end with
the truce. Terrible diseases completely filled the time between
wars and, when there was no war abroad, wrath from Heaven
raged at home. In the consulship of Fabius Gurges (his second) and of C. Genucius Clepsina,[6] a severe pestilence swept
over the city and its environs. It seized all, but attacked with
special severity the women and the flocks. By killing the un-
born in their mothers' wombs, it left no chance for future offspring; miscarriages were of common occurrence and mothers
were endangered by premature births. The terror assumed
proportions so great that they thought that human and animal life would soon be extinct, because birth in the normal
manner was no longer possible.

In the meantime the consul Curius[7] intercepted Pyrrhus
as he was returning from Sicily, and a third battle was fought
against the Epirots at Lucania in the Arusinian Plains.[8] In
their first encounter the soldiers of Pyrrhus became panic-
stricken under the attack of the Romans. Contemplating
flight, they were attempting to withdraw from the battle when
Pyrrhus ordered the elephants to be led up from the reserve.
The Romans, who were now accustomed to fight with the
beasts, prepared fire-darts, which they wound with tow,
smeared with pitch, and capped with barbed spurs. They

---

[6] Q. Fabius Maximus Gurges II and C. Genucius Clepsina, 276 B.C.
[7] M. Curius Dentatus II, 275 B.C.   [8] Near Beneventum, 274 B.C.

hurled these flaming missiles at the backs of the elephants and
at the towers on their backs, and thus without difficulty turned
back the raging and burning beasts to bring destruction upon
the army of which they were part of the reserve. They say
that the king had eighty thousand infantry and six thousand
cavalry in that battle. Of these, thirty-three thousand are reported to have been slain; thirty thousand, however, were
captured. As a result of this defeat, Pyrrhus finally left Italy
in the fifth year after his arrival. After waging many severe
wars, he was carried away by his desire to win the Spartan
kingdom. While he was in Greece at Argos, a flourishing city
of Achaia, he was struck by a rock and died.

At this same time among the Romans, Sextilia, a Vestal
Virgin, upon being found guilty of unchastity, was condemned
and buried alive at the Colline Gate.

3. IN THE four hundred and seventy-fifth year of the City,
the Tarentines, upon learning of the death of Pyrrhus, again
stirred up war against the Romans. Through ambassadors
they requested and obtained the aid of the Carthaginians. A
battle took place in which the Romans were victorious. Then
the Carthaginians fully realized for the first time that although they were not yet adjudged enemies, they could be defeated by the Romans.

In the following year Roman severity destroyed a large
part of her own vitals. Shortly before the arrival of Pyrrhus,
the eighth legion,[9] despairing of the Roman cause, ventured
to commit an unusual crime. The soldiers of this legion killed
all the people of Rhegium who had been entrusted to their
protection and claimed the town for themselves as well as the
right to all the plunder taken from it. The consul Genucius [10]
was ordered to punish these criminals and rebels. After besieging the city of Rhegium and capturing all its defenders,
he wrought a fit punishment upon the surviving deserters and
freebooters, but sent the Roman soldiers of that legion unharmed to Rome. There, by order of the people, they were

---

[9] The Campanian legion.   [10] L. Genucius Clepsina, 271 B.C.

beaten to death and beheaded in the middle of the Forum.

At that time Rome thought that she was a conqueror when she slaughtered a legion of her own with its full complement, although she would clearly have suffered a defeat if she had lost that legion in battle with the enemy.

4. IN THE four hundred and seventy-eighth year of the City, inauspicious and dreadful omens were seen or reported at Rome. Lightning destroyed the Temple of Salus, and part of the wall in the same locality, it is said, was struck. Before dawn three wolves came into the city, bringing in a half-eaten corpse. When they were frightened by the shouts of the people, they left the remains strewn in the Forum. At Formiae [11] the walls everywhere were burned and destroyed by many bolts of lightning, while in the Calenian [12] Field, a flame suddenly burst forth from an opening in the ground and blazed frightfully for three days and three nights. Five jugera of land were burnt to ashes. The moisture which brought fertility was so completely exhausted that not only the plants of the fields but even the trees, so they say, were consumed to their very roots.

In the following year the consul Sempronius [13] led an army against the Picentes. Just as the battle lines had taken their position within spear range, the earth suddenly shook with so horrible a rumbling that both lines, amazed by the miracle, grew faint and were stricken with terror. For a long time each people was dumbfounded by the realization that their undertaking had been prejudged and stood motionless. At length they began the battle with a sharp attack. So disastrous was this engagement that people rightly say that the earth, destined to receive so much human blood, at that time trembled and groaned fearfully. The few Romans who escaped death in this battle won the victory.

5. FOUR hundred and eighty years after the founding of

[11] A city of Latium on the coast of the Gulf of Caieta.
[12] Cales, a town of Southern Campania, celebrated for its good wine.
[13] P. Sempronius Sophus, 268 B.C.

the City, among many other prodigies, blood was seen to come from the ground and milk from the sky. In many places indeed blood gushed forth and flowed from springs; and from clouds, drop by drop, milk fell like a kind of rain. Ill-omened storms, as it seemed to the people, flooded the land. At that time the Carthaginians, who had given assistance to the Tarentines against the Romans, were rebuked by the Senate through ambassadors. They added to the shame and disgrace incurred in breaking the treaty by committing a premeditated perjury.

At that time, too, the Volsinians, the most flourishing of the Etruscan peoples, almost perished as a result of their wantonness. After making license a habit, they indiscriminately freed their slaves, invited them to banquets, and honored them with marriage. The liberated slaves, admitted to a share of power, criminally plotted to usurp complete rule of the state, and, relieved of the yoke of slavery, were consumed with the desire for revolution. Once free, they cursed those masters whom they as slaves had devotedly loved, because they remembered that these men had once been their masters. The liberated slaves then conspired to commit a crime and claimed the captured city for their class alone. So great were their numbers that they accomplished their rash purpose without real resistance. They criminally appropriated the property and wives of their masters, and forced the latter to go into distant exile. These wretched and destitute exiles betook themselves to Rome. Here they displayed their misery and tearfully pleaded their cause. They were avenged and restored to their former positions through the stern rule of the Romans.

In the four hundred and eighty-first year after the founding of the City, a great plague raged at Rome. Its frightfulness I am satisfied merely to indicate because I am unable to describe it adequately. If anyone should inquire how long it lasted, I should say that its ravages lasted more than two years. As to the deaths it caused, the census gives the figures, not in terms of how many perished, but of how many survived. If anyone should inquire about the violence with which it raged, let him consult the Sibylline Books as witnesses. These testify that the plague was sent by the wrath of Heaven. But lest our temptation to scoff somewhat be offensive to anyone, because we appear to have said that it was the anger of Heaven whereas the Sibyl has said that the gods were angry, let him hear and recognize that, though these things do take place for the most part through the agency of heavenly powers, nevertheless they do not take place at all without the will of Omnipotent God.

At that time Caparronia, a Vestal Virgin, upon being convicted of unchastity, was hanged. Her seducer and the slaves, who were her accomplices, were also put to death.

Behold, how many and how great are the events of which we give a continuous record. These events followed one another in separate years in which certainly it was seldom, if ever, that something tragic did not take place. And this is true even despite the fact that those who recorded these events, in their determination to please, omitted great numbers of miseries. For they were afraid that they might hurt the feelings of those for whom and about whom they were writing and also that they might appear to frighten their audience rather than instruct them by examples from the past. Moreover, we ourselves, placed at the end of these ages, are able to learn the misfortunes of the Romans only through those who have praised them. Hence you can understand how much there must have been which was purposely suppressed on account of its horror, when we find so much which, amid the praises of historians, can only partially be known.

6. SINCE the Punic wars follow at this point, it is necessary to say something of Carthage, which we find was founded by Elissa [14] seventy-two years before the founding of Rome. We must also say something about her disasters and domestic misfortunes, just as Pompeius Trogus and Justin relate them. The Carthaginians have always had domestic and internal

[14] Better known as Dido.

misfortunes. Because of this source of discord and its un-happy faculty of causing disturbance they have never yet enjoyed prosperity abroad, or peace at home. When they were suf-fering from plagues in addition to their other misfortunes, they resorted to homicides instead of to medicines; indeed they sacrificed human beings as victims and offered young children at their altars. In this way they aroused even the pity of the enemy.

Concerning this form of sacred rite—nay, rather of sacri-lege—I am perplexed as to what I should discuss in prefer-ence to all else. For if some demons have dared to order rites of this character, requiring as they did that the death of men should be propitiated by human slaughter, it must be understood that these demons acted as partners and promoters of the plague and that they themselves killed those whom the plague had not seized; for it was customary to offer healthy and undefiled sacrificial victims. In doing this they not only failed to allay, but rather anticipated, the pestilences.

When the Carthaginians—the gods being alienated, as Pompeius Trogus and Justin admit, because of sacrifices of this kind, and, as we assert, because of their presumption and impiety toward an angered God—had long fought unsuc-cessfully in Sicily, they transferred the theater of war to Sardinia, and there they were still more disastrously defeated. On account of this, they sentenced their general Malcus and the few surviving soldiers to exile. When their petition for clemency was denied, these exiles, led by Malcus, made war upon and besieged their native city. Malcus was met by his own son Carthalo, a priest of Hercules, who came clad in purple as if to insult him. Malcus had him crucified in the sight of his countrymen, still arrayed in his purple garments and wearing his sacred fillets. A few days later Malcus cap-tured the city itself. He killed many of the senators and ruled with cruelty. Afterward he was himself slain. These events took place in the days of Cyrus, king of the Persians.

Later the Carthaginian king Himilco, while waging war in Sicily, unexpectedly lost his army by a horrible pestilence.

The plague spread rapidly and the people perished in droves. As soon as anyone was smitten he fell lifeless; there was no time to bury the dead. When the news of this catastrophe was bruited about Carthage, the city, stunned by this sudden blow, became as greatly agitated as if she had been captured. The whole city resounded with wailings, the gates were closed everywhere, and all public and private business was forbidden. Everybody rushed to the harbor and plied the few who were disembarking and who had survived the disaster with questions about their friends and relatives. When told their fate, some of the unhappy men were silent while others groaned. At one time the voices of those weeping and at another the cries and the sorrowful lamentations of the unhappy mothers were heard along the entire shore. In the midst of this mourning, the commander himself, ungirt and wearing the soiled tunic of a slave, disembarked from his ship. At his appearance the weeping hands gathered in one body. He himself, lifting up his hands to Heaven, bemoaned and lamented now his own misfortune, now the misfortune of the state; and crying aloud as he was making his way through the city, he finally entered his own house. He then dismissed with a final word of encouragement all the mourners, who wept as they followed him. After barring the doors and excluding even his own sons, he ended his sorrow and his life with a sword. These events took place in the time of Darius.

Subsequently, Hanno, a Carthaginian whose private fortune exceeded that of the state, was consumed with a covetous desire to usurp control of the government. As a useful means to this end, Hanno thought of killing all the senators, whose rank he considered would block his designs. His plan was to poison their cups at a sham marriage of his only daughter. His accomplices, however, betrayed this plot to the senators, who frustrated it without recourse to vengeance. For they feared that in the case of so powerful a man the recognition of his conspiracy might cause more trouble than what he originally intended. Defeated in this plot, Hanno tried to advance his villainy by another scheme. He roused slaves to a surprise attack upon the city when she was off her guard. But before the day set for the massacre, he learned that he had been betrayed and that his attack had been anticipated. With the help of twenty thousand of his slaves he then took possession of a certain fort. There he was captured while engaged in inciting the Africans and the king of the Moors to rebellion. First he was beaten with rods, next his eyes were torn out and his hands and legs broken—just as if punishments were exacted on every limb—and finally he was publicly executed. His body, mangled with stripes, was nailed to a cross. All his children and relatives were put to death, lest any of his family should ever think of following his example or of avenging him. These events took place in the time of Philip.

Afterward the Carthaginians learned that Tyre, their mother city, had been captured and destroyed by Alexander the Great. Fearing that he would come later to Africa, they sent one Hamilcar, whose surname was Rhodanus and who was a man of extraordinary eloquence and shrewdness, to investigate thoroughly what Alexander was doing. Rhodanus was received by Parmenio as a deserter and was later admitted to the royal army; he then informed his fellow countrymen about everything that was taking place by writing on tablets and covering the writing with wax. After the death of Alexander, Hamilcar returned to Carthage, where he was put to death just as if he had really betrayed his city to the king. An envy that knew no mercy rather than an ungrateful spirit brought him to his end.

Some time after these events, the Carthaginians were waging constant but never quite successful wars against the Sicilians. When they had besieged the city of Syracuse, at that time the most flourishing city of Sicily, they were tricked by the remarkable ingenuity of the Sicilian king Agathocles, and reduced to a state of utter desperation. For when the Carthaginians were besieging Agathocles at Syracuse, he saw that his forces were not large enough to fight on even terms nor his supplies sufficient to withstand a siege. He therefore crossed to Africa with his army, concealing his maneuver even better than he had anticipated. There for the first time he disclosed to his own people what he was attempting and then indicated what further must be done. All acting in agreement, they first set fire to the ships in the place where they had landed, so that there would be no possible hope of retreat. Then, while he was devastating the country wherever he went and reducing towns and fortresses to ashes, Agathocles encountered a certain Hanno accompanied by thirty thousand Carthaginians. Hanno and two thousand of his men were slain in the battle, but Agathocles himself lost only two men.[15] This battle broke the spirit of the Africans almost beyond belief and immeasurably raised the spirit of his own men. Agathocles then stormed cities and fortresses, took an enormous amount of booty, and killed many thousands of the enemy. Next he pitched camp five milestones from Carthage, in order that the destruction of their most valuable possessions, the devastation of their fields, and the burning of their country houses might be seen from the very walls of the city.

To these evils a still gloomier report was added. It was announced that an African army with its leader had been destroyed in Sicily. Antander, the brother of Agathocles, had overwhelmed the army when it was completely off its guard and almost at ease. When this rumor had spread through all Africa, not only tributary cities but even royal allies revolted. Among the latter was Ophellas, the king of Cyrene, who at that time was eagerly endeavoring to obtain the rule of Africa. He entered into an alliance of war with Agathocles, but after the two kings had joined armies and made a common camp, he was deceived by the flattery and wiles of Agathocles and slain. In the meantime Carthaginian troops came together from all sides, eager for battle. Agathocles, who now had with him the troops of Ophellas, encountered them and won the victory after a severe battle. Much blood was shed on both sides. At the critical moment in the struggle the Carthaginians were driven to such a state of despair that, had

15 The battle was fought within sight of Carthage.

not a mutiny arisen in the army of Agathocles, the Carthaginian general Hamilcar and his army would have deserted to the side of the enemy. For this intended offense the Carthaginians fastened Hamilcar to the *patibulum* [16] in the middle of the Forum, where he furnished a cruel spectacle to his countrymen. After the death of Agathocles, the Carthaginians then fitted out a fleet and ravaged Sicily. But after being defeated frequently on land and sea by Pyrrhus, the king of Epirus, who had been summoned from Italy, they finally turned their attention to the wars against the Romans.

Oh, what tribulation! Do those who complain about recent events read about what happened in the past? They read, certainly, and then draw conclusions, yet not in a spirit of fairness but in one of bias. This is especially so because they themselves do not discern the great and ineffable spur which goads them on. It is not that the times are evil but that they are Christian. And this brings into existence that invidious ulcer which makes everything done in circumstances that are detestable seem much more horrible than it really is. We, too, are accustomed to look with just as unfriendly eyes upon those whom we detest. We, too, see in their words and deeds nothing that is not vicious, nothing that is not in excess, and nothing that is not to their own detriment. People deceive themselves in this way quite easily, for envy enslaves the heart and leads it astray to such a degree that things do not appear as they really are. These objectors belong to this number, but they are far more wretched because as enemies of God they are therefore enemies of truth. We say these things about them with tears in our eyes. If they suffer, we mercifully reprove them in order that we may restore them to health. For these people see these things with defective vision and thus what they see appears double; and being confused as it were by a fog of wickedness, they fall into a condition where by seeing less they see more, since they cannot see things as they are. Indeed, they consider the scourges

---

[16] An instrument of torture similar to the cross. The Carthaginians were famous for their cruelty and for the frequency of their executions. The Carthaginian general executed was Bomilcar, not the Hamilcar of the text.

inflicted by a father more painful than the fires started by an
enemy; they call a God who caresses, admonishes, and redeems
harsher than the devil who persecutes, bullies, and destroys
them. Yet if they knew anything of the Father, they would
delight in His chastisement and, if they had the knowledge to
foresee the ends for which He sent it, the discipline would be
bearable. Indeed, with the hope that has now been given to
the nations—this did not exist earlier—they would consider
the chastisement lighter even though they suffered more.
Nevertheless, they can also learn to despise miseries from
their own people who regard evils of the highest benefit,
whenever they lead to both a glorious and illustrious renown.
We can infer how much we, to whom a blessed immortality
is promised, must suffer for life, when they have been able to
bear so much merely for fame.

7.   IN THE four hundred and eighty-third year of the City,
that is, during the consulship of Appius Claudius [17] and Q.
Fabius, the Romans sent Appius Claudius with an army and
auxiliaries to help the Mamertines in their struggle against
Hiero, the king of the Syracusans, and the Punic troops allied
with him. At this time the Mamertines controlled Messana,
a celebrated city in Sicily. So quickly did Appius Claudius
overcome the Syracusans and the Carthaginians, that Hiero,
terrified by the extent of the conflict, admitted that he had
been beaten before battle had even begun. His power broken
and his confidence lost, Hiero humbly begged for peace. This
was granted after he had paid the fine of two hundred silver
talents demanded by the consuls.

The consuls besieged Agrigentum, a city of Sicily, and the
Punic garrison stationed there. They surrounded the city by
earthworks and a wall. The elder Hannibal, commander of
the Carthaginians, was shut in by this siege and reduced to
the direst want. Then Hanno, the new leader of the Carthaginians, unexpectedly intervened with one thousand five hun-

---

[17] Ap. Claudius Caudex. His colleague is usually given as M. Fulvius Flaccus,
264 B.C. Hannibal, son of Grisco, is not the famous general.

dred cavalry, thirty thousand infantry, and thirty elephants, and raised the siege of the city within a short time. Nevertheless, the Romans captured the city without much delay. They defeated the Carthaginians in a great battle, put them to flight, captured eleven elephants, and sold all the inhabitants of Agrigentum into slavery. But the elder Hannibal with a few men sallied forth and escaped.

In the consulship of Cn. Cornelius Asina and C. Duilius,[18] when the elder Hannibal was laying waste the seacoast of Italy with a fleet of seventy vessels, the Romans and their consuls ordered a fleet to be built and equipped. Duilius completed this order with great speed, for within sixty days from the time the trees had been cut, a fleet of one hundred and thirty ships was launched and lay at anchor. Cornelius Asina, one of the consuls, accompanied by eleven ships made for the island of Lipara. Here Hannibal, by a typical Punic trick, induced him to go to a peace conference where he captured him. Hannibal later had him put to death while in prison. When Duilius, the other consul, learned of this outrage, he set out against Hannibal with thirty ships. In the course of the naval engagement, Hannibal lost the ship on which he was sailing and escaped by stealing away in a rowboat. Thirty-one of his ships were captured, and thirteen sunk, three thousand men were killed, and seven thousand, according to the report, captured.

Later, in the consulship of C. Aquillius Florus and L. Cornelius Scipio,[19] the Carthaginians put Hanno in charge of naval operations, substituting him for Hannibal in the defense of the Sardinians and Corsicans. When Hanno was defeated by the consul Scipio and when he had lost his army, he threw himself into the midst of the dense ranks of the enemy and there lost his life. In the same year three thousand slaves and four thousand naval allies conspired to destroy the city of Rome. Had not their plan been betrayed at an opportune

[18] C. Cornelius Scipio Asina and C. Duilius, 260 B.C.
[19] C. Aquillius Florus and L. Cornelius Scipio, 259 B.C.

time and measures taken to thwart it, the city, which was without a garrison, would have perished at the hands of slaves.

8. THE following year the consul Calatinus attacked the Sicilian city of Camarina.[20] He heedlessly led his army down into a pass which the Punic troops had fortified a short time before. With no chance whatever to resist or to escape, he was rescued by the courage and the action of Calpurnius Flamma, who, with a picked band of three hundred men, seized the mound held by the enemy and diverted the entire Punic attack toward himself. In the meantime the Roman army crossed the blockaded entrances without being pressed by the enemy. In that battle all the three hundred lost their lives with the exception of Calpurnius. He, though weakened by many wounds, hid among the corpses and thus escaped.

For a second time the Carthaginians put the elder Hannibal in charge of the fleet. He had the misfortune to meet the Romans in a naval battle, was defeated, and finally during a mutiny was stoned to death by his own army. The consul Atilius[21] marched through Lipara and Melita, famous islands of Sicily, and left them in ruin. Both consuls were then ordered to transfer the war to Africa. With three hundred and thirty vessels they made for Sicily, where they were opposed by Hamilcar, the general of the Carthaginians, and by Hanno, who was in charge of the fleet. A naval engagement took place and the Carthaginians were put to flight, losing sixty-four ships. The victorious consuls crossed over to Africa and received in surrender first of all, the city of Clypea;[22] then, setting out for Carthage, they destroyed three hundred or more forts and surrounded Carthage with hostile standards. The consul Manlius[23] and his victorious fleet left Africa and

[20] A. Atilius Calatinus, 258 B.C. The city of Camarina was situated on the south coast of the island at the mouth of the Hipparis River.

[21] That is, the Atilius Calatinus mentioned above.

[22] Its Greek name was Apis; it was an important and strongly fortified city in Carthaginian territory.

[23] L. Manlius Vulso Longus, 256 B.C.

brought back to Rome twenty-seven thousand captives and a huge quantity of booty.

Regulus,[24] chosen by lot for the Carthaginian War, marched with his army to a point not far from the Bagrada River[25] and there pitched his camp. In that place a reptile of astonishing size devoured many of the soldiers as they went down to the river to get water. Regulus set out with his army to attack the reptile. Neither the javelins they hurled nor the darts they rained upon its back had any effect. These glided off its horrible scaly fins as if from a slanting testudo of shields and were in some miraculous fashion turned away from its body so that the creature suffered no injury. Finally, when Regulus saw that it was killing a great number of his soldiers with its bites, was trampling them down by its charge, and driving them mad by its poisonous breath, he ordered *ballistae* brought up. A stone taken from a wall was hurled by a *ballista;* this struck the spine of the serpent and caused its entire body to become numb. The formation of the reptile was such that, though it seemed to lack feet, yet it had ribs and scales graded evenly, extending from the top of its throat to the lowest part of its belly and so arranged that the creature rested upon its scales as if on claws and upon its ribs as if on legs. But it did not move like the worm which has a flexible spine and moves by first stretching its contracted parts in the direction of its tiny body and then drawing together the stretched parts. This reptile made its way by a sinuous movement, extending its sides first right and then left, so that it might keep the line of ribs rigid along the exterior arch of the spine; nature fastened the claws of its scales to its ribs, which extend straight to their highest point; making these moves alternately and quickly, it not only glided over levels, but also mounted inclines, taking as many footsteps, so to speak, as it had ribs. This is why the stone rendered the creature powerless. If struck by a blow in any part of

---

[24] M. Atilius Regulus II, 256 B.C.

[25] One of the largest rivers of northern Africa, but in reality so small as to be fordable in many places.

the body from its bowels to its head, it is crippled and unable to move, because wherever the blow falls, it numbs the spine, which stimulates the feet of the ribs and the motion of the body. Hence this serpent, which had for a long time withstood so many javelins unharmed, moved about disabled from the blow of a single stone and, quickly overcome by spears, was easily destroyed. Its skin was brought to Rome—it is said to have been one hundred and twenty feet in length—and for some time was an object of wonder to all.

Regulus waged an exceptionally severe campaign against three generals, that is, against the two Hasdrubals and Hamilcar, who had been summoned from Sicily. In this war seventeen thousand Carthaginians were slain, five thousand captured, eighteen elephants were led away, and eighty-two towns surrendered to the Romans.

9. THE Carthaginians, crushed in battle and exhausted by disasters, sought peace from Regulus. But when they heard of the hard and intolerable conditions of peace, believing that it was better to die in arms than to live in misery, they decided to hire Greek auxiliaries in addition to the Spanish and Gallic troops. They therefore summoned the Lacedaemonian king Xanthippus and his auxiliaries, and appointed him chief in command. After inspecting the Punic forces, Xanthippus led them down into the plain where,[26] with a vastly strengthened army, he engaged the Romans in battle. In this encounter the Romans suffered huge losses. Thirty thousand of their soldiers were slain and the renowned general Regulus, together with fifty of his men, was taken prisoner. He was cast into chains and finally in the tenth year of the Punic War shared in giving the Carthaginians a glorious triumphal procession. Xanthippus, aware of the consequences of his bold action and fearing a change in conditions already sufficiently unstable, left Africa and returned to Greece.

When the consuls Aemilius Paulus and Fulvius Nobilior [27]

[26] The plains of the Bagradus River.
[27] M. Aemilius Paulus and Ser. Fulvius Paetinus Nobilior, 255 B.C.

heard of Regulus's imprisonment and of the destruction of the Roman army, they crossed under orders to Africa with a fleet of three hundred vessels and attacked Clypea. The Carthaginians arrived immediately with a fleet of equal size. The naval battle could not be long delayed.[28] One hundred and four Carthaginian ships were sunk, thirty with their complement of soldiers were captured, and in addition thirty-five thousand soldiers were slain. The Romans lost nine ships and one thousand and one hundred soldiers perished. The consuls then pitched camp near Clypea. The two Hannos, the Punic commanders, again assembled a mighty army and, after engaging in battle with the Romans, lost nine thousand soldiers. But in those days the Romans never enjoyed long periods of good fortune, and whatever successes they won were forthwith eclipsed by a series of misfortunes. So it was that when the Roman fleet, loaded with booty, was returning to Italy, it was shattered by a storm of indescribable violence.[29] Of three hundred ships two hundred and twenty were lost; the Romans saved the remaining eighty by throwing the cargo overboard. The Punic general Hamilcar who had been sent with an army into Numidia and Mauretania, treated all the people as enemies and acted with cruelty toward them, because they were said to have received Regulus in a friendly spirit. He had the leaders of all the districts fastened to the *patibulum* and fined the rest of the people a thousand silver talents and twenty thousand cattle.

In the third year—so quickly does uncontrolled fury forget danger—the consuls Servilius Caepio and Sempronius Blaesus[30] crossed to Africa with two hundred and sixty ships and laid waste the whole maritime coast that lies near the Syrtes. Advancing inland they captured and overthrew many cities and brought a huge amount of booty back to the fleet. When they were returning to Italy, their ships were dashed to

---

[28] The battle was fought off the Hermean Promontory not far from Aspis (Clypea).

[29] Off Camarina, as the fleet was about to round Pachynus, 255 B.C. The whole coast was strewn with wreckage.

[30] Cn. Servilius Caepio and C. Sempronius Blaesus, 253 B.C.

pieces on the rocks near the Promontory of Palinurus, which extends from the Lucanian Mountains out into the deep. They lost one hundred and fifty transports and the splendid booty which they had acquired by great cruelty. The magnitude of the misfortunes which afflicted the Romans at times prevailed over their base greed. The fathers, now disgusted with the conduct of naval affairs, decreed that the fleet should not have more than sixty vessels with which to protect Italy; but under the compulsion of their ungovernable greed, they at once broke the terms of this decree. Moreover, the consul Cotta crossed to Sicily and fought many battles on land and sea against the Carthaginians and Sicilians, leaving throughout the whole of Sicily unburied heaps of the dead, not only of the enemy, but also of his own allies.

In the consulship of L. Caecilius Metellus and C. Furius Pacilus,[31] Hasdrubal, the new general of the Carthaginians, came from Africa to Lilybaeum with one hundred and thirty elephants and more than thirty thousand infantry and cavalry. He immediately engaged in battle at Panormus [32] with the consul Metellus. The latter had earlier feared the great strength of the elephants, but he now managed to put the beasts to flight or to death by a brilliant maneuver. Thus he easily won the victory despite the great numbers of the enemy. Twenty thousand Carthaginians were slain in that battle; twenty-six elephants were killed and one hundred and four captured. The Italians enjoyed a great spectacle when these elephants were led through Italy. Hasdrubal took refuge in Lilybaeum [33] with a few men and while absent from Carthage was condemned to death by the Carthaginians.

10. LATER the Carthaginians, who were now worn out by many misfortunes, decided that they must seek peace from

---

[31] L. Caecilius Metellus and C. Furius Pacilus, 251 B.C. The text erroneously has "Placidus" instead of "Pacilus."

[32] Panormus, one of the important cities of Sicily, was situated on the northwest coast.

[33] A city in the extreme western part of Sicily, and the nearest port to Africa.

the Romans. For this purpose they thought that they should send, among others, M. Atilius Regulus, the former Roman general, whom they had held a prisoner for five years. Their request for peace was rejected. They therefore killed Regulus on his return from Italy by cutting off his eyelids and binding him in a machine that prevented him from sleeping. Then the other Atilius Regulus and Manlius Vulso,[34] both consuls for the second time, proceeded to Lilybaeum with a fleet of two hundred vessels and four legions. They attempted to besiege the town, which was situated on a promontory, but were defeated after the arrival of Hannibal, the son of Hamilcar. They lost the greater part of their army and they themselves escaped only with difficulty. After this, the consul Claudius,[35] accompanied by a fleet of one hundred and twenty ships, made for the harbor of Drepanum [36] to engage the enemy. There he was soon overtaken by a Punic fleet and defeated. Claudius himself with thirty ships fled to the camp at Lilybaeum. All the rest of the ships, ninety in number, are said to have been captured or sunk. Eight thousand soldiers were slain and twenty thousand, according to report, were taken prisoner. Gaius Junius,[37] a colleague of Claudius, also lost his entire fleet through shipwreck.

The following year, a Punic fleet crossed to Italy and brought devastation to many regions throughout the length and breadth of the land. In the meantime Lutatius [38] with a fleet of three hundred ships sailed over to Sicily, where he began a battle at the city of Drepana. While fighting in the front rank, he was grievously wounded in the thigh, but he was rescued when about to be overwhelmed by the enemy. Next the Carthaginians assembled at Sicily a fleet of forty vessels and a large body of troops, both of which were under the command of Hanno. Nor was Lutatius slow to move; on the contrary he was extraordinarily quick to anticipate the plans

[34] C. Atilus Regulus Serranus (son of M.) and L. Manlius Vulso Longus, 250 B.C.   [35] P. Claudius Pulcher, 249 B.C.

[36] The name both of a promontory and a town in northwestern Sicily. The engagement was fought in 249 B.C. Lilybaeum is fifteen miles from Drepanum (or Drepana).   [37] L. Junius Pullus, 249 B.C.   [38] C. Lutatius Catulus, 242 B.C.

of the Carthaginians. The opposing fleets lay over against each other with anchors almost intermeshed all night long at the Aegates Islands.[39] At daybreak Lutatius was the first to give the signal for battle. After a violent struggle Hanno was defeated; he abandoned his ship and was the first commander to flee. With him a considerable part of his army made for Africa; the rest fled to Lilybaeum. The Romans captured sixty-three Punic ships and sank one hundred and twenty-five; they took thirty-two thousand men prisoners and slew fourteen thousand. Of the Roman ships twelve were sunk. Lutatius then went to the city of Eryx,[40] which the Carthaginians were holding, and there, after engaging in battle, killed two thousand Carthaginians.

11. AT THIS juncture the Carthaginians with all possible speed communicated with the consul Lutatius [41] and then with Rome. They sued for peace and immediately obtained it on the terms formerly proposed. These conditions were: that they should withdraw from Sicily and Sardinia, and that they should defray the expenses of the war by paying three thousand Euboic talents of pure silver in equal installments over a period of twenty years. The terms of this peace were observed for more than twenty-three years from the opening of the Punic War.

Who, I ask, can know the extent of the wars which the two cities waged for twenty-three years? Who can state how many Carthaginian kings, how many Roman consuls, how many armies, how many ships, they brought together, overthrew, and crushed? Not until we have fully considered all of these things are we in a position to pass judgment.

In the five hundred and seventh year of the City, a sudden catastrophe which befell Rome herself prevented the Romans from celebrating a triumph. Nor do I speak rashly when I

---

[39] The name given to a group of three small islands, lying off the western extremity of Sicily, nearly opposite to Drepanum and Lilybaeum. The battle took place in 241 B.C. [40] Situated six miles from Drepanum.
[41] Q. Lutatius (Cerco), 241 B.C.

say that this affliction, not so severe as sudden, crushed Rome's immoderate joy; for in the consulship of Q. Lutatius Catulus and A. Manlius [42] various disastrous fires and floods almost destroyed the city. The Tiber, swollen by unusual rains, continued to overflow its banks to such an extent and for so long a time that no one would have believed it possible. It destroyed all the buildings of Rome that were situated in the plain, but all places, regardless of their location, suffered like destruction. For wherever the lingering flood waters spread, the structures were soaked through and crumbled, and wherever the raging torrent struck, buildings were overthrown and leveled. A fire causing even greater desolation followed in the wake of this most disastrous flood. This fire (it is impossible to state definitely where it began) swept through many parts of the city and took a pitiable toll of homes and human life. Indeed more than all the wealth gained by a great number of foreign victories was at that time consumed by one fire. After destroying everything around the Forum, this ephemeral fire swept the Temple of Vesta and overwhelmed that fire which was thought to be eternal. Even the gods themselves were unable to come to its assistance. While Metellus was rescuing the burning gods, his arm was half-burnt, and he barely managed to escape with his life.

12. IN THE consulship of T. Sempronius Gracchus and P. Valerius Falto,[43] the Romans went to war with the Falisci. Fifteen thousand of the latter lost their lives in this war. In the same year war was waged, with varying success, against new enemies.[44] In the first conflict, when Valerius was consul, three thousand Romans fell; in the second, fourteen thousand Gauls were slain and two thousand captured. The consul was

---

[42] Orosius is mistaken. The consul was Q. Lutatius Cerco and his colleague A. Manlius Torquatus Atticus II, 241 B.C.

[43] Ti. Sempronius Gracchus and P. Valerius Falto, 238 B.C.

[44] The Boian Gauls had made an alliance with kindred tribes on the Po and with the Ligurians. Valerius was denied a triumph because he attacked the enemy with a defeated army before awaiting the arrival of reinforcements which were on their way.

denied a triumph, however, on account of the previous disaster.

In the consulship of T. Manlius Torquatus and C. Atilius Bulbus,[45] the island of Sardinia rebelled against the Carthaginian rule. The Sardinians, however, were soon crushed and reduced to subjection. The Romans then voted to declare war on the Carthaginians as violators of the peace that they themselves had requested. The Carthaginians for their part humbly sued for peace. After they had accomplished nothing by twice sending ambassadors and even after ten of their leading men, twice acting as suppliants had failed in their mission, they finally obtained peace through the eloquence of Hanno, the most unimportant man among their ambassadors. At this time the gates of Janus Geminus were shut because there was no war anywhere. This had happened previously only in the reign of Numa Pompilius.

At this point I had better hold my peace and pass over in silence those days to which our own can in no way be compared, lest my loud voice arouse the disparagers of our own times to censure the age rather than themselves. Behold, the gates of Janus were closed. The Romans waged no war abroad, while Rome held all her children quiet in her bosom and did not breathe a sigh. And when was this? After the First Punic War. After how long a time? After four hundred and forty years. How long did this last? One year. And what followed? The Gallic War and the Second Punic War with Hannibal, not to mention other events.

How ashamed am I to have investigated and exposed these matters! Was that one year's peace, or rather shadow of peace, an alleviation of miseries or an incentive to evils? Did that dripping oil as it fell into the midst of a great flame extinguish or kindle this fire? Did a small drink of cold water swallowed during a burning fever restore the patient to health or did it rather cause his fever to mount? During a period of almost seven hundred years, that is, from Hostilius Tullus to Caesar Augustus, there was only one year in which

---

[45] The text has "Bubulcus." T. Manlius Torquatus and C. Atilius Bulbus II, 235 B.C.

the Roman viscera did not sweat blood; amid the countless years of long centuries, the unhappy city, truly our unhappy mother, has scarcely once been wholly at rest from the fear of sorrows, not to mention from sorrows themselves. Can one say of any man who has enjoyed so little peace in his life, that he has really lived? Suppose that a man be assailed by grief and misfortune throughout a whole year and in the middle of that year passes only one day in peace without a struggle. Will that single day give him consolation for his misfortunes or will he not consider the whole year one of continuous misery? But these critics, he replies, have set up this year as a glorious example of indefatigable courage. Would that they might have passed over it and left in oblivion its uninterrupted succession of disasters. Now, we know that in the body of a man leprosy is finally diagnosed when a different color appears in various places on the healthy parts of the skin. But if the disease spreads everywhere so that the whole body assumes one color, however altered, then this method of distinguishing loses all value. Similarly, if people labor on uninterruptedly with cheerfulness and without a desire for a breathing spell, they apparently are governed both by a strong will power and the choices they have been accustomed to make. But once, during a very brief interval of peace, leisure releases their energies either for the enjoyment of the higher things or preoccupation with trifling matters, they can immediately see how much pleasure this brief interval afforded them and how much they suffered during that long period; that is, they now appreciate how much they would have enjoyed that interval of peace had it lasted a long time, and also how they would have avoided this unending succession of miseries, if they had been able in any possible way to do so.

13. In the five hundred and seventeenth year of the City, when Hamilcar, the Carthaginian general, was secretly preparing for another war against the Romans, he was killed by the Spaniards in battle.[46]

[46] He was drowned in the Vinalapó River near the town of Helice, in the winter of 229–28 B.C.

The following year, the Illyrians put to death some Roman ambassadors. For this reason the Romans waged a very savage war against them. They destroyed many of their towns, and inflicted heavy losses in battle upon them. The surviving Illyrians then surrendered to the consuls Fulvius and Postumius.[47]

Two years later, the pontiffs, who were mighty in their power to do evil, polluted the wretched city by sacrilegious rites. The decemviri, following the custom born of an ancient superstition, buried alive a Gallic man and woman and with them also a Greek woman at the Cattle Market in Rome. But this resort to magic, which was obligatory, produced an opposite effect from that desired. For a horrible massacre of their own men expiated the dreadful deaths of these strangers.

In the consulship of L. Aemilius Catulus and C. Atilius Regulus [48] the Senate became panic stricken by a rebellion of Cisalpine Gaul. At the same time they also heard of the approach of a huge army from Further Gaul. This army was composed largely of the Gaesati, which was the name not of a tribe but of Gallic mercenaries. The consuls, terror stricken, assembled the military forces of all Italy for the defense of the state. When the troops had assembled, there were, according to the historian Fabius who took part in that war, eight hundred thousand soldiers in the army of each consul. Of that number the Roman and Campanian infantry numbered 299,200 and the cavalry 26,600. There was also a vast number of allies. When battle was joined near Arretium,[49] the consul Atilius was killed. After a part of the Roman army had been slain, the rest of the eight hundred thousand took flight. But their losses were by no means sufficient to cause them any apprehension, for the historians relate that only three thousand of them were killed on that occasion.

That so many columns fled when so few were lost is all the more ignominious and shameful, because it betrayed the fact

---

[47] Cn. Fulvius Centumalus and L. Postumius Albinus II, 229 B.C.
[48] L. Aemilius Papus (not Catulus) and C. Atilius Regulus, 225 B.C.
[49] One of the chief cities of Etruria.

that they had prevailed in other victories not by the strength of their spirit but by the fortunate issue of battle. Who, I ask, in the Roman army would believe that this was really the number? And I do not mean the number of those who fled. Later a second battle was fought with the Gauls in which at least forty thousand of their number were slaughtered.[50]

The following year Manlius Torquatus and Fulvius Flaccus [51] were the first consuls to lead Roman legions across the Po. There the Romans engaged the Insubrian Gauls in battle. They killed twenty-three thousand and captured five thousand of them.

During the next year dreadful portents terrified the unhappy City. Wretched indeed was this City which was greatly alarmed by the clamor raised by the enemy on one side and by the wickedness of the demons on the other! For in Picenum [52] a river flowed blood, and in the land of the Tuscans the sky seemed to be aflame. At Ariminum,[53] late at night, a bright light shone and three moons that had arisen in the distant parts of the heaven were visible. In addition so severe earthquakes shook the islands of Caria and Rhodes that even the huge Colossus fell, while buildings collapsed everywhere. The same year the consul Flaminius,[54] disregarding the auspices which forbade fighting, fought the Gauls and defeated them. In that battle nine thousand Gauls were slain and seventeen thousand captured.[55]

Later the consul Claudius [56] destroyed thirty thousand of the Gaesati. He advanced into the first line of battle and killed with his own hand their king Virdomarus.[57] In addition to the many towns of the Insubres that he forced to surrender, Claudius also captured Milan, a very flourishing city.

[50] The battle was fought at Telamon, a city on the coast of Etruria, 225 B.C.
[51] T. Manlius Torquatus II and Q. Fulvius Flaccus II, 224 B.C.
[52] A region of central Italy.
[53] A celebrated city of Umbria, situated on the coast of the Adriatic.
[54] C. Flaminius, 223 B.C.
[55] Somewhere in the neighborhood of the modern Bergamo, about thirty-five miles northeast of Milan.   [56] M. Claudius Marcellus, 222 B.C.
[57] The Roman consul advanced to the relief of Clastidium, south of the Po, 222 B.C. During the clash of cavalry forces, the leaders of the opposing armies fought a duel.

Then new enemies, the Histri, became aroused. The consuls Cornelius and Minucius [58] subdued them only after shedding much Roman blood. Now happened an unimportant incident that illustrates the old passion of the Romans for fame, so debased as to lead to parricide. For Fabius Censorius killed his own son Fabius Buteo because he had been charged with theft: this crime the laws usually punished only by a fine or at the most by exile, whoever the guilty man might be, but the father thought it fitting and necessary to punish him by death.

14. IN THE five hundred and thirty-fourth year after the founding of the City, Hannibal, the Carthaginian commander, first attacked Saguntum, a flourishing city of Spain and a friend of the Roman people.[59] He then laid siege to the city, which endured the tortures of hunger and bore heroically all sufferings, whether deserved or undeserved, in view of the promise its inhabitants had made to the Romans. In the eighth month he finally destroyed it. Acting in a way absolutely contrary to law he also refused an audience to the accredited ambassadors of Rome. As a result of his hatred of the Roman people which he had most solemnly sworn before the altar in the presence of his father Hamilcar when he was nine years old—though in other matters he was the most faithless of men—he crossed the Pyrenees in the consulship of P. Cornelius Scipio and P. Sempronius Longus,[60] and by the sword opened a path through the fierce Gallic tribes. After a nine-day journey from the Pyrenees, he came to the Alps. There he defeated the Gallic hillsmen who strove to prevent his ascent and by employing fire and sword he cut a pass through the rocks that blocked his way. He was delayed for four days, but finally by a supreme effort he reached

---

[58] P. Cornelius Scipio Asina and M. Minucius Rufus, 221 B.C.

[59] Rome had previously entered into a defensive alliance with Saguntum. The reason given by Hannibal for the attack was that Saguntum had made an unwarranted war upon some of his Spanish allies. In Roman international relations *amicus* is a term embracing both general and varying specific obligations. The term is to be differentiated from *socius*.

[60] P. Cornelius Scipio and Ti. Sempronius Longus, 218 B.C. This Scipio is a cousin of the consul of 221 B.C., P. Cornelius Scipio Asina.

the plains on the fifth day. At that time they say that Hannibal's army did not exceed one hundred thousand infantry and twenty thousand cavalry.

The consul Scipio was the first to meet Hannibal. They joined battle at the Ticinus.[61] Scipio himself was severely wounded but he escaped impending death by the help of his son,[62] who was still wearing the *toga praetexta* and who later bore the cognomen of Africanus. In that battle almost the whole Roman army was cut to pieces. Another battle was fought by the same consul at the river Trebia.[63] Again the Romans were defeated and suffered as great losses as before. When the consul Sempronius learned of the fate of his colleague, he returned from Sicily with his army. In like manner he engaged in battle at the same river, lost his army, and was himself almost the sole survivor. Hannibal was also wounded in this battle. Later in the spring, when Hannibal's army was crossing over into Etruria and was high in the Apennines, it was overtaken by a storm, shut in fast, and so weighted down by the snow that it could not move.[64] For two continuous days both he and his army remained numb from the cold. A great number of men, many beasts of burden, and almost all the elephants died there from exposure to the wintry blasts. But the other Scipio,[65] the brother of the consul Scipio, waged many battles in Spain at this time and succeeded in defeating and capturing Mago, the leader of the Carthaginians.

15. At this time the Romans were also terrified by dreadful prodigies. To give some examples: the sun's disk seemed to be contracted and at Arpi *parmae* were seen in the sky;[66] the sun also seemed to be fighting with the moon; at Capena two moons arose in the daytime;[67] in Sardinia two shields sweated

[61] A tributary of the Po. The battle was fought in 218 B.C.
[62] P. Cornelius Scipio Africanus Major.
[63] A river joining the Po about two miles west of Placentia.
[64] Livy *Histories* xxi. 38 gives a vivid picture.
[65] Cn. Cornelius Scipio Calvus. Hanno, and not Mago, the latter escaping.
[66] Arpi is situated in Apulia. *Parmae* are small, round shields.
[67] Capena, a city of Etruria, is situated eight miles from the foot of Mt. Soracte.

blood; in the territory of the Faliscans the sky seemed to be rent in twain,[68] as it were, by a great fissure; at Antium,[69] when men were harvesting, bloody ears of corn fell into their baskets.

Hannibal, knowing that the consul Flaminius [70] was alone in his camp, moved forward in the spring and took the more direct road, even though it was marshy. By this maneuver he planned to surprise and overthrow him when he was off his guard. The Sarnus [71] happened at that time to have overflowed its banks far and wide and had left its bordering fields in ruin. Concerning this a poet has said:

> and the plains which Sarnus waters.

Hannibal, advancing with his army into this country, lost a large part of his allies and beasts of burden, particularly when the mists, which rose from the swamps, cut off his view. Hannibal himself, seated aloft on the sole surviving elephant, barely managed to avoid the hardships of the march; but as a result of the severe cold, lack of sleep, and the strain of the work, he lost the sight of one of his eyes which had long been diseased.

When Hannibal was in the vicinity of the camp of the consul Flaminius, he laid waste the surrounding country in order to provoke him to fight. A battle took place at Lake Trasimene.[72] There the Roman army had the misfortune to be tricked by a stratagem of Hannibal and was completely cut to pieces. The consul himself perished. In that battle it is reported that twenty-five thousand Romans were slain and six thousand captured. Of Hannibal's army, only two thousand fell. This battle at Lake Trasimene was especially notable, not only because of the great disaster suffered by the Romans, but also because the combatants in the tension and heat of the battle were completely unaware of a terrible

[68] In Etruria.

[69] Antium is a powerful city of Latium on the coast thirty-eight miles from Rome. [70] C. Flaminius II, 217 B.C. [71] Sarno River.

[72] One of the largest lakes of Etruria, ten miles long and eight wide, situated between Cortona and Perusia.

earthquake. This assumed so violent proportions that, according to reports, it destroyed cities, moved mountains, tore rocks asunder, and forced rivers back in their courses. The battle of Cannae [73] followed the disaster of Trasimene. During the intervening period, however, Fabius Maximus, the dictator, slowed down the attack of Hannibal by his policy of delaying action.

16.   IN THE five hundred and fortieth year of the City, the consuls L. Aemilius Paulus and P. Terentius Varro [74] were sent against Hannibal. They had the ill fortune to lose at Cannae, a village of Apulia, almost the entire resources upon which Rome had based her hope. In that battle forty-four thousand Romans were killed, although a great part of Hannibal's army also lost their lives. In no other battle of the Punic War were the Romans so close to annihilation, for in that battle the consul Aemilius Paulus perished, twenty men of consular and praetorian rank were killed, and thirty senators were either captured or killed; three hundred nobles, forty thousand infantry, and thirty-five hundred cavalry also lost their lives. The consul Varro fled to Venusia [75] with five hundred cavalry. Without doubt that would have been the last day of the Roman state had Hannibal after his victory hastened to reach Rome at once. He sent to Carthage, as proof of his victory, three pecks of gold rings that he had pulled from the hands of the slain Roman knights and senators.

So desperate was the plight of the remaining Romans that the senators thought it necessary to consider a plan of abandoning Italy and seeking new homes. This plan would have been confirmed on the motion of Caecilius Metellus, had not Cornelius Scipio, then military tribune and the same man who was later called Africanus, prevented him with drawn sword and forced him instead to swear to maintain the defense of

[73] A small town of Apulia. The date of the battle is 216 B.C.
[74] L. Aemilius Paulus II and C. Terentius Varro, 216 B.C.
[75] A city of Apulia situated about ten miles from Cannae.

his country. The Romans, daring to breathe again, and emerging, as it were, from death to the hope of life, chose Decimus Junius dictator. He made a levy of those above seventeen years of age and gathered fifteen legions of immature and untrained soldiery. With a promise of freedom he then induced slaves of proven strength and purpose to take the military oath. Some of these slaves volunteered, but others, when urgently needed, were bought with public money. The arms that were lacking were taken from the temples, and private wealth poured into the impoverished public treasury. The equestrian order as well as the frightened plebeians forgot their own interests and planned for the common welfare. The dictator Junius, resuming an ancient practice of the days of Rome's misery, in order to reinforce the army, decreed that all men subject to punishment for crime or debt should be promised immunity and turned over to the military service—opening for them, as it were, a haven of refuge. Their number amounted to six thousand. Campania, or rather all Italy, in utter despair of restoring Rome to her former position, finally went over to Hannibal's side. After this, the praetor L. Postumius, who was sent to wage war against the Gauls, was destroyed with his army.

In the consulship of Sempronius Gracchus and Q. Fabius Maximus,[76] Claudius Marcellus, the ex-praetor who had been chosen proconsul, routed the army of Hannibal in a battle.[77] He was the first man, after the great disasters to the Republic, to offer hope that Hannibal could be defeated. In Spain, moreover, the Scipios [78] crushed the Carthaginian general Hasdrubal in a hard-fought battle as he was preparing

---

[76] Ti. Sempronius Gracchus and Q. Fabius Maximus Verrocosus III, 215 B.C. L. Postumius Albinus III was first consul chosen, but he was killed in Cisalpine Gaul. M. Claudius Marcellus II was elected but was not allowed to take office, for there would have been two plebeian consuls. He resigned and was appointed proconsul with command of the army in Campania.

[77] An engagement near Nola.

[78] That is, P. Cornelius Scipio and Cn. Cornelius Scipio Calvus. The text is not clear which battle was intended. There were a series of battles, beginning with Nova Carthago in 209 B.C. and continuing until Hasdrubal, after his defeat near Baecula, left for Italy.

his army for an invasion of Italy, causing him to lose thirty-five thousand by death or capture. The Romans now bribed some Celtiberian soldiers to leave the enemy and to join them. This was the first occasion when Romans allowed foreign troops to be in their camp. Sempronius Gracchus was led into ambush by a Lucanian,[79] his host, and slain. Of his own accord the centurion Centenius Paenula asked for the command of the war against Hannibal; but he, together with the eight thousand troops that he had led to the line of battle, was slain by the Carthaginian leader. Following him, the praetor Cn. Fulvius was defeated by Hannibal and, after losing his army, barely escaped with his life.

I am ashamed to recall these things. Of what am I to speak first, the depravity of the Romans or their wretchedness? Nay more truly of their depraved wretchedness or of their wretched depravity? Who would believe that in those days, when the public treasury of the Romans was soliciting trifling contributions from private citizens there was not a single soldier in camp who was not either a boy, a slave, a criminal, or a debtor, that even then the number was insufficient, that the Senate in the Curia seemed composed almost wholly of new members, and finally that, in the face of all their losses and defeats, despair so overwhelmed them that a plan of abandoning Italy was submitted? And who would believe that at this time when, as we have said, they could not wage even one war at home, they undertook three more wars across the seas: one in Macedonia against Philip, the very powerful king of Macedonia; another in Spain against Hasdrubal, the brother of Hannibal; a third in Sardinia against the Sardinians and the other Hasdrubal, the Carthaginian general. Besides these wars, they undertook a fourth against Hannibal, who was pressing them hard in Italy. And yet a display of courage, bred of desperation, led to better fortune in every case; for in all these wars it was desperation that made them fight, and fighting that made them victorious. From this it is

[79] Flavius, the head of the Roman party among the Lucanians, betrayed Gracchus into the hands of the Carthaginian commander Mago.

clearly evident that the times then were not more peaceful
for the pursuits of leisure than they are at present, but that
the men were braver as a result of their miseries.

17. IN THE five hundred and forty-third year of the City,
Claudius Marcellus took Syracuse, the richest city in Sicily.
He barely succeeded in this and then only after a second
assault. His earlier attempt to besiege this city had failed,
for he had been driven back by a machine of remarkable ingenuity made by Archimedes of Syracuse. In the tenth year
after his arrival in Italy and during the consulship of Cn.
Fulvius and P. Sulpicius,[80] Hannibal moved his army from
Campania, and as he proceeded through the territory of the
Sidicini and Suessani by way of the Via Latina to the Anio
River, he slaughtered great numbers of the people. He encamped three miles from the City and terrified all the inhabitants beyond belief. The Senate and the people became panic
stricken and were unable to perform their several duties. The
women, frantic with anxiety, ran along the fortifications,
brought stones to the walls, and excelled all others in eagerness to fight in defense of the walls. Hannibal himself with
his light-armed cavalry then advanced in hostile array to the
Colline Gate [81] and drew up his entire forces in battle line.
The consuls and the proconsul Fulvius did accept the challenge
to battle. But just as both battle lines stood ready within plain
sight of Rome, which was destined to be the prize of the
victor, a hailstorm suddenly burst forth from the clouds with
so terrific force that the disorganized lines barely managed to
save their arms and reach their camps in safety. Fair weather
returned and the troops again took their positions in battle
line. A still more violent storm then arose. This inspired an
even greater fear and curbed the presumption of mortal men,
forcing the terror stricken armies to flee back to their tents.
At that time Hannibal was overcome by religious awe. He is
reported to have said that on the one occasion he did not

80 Cn. Fulvius Centumalus and P. Sulpicius Galba Maximus, 211 B.C.
81 A gate in Rome near the Quirinal Hill.

desire to take Rome, but that on the other he did not have
the power.

Let the defamers of the true God answer me at this point.
Did Roman bravery or did Divine compassion prevent Hannibal from seizing and overthrowing Rome? Or perhaps those
left unharmed are loath to confess that Hannibal became terrified in the hour of victory and proved it by retreating. If it
is clear that this Divine protection came from Heaven in the
form of rain but that it only rained at the opportune and
necessary moment through the intervention of Christ, Who is
the true God, I think then that this fact is sufficiently well
established and cannot be denied. This truth is now completely proved by a further demonstration of His power.
During a period of distressing drought, continuous interces-
sions of rain were made. In turn the Gentiles and the Christians prayed, but the desired rain fell, as they themselves
testified, only on the day when it was agreed that Christ should
be the object of their prayers and that Christians should pray.
It is therefore beyond dispute that it was the intercession of
this same true God, Who is Jesus Christ, Who governs according to the dictates of His ineffable judgment, that in those days
saved the city of Rome, so that it might accept the faith in
the future and yet now be partially punished for her unbelief.

In Spain, however, both Scipios [82] were killed by Hasdrubal's brother.[83] In Campania, Q. Fulvius, the proconsul,
captured Capua. The leaders of the Campanians committed
suicide by taking poison and Fulvius put to death the entire
Senate of Capua despite the order of the Roman Senate to
spare them. After the death of the Scipios in Spain, action
was delayed because everyone was terror stricken. At this
juncture, Scipio,[84] though still a young man, volunteered his

---

[82] P. Cornelius Scipio who was consul with T. Sempronius Longus in 218 B.C.
and Cn. Cornelius Scipio Calvus who was consul with M. Claudius Marcellus
in 222 B.C.

[83] P. Scipio was defeated by Mago and Hasdrubal, son of Gisco; Cn. Scipio
was later crushed by combined forces of these Carthaginian generals and
Hasdrubal, son of Barca.

[84] P. Cornelius Scipio Africanus Major, on death of his father and uncle,
was sent as propraetor, and next year as proconsul, to command the army in
Spain.

services. In the meantime the scarcity of money in the public treasury had become a source of shame. On the proposals of Claudius Marcellus and Valerius Laevinus [85] who were consuls at that time, all the senators openly brought gold and silver coins to the quaestors at the treasury. Nothing except individual rings and bullae [86] remained for themselves and for their sons, and for their daughters and wives they left only a single ounce of gold and not more than a single pound of silver.

18. SCIPIO, when twenty-four years old, was chosen with the rank of proconsul for the command in Spain. He crossed the Pyrenees with his mind bent upon avenging his father and uncle especially. On the first assault he captured New Carthage,[87] where the Carthaginians had vast tributes from tax payments, strong defenses, and great stores of gold and silver. There Scipio also captured Mago, the brother of Hannibal, and sent him with others to Rome. The consul Laevinus, returning from Macedonia, took the Sicilian city of Agrigentum by storm and there made a prisoner of Hanno, the African commander. He also accepted the surrender of forty cities and took twenty-six by storm. In Italy, Hannibal killed the proconsul Cnaeus Fulvius, and also eleven tribunes and seventeen thousand soldiers. The consul Marcellus fought with Hannibal continuously for three days.[88] On the first day the battle was drawn and on the following the consul was defeated; but on the third he was victorious and killed eight thousand of the enemy, forcing Hannibal himself and other survivors to flee to their own camp. The consul Fabius Maximus [89] stormed Tarentum a second time and captured the city, which had withdrawn from its alliance with Rome. On that occasion he destroyed huge numbers of Hannibal's army and also killed their general Carthalo. He sold thirty thousand

---

[85] M. Valerius Laevinus and M. Claudius Marcellus IV, 210 B.C.
[86] A kind of amulet worn up the neck.
[87] The celebrated city of Hispania Tarraconensis; it had an excellent harbor. This Mago is the commander of the garrison, not the brother of Hannibal.
[88] The engagement was fought at Herdonea in Apulia in 210 B.C.
[89] Q. Fabius Maximus Verrucosus V, 209 B.C.

of the captives and remitted the proceeds of the sale to the state treasury.

In Italy, the following year, the consul Claudius Marcellus [90] was slain and his army destroyed by Hannibal.[91] In Spain, however, Scipio defeated the Carthaginian leader Hasdrubal and sacked his camp.[92] In addition Scipio reduced to subjection eighty cities. Some of these cities surrendered while others were taken in battle. He sold the Carthaginians into slavery, but let the Spaniards go without ransom. Meanwhile Hannibal lured both consuls, Marcellus and Crispinus, into ambush and killed them.

In the consulship of Claudius Nero and M. Livius Salinator,[93] Hasdrubal, Hannibal's brother, made his way from Spain through the Gallic provinces to Italy. He had been ordered by the Carthaginians to join his forces to his brother's and was bringing with him great bodies of Spanish and Gallic auxiliaries. But when it was reported to the consuls that he had already descended from the Alps by a forced march, the Roman army, anticipating his plans, killed him and destroyed his whole army.[94] Hannibal knew nothing of this disaster. The issue of the battle was long in doubt because the elephants proved very troublesome to the Roman battle line. In the Roman army there were soldiers called *velites,* so termed from their practice of flying to and fro. This mode of warfare had been developed a short time before. Young men, chosen for their agility, would take weapons and mount horses, seating themselves behind the cavalrymen; as soon as they came in contact with the enemy, after leaping from the horses, they would immediately become real infantrymen and fall upon the enemy; the cavalry, who had brought them, would fight in another part of the battle field. These *velites,* then, drove back the elephants when these beasts got out of the

---

[90] M. Claudius Marcellus in his fifth consulship, 208 B.C.
[91] In a skirmish near Venusia in Apulia, 208 B.C.
[92] At Ilipa, near Seville, 207 B.C.
[93] C. Claudius Nero and M. Livius Salinator II, 207 B.C.
[94] Battle of the Metaurus, 207 B.C. The Metaurus, a river of Umbria, flows into the Adriatic Sea.

control of their own masters, and finally killed them by driving artificer's knives through their ears. This method of killing elephants, when need arose, was first discovered by this same general Hasdrubal.

The Metaurus River, where Hasdrubal was overwhelmed, proved as disastrous to the Carthaginians as Lake Trasimene, the city of Cesena in Picenum, and that famous village of Cannae had been to the Romans. Fifty-eight thousand of Hasdrubal's army were slaughtered there and five thousand four hundred were captured. Among the latter were found four thousand Roman citizens who were repatriated. This was a source of consolation to the victorious consuls, for they themselves had lost eight hundred of their own army. Hasdrubal's head was thrown out in the sight of Hannibal's camp. When Hannibal saw his brother's head, he at once knew that the Carthaginians had met disaster and he himself took refuge among the Bruttians. These events took place thirteen years after his arrival in Italy. Following this period of violence and of war, peace between Hannibal and the Romans seems to have prevailed for a whole year, because there was fever and disease in the camps and a very severe pestilence was taking its toll from both armies.

In the meantime, Scipio had reduced all Spain from the Pyrenees to the Ocean to the status of a province. He now returned to Rome and was elected consul along with Licinius Crassus.[95] He then crossed to Africa, killed the Punic general Hanno, the son of Hamilcar, and scattered his army, slaughtering part and capturing the remainder. Eleven thousand Carthaginians fell in that battle.[96] Meanwhile the consul Sempronius [97] met Hannibal, was defeated, and fled back to Rome. In Africa, Scipio attacked the winter quarters of the Carthaginians and also those of the Numidians, both of which were not far from Utica. In the early hours of the night he set these quarters on fire. The Carthaginians, in their alarm, imagined that

---

[95] P. Licinius Crassus Dives, 205 B.C.
[96] A cavalry skirmish near Utica, 204 B.C.
[97] P. Sempronius Tuditanus, 204 B.C.

the fire had started by accident and ran out to extinguish it.
Therefore the Romans, who were armed, easily conquered
them. In the two camps forty thousand men met death either
by fire or by sword and five thousand were captured. The
leaders themselves, in a pitiful condition from their burns,
barely escaped. Hasdrubal, the commander, came to Carthage
as a fugitive. Then Syphax and Hasdrubal recruited a great
army and at once engaged in a second battle with Scipio.
They were defeated and fled.[98] Laelius and Masinissa captured Syphax as he was fleeing. The rest of the great army
took refuge in Cirta,[99] which, after being stormed, surrendered
to Masinissa, who led Syphax, bound in chains, to Scipio. The
latter handed him over for safe conduct to Laelius, together
with huge spoils and many captives.

19.   HANNIBAL was ordered to return to Africa to give assistance to the worn-out Carthaginians. After killing all soldiers of Italian stock who were unwilling to accompany him,
he abandoned Italy, shedding tears as he departed. As the
African coast drew near, one of the sailors was ordered to
climb a mast and from that vantage point to observe what
land they were approaching. He answered that he saw in the
distance a ruined sepulchre. Hannibal regarded this report
as an ill omen, changed his course, and disembarked his forces
at the town of Leptis.

While his army was resting, Hannibal proceeded at once
to Carthage and there sought a conference with Scipio. On
meeting, the two famous generals regarded each other for
a long time in wonder and mutual admiration. After they had
failed to negotiate peace, they engaged once more in battle.
This battle,[100] arranged in advance carefully and with great
skill by the commanders, was waged by large masses of troops,
and ended with a great display of spirit on the part of the
soldiers. The Romans were victorious. Eighty elephants were

98 The battle was fought on the great plains of the Bagradas River, 203 B.C.
99 A city of Numidia about 48 miles from the sea.
100 The battle of Zama, 202 B.C.

captured or killed and twenty thousand five hundred Carthaginians lost their lives. After vainly trying every possible expedient both before and during the conflict, Hannibal with a few men, that is, with only four horsemen, slipped away amid the din of battle and took refuge in Hadrumentum. Later he returned to Carthage, which he had left as a small boy with his father thirty-six years earlier. He persuaded the Senate, which was then in session, that their only hope was to make peace.

In the consulship of C. Cornelius Lentulus and P. Aelius Paetus,[101] through the good offices of Scipio, the Romans granted peace to the Carthaginians by the vote of the Senate and of the people. They convoyed more than fifty ships out to sea and burned them in sight of the City. Scipio, who now bore the cognomen of Africanus, entered the City in a triumph. Terentius,[102] one of the noble Carthaginian captives and later a comic poet, wore the *pilleus*—which was a symbol of the liberty granted him—and followed the chariot of the conqueror.

20. IN THE five hundred and forty-sixth year after the founding of the City, the Second Punic War, which had been waged for seventeen years, came to an end. The Macedonian War followed immediately. Quintius Flamininus [103] was chosen consul. After he had defeated the Macedonians in many severe battles, he granted peace to Philip. He then fought against the Lacedaemonians. After defeating their leader Nabis,[104] he led before his chariot Demetrius, the son of Philip, and Armenes, the son of Nabis, who were the noblest of the hostages. The Roman captives, who had been sold throughout Greece by Hannibal, were all restored to freedom and followed the chariot of the conqueror with their heads shaven as a sign of their new liberty. At the same time the Insubres,

---

101 Cn. Cornelius Lentulus and P. Aelius Paetus, 201 B.C.

102 Terentius Afer, a poet born in 195 B.C. at Carthage, who later won a reputation in Rome as a writer of comedies.

103 T. Quintius Flamininus, 198 B.C.

104 "Nabis," not "Navid," as the text reads.

the Boii, and the Cenomani united their forces under the leadership of the Punic Hamilcar, who had remained in Italy. After laying waste Cremona and Placentia,[105] they were overcome by the praetor L. Furius[106] in a very hard-fought battle.[107] Later the proconsul Flamininus vanquished King Philip in battle[108] and also the Thracians, Macedonians, and Illyrians, besides many other tribes that had come to their assistance. The Macedonians were defeated and lost their camp. According to Polybius, eight thousand Macedonian soldiers were slain on that day and five thousand were captured. Valerius says that forty thousand were slaughtered; but Claudius tells us that the number was thirty-two thousand.

This inconsistency of the historians is certainly an evidence of falsehood. But flattery is surely the cause of their misrepresentation, since they eagerly heap praises upon the victor and extol the virtue of their own country for the edification of present and future generations. Otherwise, if the number had not been investigated, it never would have been spoken of at all. But if it is glorious for a commander and a country to have destroyed so many of the enemy, how much more joyful is it for a country and how much happier for a commander if they have lost none or very few of their men. The intent to deceive becomes absolutely plain, because with like shamelessness they lied by exaggerating the number of the enemy dead while they either minimized the losses suffered among their own allies or kept them entirely secret.

Shortly after this battle, Sempronius Tuditanus was crushed in a battle in Hither Spain. He was killed and the entire Roman army was destroyed. The consul Marcellus[109] was defeated by the Boii in Etruria and lost a great part of his army. The other consul Furius, however, later brought assistance to

[105] These cities were situated on the left and right banks of the Po River in Cisalpine Gaul.

[106] "Furius," not "Fulvius." L. Furius Purpurio.

[107] Under the walls of Cremona, 200 B.C.

[108] Battle of Cynoscephalae, 197 B.C. The name is so called from the resemblance of the two ranges of hills to the heads of dogs. There is some doubt as to the exact location of the field of battle.

[109] M. Claudius Marcellus, son of the great Marcellus, and Furius Purpurio, 196. B.C.

him and together they ravaged the entire Boii nation with fire and sword, almost annihilating this people.

In the consulship of L. Valerius Flaccus and M. Porcius Cato,[110] Antiochus, the king of Syria, prepared for war against the Roman people and crossed from Asia into Europe. At that time also, the Senate ordered Hannibal to be brought to Rome, because rumors were circulating among the Romans that he was stirring up war. Hannibal secretly set out from Africa and went to Antiochus. He met the latter tarrying at Ephesus and urged him to begin war immediately. At that time, too, the law, that no woman should have more than a half ounce of gold, or should wear a colored garment or use a carriage anywhere in the City, which had been proposed by Oppius, a tribune of the plebs, was repealed after being in force for twenty years.

In the second consulship of P. Scipio Africanus and T. Sempronius Longus,[111] the Romans slew ten thousand Gauls at Milan. In a later battle eleven thousand Gauls were slain, but only five thousand Romans lost their lives. The praetor Publius Digitius lost almost his entire army in Hither Spain. The praetor M. Fulvius defeated the Celtiberi together with neighboring peoples and captured their king. Minucius was drawn into a situation of extreme peril by the Ligurians. He was surrounded by enemy ambuscades and barely managed to escape as a result of the activity of the Numidian cavalry. Scipio Africanus with other ambassadors was sent to Antiochus and had a private talk with Hannibal. Peace negotiations failed, however, and Scipio parted from Antiochus. In both Spains, the praetors Flaminius and Fulvius waged wars that brought terror and destruction to each people.

During the consulship of P. Cornelius Scipio and M. Acilius Glabrio,[112] Antiochus seized the passes of Thermopylae, the fortification of which, in view of the uncertain issue of battle, gave him a greater measure of safety. Nevertheless, when

---

[110] M. Porcius Cato and L. Valerius Flaccus, 195 B.C.
[111] P. Cornelius Scipio Africanus II and Ti. Sempronius Longus, 194 B.C.
[112] P. Cornelius Scipio Nasica and M. Acilius Glabrio, 191 B.C.

battle began,[113] he was overcome by the consul Glabrio and was barely able to escape with a few men from the battlefield and to reach Ephesus. Antiochus is said to have had sixty thousand troops; of these forty thousand were slain and more than five thousand, according to the report, were captured. Scipio, the other consul, engaged in war with the Boii nation and slew twenty thousand of the enemy in battle.

The following year Scipio Africanus and his ally Eumenes, the son of Attalus, engaged in a naval battle against Hannibal, who was then in command of the fleet of Antiochus. Hannibal was defeated, put to flight, and lost his entire army. Antiochus therefore sued for peace. Of his own free will he sent back the son of Africanus, whom he had taken prisoner. It is uncertain whether this son of Africanus was captured while he was scouting or while he was fighting in battle. In Further Spain the proconsul L. Aemilius perished after his whole army had been slaughtered by the Lusitani. L. Baebius, who had set out for Spain, was surrounded by the Ligurians; he and his entire army were destroyed. Since it was certain that not even a messenger had survived this battle, the Massilians took it upon themselves to inform Rome of the disaster.

The consul Fulvius [114] traveled from Greece to Gallo-Greece, which is now Galatia, and came to Mount Olympus,[115] on which all the Gallo-Greeks with their wives and children had taken refuge. There they fought a very bitter battle. The Romans suffered serious losses from arrows, leaden balls, rocks, and other missiles sent from the higher ground. Finally, however, they forced their way through to meet the enemy. It is reported that forty thousand Gallo-Greeks lost their lives in that battle. The consul Marcius [116] set out against the Ligurians, was defeated, and lost four thousand troops; had he not quickly fled back to his camp after his defeat, he would have met the same fate as that which overtook Baebius

---

[113] The battle of Magnesia, 190 B.C.
[114] M. Fulvius Nobilior, 189 B.C.
[115] A mountain situated in northern Galatia; it is a part of the Mysian Olympus chain.
[116] Q. Marcius Philippus, 186 B.C.

a short time before when he was slaughtered by these same enemies.

In the consulship of M. Claudius Marcellus and Q. Fabius Labeo,[117] King Philip, who had put to death the ambassadors of the Roman people, was pardoned after his son Demetrius, whom he had sent as his envoy, had pleaded most humbly in his behalf. Despite this service, Philip almost at once poisoned and killed him on the pretext that he had acted as a friend of the Romans and had been a traitor to his own father. Another son aided the father in the murder of his brother who, poor wretch, suspected nothing evil from either of them.

In the same year Scipio Africanus, long an exile from his ungrateful city, died of disease in the town of Liternum.[118] At this time also Hannibal committed suicide at the court of Prusias,[119] the king of Bithynia; he took poison when the Romans demanded his surrender. Philopoemen,[120] the king of the Achaeans, was captured and executed by the Messenians. Near Sicily, the island of Vulcan, which had not been visible before, suddenly, to everyone's astonishment, emerged from the sea and it remains there even to this day. In a great battle in Hither Spain the praetor Q. Fulvius routed twenty-three thousand men and took captive four thousand, while in Further Spain Tiberius Sempronius Gracchus forced into surrender one hundred and five towns that had been weakened and shattered by war. During the same summer, L. Postumius killed forty thousand of the enemy in battle in Hither Spain, and in the same region the praetor Gracchus in a second campaign stormed and captured two hundred towns.

In the consulship of Lepidus and Mucius,[121] a very savage

---

[117] M. Claudius Marcellus and Q. Fabius Labeo, 183 B.C.

[118] A town situated on the seacoast of Campania.

[119] Though formerly an ally of Rome, his hostility to Eumenes of Pergamum made him lukewarm to Rome, but though a host he did not dare refuse the urgent request for the surrender of Hannibal.

[120] He was the famous leader of the Achaean League and called "the last of the Greeks." In battle he was stunned by a fall from his horse, taken prisoner, and executed by being required to drink a cup of poison.

[121] M. Aemilius Lepidus II and P. Mucius Scaevula, 175 B.C.

people, the Basternae, met destruction in this way. They followed the advice of Perseus, son of Philip, and were also attracted by the prospect of booty and the possibility of crossing the Ister River without encountering the enemy. For at that time the Danube, which is also called the Ister, happened to be covered with solid ice and hence could easily be crossed on foot. A vast number of men improvidently crossed with their horses, advancing all together in one great column. Under the enormous weight and the impact of those moving over it, the icy, frozen surface gave way and cracked. The ice, which had so long supported the entire column, finally crumbled in midstream and broke up into small pieces. These pieces of ice, passing over them and preventing them from reaching the surface, caused them to drown. Thus, out of the entire number only a few, badly cut up, managed to reach the shore.

In the consulship of P. Licinius Crassus and C. Cassius Longinus,[122] the Macedonian War was waged. This war must rightly be classed among the really important ones. Those who aided the Romans were as follows: first, all of Italy; then, Ptolemy the king of Egypt; and finally, Ariarathes of Cappadocia, Eumenes of Asia, and Masinissa of Numidia. Perseus and the Macedonians had as allies the Thracians and their king Cotys, and the Illyrians united under their king Gentius.

When the consul Crassus was approaching, Perseus advanced to meet him and engaged him in battle. The Romans suffered a miserable defeat and fled. In a later battle both sides met with almost equal losses and they then retired to winter quarters. Having conquered the Roman army in many battles, Perseus went over into Illyricum, where he attacked and captured Uscana, a town defended by a Roman garrison. Some members of the large Roman garrison he killed, others he sold into slavery, and the rest he took with him to Macedonia.

Later the consul L. Aemilius Paulus fought and conquered

---

[122] P. Licinius Crassus and C. Cassius Longinus, 171 B.C.

Perseus in a battle in which the consul's forces killed twenty thousand of the enemy's infantry.[123] The king, who escaped with his cavalry, was soon captured and with his sons was led in triumph before the chariot. Subsequently he died in a prison at Alba. The younger son of Perseus, on account of his dire want, learned the art of working brass in Rome and later died there. For the sake of brevity I have omitted the most of the wars which many peoples in different places fought with varying results.

21.   IN THE six hundredth year of the City, in the consulship of L. Licinius Lucullus and A. Postumius Albinus,[124] the Celtiberi greatly terrified all the Romans. Not one Roman, either tribune or legate, dared to go into Spain. P. Scipio,[125] who later was to be called Africanus, volunteered his services for the Spanish campaign, although he had already been chosen by lot for the Macedonian command. He then set out for Spain and overthrew many tribes. Taking the part of a soldier more often than that of a general, he met and killed in single combat a barbarian who had challenged him. The praetor Sergius, however, was defeated by the Lusitani in a great battle, and after the loss of his entire army he himself barely managed to slip away and escape. This same year the censors decided to build a stone theater in the city. Scipio Nasica made an impressive speech opposing its construction at that time; he maintained that this measure would foster wantonness and laziness and would be most harmful to a warlike people. He therefore moved that the Senate should not only order the sale of everything prepared for the theater but should even prohibit the tiers of seats for the games from being put into place.

Today our people consider whatever runs counter to the satisfaction of their lusts to be a misfortune. As a result they feel weaker, and even admit that they are weaker, than their

---

[123] L. Aemilius Paulus. The battle of Pydna, 168 B.C.

[124] Licinius Lucullus and A. Postumius Albinus, 151 B.C.

[125] The son of Paulus and, by adoption, grandson of the elder Africanus. He is known as P. Cornelius Scipio Aemilianus Africanus Minor. The Scipio Nasica is Scipio Nasica Corculum.

enemies. Let them understand, then, that they should blame the theaters and not the times. Neither should they blaspheme the true God Who has ever forbidden these unlawful pleasures. Rather let them detest their own gods or demons who have required these pleasures. Indeed these gods have given sufficiently clear evidence of their malignity by demanding this kind of a sacrifice, since they fed on the corrupt nature of men no less than on the spilt blood of cattle. Surely in former days there was no lack of enemies, famines, diseases, and prodigies; on the contrary there were a great number. But there were no theaters in which—however difficult it may be to believe—virtues were slaughtered like victims on the altar of voluptuousness. It is true that at one time the Carthaginians thought it right to sacrifice human beings, but they soon discarded this belief which they had so wickedly conceived. The Romans, however, demanded that men should apply themselves to their own destruction. It has happened, it is happening. People love it and cry aloud that it should continue. Those who perhaps might be offended by the sacrificing of cattle from their herds rejoice at the slaughter of the virtue of their own hearts. Nay, let those who think that the Christians ought to be reproached rather be ashamed in the presence of Nasica. And let them not complain to us about enemies who have ever been with them, but to Nasica about the theater which he prevented from being built.

In Spain, the praetor Sergius Galba accepted the voluntary surrender of the Lusitani who were living on the nearer side of the Tagus River.[126] Later he committed a crime by putting them to death. Although he had pretended that he would act in their interest, he surrounded them with troops and destroyed them while they were unarmed and off their guard. This treachery on the part of the Romans was later the source of the greatest disturbance throughout all Spain.

22. THE Third Punic War began six hundred and two years after the founding of the City in the consulship of L. Cen-

[126] One of the principal rivers of Spain; it empties into the Atlantic Ocean.

sorinus and M. Manilius.[127] The Senate voted that Carthage
must be destroyed. The consuls and Scipio, who was then
tribune of the soldiers, then proceeded to Africa and reached
the camp of the elder Africanus near Utica. There they summoned the Carthaginians and ordered them to surrender both
their arms and ships without delay. The quantity of arms
hastily surrendered was easily great enough to arm all Africa.
But after the Carthaginians had surrendered their arms, they
were ordered to abandon the city and to withdraw inland ten
miles from the sea. Grief brought them to despair. Resolv-
ing either to defend the city or to be buried with her in her fall,
they chose two Hasdrubals [128] as their leaders. Then they
set about to manufacture arms, using gold and silver to supplement the scarce supply of bronze and iron. The consuls
decided to attack Carthage, the situation of which is said to
have been somewhat as follows: [129] the city was surrounded
by a wall nearly twenty-two miles long and was almost entirely
enclosed by the sea except for a neck of land. This extended
for three miles and had a wall thirty feet wide constructed
of hewn rock forty cubits in height. The citadel, the name of
which was Byrsa, was a little more than two miles long. On
one side, a continuous wall, connecting the city with Byrsa,
towered above the Stagnum Sea. This was so named because
a projecting strip of land formed a breakwater and thus made
its waters calm.

Although the consuls by means of machines had shattered
and demolished a considerable part of the wall, nevertheless
they were defeated and driven back by the Carthaginians.
Scipio, however, drove the enemy behind their walls and came

[127] L. Marcius Censorinus and M. Manilius, 149 B.C.

[128] One of the Hasdrubals was in exile to which he had fled to escape a death
penalty. He had at this time gathered a strong army to combat his enemies.
In view of the desperate situation at Carthage, he was asked in the name of
patriotism to fight on behalf of his native city and to assume leadership of the
forces outside of the city. The other Hasdrubal was placed in charge of the
forces within the city.

[129] A map of ancient Carthage is necessary in order to understand the description of Orosius. Appian *Punic Wars* xvi. 95 gives a clear picture of the
city and the defenses.

to the rescue of those who were fleeing.[130] Censorinus returned to the City. Manilius passed by Carthage and directed his forces against Hasdrubal. In the meantime Masinissa died, and Scipio divided the Numidian kingdom among Masinissa's three sons.[131] When Scipio had returned to the vicinity of Carthage, Manilius stormed and plundered the city of Tezaga, slaying twelve thousand Africans and capturing six thousand. Hasdrubal,[132] the Punic general and the grandson of Masinissa, was suspected of treachery. His own countrymen wielded pieces torn from the benches in the Senate House and beat him to death. At the same time the praetor Juventius fought an engagement with Psuedo-Philip in Macedonia. He was slain and the entire Roman army suffered very heavy losses.

23.　In the six hundred and sixth year of the city, that is, in the fiftieth year after the Second Punic War, in the consulship of Cn. Cornelius Lentulus and L. Mummius,[133] P. Scipio,[134] the consul of the year before, tempted fortune for the last time in an effort to destroy Carthage. He advanced to Gothon,[135] where he fought a battle lasting six days and six nights. Utter despair forced the Carthaginians to surrender. They begged that the survivors of the disastrous battle might at least be permitted to become slaves. First a line of women came down [136]—a wretched enough sight—and following them a still more miserable looking body of men. Tradition says that there were twenty-five thousand women and thirty thousand men. Hasdrubal, the king, voluntarily surrendered himself. The Roman deserters, who had taken possession of the temple of Aesculapius, now of their own accord hurled them-

---

[130] Some over-zealous soldiers had rushed through a breach in the wall to attack the enemy. Scipio covered their retreat by stationing soldiers on the wall.

[131] Scipio was in the complete confidence of Masinissa, whose three sons were Micipsa, Gulussa, and Mastanabal.

[132] The Hasdrubal who had directed operations from the city.

[133] Cn. Cornelius Lentulus and L. Mummius Achaicus.

[134] P. Cornelius Scipio Africanus Aemilianus, 146 B.C.

[135] The name of the war harbor of Carthage.

[136] That is, from Byrsa, the citadel of Carthage, where they had taken refuge.

selves down from the walls and were burned to death. The
wife of Hasdrubal, acting as would a man in grief and a
woman in rage, threw herself and her two sons into the middle
of the fire. Thus the last queen of Carthage came to her end
by the same death as that which in ages past had claimed the
first queen. The city burned for seventeen consecutive days,
furnishing the conquerors with a pitiable spectacle to illustrate
the fickleness of human fortune. Thus Carthage was destroyed
and her entire stone wall reduced to dust seven hundred years
after her foundation. With the exception of a few leading
men, every one of the captives was sold into slavery. The
Third Punic War now came to an end in the fourth year
after it had begun.

In regard to the Third Punic War it has never appeared to
me, a very diligent but not brilliant inquirer, that Carthage
was so far instrumental in causing the war that her destruction
was justly decreed. And I am especially moved by the fact
that there would have been no need for deliberation, if, as
in previous wars, an obvious cause and resentment had inflamed the Romans against a rising power. But there was
deliberation. While some of the Romans proposed that Carthage be destroyed to insure the permanent safety of Rome,
there were others who, with a view to the permanent school-
ing of Roman courage—a task they always imposed upon
themselves through suspicion of a rival city—held that Carthage should be left to herself intact, lest Roman energy, always
trained in war, should relax through peace and leisure into
listless indolence. Consequently I find the cause, not in unfair
aggression on the part of Carthage, but in the loss of stead-
fastness and morale among the Romans. Such being the case,
why do they charge to Christian times the dullness and rust
with which they themselves are outwardly stolid and inwardly
corroded? Moreover, some six hundred years ago the Romans lost, as their men of wisdom and caution had predicted,
that great whetstone of their brilliance and keenness—
Carthage.

So I shall close this book, lest I meet with unnecessary harshness. For though I may remove rust for the moment by the violence of the encounter, I will be unable to stimulate the keen judgment that is needed. Yet I should have no fear of open and harsh attack if I could discover a hope of that keen judgment within.

THE FIFTH BOOK

1. IN THE light of the events directly following those I have just related, I realize that some people may be influenced by the fact that Roman victories continued to grow more numerous as the result of the overthrow of many peoples and cities. If they weigh the evidence carefully, however, they will find that more harm than good resulted. For none of these wars against slaves, allies, citizens, or fugitives should be dismissed lightly, since they certainly brought no benefits, but only great disasters. Nevertheless, I shall ignore this fact in order to treat the situation in the light in which these people saw it. I think that they would say: Has there ever been an age happier than this with its continuous triumphs, famous victories, rich prizes of war, imposing processions, and with kings and conquered peoples marching in a long line before the triumphal chariot? I shall answer them briefly and point out that they are pleading for, and that we are talking about, times and events which must be considered not merely from the point of view of one city but by taking the whole world into consideration. It will then appear that whenever Rome conquers and is happy the rest of the world is unhappy and conquered. Should we therefore attach too much importance to this small measure of happiness when it has been obtained at so enormous an expenditure of effort? Granted that these times did bring about some happiness to a particular city, did they not also weigh down the rest of the world with misery and accomplish its ruin? If these times are to be considered happy because the wealth of a single city was increased, why should they not rather be judged as most unhappy in view of the wretched destruction and downfall of mighty realms, of numerous and civilized peoples?

Did Carthage perhaps not view the situation differently at

that time? Over a period of one hundred years the city alternately dreaded the disasters of war and the terms of peace. At one time deciding to renew war and at another to sue humbly for peace, Carthage was continually exchanging peace for war and war for peace. In the end her wretched citizens throughout the city were driven to desperation and threw themselves into the flames. The whole city became one funeral pyre. The city is now small in size and destitute of walls, and it is part of her unhappy lot to hear of her glorious past.

Let Spain present her opinion. For two hundred years Spanish fields were drenched with her own blood. The country was unable either to drive back or to withstand a troublesome enemy that was persistently attacking on every frontier. Towns and country districts everywhere were in ruins. The inhabitants were crushed by the carnage of battle and exhausted by the famines accompanying sieges. Men killed their wives and children, and to end their own sufferings, ran at one another, cut one another's throats, and suffered wretched deaths. What was Spain, then, to think about her own condition?

And now let Italy speak. Why should Italy have oppressed, resisted, and placed all sorts of obstacles in the way of her own Romans over a period of four hundred years? She certainly could not have acted in this way had the happiness of the Romans not spelled her own disaster and had she not felt that she was promoting the welfare of all by preventing the Romans from becoming masters of the entire world.

I am not now raising the question concerning innumerable peoples of various countries, who, after enjoying long periods of freedom, had been defeated in war, forcibly carried away from their native lands, sold into slavery, and dispersed far and wide. I do not ask what they would have preferred for themselves, what they thought of the Romans, and how they judged the times. I am not mentioning one word about kings of vast wealth, great power, and widespread renown, who, after enjoying a long supremacy, were later captured, chained like slaves, sent under the yoke, led before the triumphal chariot, and slaughtered in prison. To inquire their opinion is as foolish as it is difficult not to pity their misery.

Let us question ourselves then, I say, about the way of life which we have chosen and which we are accustomed to live. Our forefathers waged wars, sought peace, and offered tribute; for tribute is the price of peace. We ourselves pay tribute to avoid war and by this means have come to anchor and are remaining in the harbor in which our ancestors finally took refuge in order to escape the storm of evils. Therefore I should like to know whether our times are not happy. Certainly we, who continuously possess what our forefathers finally chose, consider our days happier than those earlier days; for the tumult of wars that exhausted them is unknown to us. We ourselves are also born and raised in a state of peace that they enjoyed only for a brief time after the rule of Caesar and the birth of Christ. The payment which subjection compelled them to make we contribute freely for the common defense. How great is the difference between the present and the past can best be judged by the fact that what Rome once extorted from our people by the sword merely to satisfy her thirst for luxury, she now contributes with us for the maintenance of government. And if anyone asserts that the Romans at that time were much more tolerable enemies to our forefathers than the Goths are now to us, his knowledge and understanding of conditions are quite at variance with the facts.

In former days the entire world was ablaze with wars, and each province was governed by its own king, laws, and customs. A feeling of common fellowship was also lacking when different powers were disagreeing with one another. What was it then that could finally draw into one bond of fellowship barbarian tribes which were scattered far and wide and, moreover, separated by differences in religion and ritual? Suppose that in those days a person was driven by the bitterness of his misfortune to utter desperation and that he decided to abandon his own country and to leave in company with the enemy. What strange country, would he, a stranger, approach? What people, usually enemies, would he, an enemy supplicate? In what man, at first meeting, would he place his confidence? He would not be invited because he belonged to the same race, he would not be induced to come because he obeyed the same law, and he would not be made to feel secure because he believed in the same religion. We have plenty of examples to illustrate what happened. Did not Busiris most brutally offer as sacrifices all strangers who had the misfortune to cross his path?[1] Did not the people on the shores of Taurian Diana act most cruelly toward visitors and perform sacred rites that were crueler still?[2] Did not Thrace and its own Polymestor treat guests, who were at the same time their relatives, in a most criminal fashion?[3] Without dallying too long on events of antiquity, I shall merely cite the testimony of Rome with regard to the murder of Pompey and the testimony of Egypt with regard to Ptolemy, his murderer.

2.   AT THE present, however, I feel no apprehension over the outbreak of any disturbance, since I can take refuge anywhere. No matter where I flee, I find my native land, my law, and my religion. Just now Africa has welcomed me with a warmth of spirit that matched the confidence I felt when I came here. At the present time, I say, this Africa has welcomed me to her state of absolute peace, to her own bosom, and to her common law—Africa, concerning whom it was once said and truly said:

> We are debarred the welcome of the beach,
> They stir up wars and forbid us to set foot even on the land's edge.[4]

[1] One story states that when Egypt had suffered nine years from famine, Phrasius, a soothsayer from Cyprus, suggested to Busiris that the famine would cease if he would sacrifice one foreigner to Zeus each year. Busiris proceeded to sacrifice all foreigners until Heracles, a bound victim, escaped from his fetters and slew him.

[2] The Tauri, a wild and savage people of the Crimea, sacrificed all strangers to a goddess whom the Greeks identified with Artemis or Diana.

[3] The Greek tragedians, following one legend, made Polydorus the son of Priam and Hecuba. When the fall of Troy was imminent, they gave a rich treasure to him to take to their guest-friend, the Thracian king Polymestor. The latter slew Polydorus to obtain the treasure.   [4] Vergil *Aeneid* i, 540-41.

Africa of her own free will now opens wide her kindly bosom to receive friends of her own religion and peace,[5] and of her own accord invites those weary ones whom she cherishes.

The width of the East, the vastness of the North, the great stretches of the South, and the largest and most secure settlements on great islands, all have the same law and nationality as I, since I come there as a Roman and Christian to Christians and Romans. I do not fear the gods of my host. Neither do I fear that his religion will bring death to me. Nor am I afraid of any place where a native may do whatever he wishes and a stranger may not do whatever is lawful, where my host's law will not be my own. One God, Who established the unity of this realm in the days when He willed Himself to become known, is loved and feared by all. The same laws, which are subject to this one God, hold sway everywhere. Wheresoever I go, stranger though I be, I need harbor no fear of sudden assault as would a man without protection. Among Romans, as I have said, I am a Roman; among Christians, a Christian; among men, a man. The state comes to my aid through its laws, religion through its appeal to the conscience, and nature through its claim of universality.

For a time I enjoy any country as if it were my own, because that native land, which is my real home and the one which I love, is not wholly on this earth. I have lost nothing where I have loved nothing. I have everything when I have with me Him whom I love; especially since He is the same among all. He made me not only known to all but also very near to all. Neither does He forsake me when I am in need, because the earth is His and its fullness, whereof He has ordered all things to be common to all men. The blessings of our age, which our ancestors never had in their entirety, are these: the tranquillity of the present, hope for the future, and possession of a common place of refuge. Our ancestors had to wage incessant wars, because, not feeling free to move as a body and to change their abodes, they continued to remain at home where they had the misfortune to be slaughtered or to be

[5] That is, the Christian religion and the Roman peace.

basely enslaved. This will appear clearer and more evident when the actual deeds of our ancestors are unrolled in due order.

3. IN THE six hundred and sixth year of the City, that is, in the same year that Carthage was destroyed, and in the consulship of Cn. Cornelius Lentulus and L. Mummius,[6] the overthrow of Corinth followed the destruction of Carthage. The conflagrations of two of the most powerful cities—pitiable sights—were separated from each other by only a short interval of time and illuminated parts of the world at great distances from each other. The praetor Metellus won two victories over the Achaeans and the Boeotians who had joined them. The first took place at Thermopylae and the second in Phocis. The historian Claudius[7] tells us that twenty thousand fell in the first battle and that seven thousand were killed in the second battle. Valerius Antias[8] confirms the statement that a battle was fought in Achaia and that twenty thousand Achaeans and their leader Diaeus were slain. But although Polybius of Achaia[9] was at that time in Africa with Scipio, he was unable to ignore a disaster suffered by his native land. He claimed that one battle had been fought in Achaea under the leadership of Critolaus, but hastened to add that Diaeus and the army which he had brought with him from Arcadia had been crushed by this same praetor Metellus. Now I have already made some remarks about the variety of opinions expressed by disagreeing historians. Let it suffice to say that these historians have been exposed and branded as liars, because if writers present entirely different accounts of events which they themselves saw as eyewitnesses it indicates very clearly that their opinions of other events are worth very little.

[6] Cn. Cornelius Lentulus and L. Mummius Achaicus, 146 B.C.
[7] Claudius Cornelius Tacitus.
[8] The text has Valerius and Antias, but the reference is clearly to Q. Valerius Antias, a Roman historian living in the first century before Christ. He had the reputation of being most untrustworthy.
[9] The famous historian who wrote a history covering the years 220–146 B.C.

After the annihilation of garrisons over all Achaia and after the destruction of defenseless cities, the consul Mummius with a few men suddenly went into camp in accordance with the plan formed by the praetor Metellus. After the latter had been sent away, Mummius stormed Corinth without delay. This city was by far the wealthiest of all cities in the world at that time and for centuries back had been a kind of laboratory for all crafts and craftsmen as well as the common market of Asia and Europe. He cruelly granted the captives permission to plunder. The whole city was filled with carnage and ablaze with fires which formed a single great flame that shot forth from the circumference of the walls as if from a chimney. When most of the population had been destroyed by fire and sword, the survivors were sold into slavery. A huge quantity of booty was carried away just before the city was burned to the ground, her walls leveled, and the stones in the walls reduced to dust. The presence of a great number of statues and images of all sorts in the burning city was responsible for the formation of a new type of metal consisting of gold, silver, and copper, and representing an alloy of all the metals melted down and dissolved. Hence even to this day, as tradition tells us, this metal has been called Corinthian bronze either because of its origin in Corinth or because it is an imitation of that metal. I might add that people also speak of Corinthian vases.

4. In Spain, during the same consulship,[10] Viriathus, a Lusitanian by birth but a shepherd and robber by calling, infested the roads and devastated the provinces. He also defeated, routed, and subdued armies commanded by Roman praetors and consuls. As a result the Romans became greatly terrified. Then Viriathus encountered the praetor C. Vetilius as the latter was passing through and roaming over the broad territories of the Ebro and Tagus, rivers that were very large and widely separated from each other. He defeated the army of Vetilius and slaughtered its soldiers almost to a man; the

[10] That is, in the consulship of Cn. Cornelius Lentulus and L. Mummius.

praetor himself barely managed to slip away and escape with a few followers.[11] He also put to flight the praetor C. Plautius, whose power had previously been broken by many battles.[12] Later he encountered a large and well-equipped army which the Romans had dispatched under the command of Claudius Unimammus, whose evident purpose was to wipe out the stain of the earlier disgrace, but who managed only to add to the dishonor; for he lost all the supplies that he had brought with him as well as the strongest division of the Roman army. As trophies, Viriathus displayed robes, fasces, and other Roman insignia [13] on a mountainside of his own country.

In these same days, three hundred Lusitani fought an engagement against a thousand Romans in a mountain valley. Claudius reports that in this battle seventy Lusitani and three hundred and twenty Romans lost their lives. When the victorious Lusitani had scattered and were withdrawing in safety, one of them, a foot soldier, was cut off at some distance from his companions. When Roman cavalrymen suddenly surrounded him, he pierced the horse of one of his assailants with his spear and beheaded the rider with a single blow of his sword. All the others were so terrified that he was able to walk off leisurely and in a contemptuous manner while they looked on.

In the consulship of Appius Claudius and Q. Caecilius Metellus,[14] the former encountered the Salassian Gauls. He met defeat and lost five thousand men, but when the struggle was renewed he killed five thousand of the enemy. He now sought a triumph in accordance with the law that stated that anyone who had destroyed five thousand of the enemy should be granted the privilege of holding a triumph. His request, however, was refused on account of the losses he had previously suffered. Nevertheless, in his desire for glory he stooped to

---

[11] In reality, Vetilius was killed. The battle was fought in a defile of the Sierra Ronda near Tribola, a town to the south of the Tagus in Lusitania.

[12] Plautius lost the camp he had established on the "Hill of Venus."

[13] The text follows Florus *History* i. 33.

[14] Appius Claudius Pulcher and Q. Caecilius Metellus Macedonicus, 143 B.C.

infamy and impudence and celebrated a triumph at his own expense.

During the consulship of L. Caecilius Metellus and Q. Fabius Maximus Servilianus,[15] an hermaphrodite, among other prodigies, was seen at Rome. At the order of the haruspices the hermaphrodite was thrown into the sea; but this act of expiation proved of no avail. Immediately so great a pestilence broke out that the insufficient number of undertakers was at once overtaxed; soon no undertakers at all were left to prepare bodies for burial. The great mansions remained, but they were now empty of all life and filled with the dead; within there were vast inheritances but not a single heir was to be found. It finally became impossible to live in the city or even to approach it, so awful were the odors given off from bodies decaying in houses and on the streets.

That expiation which required the cruel death of a human being resulted in the roads being piled high with the dead. In the midst of their miseries the Romans became overcome with shame and finally realized how vile and utterly useless that act had been. For they had performed this expiation to ward off impending disaster; but, as you see, a pestilence immediately followed. After running its course, it subsided in accordance with the decision of an inscrutable Providence without further resort to expiatory sacrifices. If the haruspices, those master craftsmen in the art of deceit, had by chance carried out that expiation—a customary procedure on their part when diseases were abating—they would have indubitably claimed for themselves, their gods, and their rites, the credit for the return to normal conditions. And so that wretched City, whose evil religion did not shrink from sacrilege, was deceived by falsehoods from which it could not free itself.

The consul Fabius in the course of his struggle against the Lusitani and Viriathus drove off the enemy and freed the town of Buccia, which Viriathus was besieging. He received in surrender not only this city but also many other strongholds.

---

[15] L. Caecilius Metellus Calvus and Q. Fabius Maximus Servilianus, 142 B.C.

He then committed a crime that would have been detestable even to the barbarians dwelling in farthest Scythia, not to mention its affront to the Roman sense of honor and moderation. He cut off the hands of five hundred Lusitanian chiefs who had been tempted by his offer of an alliance and had been received in accordance with the law of surrender.

Pompey,[16] the consul of the following year, invaded the territories of the Numantines and after suffering a great disaster withdrew. Not only was his entire army almost annihilated, but also many nobles serving with him were slain.

Viriathus, however, after defeating Roman generals and armies over a period of fourteen years, was finally killed, a victim of an act of treachery. In this instance alone the Romans acted as men toward Viriathus in that they judged his assassins undeserving of a reward.

Not only now but also frequently in the past I have found myself able to interweave in my story those extremely complicated wars of the East, which rarely ever either begin or end without crimes. But the crimes of the Romans, with whom we are now concerned, are so monstrous that we may justly scorn those of other peoples.

In the days of which we are writing, Mithridates, the sixth king of the Parthians in line from Arsaces, conquered the prefect Demetrius.[17] Now victorious, he attacked the city of Babylon and invaded all her territories. He next subdued all the tribes that dwelt in the country between the Hydaspes and Indus rivers and extended his bloody rule even to India. He fought Demetrius a second time, defeated, and captured him. Whereupon a certain Diodotus and his son Alexander usurped the throne of Demetrius and took over the name of his dynasty. But Diodotus did not wish to share the throne with his son who had participated in all the dangers involved in winning the crown. Therefore he later had him put to death.

During the consulship of M. Aemilius Lepidus and C.

---

[16] Q. Pompeius, 141 B.C. The other consul was Cn. Servilius Caepio. He made several unsuccessful attempts to capture Numantia and lost heavily.

[17] Demetrius Nicator, king of Syria.

Hostilius Mancinus,[18] various prodigies appeared. The consuls, so far as they were able, offered expiation according to
the usual custom. But chance events did not always come
opportunely to the aid of the haruspices, those weavers of
lies and observers of events. For the consul Mancinus, after
taking over the command of the army from Popillius at
Numantia, met with constant reverses on the field of battle.
He was reduced to such desperate straits that he was forced
to make a most disgraceful treaty with the Numantines. Although Pompey had also but a short time before concluded
an equally dishonorable treaty with these same Numantines,
the Senate ordered the treaty to be abrogated and handed
Mancinus over to the Numantines. They stripped him of his
clothes, tied his hands behind his back, and exposed him to
public view before the Numantine gates, where he remained
far into the night. Deserted by his own people and rejected
by the enemy, he furnished a spectacle that caused friend and
foe alike to weep.

5.   GRIEF compels me to cry out at this point. Why, O Romans, do you undeservedly ascribe to yourselves those great
attributes of justice, good faith, courage, and mercy? Learn
the true nature of these virtues from the Numantines. Was a
display of courage required? The Numantines conquered by
fighting. Was good faith demanded? Trusting others to act
as they themselves would have acted, the Numantines concluded a treaty and set free those whom they might have
killed. Was justice to be put to the test? The very silence of
the Senate bore witness to that justice when these same Numantines through their own envoys kept demanding either an
inviolable peace or else, according to the agreement made, the
return of all those whom they had released alive. Was it
evident that the spirit of mercy needed examination? The
Numantines have given evidence enough by granting life to
a hostile army and by not punishing Mancinus. Ought Mancinus, I ask, to have been surrendered? It was he who saved

[18] M. Aemilius Lepidus Porcina and C. Hostilius Mancinus, 137 B.C.

his defeated army from impending slaughter by shielding them under the cover of a peace treaty and it was he who preserved for better times the imperiled forces of his fatherland. If the treaty concluded did not meet with approval, why was the army set free by this pledge, or, when the army came back, why was it received? When the return of the army was demanded, why was it not sent back? Or if any possible arrangement for saving the army met with approval, why was Mancinus, who concluded this treaty, alone surrendered?

Somewhat earlier, Varro, in order to precipitate the conflict, had overcome the reluctance of his colleague Paulus and forced him to take action. Varro rushed forward his own army which thus far had been afraid to risk battle and at Cannae—notorious for that famous Roman disaster—drew up his luckless troops, not to fight a battle but to expose them to death. He lost more than forty thousand Roman soldiers solely because of his own impatience, a trait upon which Hannibal had long relied to achieve victory for himself. After the death of his colleague Paulus (and what a man he was!) Varro finally had the impudence to return practically alone to the City. There he earned the reward of his self-assurance. He was publicly thanked by the Senate for not despairing of the Republic, which, however, he himself had brought to dire straits.

At a later date Mancinus did his very best to save the army which, in the fortunes of war, had been surrounded. Nevertheless this same Senate condemned him to be surrendered to the enemy. I know, O Romans, that you disapproved in the case of Varro, but you yielded to the emergency. You made the present decision in the case of Mancinus and again cited the pretext of an emergency. Thus your actions from the very beginning have been such that no citizen could consistently have any regard for so ungrateful a people nor could an enemy place any trust in those proven to be so untrustworthy.

In the meantime Brutus [19] in Further Spain crushed sixty

[19] Decius Junius Brutus. The battle took place in 136 B.C.

thousand Gallaeci who had come to the assistance of the Lusitani. He was victorious only after a desperate and difficult battle, despite the fact that he had surrounded them unawares. According to report, fifty thousand of them were slain in that battle, six thousand were captured, and only a small number escaped by flight. In Nearer Spain the proconsul Lepidus, against the Senate's orders, stubbornly tried to subdue the Vaccaei, a harmless and submissive tribe. But he paid the penalty for his effrontery and stubbornness, for shortly afterward he suffered a severe defeat: [20] no less than six thousand Romans met a just death in this unjust war; the rest, having stripped their camp and thrown away their arms, escaped.

This disaster of Lepidus was not one whit less disgraceful than that suffered under Mancinus. Let the Romans themselves, overcome by constant disasters and defeated time and again—to say nothing of the Spaniards who were beaten and worn out by so many battles—now ascribe, if they can, happiness to this period. In order not to make it a matter of reproach by revealing the number of the Roman praetors and of their lieutenant-generals, consuls, legions, and armies that were lost, I simply repeat: what kind of madness, arising from fear, was it that so weakened the Roman soldier that he could no longer stand firm nor steel his courage for further trials of warfare, but took to his heels as soon as he caught a glimpse of a Spaniard, his special enemy, and practically considered himself defeated before the enemy was even sighted? From what I have said it is clear that both sides judged their times wretched, since the Spaniards, though quite able to conquer, were loath to relinquish the pleasures of their idle life and to engage in foreign wars, whereas the Romans suffered more disgraceful defeats the more outrageously they encroached upon the peace of a foreign power.

6. DURING the consulship of Servius Fulvius Flaccus and Q.

[20] After initial successes, want of provisions compelled a retreat during which the Romans lost many troops. 136 B.C.

Calpurnius Piso,[21] a maid servant at Rome gave birth to a boy who had four feet, four eyes, as many ears, that is, double the number that an ordinary human being has. About this time Mount Etna in Sicily erupted and poured forth vast streams of fiery lava, which, like torrents, rushed precipitously down the slopes. The flames consumed everything nearby, while glowing ashes, which gave off a dense vapor as they flew far and wide through the air, scorched more distant places. This type of prodigy, ever native to Sicily, is wont not so much to portend as to bring misfortune.

In the territory of Bononia [22] the produce of the field sprouted forth on trees. In Sicily a slave war arose which was particularly severe and bitterly fought on account of the large number of slaves participating, the amount of their equipment, and the imposing strength of their forces. Roman praetors were completely routed and even the consuls were terrified, for at that time seventy thousand slaves, according to report, were in the army of the conspirators. This number did not include slaves from the city of Messana, which kept its slaves peaceful by treating them with kindness. In another respect, also, Sicily was rather unfortunate. As an island Sicily never had a law adapted to her own conditions. Therefore she fell under the control of tyrants at one time and at another of slaves. The evil rule of the former resulted in slavery, whereas the perversity and presumption of the latter effected an interchange of liberty and slavery between the classes. Sicily was in an especially unfavorable position since she was surrounded by the sea and therefore able only with the greatest difficulty to purge herself of intestine evils. To her ruin, Sicily sustained a viperous growth that was strengthened by her own lust and destined to live on after her death. In such a situation, the emotions of a slave mob are more truculent than free men's in the degree that their display is rarer. For a crowd of free men is motivated by an urge toward their country's welfare whereas a slave mob desires the country's ruin.

[21] Consuls in 135 B.C.   [22] Cispadane Gaul.

7. DURING the six hundred and twentieth year of the City,
the disgrace of the treaty concluded at Numantia added to
the shame which the Roman brow already carried. This disgrace was almost greater than that involved in the treaty formerly made at Caudine Forks. Scipio Africanus was now
unanimously elected consul [23] by the tribes and dispatched with
an army to storm Numantia. This was the farthest city of
the Celtiberi and was situated in Hither Spain on a high point
of Gallaecia not far from the lands of the Vaccaei and Cantabri. For a period of fourteen years Numantia, with only
four thousand troops, not only had held her own against forty
thousand of the Romans but even defeated and forced them
to conclude humiliating treaties. Therefore, when Scipio
Africanus entered Spain, he did not immediately engage the
enemy, thinking that he might overthrow them when they
were off their guard. He knew that this race of men never
allowed their bodies and minds to become so relaxed in times
of leisure that the state of their training was not, even then,
superior to the preparations of others. On the contrary, he
confined his own army to its camp for some time and drilled
his soldiers as if they were in a training school. Even though
Scipio passed part of the summer and the whole winter without attempting even one battle, he gained very little advantage
from his diligence. In fact, when an opportunity for battle
presented itself, the Roman army was overwhelmed by the
attack of the Numantines, and it fled. After the consul had
checked its flight by upbraiding his soldiers with reproaches
and threats, the army rallied, turned against its pursuers, and
compelled them to flee. It is difficult at this point to relate
the truth of this affair. The Romans both turned back the
Numantines and witnessed their flight. Hence although Scipio
had rejoiced and boasted that this victory had exceeded his
expectations, nevertheless he openly acknowledged that it
would have been rash to continue this particular battle.
Thinking, however, that he ought to take further advantage
of his unexpected success, he closely besieged the city itself,

[23] P. Cornelius Scipio Africanus Aemilianus II, 134 B.C.

surrounding it with a trench ten feet wide and twenty feet deep. By means of numerous towers he then set about to reduce the rampart, which had been constructed with stakes, so that, if the enemy should sally forth and make an attack upon him, he might at once carry on the struggle not as a besieger against the besieged, but vice versa, that is, as the besieged against the besieger.

Numantia, situated on an eminence not far from the Durius River, was surrounded by a wall three miles in circumference. Nevertheless there are some who assert that the city was without walls and that its area was very small. The latter opinion is credible for this reason: although the Numantines enclosed the large space mentioned in order to take care of the feeding and protection of their flocks and also to provide satisfactory means for the cultivation of the land when hard pressed in war, they themselves occupied a small citadel fortified by its natural position. Otherwise so large an area would have seemed not to protect the city's inhabitants but rather to betray its small population.

The Numantines were shut in for a long time and became completely exhausted by hunger. They then offered to surrender on the condition that they obtain reasonably satisfactory terms. They also repeatedly begged for an opportunity to engage in a regular battle, so that they might die like men. Finally they all suddenly burst forth from two gates. They had just drunk their fill not of wine—this place was not favorable to viticulture—but of the juice of a weed. This drink is skilfully concocted, and it is called *caelia* because it is heated. The potency of the moistened fruit bud is first intensified by heat. The bud is then dried, ground to powder, and mixed with a mild juice. When this ferments, it becomes sour and when consumed produces that feeling of warmth characteristic of drunkenness. They drank this potion after their long fast and as soon as it took effect presented themselves for battle.

The struggle raged long and fiercely and even jeopardized the safety of the Romans. Had they not been under the command of Scipio, the Romans would have proved by fleeing that they were fighting against the Numantines. When the bravest of their men had been killed, the Numantines withdrew from battle, but they returned to their city with ordered ranks and not as fugitives. They were unwilling to receive the bodies of the slain offered for burial. With their last hope gone and only death awaiting them, they became desperate and set fire to their besieged city. Each died either by sword, by poison, or by fire. So the Romans gained absolutely nothing from their victory except their own security; for when Numantia had been overthrown, they did not consider that they had defeated the Numantines but that they had escaped from them. The fetters of the victor held not a single Numantine, so that Rome saw no sufficient reason for granting Scipio a triumph. The Numantines were so poor that they had no gold or silver that could have survived the fire, which had consumed their weapons and their clothing.

8. WHILE these events were taking place at Numantia, the seditions stirred up by the Gracchi [24] were agitating Rome. After the destruction of Numantia, Scipio entered into peace treaties with other Spanish tribes. Once he consulted a certain Thyresus, a Celtic chieftain, and asked him how it happened that the Numantine state had remained so long unconquered and how later it came to be overthrown. Thyresus replied: "When harmony reigned the state was unconquerable, but once lack of harmony began to prevail the state was destroyed." The Romans took this statement as a warning applying to themselves, for presently they received news that seditions were throwing the whole City into discord. Indeed once Carthage and Numantia were destroyed, that useful spirit of coöperation, the consequence of their foresight, perished among the Romans, and a disastrous spirit of contention, the natural outgrowth of their ambition, sprang up.

T. Gracchus, the tribune of the plebs, became angry at the nobility because he was charged with being one of the authors

[24] Tiberius Sempronius Gracchus and Caius Sempronius Gracchus.

of the Numantine treaty. He decided that the land which
heretofore had been held by private interests should now be
divided for the benefit of the people. He took away the imperium from Octavius, a tribune of the plebs, who was opposing him, and made Minucius the latter's successor. These
acts angered the Senate and made the people arrogant. At
this time it chanced that on his deathbed, Attalus, the son of
Eumenes, had provided in his will that the Roman people
should fall heir to the rule of the province of Asia. Gracchus,
seeking to win the favor of the people by bribery, put through
a law stipulating that the money obtained from Attalus should
be distributed among the people. When Nasica [25] opposed
this measure, Pompey promised that he would also bring
charges against Gracchus, as soon as the latter had left his
magistracy.

9. WHEN Gracchus was striving to remain a tribune of the
plebs for the following year and was stirring up riots among
the people on election day, the nobles became greatly incensed. On the order of Nasica they wielded pieces of wood
torn from the benches and put the plebeians to flight. As
Gracchus, his cloak torn off, fled along the steps that were
above the Calpurnian Arch, he was struck by one of these
pieces and fell to the ground. When he rose to his feet, another blow of a cudgel smashed his skull and killed him. In
that riot two hundred were killed and their bodies were
thrown into the Tiber. The unburied corpse of Gracchus
vanished.

In addition, the contagion of the Slave War that had arisen
in Sicily infected many provinces far and wide. At Minturnae,[26] the Romans crucified five hundred slaves, and at
Sinuessa,[27] Q. Metellus and Cn. Servilius Caepio overwhelmed
about four thousand slaves. In the mines of the Athenians,
the praetor Heraclitus broke up a slave uprising of like char-

---

[25] P. Scipio Nasica, the leader of the aristocracy.
[26] A city of Latium on the border of Campania.
[27] A maritime colony founded in Latium about 296 B.C.

acter. At Delos, citizens, anticipating the movement, crushed the slaves when they arose in another rebellion. These riots, if I may so express myself, represented but additional sparks which, set ablaze by that trouble in Sicily, leaped forth and started all these different fires. For in Sicily the consul Piso,[28] who succeeded the consul Fulvius, took the town of Mamertium [29] and killed eight thousand fugitives; those whom he was able to capture he had fastened to the *patibulum*. Rupilius,[30] who had succeeded Piso as consul, stormed and recaptured Tauromenium and Henna,[31] the strongest places of refuge held by the fugitive slaves. More than twenty thousand slaves, according to report, were slaughtered at that time.

Of such a war as this the cause is pitiable and the issues hopelessly involved. For undoubtedly the masters would have had to die had they not met the insolence of the slaves with steel. Nevertheless if one takes into account the unfortunate losses of battle and the still more unfortunate gains of victory, the conquerors lost in proportion to the number of the conquered who perished.

10. IN THE six hundred and twenty-second year of the City, P. Licinius Crassus,[32] consul and pontifex maximus, was dispatched with a well-equipped army against Aristonicus, the brother of Attalus. Aristonicus had invaded the province of Asia, which had been left as a legacy to the Romans. The consul was also supported by the powerful kings, Nicomedes of Bithynia, Mithridates of Pontus and Armenia, Ariarathes of Cappadocia and Pylaemenes of Paphlagonia, all of whom contributed great forces. Nevertheless, Crassus was defeated in a pitched battle,[33] and his army was compelled to flee after

[28] L. Calpurnius Piso Frugi, 133 B.C.
[29] A city in the interior of the Bruttian peninsula.
[30] P. Rupilius, 132 B.C.
[31] Henna or Enna is in the center of Sicily; Tauromenium is on the east coast.
[32] P. Licinius Crassus Mucianus, 131 B.C.
[33] In the neighborhood of Lencae, a small town of Ionia near Phocaea. 131 B.C.

suffering heavy losses. When the consul himself was surrounded by the enemy and was about to be captured, he thrust
the whip, which he had used on his horse, into the eye of a
Thracian. The barbarian, smarting from the pain and burning with rage, stabbed him through the side with a sword.
Thus Crassus escaped both dishonor and slavery by meeting
death in the way he had chosen to die.

Upon hearing of the death of Crassus and of the slaughter
of the Roman army, the consul Perperna,[34] who had succeeded
Crassus, speedily marched over into Asia and surprised Aristonicus who was resting after his recent victory. Perperna annihilated his army and forced him to flee. Next he besieged
the city of Stratoniceia to which Aristonicus had fled for
refuge. He compelled the latter, now emaciated from hunger,
to surrender. The consul was later taken ill at Pergamum and
died. Aristonicus, by order of the Senate, was strangled in
a prison at Rome.

In the same year, the miserable life of Ptolemy, the king
of the Alexandrians, was brought to an end still more
wretched. He first seduced his own sister, then married her,
and finally divorced her—the last act being more disgraceful
than the marriage. He next took to wife his own stepdaughter, that is, the daughter of his sister and wife. He put
to death his own son, who was born of his sister, and also
killed one of his brother's sons. Because of these acts of
incest and parricide he was detested by the Alexandrians who
drove him from the kingdom.

During those same years, Antiochus,[35] not content with
Babylon, Ecbatana, and the whole Median Empire, engaged
in battle with the Parthian king, Phraates II,[36] and was defeated. Though Antiochus apparently had only a hundred
thousand soldiers in his own army, he carried along with him
two hundred thousand servants and camp followers, among
whom were prostitutes and actors. Therefore he and his en-

---

[34] M. Perperna. The other consul was C. Claudius Pulcher Lentulus, 130 B.C.
[35] Antiochus VII, surnamed Sidetes.
[36] Arsaces VII, also known as Phraates II.

tire army fell an easy prey to the Parthian troops and all perished.[37]

I have no hesitation in saying that one of the worst disgraces that can be charged to the Romans occurred in the consulship of C. Sempronius Tuditanus and M. Acilius.[38] On the day before his death P. Scipio Africanus learned that he would be accused in court by evil and ungrateful men notwithstanding the efforts he had made in behalf of his country. He therefore testified before the Assembly that his life was in danger. Early the next day he was found dead in his own bedroom. I make special mention of this because Africanus enjoyed so great a reputation in the City for strength and moderation that people readily believed that had he lived there could have been no war against the allies nor any civil war. It was a common saying that Africanus was treacherously murdered by his wife Sempronia, a sister of the Gracchi. They said this, I believe, so that a family already steeped in crime and fated to bring ruin on its own country might have, in the midst of the wicked seditions raised by its men, a reputation even more monstrous because of the crimes committed by its women.

In the consulship of M. Aemilius and L. Orestes,[39] Etna was shaken by a severe tremor and poured forth masses of glowing lava. Again, on another day, on the island of Lipara and around its adjacent waters, the volcano boiled over to such an extent that it dissolved rocks already burned, scorched the planks of ships after first causing the binding wax to liquify, and boiled alive fish swimming near the surface. It also suffocated human beings who by constantly breathing hot air burned their vital organs. Only those who were able to withdraw to some distance escaped death.

11. IN THE consulship of M. Plautius Hypsaeus and M. Fulvius Flaccus,[40] Africa had only just become peaceful and

[37] 128 B.C. [38] C. Sempronius Tuditanus and M. Aquillius, 129 B.C.
[39] M. Aemilius Lepidus and L. Aurelius Orestes, 126 B.C.
[40] Consuls in 125 B.C.

free from the ravages of war when a horrible and unusual
catastrophe overtook her. Huge numbers of locusts swarmed
over the whole land. They not only completely destroyed all
hope of any crops by consuming all the plants and part of
their roots and the leaves of the trees along with the tender
shoots of their branches, but even gnawed away the bitter
bark and dry wood. The locusts were then swept away by the
wind and driven together into dense masses. After being carried through the air for a long time they finally were drowned
in the African Sea. The great waves deposited enormous
heaps of them along wide stretches of the shore where the decaying and putrifying masses gave out a stench foul beyond
belief and very infectious. The plague that followed was so
severe that it affected all living creatures. Everywhere the
putrifying bodies of the birds, domestic animals, and wild
beasts destroyed by the contaminated atmosphere increased
the virulence of the pestilence. Indeed the human toll taken
by the plague was so frightful that my whole body trembles
as I refer to it. In Numidia, where King Micipsa was ruling
at that time, it is recorded that eight hundred thousand men
perished, while along the maritime coast closely adjacent to
Carthage and to Utica more than two hundred thousand lost
their lives. In the city of Utica itself, thirty thousand soldiers
who were stationed there to protect all Africa were killed and
wiped off the face of the earth. This disaster came so suddenly and with so great violence that at Utica in a single day
and through one gate alone more than fifteen hundred bodies
of young men and women were said to have been carried out
for burial.

Nevertheless, as a result of the favor and kindness of
Almighty God, by Whose mercy and in whose trust I speak
of these matters, I should say this. Although locusts in our
times have appeared unexpectedly now and then—and this
has happened in various places—for the most part they have
been endurable even though they did some harm. But never
has there been a plague of locusts like this. So long as these
locusts were alive they were utterly unbearable, but when they

were dead they became even more so. For while they were still alive, everything seemed about to perish, but once they were destroyed, even those creatures nearing death wished that the locusts had not perished.

12. IN THE six hundred and twenty-seventh year of the City, during the consulship of L. Caecilius Metellus and Q. Titius Flamininus,[41] the city of Carthage in Africa, which had been destroyed twenty-two years earlier, was now ordered to be restored. But before the city was rebuilt and settled by families of Roman citizens brought there to live, an extraordinary prodigy occurred. Surveyors sent to determine the boundaries of the territory belonging to the city of Carthage discovered that the posts erected to mark the boundaries had been torn up, bitten, and gnawed to pieces by wolves during the night. The Romans then were for some time in doubt whether the restoration of Carthage would be advantageous to the peace of Rome.

In that same year, Caius Gracchus, the brother of that famous Gracchus [42] who had previously been killed in a domestic riot, was aided in his election to the office of tribune of the plebs by an uprising of the people. This brought great harm to the Republic. For Gracchus continuously incited the Roman people to bitter dissension by his largesses and immoderate promises, especially those made in the interests of the agrarian law in behalf of which his brother, Tiberius Gracchus, had met his death. Finally, however, he withdrew from the tribunate. As the tribune of the plebs, he was succeeded by Minucius, who proceeded to tear up most of his statutes and to repeal the greater part of his laws. C. Gracchus, accompanied by Fulvius Flaccus and surrounded by a huge crowd, then went up to the Capitol where an assembly was in session. A great tumult arose there. The killing of a certain herald by the partisans of Gracchus was a summons to battle. Flaccus, escorted by his two sons who were armed and also accompanied by Gracchus who was wearing a toga and concealing a

41 Consuls in 123 B.C. T. Quintus Flamininus, not Q. Titius. 42 Tiberius Gracchus.

poniard under his left arm, sent a herald ahead to offer the slaves their freedom. When they did not accept his offer, he seized the temple of Diana as a citadel.

As a counter move, D. Brutus, a man of consular rank, rushed down the sloping Publican Road and made a spirited attack upon him, but Flaccus fought most stubbornly for a long time. Gracchus, meanwhile, withdrew to the Temple of Minerva and planned to fall on his sword but was restrained by the intervention of Laetorius. The battle raged a long time, the issue ever hanging in the balance. Finally, however, the bowmen dispatched by Opimius scattered the crowd which was engaged in hand-to-hand fighting. The two Flacci, father and son, fled through the Temple of Luna, leaped down into a private house, and barricaded the doors. Their pursuers tore down the walls made of wickerwork and stabbed them both to death.

When his friends had fought a long time and many of them had laid down their lives in his behalf, Gracchus barely managed to reach the Sublician Bridge, where, in order to avoid being captured alive, he offered his neck to his slave. The head of Gracchus, which had been cut off, was brought to the consul; his body was sent to his mother Cornelia who lived in the town of Misenum.[43] This Cornelia, the daughter of the greater Africanus, had withdrawn to Misenum, as I have said, upon the death of her elder son. The property of Gracchus was confiscated and the youthful Flaccus was put to death in prison, while two hundred and fifty of the faction of Gracchus, according to report, were slain on the Aventine Hill. The consul Opimius[44] was as cruel in the judicial investigations as he had been brave in battle. He executed more than three thousand men, most of whom, having been denied even a chance to defend themselves, were killed in spite of their innocence.

13. IN THOSE same days, Metellus[45] overran and subdued

---

[43] A town in Campania, situated on one extremity of the Bay of Naples.
[44] L. Opimius was consul in 121 B.C.
[45] Quintus Caecilius Metellus was consul in 123 B.C.

the Balearic Islands. By slaughtering a great many of the inhabitants, he suppressed a dangerous outbreak of piracy that had arisen at this time among the people. The proconsul Gnaeus Domitius also defeated the Allobrogian Gauls in a severe battle near the town of Vindalium.[46] The principal reason for his victory was the terror that the strange appearance of the elephants aroused in the horses of the enemy and in the enemy themselves, causing them to flee in every direction. Twenty thousand of the Allobroges, according to report, lost their lives there and three thousand were captured.

At this same time an eruption of Mount Etna took place. It was more violent than usual. Fiery torrents overflowed and spread far and wide. The city of Catana and its territory were overwhelmed to so great an extent that the roofs of the houses, scorched and weighed down by the hot cinders, crumbled in ruins to the ground. For the sake of relieving the suffering that this disaster had brought to the people of Catana, the Senate released them from the obligation of paying any tribute for ten years.

14.   IN THE six hundred and twenty-eighth year of the City, the consul Fabius [47] encountered Bituitus,[48] king of the Arverni, a people of the Gallic state. At this time the king was making extensive preparations for war. The army of the consul was so small that Bituitus boasted that the small number of the Romans would scarcely suffice to feed the dogs that were with his army. Realizing that the one bridge over the Rhone River was too small for him to lead his troops across, Bituitus had another constructed by chaining together small boats over which he spread boards and fastened them down. A battle was begun [49] which raged long and fiercely, finally ending in the defeat and rout of the Gauls. For the Gauls, while each man was thinking of his own safety, thoughtlessly allowed too great a concentration of their col-

---

[46] Located in Gallia Narbonensis.
[47] Q. Fabius Maximus, who was later called Allobrogicus. 121 B.C.
[48] On inscriptions the name is written "Betuetus."
[49] Where the Isara empties into the Rhone, 121 B.C.

umns and in their haste to cross broke the chains binding the
bridge. Boats and men immediately sank. Of the one hundred and eighty thousand soldiers reported in the army of
Bituitus, one hundred and fifty thousand were slain or
drowned.

The consul Q. Marcius [50] made war upon a tribe of Gauls
living at the foot of the Alps. When they saw themselves
surrounded by the Roman troops and realized that they
would be an unequal match for them in battle, they killed their
wives and children and then threw themselves into blazing
fires. Those whom the Romans had made captive before they
had had any opportunity of taking their own lives later did
away with themselves, some by the sword, some by hanging,
and others by starvation. Not one survived, not even one
small boy who, in his love for life, might have been willing
to endure the state of slavery.

15.   IN THE six hundred and thirty-fifth year of the City,
during the consulship of P. Scipio Nasica and L. Calpurnius
Bestia,[51] the Senate, acting with the consent of the Roman
people, declared war on Jugurtha, the king of the Numidians.

But I myself shall touch but briefly on Jugurtha and then
only to mention him in order to follow an orderly arrangement in my narrative. Owing to the excellent work of historians, people are generally sufficiently well informed not
only of his fickle and insufferable character but also of the
exploits which he carried out with a treachery that matched
his great energy.

When Jugurtha, the adopted son of the Numidian king
Micipsa, was made co-heir with the king's natural children,
he first put to death Hiempsal, one of the heirs and then
after defeating Adherbal, the other heir, drove him from
Africa. By offering a bribe of money, he then corrupted the
consul Calpurnius, who had been dispatched against him, and
persuaded the consul to agree to most disgraceful conditions

---

[50] Q. Marcius Rex, 118 B.C.
[51] P. Cornelius Scipio Nasica and L. Capurnius Bestia, 111 B.C.

of peace. Moreover, when Jugurtha came to Rome, he corrupted or tried to corrupt everybody with money, and thus involved all in sedition and dissension. When he was on the point of leaving, he branded Rome with these shameful words, which well describe the City: "O venal city, doomed to quick perdition, if it can only find a buyer!" [52]

The following year Jugurtha overwhelmed A. Postumius [53] in battle at the city of Calama. The Roman general had been placed in command of an army of forty thousand soldiers by his brother, the consul Postumius, [54] and was very eager to seize this city because it was the repository of the royal treasury. Jugurtha, after defeating him, exacted a most humiliating treaty. Then he added to his own kingdom almost all the African territories that were trying to free themselves from the Roman rule. Later, however, he was checked by the integrity and military ability of the consul Metellus, who defeated him in two battles. With his own eyes he now saw his Numidia ravaged and himself powerless to defend it. Forced by Metellus to surrender, Jugurtha gave three hundred hostages and promised that he would turn over to him grain and other supplies. He failed, however, to live up to the terms of the treaty and continued his unwarranted attacks until he was finally overcome by the Roman forces and the astuteness of Marius, [55] who was just as clever as Jugurtha himself. Marius gave an excellent example of this trait when he outwitted the enemy and captured the city of Capsa, which, they say, was founded by the Phoenician Hercules and which now was filled with royal treasure.

Jugurtha finally despaired of his own affairs and resources and made an alliance with Bocchus, the king of the Moors. Greatly strengthened by the cavalry contingents of the latter, he harassed the Marian army by frequent raids. Finally at Cirta, an ancient city and the capital of Masinissa, he encountered the Romans, who were preparing an assault upon

[52] Sallust *Bellum Jugurthinum* 35. 10.   [53] Aulus Postumius.
[54] Sp. Postumius Albinus, 110 B.C. The city is not Calama but Suthul.
[55] C. Marius, 107 B.C. The other consul was L. Cassius Longinus.

that city. He drew up his forces in battle array against a cavalry force numbering sixty thousand. No battle was ever more turbulent or more harrowing to a Roman soldier. A cloud of dust, raised by the galloping and snorting of the horses as they circled about in the attack, veiled the heavens, shut out the daylight, and brought on darkness; so great a shower of missiles poured down upon the Romans that no part of the body was safe. Moreover, the density of the atmosphere prevented them from seeing any distance ahead, while their great numbers, as they crowded together, made maneuvers for defending themselves difficult to execute. The Moorish and Numidian cavalry did not have to exert themselves much to carry out a well-timed javelin attack designed to break up the ranks of their opponents who were occupying a favorable position. They kept on discharging their darts blindly in the confident assurance that the missiles must of necessity strike their mark. Driven into one space, the Roman infantrymen pressed closely against one another.

Night afforded the Romans a temporary relief from their perilous situation, but the next day the same conditions of war and of danger prevailed. It was useless for a soldier to rush against the enemy with drawn sword, for he would be driven back by darts hurled from a distance; the infantrymen could not flee, since the cavalry, which had completely hemmed them in, could swiftly overtake them. When the third day came and there was no help from any source, the dread appearance of death presented itself on all sides. Finally the consul Marius offered a means of escape by undertaking a brave and desperate move. His entire army in battle formation rushed forth simultaneously from valley and open plain, and offered battle everywhere at the same time. The enemy, again circling around them, not only cut to pieces the flanks of the line but also kept overwhelming the center with darts that reached their mark though hurled from a distance; and what is more, the heat of the sun, unbearable thirst, and the presence of death all around them exhausted the disorganized Romans and reduced them to a state of complete

despair. At this point a storm of wind and rain was sent from
Heaven against the Africans.   This kind of assistance, which
was well known to the Romans, brought unexpected deliverance. The sudden downpour cooled the thirsty and heated
Romans and gave them drink, but so far as the Numidians
were concerned, it made slippery the shafts of their darts,
which they were accustomed to hurl with their hands without
ammenta.[56] Thus their darts became useless. The shields,
too, which they usually carried and which were made from
stretched and toughened elephant hide, though easy to handle
and offering adequate protection, were of such a nature that
they absorbed rain like a sponge. This added weight rendered them unmanageable and quite useless in affording protection, since they could not be manipulated with ease. When
the Moors and Numidians had thus been unexpectedly
thrown into confusion and rendered helpless, Bocchus and
Jugurtha took flight. Later, however, these same kings threw
ninety thousand soldiers into a final struggle. When the
Romans conquered them, their forces, it is said, were slaughtered almost to the last man. Bocchus despaired of any hope
of further success in war and sued for peace. As the price of
peace he turned over Jugurtha to Sulla who brought him to
Marius. Jugurtha, who had been captured by a ruse, was
now weighed down by chains and driven with his two sons
before the chariot in a triumph. Shortly afterward he was
strangled to death in prison.

In those same days an ominous and sad prodigy was seen.
As L. Helvius, a Roman knight, accompanied by his wife and
daughter, was returning from Rome to Apulia, he was overtaken by a storm. When he saw that his daughter was terrified, he abandoned the carriages and took to horse in order
to reach the nearest shelter more quickly. As soon as his
unmarried daughter began to ride in the center of the caval-
cade, she was knocked senseless by a bolt of lightning. Despite
the fact that all her clothes were stripped from her body

---

[56] *Ammenta,* or *amenta,* were leather thongs tied to the middle of the shaft
to assist in throwing the spear.

without being torn, that the bands at her breast and feet were loosened, and that her necklaces and bracelets were broken, her body remained unharmed except that it lay shamefully exposed with her tongue protruding a little. The horse that she had been riding lay lifeless some distance away. Its loosened trappings, reins, and surcingles were widely scattered.

Shortly thereafter, L. Veturius, a Roman knight, secretly defiled Aemilia, a Vestal Virgin. This same Aemilia also led into temptation and corrupted two other Vestal Virgins, whom she had induced to enter into sexual relations with the comrades of her own betrayer. When a slave disclosed the affair, all suffered punishment.

In these days of the Jugurthine War, the consul L. Cassius,[57] who was in Gaul, pursued the Tigurini as far as the Ocean. When he was on his way back, he was surrounded and slain in an ambush laid by the enemy.[58] Lucius Piso, a man of consular rank and at the same time the legate of the consul Cassius, was also killed. The other legate, C. Publius, in accordance with the terms of a most disgraceful treaty, was handed over to the Tigurini together with hostages and a half share of all their property. This was done in order to save the surviving part of the army, which had fled for refuge to the camp. On returning to Rome, Publius was summoned to trial by the plebeian tribune Caelius on the charge that he had given hostages to the Tigurini. Consequently he had to flee into exile. The proconsul Caepio [59] captured a city of the Gauls, Tolosa by name, and carried away from the Temple of Apollo one hundred thousand pounds of gold and one hundred and ten thousand pounds of silver. He then sent this treasure under guard to Massilia, a city friendly to the Roman people. But the men whom he had commissioned to guard and transport it were secretly slain, as some bear witness, and Caepio is said then to have criminally appropriated all the treasure.

[57] L. Cassius Longinus consul with Marius in 107 B.C.
[58] The battle was perhaps fought to the southeast of Bordeaux.
[59] Q. Servilius Caepio.

On account of his action an investigation, far reaching in scope, was later held at Rome.

16. IN THE six hundred and forty-second year of the City, the consul C. Manlius [60] and the proconsul Q. Caepio were dispatched against the Cimbri, Teutones, Tigurini, and Ambrones, Gallic and German tribes which at that time had formed a conspiracy to destroy the Roman Empire. The Roman leaders divided the provinces between themselves, making the Rhone River the boundary. While they were disputing and contending over their claims with much ill will, they suffered defeat, thereby bringing great disgrace as well as peril to the Roman nation. In this battle,[61] M. Aemilius, who was of consular rank, was captured and killed, and the two sons of the consul were slain. Antias writes that eighty thousand of the Romans and their allies were slaughtered in that disaster and that forty thousand servants and camp followers were killed. Of the entire army it is said that only ten men have survived. These men reported the sad news and thereby increased the distress of the people. Having gained possession of both camps and of a huge amount of booty, the enemy seemed driven by some strange and unusual animus. They completely destroyed everything they had captured; clothing was cut to pieces and strewn about, gold and silver were thrown into the river, the breastplates of the men were hacked to pieces, the trappings of the horses were ruined, the horses themselves were drowned in whirlpools, and men, with nooses fastened around their necks, were hanged from trees. Thus the conqueror realized no booty, while the conquered obtained no mercy. At Rome there was not only very great sorrow, but also the fear that the Cimbri would immediately cross the Alps and destroy Italy.

During those same days Q. Fabius Maximus sent his youthful son away to his country estate and there had him put to

[60] Cn. Mallius Maximus, consul in 105 B.C.

[61] Fought close by the town of Arausio, north of Arles. The battle took place on the sixth of October, 105 B.C.

death by two slaves who were accomplices in this parricide. He at once manumitted these slaves as a reward for their part in the crime. Upon the accusation of Cn. Pompey, he was tried and found guilty.

Marius, now consul for the fourth time, pitched his camp near the confluence of the Isère and Rhone rivers. The Teutones, Cimbri, Tigurini, and Ambrones fought continuously for three days in the neighborhood of the Roman camp, trying by every means to dislodge the Romans from their ramparts and drive them out on level ground. They then resolved to invade Italy in three armies. After the departure of the enemy, Marius also moved his camp and occupied the hill overlooking the river and the plain where the enemy had spread themselves. When his army lacked drinking water, complaints arose on all sides against him; he answered that there was certainly water in plain sight but that it would have to be claimed by the sword. The camp servants, shouting loudly, were the first to rush into the fray; then the army immediately followed. Lines of battle were quickly formed for regular combat.[62] An engagement was fought in which the Romans were victorious. On the fourth day both sides again drew up lines of battle upon the field. The struggle raged on almost equal terms until midday. Under the burning rays of the sun, the flabby bodies of the Gauls melted like snow, and a massacre rather than a battle continued into the night. Two hundred thousand of the Gallic soldiers, according to report, were slain in that battle, eight thousand were captured, and barely three thousand fled. Their general Teutobodus was killed.

Exhibiting a more steadfast spirit than they would have shown if their husbands had been victorious, the wives advised the consul that if their chastity remained inviolate and if they were assigned the duty of serving the Vestal Virgins and the gods, they would not take their own lives. When their petition was refused, they dashed their children upon the rocks

[62] In the neighborhood of Aquae Sextiae (Aix), about eighteen Roman miles north of Massilia. 102 B.C.

and then took their own lives by the sword or by hanging. Such was the fate of the Tigurini and Ambrones.

The Teutones and Cimbri, however, passed over the snows of the Alps with forces intact and swept across the plains of Italy. These hardy peoples became effeminate there under the influence of a milder climate and of an abundance of drink, food, and baths. Catulus and Marius, who was consul for the fifth time, were dispatched against them. Following Hannibal's clever plan of selecting not only the day for battle but also the field, the consuls arranged their battle line under the cover of a mist but later fought the battle in the sun. The first sign of disorder arose on the side of the Gauls, because they realized that the Roman line of battle had already been drawn up ready for action before they came on the field. In the battle, wounded cavalrymen, driven backward upon their own men, threw into confusion the entire force that was advancing to the battlefield in irregular formation. The sun, too, was shining brightly in their faces and at the same time a wind arose. As a result, dust filled their eyes and the brilliant sun dimmed their sight. Under these conditions the casualties suffered were so terrible that only a few survived the disaster, whereas the losses of the Romans were very slight. A hundred and forty thousand, according to report, were slain in that battle,[63] while sixty thousand were captured.

The women provoked a battle that was, if anything, more severe. Surrounded by their wagons drawn up in the form of a camp, they defended themselves from their higher position and held the Romans at bay for a long time. They finally became terrified by a new method employed by the Romans in killing enemies. The Romans scalped the women and left them in an unsightly condition from their shameful wounds. The women now turned the sword, which they had taken up against the enemy, against themselves and against their own children. Some cut each other's throats; others tied cords to the legs of horses and then placing around their own necks these same cords with which they had tied the horses, they

---

[63] Near Vercellae, west of Milan, at a place called Campi Raudii. 101 B.C.

goaded their horses on, and were thus dragged along and choked to death; others hanged themselves with nooses suspended from the wagon poles which had been raised high in the air. One woman indeed was found who first had slipped nooses over the necks of her two sons and then had bound the ropes to her own feet. When she cast herself off to meet her own death by hanging, she carried her sons along with her to destruction.

Among these many wretched forms of death, it is reported that two chieftains rushed upon each other with drawn swords. The kings Lugius and Boiorix fell on the battlefield; Claodicus and Caesorix were captured. In these two battles three hundred and forty thousand Gauls were slain, and one hundred and forty thousand were captured. This does not include the countless number of women who, in a fit of feminine frenzy but with manly strength, put themselves and their little children to death.

An unbelievable crime and one never previously experienced among the Romans was suddenly perpetrated at Rome. It turned the great triumph of Marius and the Roman victory to horror and grief and cast a pall over the entire city. Publicius Malleolus with the assistance of slaves killed his own mother. He was condemned for parricide, sewed up in a sack, and thrown into the sea. Thus the Romans provided a penalty and punished a crime for which even the Athenian Solon had not ventured to prescribe a penalty because he did not imagine such an outrage possible; the Romans, however, realizing that they were descended from Romulus and knowing that even such a deed was possible, enacted a unique punishment for it.

17. IN THE six hundred and forty-fifth year of the City, following the Cimbrian and Teuton War and the fifth consulship of Marius, the constitution of the Roman Empire was judged to be legally in force. In the sixth consulship of this same Marius,[64] the state was so violently shaken that it was

[64] In the year 100 B.C.

almost destroyed through internal conflict. To unravel and to run through the ambiguities of the quarrels and the inextricable causes of seditions seems to me unnecessary as well as tedious. Therefore let it suffice that I have touched briefly upon the fact that Apuleius Saturninus stood forth as the first instigator of the insurrection that broke out. He was a very bitter enemy of Q. Metellus Numidicus, who, it must be granted, was a man of the first rank. When Metellus was elected to the office of censor, Saturninus had him dragged from his home and, when he fled to the Capitol for refuge, had him besieged by an armed mob. After much blood had been shed before the Capitol, Metellus was thrown out of the building because he had incurred the displeasure of the Roman knights. Saturninus and Glaucia, aided by treachery on the part of the consul C. Marius, then slew their rival A. Nunius.[65]

The following year Marius, who was consul for the sixth time, Glaucia, who was praetor, and Saturninus, who was tribune of the plebs, formed a conspiracy. They used every available means to drive Metellus Numidicus into exile. On the day set for the trial, Metellus, though innocent, was condemned to exile by the criminal action of the judges who had been illegally substituted for others and who belonged to the conspirators' faction. In the course of a riot that suddenly broke out, this same Saturninus, fearing that Memmius,[66] a man of shrewdness and of integrity, would be made consul, ordered P. Mettius, one of the followers of Saturninus, to kill him. He did this by crushing Memmius with an unshapely bludgeon as he fled.

The Senate and the Roman people now began to complain loudly about the great evils afflicting the state. The consul Marius, adapting his genius to the occasion, allied himself with the cause of the patriots and calmed the aroused plebeians by addressing then with soothing words. Saturninus, after daring to commit these infamous deeds, held a meeting

---

[65] Aulus Nonius, a candidate for the tribuneship of the plebs in 100 B.C.

[66] C. Memmius, the tribune of the plebs, who had exposed the corruption of the oligarchical party in Rome during the Jugurthine War.

at his own house and there was acclaimed "king" by some and "general" by others. Marius divided the plebeians into maniples and then stationed the other consul [67] and a garrison on the hill, while he himself barricaded the gates. The battle took place in the Forum. Marius drove Saturninus from the Forum to refuge in the Capitol. Marius then cut the pipes which furnished that place with water. Thereupon a savage battle took place at the entrance of the Capitol. Many around Saufeius and Saturninus were slain. Saturninus cried out loudly and called the people to witness that Marius was the cause of all their difficulties. Marius next forced Saturninus, Saufeius, and Labienus to flee for refuge to the Senate house, where some Roman knights broke down the doors and killed them. C. Glaucia was dragged from the home of Claudius and killed. Furius, the tribune of the plebs, decreed that the property of all these men should be confiscated. Cn. Dollabella, the brother of Saturninus, while fleeing with L. Giganius through the Forum Holitorium, was put to death.

When the instigators of this uprising were dead, the people calmed down. Much to the joy of the entire city, Cato and Pompey now proposed a decree that Metellus Numidicus should be asked to return. To prevent this decree from being approved, the factions of the consul Marius and of Furius (the latter was a tribune of the plebs) blocked its passage. Rutilius [69] also, a man of great integrity, so firmly maintained his spirit of good faith and uprightness that, until the day which his accusers had set for the trial, and indeed up to the very moment of the judicial examination, he did not let his hair or beard grow. Nor did he court the favor of his jurors by wearing shabby clothing or by displaying a humble mien. Neither did he flatter his enemies nor did he try to moderate his judges. On the contrary, upon being given permission by the praetor, he delivered a speech that was just as defiant as was his spirit. When charges that were plainly malicious

---

[67] L. Valerius Flaccus.   [68] C. Saufeius, the quaestor in 100 B.C.
[69] P. Rutilius Rufus. He was *legatus* in Asia under Q. Mucius Scaevola in 95 B.C.

were preferred against him, although all good men believed
that in justice he should be acquitted, nevertheless he was found
guilty by the judges who had perjured themselves. He then
emigrated to Smyrna where he lived to an advanced age, devoting himself to literary pursuits.

18. IN THE six hundred and fifty-ninth year of the City and
during the consulship of Sextus Julius Caesar and L. Marcius
Philippus,[70] all Italy was in the throes of the war against
allies. This war was caused by domestic quarrels. For Livius
Drusus, a tribune of the plebs, was unable to appease the
Latins by a decree after they had been deceived in their hope
of gaining liberty and thus he roused them all to arms. Things
came to such a pass that awful prodigies terrified the sad-
dened city. At sunrise a ball of fire, accompanied by a tre-
mendous clap of thunder, shone forth from the northern
region. While the inhabitants of Arretium [71] were breaking
bread at banquets, blood flowed from the center of the loaves
as if from bodily wounds. Moreover, a shower of stones,
intermingled with pieces of brick, lashed the earth far and
wide for seven continuous days. Among the Samnites, a flame
broke forth from a vast fissure in the ground and seemed to
shoot upwards into the sky. Furthermore, several Romans on a
journey saw a golden globe falling headlong from the sky to
the earth; when it had become large in appearance, they saw it
again carried aloft from the earth toward the rising sun,
where its huge bulk hid the sun itself from view. Drusus, who
was worried by these ill-boding portents, was killed by an
unidentified assassin in his own house.

The Picentes, Vestini, Marsi, Paeligni, Marrucini, Samnites,
and Lucani, who had long since been planning a secret rebellion, put to death at Asculum [72] the praetor C. Servius, who
had been sent to them as an ambassador. The inhabitants
immediately closed the city, proclaimed a slaughter, and cut
the throats of all Roman citizens. Notorious prodigies directly

[70] Consuls in 91 B.C.   [71] A large city in Etruria.
[72] A city situated in the interior of Apulia.

preceded this frightful massacre. Animals of all kinds, which
were accustomed to accept caresses from the hands of men
and to live among men, left their stables and pastures; even
the dogs, whose nature is such that they must live among men,
wandered about, howling mournfully and loping in the manner
of wolves.

The Samnites placed Papius Mutilus in command of their
forces, and the Marsi for their part chose as leader the
arch-pirate Agamemnon. The praetor Cn. Pompey, under
orders from the Senate, waged war with the Picentes and
was defeated. Julius Caesar fled after his defeat and the
slaughter of his army in a battle with the Samnites. The
consul Rutilius [73] chose his kinsman Marius as his lieutenant.
Inasmuch as Marius was constantly suggesting in private that
a delay would prove beneficial to the conduct of the war and
that the young recruits ought to be drilled in camp for a
short time, Rutilius thought that the action of Marius was
prompted by some hidden motive. He therefore made light
of his advice and carelessly brought himself and an entire
column of his army into an ambuscade set by the Marsi.
There the consul himself and many nobles were killed and
eight thousand Roman soldiers were slaughtered. The Tolenus
River [74] carried the arms and bodies of the dead within sight
of the legate Marius, and thus furnished proof of the disaster.
After quickly gathering together troops, Marius took the
victors by surprise and slew eight thousand of these Marsi.
Caepio was led into an ambush by the Vestini and Marsi;
he and his army were cut to pieces. But after L. Julius
Caesar had fled following his defeat at Aesernia,[75] he collected
troops from all quarters and fought against the Samnites and
Lucani, slaying many thousands of the enemy. When he had
been saluted by the army as imperator, he sent messengers to
Rome to announce his victory. With this good fortune smiling
upon them, the senators took off their sagas, that is, the garment of mourning which they had put on at the beginning of

[73] P. Rutilius Lupus, 90 B.C.   [74] A river in central Italy.
[75] A city of Samnium, situated in the valley of the Vulturnus.

the Social War,[76] and resumed the graceful toga of old. Next
Marius killed six thousand of the Marsi and disarmed seven
thousand. Sulla [77] was sent with twenty-four cohorts to Aesernia, where Roman citizens and soldiers were being hard
pressed by a very close siege. He saved the city and its allies
after he had fought a great battle and inflicted a terrific
slaughter upon the enemy. As a result of the victory in which
Cn. Pompey routed the Picentes in a severe battle, the Senate
now assumed the broad purple stripes on the tunic and other
marks of dignity. Previously the Senate had resumed their
togas only when the victory of Caesar had given them a
respite. The praetor Porcius Cato conquered the Etruscans
and the lieutenant Plotius conquered the Umbrians. Both
victories entailed most distressing hardships and much
bloodshed.

During the consulship of Cn. Pompey and L. Porcius Cato,[78]
Pompey besieged the city of Asculum [79] for a long time. Had
he not first overcome and severely defeated the people who
had rushed out on an open field, he would not have captured
it. Eighteen thousand of the Marsi and their general Fraucus
were slain in this battle and three thousand captured. Four
thousand Italians, fleeing from the slaughter, chanced to
ascend the summit of a mountain with their column in close
formation. Overwhelmed and weakened by the snows there,
they suffered a miserable death from exposure. They had
taken a stand just as if they had been stricken with fear of
the enemy, some reclining on stumps or rocks, others leaning
on their weapons. The eyes of all were open wide and their
teeth exposed. All appeared alive and their continuous im-
mobility, a state which a living being could in no wise maintain
for long, was the only indication of death apparent to an ob-
server at a distance. On the same day the Romans encountered
and defeated the Picentes. Their leader Vidacilius gathered

[76] This war against allies is sometimes called the Marsic War.
[77] L. Cornelius Sulla Felix.
[78] Cn. Pompeius Strabo and L. Porcius Cato. 89 B.C.
[79] A city of Picenum, not to be confused with Asculum in Apulia where
Pyrrhus and the Romans fought a celebrated battle in 269 B.C.

together his chiefs and, after a magnificent feast accompanied by heavy drinking, challenged all to follow his example. He then drank a poisonous draught and died. All praised his action, but not one followed it.

In the six hundred and sixty-first year of the City, a Roman army went to besiege the Pompeys. The lieutenant of L. Sulla, Postumius Albinus, a man of consular rank, at that time so aroused the hatred of all the soldiers against him by his insufferable arrogance that they stoned him to death. The consul Sulla gave it as his opinion that civil bloodshed could be atoned for only by shedding the blood of the enemy. Fully aware of the truth of this opinion, the army began battle, each soldier feeling that he must die unless he was victorious. Eighteen thousand Samnites were slain in that battle. Sulla also pursued and killed L. Cluentius, an Italian leader, and a great number of his people. The consul Porcius Cato, accompanied by the Marian forces, fought a number of hard battles. Indeed, he boasted that even C. Marius had not accomplished greater deeds. On account of this, when he was waging war against the Marsi at Lake Facinus, the son of C. Marius, as if an unknown champion, struck him down in the tumult of battle. The lieutenant C. Gabinius was killed while he was storming the enemy's camp. The attack of Sulpicius, Pompey's legate, overwhelmed and destroyed the Marrucini and the Vestini. This same Sulpicius killed the Italian generals Popaedius and Obsidius in a frightful battle at the Teanus River. Pompey entered Asculum and had the prefects, centurions, and all the leading men beaten with rods and beheaded. He sold the slaves and all the booty at auction and ordered the remaining people to depart, free indeed, but stripped and destitute. Though the Senate expected that the proceeds of the booty would somewhat increase the public income, Pompey did not contribute anything from it to the needy treasury.

The treasury at that time was thoroughly depleted and funds for the payment of grain were lacking. The public properties within the circuit of the Capitol, the ancient possessions

of the pontifices, augurs, decemvirs, and flamines, were therefore sold under the pressure of necessity. These brought
enough money to relieve the deficit for the time being. Indeed
all the wealth that had been seized from conquered cities and
from lands stripped bare was heaped up in the lap of Rome
at the time when the City herself, compelled by the urgency of
her shameful need, was putting up at auction her own most
valuable properties. Therefore let Rome now reflect upon her
own past. Like an insatiable stomach that consumes everything and yet remains always hungry, the City herself, more
wretched than all other cities that she was making wretched,
left nothing untouched and yet had nothing; and she was forced
by the pinch of hunger at home to continue in that state of
unrest which war engenders.

In those same days, King Sothimus, accompanied by a large
force of Thracian auxiliaries, invaded Greece and ravaged
all the territory of Macedonia. The praetor C. Sentius finally
defeated him and forced him to return to his own kingdom.

19.   IN THE six hundred and sixty-second year of the City,
before the Social War had come to an end, the First Civil
War broke out at Rome. In that same year the Mithridatic
War also began. This war, although less dishonorable, was
certainly no less serious. Indeed we have varying accounts of
its length. Some say that it was waged for thirty years, others
say forty years, depending upon whether its beginning is dated
from the time mentioned above or from the time when it
blazed forth in full strength. But however complicated the
history of those times on account of the great numbers of
evils that flared up, nevertheless I will attempt to list them,
albeit briefly, one by one.

When the consul Sulla and his army were about to leave
for Asia to war against Mithridates but were still in Campania engaged in various matters connected with the prosecution of the Social War, Marius endeavored to obtain the
consulship for the seventh time and also the command of the
war against Mithridates. Upon learning of this, Sulla, who

was a very impatient youth, was seized by an uncontrollable fit of anger. With four legions he at once encamped before the City and there killed Gratidius, the legate of Marius—the first victim, so to speak, of the Civil War. Then with his army he quickly broke into the City and demanded firebrands in order that he might set it on fire. Since all the people had hidden themselves in terror, he marched rapidly along the Sacred Way and came to the Forum. Marius tried first to arouse the nobility, then to inflame the people, and finally to arm the equestrian order against Sulla. But when he had failed, he tried as a last resort to tempt the slaves to take up arms by offering them liberty and booty. When he saw that his attempt to resist was useless, he finally withdrew to the Capitol, where the Sullan cohorts charged upon him. After suffering heavy casualties he took flight. At this time Sulpicius, a colleague of Marius, was betrayed by one of his own slaves and killed. Although the consuls agreed that this slave deserved freedom in return for his services in giving information about the enemy, nevertheless they decreed that he should be hurled from the Tarpeian Rock because he had betrayed his master.

As a result of the persistence of his pursuers, Marius was finally surrounded during his flight. He hid himself in the swamps of Minturnae,[80] where he had the bad luck and the humiliation to be dragged out entirely covered with mud. When he had been brought to Minturnae (an unsightly spectacle) he was thrust into prison. His stern expression terrified the man sent to execute him. Later he escaped from his fetters and fled to Africa. Accompanied by his son, whom he forcibly removed from Utica where the latter was being held under guard, he returned without delay to Rome and there formed a criminal alliance with the consul Cinna.[81] The conspirators then divided the army into four parts for the

[80] A city of Latium situated on the right bank of the Liris about three miles from the sea.

[81] L. Cornelius Cinna, 87 B.C. In the following year he was consul with Marius.

purpose of overthrowing the whole Republic. Three legions were given to Marius; Cn. Carbo was placed in command of a second part of the forces; and Sertorius received a third. The latter was that well-known Sertorius who had already been an instigator of and a participant in the Civil War and who later, after the close of this war, stirred up in Spain another war which lasted many years and which wrought terrible losses upon the Romans. The remaining part of the army followed Cinna. On the other hand, Cn. Pompey, who with his army had been summoned by the Senate to bring aid to the Republic and who for a long time had kept himself aloof from any participation in the revolutionary movement, was slighted by Marius and Cinna. He therefore joined Octavius and promptly engaged in battle with Sertorius. Night ended the unfortunate conflict in which six hundred soldiers on each side were slain.

On the following day when the bodies, which were all piled together, were being identified for burial, a Pompeian soldier recognized the body of his brother whom he had killed with his own hand; for in the battle their helmets had prevented them from recognizing each other's faces, and they were so enraged that they failed to look closely at each other. Although the guilt is somewhat lessened by ignorance, since he apparently did not know that the soldier was his brother, there is no doubt that he did know that his opponent was a citizen. Therefore the victor, more unhappy than the victim, when he recognized the body of his brother and realized that he was guilty of fratricide, cursed civil wars and then on that very spot pierced his own breast with his sword. While his life blood was pouring forth and the tears were flowing from his eyes, he flung himself down over his brother's corpse.

And what help did it give toward putting an end to this cruel enterprise that at the very beginning of the civil wars a disgraceful report had spread abroad to the effect that men had fought against each other, ignorant, to be sure, that they were brothers but entirely aware of the fact that they were citizens; that one among them, victorious in his crime, had endeavored to obtain the armor belonging to his slain brother and that, responsible for this monstrous outrage, he had atoned for the fratricide that he had committed by taking his life with his own sword and by his own hand? Did so sad an example have any influence upon the animosities of the combatants whose nerves were on edge? Did the fear resulting from this mistake restrain anyone from the possibility of committing a like crime? Did piety and a reverence for nature insist on standards that are universally held, even among animals? [82] Did this example of murder and suicide make anyone afraid that the same experience might happen to him, and did it therefore restrain the conscience-stricken from similar enterprise? Not at all! Over the ensuing period of almost forty years civil wars were so continuous that people came to believe that the measure of glory depended directly upon the gravity of the crime. For after such an example in a war all would have fled from the risk of committing parricide had it not been for the fact that they welcomed these very parricides.

As I have said, Marius then forced his way into the colony of Ostia [83] and there committed all kinds of lust, avarice, and cruelty. Pompey was killed by a bolt of lightning and his men were attacked by a pestilence which destroyed almost the entire army. Eleven thousand from Pompey's camp died, while six thousand from the division of the consul Octavius were driven mad. As if he were an enemy, Marius broke into the cities of Antium and Aricia [84] and there killed everybody except the traitors; his soldiers he allowed to plunder the property. The consul Cinna with his legions and Marius with his fugitives later entered Rome and killed all the noblest men of the Senate and many men of consular rank.

What a small part of the whole story are these unhappy events that I have described! [85] Would it have been possible

---

[82] There is a lacuna in the text at this point.
[83] A city of Latium, situated at the mouth of the Tiber.
[84] Antium in Latium on the seacoast about thirty-two miles from Rome; Aricia is situated about sixteen miles from Rome at the foot of Mount Alba.
[85] There is a lacuna in the text.

for me to do justice in a word to this massacre of good citizens characterized as it was by the death of so many men, by its long duration, and by such a variety of cruelty? Regardless of whether this account is to be set before experienced or inexperienced persons, I have certainly shown a truly great spirit of fairness by omitting facts which might have strengthened my point in preference to introducing too much horror into my description. Indeed, I am telling things about my own native land, its citizens, and my own ancestors, who, harassed by these evils, did so much that must needs be abhorred that at the mere recital of their deeds our descendants may well shudder. Our ancestors were obviously unwilling that these events should be too greatly exaggerated; they were guided either by the moderation that comes from sufficient knowledge, if they knew the facts, or by the consideration that comes from a sense of pity and reverence, if they did not know them.

Marius now gathered together the heads of the slain citizens for purposes of display and ornamentation. These he had previously exhibited in the banquet halls, exposed before the Capitoline temples, and collected at the Rostra.[86] At this time he had reached his own seventh consulship and the third with Cinna as his colleague. But at the very beginning of the exercise of his consular authority, when he was at a ripe old age, he was carried off by death. Cinna, who had murdered good citizens, now completed his regime of slaughter by murdering bad citizens; for when the band of fugitives recruited by Marius continued its policy of plunder and greed and failed to hand over any part of the booty to the consuls who had authorized the procedure, he summoned the band to the Forum under the pretext of paying its members. He then surrounded them with soldiers and, although they were unarmed, slaughtered them. Eight thousand of the fugitives were slain on that day in the Forum of the City. This same Cinna, consul for the fourth time, met his death at the hands of his own soldiers.

[86] There is a play on words in Latin: *capita inlata conviviis, oblata Capitoliis, collata Rostris.*

20.   IN THE meantime, the rest of the senators, who had fled and had thus escaped the political power of Cinna, the cruelty of Marius, the insanity of Fimbria,[87] and the audacity of Sertorius, crossed over to Greece. There by their entreaties they forced Sulla to bring help to his native land, now in danger and on the verge of utter ruin. Not long after this Sulla landed on the shores of Campania and overcame the consul Norbanus [88] in battle. Sulla's men slew seven thousand other Romans and captured six thousand; Sulla's losses amounted to one hundred and twenty-four killed. Fabius Hadrianus, however, who had the powers of a propraetor, strove with the aid of an army of slaves to obtain the rule of Africa but met his death at Utica. The masters of these slaves burned him and his entire household on a pyre of fagots. At the instigation of the consul Marius, the praetor Damasippus cruelly put to death Q. Scaevola, C. Carbo, L. Domitius, and P. Antistius, who had been summoned to the Curia upon the pretext that they were to attend a conference. The executioners dragged away their dead bodies by means of hooks and threw them into the Tiber.

At the same time, Sulla's generals waged a great many battles against the Marian party with most unfortunate good fortune.[89] Q. Metellus destroyed the forces of Carrinas and captured his camp, while Pompey inflicted heavy losses upon Carbo's cavalry. The greatest battle of the war was fought between Sulla and the young son of Marius at Sacriportus,[90] where, according to Claudius, the army of Marius lost twenty-five thousand troops. Pompey also forced Carbo to abandon his camp, and attacking him as he fled, gradually divested him of most of his troops, either slaughtering them or compelling them to surrender. Metellus crushed an army commanded by Norbanus in an encounter in which nine thousand of the Marian faction were killed. When Lucullus was being

[87] C. Flavius Fimbria, the partisan of Marius and Cinna. He raged through the province of Asia and wrought terrible destruction.

[88] C. Norbanus Bulbus, 83 B.C.

[89] *Infelicissima felicitate.*

[90] A place in Latium situated between Signia and Praeneste. 82 B.C.

besieged by Quintius, he sallied forth and by a sudden attack destroyed the besieging army. More than ten thousand, according to report, were slain. Accompanied by the Samnite general Campanius and by the remaining forces of Carrinas, Sulla, at the ninth hour of the day, assembled the standards before the very city of Rome and the Colline Gate. There he finally won the victory after a very severe battle in which eighty thousand men, according to report, were routed while twelve thousand surrendered. The victorious citizens, in a spirit of rage that knew no bounds, completed the destruction of the remaining force that now had turned to flight.

21. As soon as the conquering Sulla had entered the City, he put to death, contrary to divine law and his given pledge, the three thousand men who had surrendered through envoys, and who, unarmed, felt perfectly safe. Also, a great many other people were slain, who, it is needless to mention, were not only innocent, but, what is more, were members of Sulla's own party; it is said that their number exceeded nine thousand. Uncontrolled massacres raged throughout the city. Assassins roamed everywhere, some driven by hatred and others lured by the promise of booty. When all the citizens were loudly and openly bewailing the fate that each one individually feared, Q. Catulus then said publicly to Sulla: "If we kill armed men in time of war and unarmed men in time of peace, with whose help shall we finally conquer?"

In these days, at the instance of L. Fursidius, centurion of the first maniple, Sulla became the first man to introduce the infamous proscription list. The first list contained eighty names, among which were the four consuls, Carbo, Marius, Norbanus, and Scipio. Among the proscribed Sertorius was at that time especially to be feared. Another list of five hundred names was also posted. When Lollius was reading it, entirely unconscious of having done anything amiss and so feeling absolutely safe, he suddenly discovered his own name. While he was stealing away from the Forum in terror and with his head covered, he was put to death. Not even the

publication of these lists restored confidence and put an end
to evils. For the assassins continued to slaughter some whom
they had proscribed and proscribed others after they had
slaughtered them. The victims died in various ways. In killing
citizens, the assassins, indeed, failed to observe the law that
applies even in the case of enemies—that the conquered should
simply be deprived of their lives. For Sulla gave orders that
M. Marius [91] should be dragged out of the shed where the goats
were kept. He was then put into chains and led across the
Tiber to the tomb of the Lutatii, where, after his eyes had
been torn out and his limbs broken and hacked into small
pieces, he was finally killed. Following his death, the senator
P. Laetorius and the triumvir Venuleius were executed. The
head of M. Marius was sent to Praeneste, where C. Marius
was being besieged by Lucretius. When C. Marius saw the
head, he became utterly despondent and in order to avoid
falling into the hands of enemies, tried to take his own life
in a double suicide with Telesinus. [92] He drove his weapon
so violently into the body of Telesinus who was rushing at
him, that the wounded Telesinus was powerless to inflict a
mortal wound upon him. Telesinus died, but Marius himself
was only slightly wounded. He therefore offered his neck to
his slave.

Sulla also had the praetor Carrinas murdered. He then set
out for Praeneste and there gave orders that the leaders of
the Marian army, that is, legates, quaestors, prefects, and
tribunes, should all be killed. Carbo, who was attempting to
flee from the island of Cossura [93] to Egypt, was brought back
to Sicily by Pompey and put to death together with many of
his companions. Sulla was made dictator so that his inordinate
desire for power and cruelty might be both armed and
cloaked by the reverence due to an honorable and distinguished title.

After crossing to Africa, Pompey killed eighteen thousand
men after they had made a sortie near Utica. In this battle

---

[91] A relative of the great C. Marius.   [92] The brother of the Samnite general.
[93] A small island in the Mediterranian halfway between Sicily and the coast
of Africa.

the Marian leader Domitius was slain while fighting in the vanguard. This same Pompey also pursued Hiarbas, the king of Numidia, and forced Bogudes, the son of Bocchus, who was king of the Moors, to deprive Hiarbas of all his troops. Pompey put Hiarbas to death as soon as he had captured the town of Bulla to which the latter had returned.

22. WHEN P. Servilius and Appius Claudius had been elected consuls,[94] Sulla finally became a private citizen. This settlement concluded two most destructive wars—the Italian Social War and the Sullan Civil War. These wars, which lasted ten years, took a toll of more than one hundred and fifty thousand Romans. The census taken in the different ages reveals the fact that in this Civil War Rome lost as many of her best citizens and soldiers as she formerly possessed when she was surveying her resources with a view to combating Alexander the Great. The census also shows that twenty-four men of consular rank, six of praetorian rank, sixty with the rank of aediles, and almost two hundred senators were destroyed. This does not include innumerable peoples over all Italy who were slaughtered without any consideration. Therefore let anyone deny, if he can, that Rome's victory did not entail as great a loss as the one Italy suffered when she lost these peoples.

For shame! Is there need at this point for a dubious comparison of the two periods? Yes, they say, there most certainly is; for with what can civil wars be so aptly compared as with civil wars? Or perhaps someone will say that indeed in these present times civil wars have not existed? To this we answer, we might with more justice call them wars against allies, but it suits our purpose better if we allow them to be called civil wars. Now if all these wars can be proven similar in respect to cause, name, and aims, then in these recent wars the reverence for the Christian religion can make greater claims for itself in so far as the power of the victor has taken less cruel

[94] P. Servilius Vatia and Ap. Claudius Pulcher, 79 B.C.

vengeance. Now wicked tyrants, set up by Britannic and Gallic populations, have wantonly attacked the commonwealth, usurping royal power, and have torn apart the body of the Roman Empire; and on that account they have either invited wars from without that were in themselves unjust or else have stirred up just wars against themselves. What else can these conflicts, which were very much like foreign wars and not at all like civil strife, be rightly called except wars against allies? Indeed the Romans themselves did not dignify the struggles against Sertorius, Perperna, Crixus, and Spartacus, by styling them civil wars. Consequently in this case, whether it be called properly defection or treason of allies, less hatred would exist if it should happen that either a severe battle or a bloody victory should take place. Nevertheless, in our own days everything that we do is more apt to be necessary than a source of shame, and so cause, battle, and victory derive from efforts either to wipe out the insolence of tyrants, to restrain the defection of allies, or to set an example of deserved vengeance. Who, therefore, can doubt that the wars kindled today (I mean, those civil disturbances which are repressed rather than actually waged) are waged in a much milder and more merciful manner? For who now-a-days ever heard of a single civil war that has caused a commotion lasting ten years, or of a single war in which one hundred and fifty thousand men were killed, of enemies slain by enemies, let alone of citizens killed by citizens? Who would believe that this great number of distinguished and famous men, to mention whom individually would be a long task, were slaughtered in times of peace? Lastly, who today would fear, who could read, who could comprehend those monstrous lists of the proscribed? Is it not rather obvious to everyone that all men have been reconciled by one peace and made secure by the same safety, and that conquered and conquerors alike exulted in common gladness, while even in the great provinces, in the cities, and among the peoples of the entire Roman Empire only a few have ever existed whom a just vengeance condemned though the victor willed it otherwise? And not to increase the force

of my words by more words, I may safely say that the number
of the common soldiers wiped out in the present war was only
as large as the number of nobles slain at that time amid peace.

On the death of Sulla, Lepidus, a supporter of the Marian
party, rose up against Catulus, the Sullan leader, and fanned
the coals of civil war into flame. Two battles were then
fought. Many of the Romans, now exhausted by their very
lack of numbers and up to now utterly distracted by the fury
of that struggle, were slain. The city of the Albans,[95] besieged
and suffering terribly from hunger, was saved by the surrender
of its wretched survivors. Scipio, the son of Lepidus, was
captured there and put to death. Brutus, while fleeing to
Cisalpine Gaul with Pompey in pursuit, was killed at Rhegium.
Thus this civil war, like a fire in straw, subsided with the same
speed with which it had blazed forth, as much because of the
clemency shown by Catulus himself as because of the disgust
aroused by the cruelty of the Sullan faction.

23.   IN THE six hundred and seventy-third year of the City,
the clamors of war were resounding on all sides. One of these
wars was in Spain, another in Pamphylia, a third in Macedonia, and a fourth in Dalmatia. At this time the Roman state,
as if fever-ridden, was in a weakened and exhausted condition
as the result of internal disasters. Yet Rome was forced to
repel with arms the strongest peoples of the West and North.
For Sertorius, a man who excelled in both trickery and
audacity and a member of the Marian faction, fled before
Sulla. He escaped from Africa to the Spains, where he roused
the most warlike tribes to arms. Against Sertorius, as I shall
explain briefly, the Romans dispatched two generals, Metellus
and Domitius. Hirtuleius, a general of Sertorius, overcame
Domitius and his army. Manlius, the proconsul of Gaul, accompanied by three legions and one thousand five hundred
cavalry, crossed to Spain where he engaged in an unequal
battle with Hirtuleius. Deprived of his camp and troops by
the latter, Manlius, almost alone, fled for refuge to the town

[95] The inhabitants of Alba Longa.

of Ilerda. Exhausted by many battles, Metellus wandered through out-of-the-way places and wearied the enemy by his policy of delay until he was able to join the camp of his ally Pompey. After concentrating an army at Pallantia, Pompey attempted in vain to defend the city of Lauron,[96] which Sertorius was then attacking. He brought the remaining body of the Lauronians, who had survived the slaughter to Lusitania as miserable captives. He boasted that he had conquered Pompey, the famous general of the Romans, whom Rome had dispatched, full of great confidence, to this war, not in the capacity of a consul, but in the capacity of consuls. Galba writes that Pompey had thirty thousand infantry at that time and a thousand cavalry, but also mentions the fact that Sertorius had sixty thousand infantry and eight thousand cavalry.

Later, however, Hirtuleius engaged in battle with Metellus near the city of Italica Baetica [97] and lost twenty thousand soldiers. After his defeat he fled with a few followers to Lusitania. Pompey captured Belgida, a celebrated city of Celtiberia. Sertorius then met Pompey in battle and killed ten thousand of his soldiers. When Pompey was conquering on the opposite wing, Sertorius himself suffered losses in almost exact proportion to the former's gains. Moreover, these two generals fought many other battles. Memmius, the quaestor of Pompey and the husband of his sister, was slain, the brothers of Hirtuleius were killed, and Perperna, who had joined Sertorius, was crushed. Finally, two years after the beginning of the war, Sertorius himself was killed by these two generals, and Viriathus was put to death by the treachery of his own men. This brought the war to an end and gave the Romans a victory without glory. Later, however, a part of the army of Sertorius followed Perperna. Pompey, however, defeated him and slaughtered his whole army. He at once received the voluntary surrender of all the cities with the exception of Uxama[98] and Calagurris[99] which continued their resistance.

[96] A town of Hispania Tarraconensis near Sucro, and not far from the sea.
[97] A city six miles from Hispalis (Seville).   [98] Fifty miles north of Numantia.
[99] Also in the same province; it stood on the right bank of the Iberus.

Of these cities, Pompey overthrew Uxama, while Afranius
destroyed Calagurris with a final slaughter and burning, after
the city had been worn down by a continuous siege and compelled by its pitiable hunger to eat unmentionable food.[100] The
assassins of Sertorius did not even think of asking for a
reward from the Romans, remembering as they did that a
similar reward had previously been denied to the assassins of
Viriathus.

Although these assassins had brought about security for
the Romans without earning any reward for themselves at
the time, yet Spain, ever steadfast in faith and strength,
though she has given the best and unconquered rulers to the
state, never sent forth a single tyrant from the beginning of
her existence to the present day. She never sent away alive
and still powerful any person who attacked her from without.

In the meantime, Claudius [101] was assigned by lot to the
Macedonian War. At that time the various tribes, which
were hedged in by the Rhodopaean Mountains, were most
cruelly devastating Macedonia. Among other brutalities,
dreadful to speak of and to hear, which these tribes inflicted
upon captives, I may mention this. When they needed a cup,
they were wont to seize and use greedily and without any
feeling of repulsion, in place of real cups, human skulls, still
dripping with blood and covered with hair, whose inner cavi-
ties were bedaubed with brain matter badly scooped out. The
bloodiest and most inhuman of these hordes were the Scor-
disci. These tribes then, as I have said, Claudius tried to
drive from the boundaries of Macedonia and in so doing
brought upon himself many misfortunes. On this account he
became ill in mind and weighed down by worries. He finally
fell a victim to disease and died.

His successor Scribonius,[102] not wishing to test again the
power of the tribes whose valor he had tried in an earlier war,
turned his arms against Dardania [103] and captured it. The

---

[100] They slaughtered the women and children, and later ate their flesh.
[101] Ap. Claudius Pulcher, consul in 79 B.C.   [102] C. Scribonius Curio.
[103] In upper Moesia.

ex-consul Publius Servilius, however, who was eager to bring
Cilicia and Pamphylia under his control, attacked and almost
destroyed these lands. He also captured Lycia and its cities,
which had been besieged and hard pressed. In addition, after
wandering about Mount Olympus,[104] he overthrew Phaselis [105]
and demolished Corycus; [106] and also, after combing those
slopes of the Taurian Range which incline toward Cilicia,
he subjugated the Isaurians, whose power had been broken
in battle. He was the first Roman to lead an army over the
Taurus and to make it the terminus of a march. Three years
after the beginning of the war, he assumed the name of
Isauricus. The proconsul Cosconius was awarded Illyricum.
Two years after he had crushed and subdued Dalmatia, he
finally stormed and captured Salonae,[107] a most flourishing
city.

24. IN THE six hundred and seventy-ninth year of the City
and during the consulship of Lucullus and Cassius,[108] seventy-
four gladiators escaped from the training school of Cnaeus
Lentulus at Capua. Under the leadership of Crixus and
Oenomaus, who were Gauls, and of Spartacus, a Thracian,
the fugitives occupied Mount Vesuvius. From there they
later sallied forth and captured the camp of the praetor
Clodius, who had previously surrounded and besieged them.
After forcing Clodius to flee, the fugitives concentrated their
entire attention on plundering. Marching by way of Consentia
and Metapontum,[109] they collected huge forces in a short
time. Crixus had an army of ten thousand according to report,
and Spartacus had three times that number. Oenomaus had
previously been killed in an earlier battle.

While the fugitives were throwing everything into confusion by massacres, conflagrations, thefts, and attacks upon

[104] A mountain range in Mysia.
[105] A maritime town of Lycia on the Pamphylian Gulf.
[106] On the coast of Lycia.   [107] A town and harbor of Dalmatia.
[108] M. Terentius Varo Lucullus and C. Cassius Varus, 73 B.C.
[109] Consentia, an inland city of Bruttium; Metapontum was situated twenty-
four miles from Tarentum.

women, they gave a gladiatorial exhibition at the funeral of a captured woman who had taken her own life in grief over her outraged honor. They formed a band of gladiators out of the four hundred captives. Indeed, those who formerly had been participants in the spectacle were now to be the spectators, but as the trainers of gladiators rather than as the commanders of troops. The consuls Gellius and Lentulus were dispatched with an army against these fugitives. Gellius overcame Crixus in battle, though the latter fought with great bravery; Lentulus, however, was defeated and put to flight by Spartacus. Later the consuls joined forces, but to no avail, and after suffering a severe defeat both took to flight. Then this same Spartacus killed the proconsul C. Cassius after defeating him in battle.

The City now became almost as terrified as she had been when Hannibal was raging about her gates. The Senate at once dispatched Crassus with the legions of the consuls and with fresh reinforcements. Crassus quickly engaged the fugitives in battle, slew six thousand of them, but captured only nine hundred. Before advancing against Spartacus in person, who was laying out his camp at the head of the Silarus River,[110] Crassus defeated the Gallic and German auxiliaries of Spartacus and slaughtered thirty thousand of them together with their leaders. Finally he encountered Spartacus. After drawing up his battle line, he killed most of the forces of the fugitives as well as Spartacus himself. Sixty thousand, according to report, were slain and six thousand captured, while three thousand Roman citizens were recovered. The remaining gladiators, who had escaped from this battle and were wandering at large, were gradually killed off by many generals who constantly pursued them.

But I myself repeat again and again: do the times really need at this point to be made the subject of any comparison? Who, I ask, does not shudder to hear, I do not say of such wars, but of such titles of wars—foreign, servile, wars

---

[110] A river forming the boundary between Campania and Lucania, and flowing into the gulf of Posidonia.

with allies, civil, and fugitive wars? Moreover, these wars do
not follow one another like the stormy waves of the sea, however great their force may be, but these waves of strife, stirred
up by various causes, pretexts, forms, and evils arising on all
sides and heaped together into a mass, dash upon one another.
I now take up where I left off and cease my discussion of that
notorious Slave War.

The thunders of the Jugurthine War from Africa had not yet
been stilled when from the northwest the lightning bolts of the
Cimbrian War were hurled. In addition to the vast and horrible torrents of blood raining down from those Cimbrian
clouds, Italy in her misery was now sending forth the clouds of
the Social War destined to merge into a great storm of evils.
Furthermore, after the endless and repeated storms of the
Italian War, one could not travel in safety throughout Italy.
All the inhabitants except the people of hostile cities, most
dangerous whirlpools I might call them, were reeling about
as a result of an insecure and hazardous peace. Rome was at
that time in the throes of giving birth to the Marian and
Cinnan conflagration, while another, the Mithridatic, was
threatening from a different direction, the east and north.
This Mithridatic War started, to be sure, from troubles of
an earlier period, but flared up again in later times. The
funeral pyre of the Sullan disaster was set ablaze by the
Marian torch; from that pyre of the Sullan and Civil War,
which was so destructive, flames were scattered throughout
most of the parts of the earth and many conflagrations spread
from this one blaze. Lepidus and Scipio in Italy, Brutus in
Gaul, Domitius, the son-in-law of Cinna, in Africa, Carbo
in Cossura and Sicily, Perperna in Liguria, and later Sertorius in
Spain—he was the most dangerous of them all in that same
Spain—stirred up civil wars, or whatever name these wars
should be called, causing many other wars to arise, all from
that one war. Apart from those three vast wars which at
that time were called "foreign", that is, the Pamphylian, the
Macedonian, and the Dalmatian, there was also that great
Mithridatic War, which, though by far the longest, the most

dangerous, and most formidable of all, long kept its true character concealed. After this, but before the end of the Sertorian War in Spain and while Sertorius was still living, that war against the fugitive slaves and, in order to express myself more accurately, that war against the gladiators, sent forth its horrors that were not to be seen only by a few but were to be feared everywhere. Although it was called a war against fugitives, one cannot judge its importance by the name; in that war frequently one consul and occasionally both consuls who had joined forces in vain, were defeated and a great number of nobles slain, but so far as the fugitives themselves were concerned, they lost more than one hundred thousand. Hence we must bear in mind that Italy has reason to find consolation when she compares the sufferings incurred by the present foreign war with the recollection of past wars begun by herself and directed against herself and of wars that tore to pieces her very being in a manner incomparably more cruel.

Wherefore I shall bring to an end this fifth book of mine, so that the civil wars—always interrelated with foreign wars—both those which have been mentioned and those which are to follow, although closely connected by the chain of circumstances and by related evils, may be separated at least by the end of the book.

THE SIXTH BOOK

1. ALL men, whatever their convictions, mode of life, or country, are actuated by a quite natural disposition to follow the dictates of good sense, so that, even if their actions at times do not seem to indicate that the reasoning power of the mind was preferred to the gratification of the flesh, their judgment tells them that it ought to have been. The mind, enlightened by the guidance of reason, rises in the midst of virtues to which it is inclined by an innate predilection, however much it is abased by vices, and beholds the knowledge of God which towers like a citadel. Any man may despise God for a time, but he cannot forever be ignorant of Him. For this reason some people, envisaging God in many things, were driven by an undiscerning reverence to fashion many gods. But the operations of authoritative truth and the arguments of reason itself have very generally led to the abandonment of their position at the present time. Furthermore, their own philosophers also, to say nothing of our saints, exerting their mental powers to the utmost and investigating everything, have discovered one God to be the author of all things, to Whom alone all things should be traced. Hence even now the pagans, whom at this time revealed truth convicts of stubbornness rather than of ignorance, grant, when we dispute with them, that they do not follow many gods but worship many subordinate beings under one great god. Although it is true that the manifold ways of reaching a real understanding of God have necessarily brought about a good deal of confusion and a variety of opinion as to His true nature, there is almost universal agreement that God is one. Thus far human investigation has been able to proceed, even if with difficulty. But where reason fails, faith comes to the rescue; for unless we believe, we shall not understand. Hearken to

the words of God Himself and thus learn the truth that you wish to know concerning Him.

Now this one true God, on Whom, as we said, all schools agree even though differing in their interpretations, this God, Who changes kingdoms, orders the times, and also punishes sin, has chosen the weak of the world to confound the mighty and has laid the foundation of the Roman Empire by choosing a shepherd of the humblest station. After this empire had prospered for many years under kings and consuls and had gained the mastery of Asia, Africa, and Europe, He conferred all things by His decree upon a single emperor, who was pre-eminent in power and mercy. Under this emperor, to whom almost all nations rendered respect and due honor with mingled love and fear, the true God, Who was worshipped with scrupulous observance of rites by those who did not know Him, opened that great fountainhead of His knowledge. For the purpose of teaching men more quickly through a man, He sent His Son to work miracles that surpassed man's power and to refute the demons, whom some had thought to be gods, in order that those very men who had not believed in Him as a man should believe in His works as of God. He did this also that the glory of the new name and the swift report of the promised salvation might spread abroad quickly and without hindrance in the midst of the state of great tranquillity and universal peace that prevailed and also that His disciples, as they passed through different nations and freely offered the gifts of salvation to all, might have security and liberty to go about and speak as Roman citizens among Roman citizens. I have thought it necessary to mention this because this sixth book extends to the time of Caesar Augustus, to whom these remarks apply.

Now some people think that this absolutely clear reasoning is unsound and instead give credit to their own gods, whom, as they believe, they first had the good sense to choose and then won over by their extraordinary devotion so that they established for them this extensive and magnificent empire. For these pagans indeed are always boasting that they themselves gained the special favor of the gods by the excellent character of their sacred rites, and that when these rites were abolished or neglected, all the gods went away

> from sanctuary and abandoned altar,
> gods, through whom this Empire had stood firm.[1]

Hence, although your holy reverence [2] has already treated many matters most courageously and truthfully, the situation demands that I add a few considerations. If the Romans gained the favor of the gods by worshipping them and lost it by not worshipping them, then who through worship assured the safety of Romulus himself, the founder of Rome, amid all the evils that assailed him from his very birth? Was it his grandfather, Amulius, who exposed him to die? His father, whose identity was unknown? His mother, Rhea, convicted of fornication? [3] His Alban kinsmen, who persecuted the rising power of Rome even from the very beginning? All Italy, which for four hundred years (as long as it dared) yearned for Rome's destruction? No, they answer. It was the gods themselves, who, knowing that they would be worshipped, protected their future worshippers. The gods, therefore, know the future. If they do know the future, why during all these centuries have they brought this empire to the highest pinnacle of its power just at the time when He willed Himself to be born among men and to be known as a man? For after His advent these gods fell into contempt as worthless and departed with their whole world, even those whom the gods had made mighty. But the answer is given. He crept into this world as one meanly born and entered unregarded. If unregarded and meanly born, whence His universal fame, His undoubted honor, His manifest power? It was by unmistakable signs and miracles that He captured and held fast the minds of men distracted by superstitions. But if a mere man had such power, surely the gods should have wielded still greater power. Inasmuch as He declared that this power was given Him by His Father, has anyone ever

---

[1] Vergil *Aeneid* ii. 351–52.   [2] St. Augustine.   [3] An *Rhea* mater stupri *rea*?

been able to attain to the knowledge of that known and unknown God, which knowledge, as I have said, none can apprehend save through Him? No one can do this except the man who, after a thorough self-examination and a humbling of self, has become converted to the wisdom of God, and has exchanged all the reason of a searcher for the faith of a believer.

I shall, however, argue the matter briefly as follows. The gods of the pagans are represented as being so powerful that the Roman state was thought to have been exalted by their favor and brought low by their displeasure. Now it is a well-established fact that, at the time when Christ willed to be born and to make Himself known to the nations, the gods were worshipped with the utmost devotion and fervor. Hence, assuming that they were consulting their own interest and that of their worshippers, why were they unable to repress or repel His "superstition," which, as they saw, must leave them scorned and their worshippers utterly forsaken? However, if the people did not act willingly, the gods should have pardoned instead of abandoned them; if they acted willingly, the gods should have made use of their own foreknowledge and aided them earlier. This is what was done, they answer; we roused nations, we inflamed kings, we established laws, we appointed judges, we made preparations for punishment by torture and crucifixion, we searched the whole world to see if it was possible in any way to wipe the Christian name and religion off the face of the earth. These things went on for a long time until this barbarity, multiplying its kind, made such progress amid tortures and through tortures that it finally seized the imperial throne itself, by which alone it might have been restrained. Then what ensued? The Christian emperors, they say, ordered the sacrifices to cease and the temples to close and thus

> they all went forth from sanctuary and abandoned altar,
> The gods, through whom this empire had stood firm.[4]

Oh, how great, how constant is the light of truth, if weak

[4] Vergil *Aeneid* ii. 351–52.

eyes were not unhappily, alas, closed to its radiance, which so freely offers itself! Now the Christian religion could not in any way be stamped out, although for many generations it was exposed on all sides to the fury of nations, kings, laws, slaughter, crucifixion, and death, but on the contrary, as I have said, it grew in the midst of and because of these things. Yet the worship of idols, which was already somehow failing of its own accord and feeling ashamed of itself, came to an end at the issue of a single most merciful command given without any threat of punishment. Who, then, can doubt that by this demonstration of wisdom those created finally learned those things about their Creator which up to then they had been seeking, however eagerly, through the employment of various forms of reasoning? Though their reasoning was be-clouded by other matters, yet they immediately clung fast to their love for Him Whom they had cherished even in igno-rance. In the same way it is not at all strange that in a large household there will be found some slaves who, having be-come accustomed to the loose society of their corruptors, con-temptuously abuse the patience of their master. Rightly, therefore, does God reprove the ungrateful, the unbelieving, and also the disobedient with various chastisements. Such, we must agree, has always been the case; but it was especially so at the time when there was as yet no Church in all the world which, by the intercessory prayers of her faithful, might have tempered the deserved penalties of the world and the just judgment of God by entreating His mercy. Hence, it is that all the things that men now regard as misfortunes, of what-ever kind they may be, were without doubt more severe in times past, as now will be shown in the order I have already begun.

The Mithridatic War or, to be more exact, the disasters of the Mithridatic War, involving as it did many provinces at the same time, was long drawn out, extending over a period of forty years. For the Mithridatic War first blazed forth in the six hundred and sixty-second year [5] of the City, as I have

---

[5] The exact reading is not clear.

said, at the time when the First Civil War also began. In the consulship of Cicero and Antony, however, to quote the words of the master poet,

> the city was almost consumed by barbaric poison.[6]

Since the records of these days mention thirty years of warfare, one cannot easily explain why some speak of the war as lasting forty years.

2. MITHRIDATES, the king of Pontus and Armenia, now strove to deprive of his kingdom Nicomedes, the king of Bithynia and the friend of the Roman people. When he had been warned by the Senate that if he should attempt to do this the Roman people would be forced to declare war against him, he became angry and at once invaded Cappadocia. He drove out its king, Ariobarzanes, and devastated the whole province with fire and sword. Bithynia next underwent the same destruction. Paphlagonia then suffered the same fate, for her kings, Pylaemenes and Nicomedes, were expelled. Mithridates, coming later to Ephesus, issued a cruel edict ordering that wherever Roman citizens were found throughout the entire province of Asia, they were all to be slaughtered on the same day. And this was done. Words cannot in any way set forth or make clear the number of Roman citizens slaughtered at that time, the mourning that overtook most of the provinces, and the groans of the slain and of the slayers alike when individuals were forced either to betray innocent guests and friends or themselves to risk the punishment intended for their guests.

Archelaus, a general of Mithridates, was sent in advance into Achaia with one hundred and twenty thousand infantry and cavalry. Sometimes employing force and at other times accepting surrender, he won control over Athens and all Greece. Sulla, to whose lot the Mithridatic War had fallen after he had completed his consulship, long besieged Archelaus at Piraeus, the Athenian port fortified with a sevenfold wall;

---

[6] Lucan 1. 337.

he later took by storm the very city of the Athenians. Some time afterward he engaged Archelaus in a pitched battle. It was reported that Archelaus lost one hundred and ten thousand of his army and that barely ten thousand survived the battle.[7]

When Mithridates learned of this disaster, he sent seventy thousand of his choicest troops from Asia to reinforce Archelaus. In a second battle fifty thousand of these were slain;[8] and Diogenes, the son of Archelaus,[9] also lost his life. In a third battle the entire force of Archelaus was wiped out. Twenty thousand of his soldiers were driven into a swamp[10] and, though they begged for mercy from Sulla, were killed because his wrath could not be appeased. An equal number were driven into the river[11] and slaughtered, while the wretched remnant was destroyed at random. Furthermore, Mithridates made up his mind to kill the leading men of the most famous cities of Asia and to confiscate their property. When he had already slaughtered one thousand six hundred in this manner, the Ephesians, fearing that they would undergo the same fate, expelled the garrison of Mithridates and barred their gates. The inhabitants of Smyrna, Sardis, Colophon, and Tralles did likewise. Mithridates, now alarmed, concluded through his general Archelaus a treaty of peace with Sulla.

In the meantime Fimbria, an accomplice of the Marian criminals and the boldest of them all, killed the consul Flaccus at Nicomedia, where he had gone to join his staff as a legate. As soon as he had taken over the consul's army, Fimbria forced the son of Mithridates to flee from Asia to Miletopolis; he then attacked the quarters of the king, drove him from Pergamum, and following him in his flight to Pitane, laid siege to that city. Fimbria would certainly have captured the king had L. Lucullus placed the safety of the Republic

[7] The battle was fought in the neighborhood of Chaeronea in Boeotia, 86 B.C.
[8] Near Orchomenos. The battle lasted two days.
[9] The stepson, not son, as Orosius has assumed from Eutropius v. 6.
[10] The marshes of Lake Copais.
[11] The Cephissus River, which flows into Lake Copais.

before civil discords and had he been willing to exert full
pressure on the besieged king by having the fleet block his
escape by sea.

Fimbria became enraged at the inhabitants of Ilium, who,
in their loyalty to the Sullan faction, had repulsed him, it
seemed, by barring their gates. He visited the city with fire
and slaughter and utterly destroyed that ancient foster mother
of Rome. But Sulla at once rebuilt the city. When this same
Fimbria was besieged by the army of Sulla at Thyatira, he
was driven by despair to commit suicide in the Temple of
Aesculapius. Fannius and Magius fled from the army of Fimbria and joined Mithridates. On their advice the latter made
a treaty with Sertorius through the offices of ambassadors
whom he had sent to Spain. Sertorius sent M. Marius to him
for the purpose of ratifying the treaty. Mithridates kept him
at his side and in a short time appointed him general in place
of Archelaus, who had betaken himself with his wife and
children to Sulla. Marius and Eumachus, who were dispatched
by Mithridates as generals against Lucullus, assembled a great
army in a short time and engaged in battle with P. Rutilius
near Chalcedon; he and the greater part of his army were
slain there. By constructing a trench, Lucullus surrounded
Mithridates while the latter was besieging the inhabitants of
Cyzicus, and forced him to suffer what they had suffered. He
also sent one of the soldiers, who was an expert swimmer,
as a messenger to the Cyziceni to bid them be of good cheer.
Supported by two inflated bladders, this soldier held a pole
in the middle and, propelling himself along by his feet, covered a distance of seven miles. Mithridates, who was suffering from want, ordered part of his army to leave for home.
But Lucullus overtook and destroyed all of this force. It is
said that more than fifteen thousand men were killed at that
time.

In those days also, not only Fannius, who had joined
Mithridates, but also the royal praetor Metrophanes, was
defeated by Mamercus. They fled with two thousand cavalry
to Moesia and, turning aside from there to Malonia, came

unexpectedly upon the hills and fields of the Inarimi. In that region not only did the mountains look scorched and the rocks darkened by some kind of soot, but over a space of fifty miles the fields, wretched in appearance because the soil had been burned by fire, were covered with a deep layer of decaying ashes, although there was no sign of either fire or crater. In three places dry chasms, which the Greeks call freaks of nature, were visible. The troops, wandering about these places for a long time, were at length delivered from unexpected dangers and secretly came to the king's camp. Deiotarus, the king of the Gallo-Greeks, slew the royal prefects in battle.

In the meantime, Mithridates was blockaded at Cyzicus and underwent as long a siege as had those whom he had blockaded. His army was reduced to great want and became a prey to disease. He is said to have lost more than thirty thousand men from hunger and disease during that siege. Mithridates himself and a few companions seized a ship and secretly fled from the camp. Lucullus, an eyewitness of his enemy's disaster, won a novel victory since he himself did not lose a single soldier. Soon afterward he attacked and defeated Marius and put him to flight in a battle in which more than eleven thousand of Marius's troops, according to report, were killed.[12] Lucullus later met this same Marius in a naval encounter and sank or captured thirty-two of the royal ships and also a great many transports.[13] Many of those whom Sulla had proscribed were killed in that battle. On the next day Marius was dragged out from a cave in which he was hiding and paid the penalty that his hostile intentions merited. In the same campaign, Lucullus desolated Apamia; after storming and capturing the heavily fortified city of Prusa, situated at the foot of Mount Olympus, he destroyed it. A storm overtook the fleet of Mithridates as it was sailing in battle array toward Byzantium; eighty beaked ships were lost. When his own ship was shattered and was sinking, he

[12] In crossing the Aesepus and Granicus rivers.
[13] Near a barren island not far from Lemnos.

leaped aboard a *myoparo* belonging to a pirate named Seleucus, who went to his aid. Mithridates then managed with great difficulty to reach Sinope and later, Amisus.

3. IN THE same year at Rome, Catiline was accused of an incest which he was charged with having committed with Fabia, a Vestal Virgin. His friend Catulus, however, exerted influence in his behalf and thus he escaped punishment.

Lucullus laid siege to Sinope, intending to take it by storm. The arch-pirate Seleucus and the eunuch Cleochares, who were in command of the defense, abandoned the city after pillaging and burning it. Disturbed by the destruction now being wrought within the city's walls by his wretched enemy, Lucullus took swift measures to extinguish the fire that had been set ablaze. Thus the unfortunate city, alternately · exposed to enemies and allies, was ruined by those whose duty it was to defend it and was saved by those who had sought to destroy it. M. Lucullus, who had succeeded Curio in Macedonia, accepted the surrender of the whole nation of the Bessi with whom he had been at war.

At that time, Metellus, the praetor of Sicily, discovered that the island had been ruined under the disgraceful praetorship of C. Verres. He also found that she had been torn to pieces by the criminal depredations and slaughters of the arch-pirate Pyrganion, who had secured control of the port of Syracuse after the defeat of the Roman fleet. Metellus quickly crushed this man in a naval and land battle and forced him to leave Sicily.

Moreover, Lucullus crossed the Euphrates and Tigris, encountered Mithridates and Tigranes at Tigranocerta,[14] and with a very small force killed a great number of the enemy. Thirty thousand men were reported to have fallen in that battle. Tigranes barely escaped with an escort of one hundred and fifty horsemen. To conceal his identity, he threw away his diadem and tiara. At this juncture envoys from almost

[14] There is doubt as to the location of the city. The battle was fought in 69 B.C.

the entire East came as suppliants to Lucullus. On the approach of winter, Lucullus retraced his march through Armenia to Mesopotamia and there stormed and captured Nisibis, a city which was then famous in those parts.

4.   IN THESE days pirates were scattered over all the seas and were not only intercepting the supply ships but were also laying waste islands and provinces. Their numbers were constantly being swelled by people who, prompted by greed for booty and by the opportunity of committing crime without risk of punishment, were everywhere joining their ranks. After they had long wrought much havoc on land and sea, Cn. Pompey crushed these men so quickly that people were utterly astonished.

At the same time Metellus for two years wrought destruction upon the island of Crete, which he eventually brought under his power when its resistance had been broken by long wars. He then substituted the laws of Rome in place of the laws of Minos.

Pompey, the successor of Lucullus, later invested the camp of the king in Lesser Armenia near Mount Dastarcum. After sallying forth in the night with all his troops, the king decided, as the next move, to repel his pursuer by engaging him in battle. Pompey did his best to overtake them as they fled. Battle was then joined at night.[15] The moon had risen behind the Romans. The royal soldiers, judging the nearness of the Romans by the length of their shadows, hurled their darts in vain. Quite unharmed, the Romans later attacked and easily conquered them. Forty thousand of the royal army were slain or captured, while of the Romans only a thousand were wounded and barely forty killed. The king slipped away amid the din of battle and, aided by the faint light of the night, made good his escape. Abandoned by all of his friends, philosophers, historians, poets, and doctors, alone he led his

---

[15] This battle is known as the battle of Nicopolis, a name not very appropriate. Perhaps the battle of the Lycus would be a better name. The date was 66 B.C.

horse through unfrequented ways, terrified by all the noises of the night. He finally took refuge in a certain stronghold and from there hastened to Armenia.

That he might follow the king between the two rivers, the Euphrates and the Araxes, which rise from one mountain though from different caverns, Pompey founded the city of Nicopolis, where he left the aged people, the camp followers, and the sick who wished to stay. He pardoned Tigranes at the latter's entreaty and three times defeated in battle the army of Orodes,[16] the king of the Albanians, and his prefects.[17] Later he was happy to receive a letter from Orodes and the presents sent by the Albani as a peace offering. He then fought and routed Artoces, the king of Iberia, and received all Iberia in surrender. After he had pacified and reorganized Armenia, the Colchians, Cappadocia, and Syria, he pushed on from Pontus into Parthia to Ecbatana, the capital of the Parthian kingdom, arriving there on the fifteenth day.

5. WHILE Mithridates was celebrating the sacred rites of Ceres in Bosporus, an earthquake suddenly occurred of so great violence that it caused much damage to both city and country. At the same time Castor, who was the prefect of Mithridates and in command of Phanagorium, seized the citadel. After slaying the king's friends he turned over the four children of Mithridates to the Roman garrison. Mithridates, fired with anger, blazed forth in a series of crimes, murdering a great number of his friends at the time and also his own son Exipodra. He had already committed another parricide by putting Machares to death. Pharnaces, another son of his, now terrified by the fate of his brothers, won over to his side the army sent to attack him, and soon led it against his father. Mithridates, standing on the top of the wall, long pleaded in vain with his son. When he found him relentless, he is reported to have exclaimed when about to die: "Since

---

[16] He is called Oroeses by some Greek writers.

[17] Pompey's army was divided and quartered in three separate cantonments. (66 B.C.).

Pharnaces orders my death, I beseech you, O gods of my native land, if you do exist, that he himself may also some day hear this utterance from his own children." Straightway he went down to his wives, concubines, and daughters, and gave poison to them all. Mithridates himself was the last to swallow the poison, but because he had taken antidotes over a long period, thus rendering his vital organs immune to the effects of poisonous juices, the poison could not kill him. He ran up and down in a vain attempt to see, as a final measure, whether the deadly drink would not now spread through his veins under the stimulus of vigorous exercise. Finally he summoned a certain Gallic soldier who happened to be running by after the wall had been broken down, and offered his throat to him. Such was the death suffered by Mithridates who, reputed to be one of the most superstitious of all men, left us an impressive example of his way of thinking. He was seventy-two years of age at the time of his death and had always surrounded himself with philosophers, skilled in all the arts.

"If you exist," he said, "O gods of my native land." Thus he had come to the conclusion after a long period of worship and of search, that those gods, who were usually thought to exist, could not with absolute certainty be proved to exist. A king of rich experience and one old in years did not grasp the fact that there was a true God, to the knowledge of Whom one comes only by hearing His Word in faith. He had perceived by the light of his reason that these gods were false, but he yielded to some extent to custom as well as asserting his own convictions. "If you exist, O gods," he said, thereby meaning: "I myself feel that there exists above mankind a power mightier than man himself. Being influenced by the need for prayer, I commend to them my scrupulousness, and I apologize for my own ignorance; for although I invoke a God who exists, actually I find one who does not exist." For this reason, this question must be sorrowfully and anxiously considered: what punishment or what judgment will they deserve who, contrary to the command of a truth that is at present widely diffused and known to all, eagerly follow and worship those gods whose credibility was already open to doubt in those days when people could have known no divinity other than those same gods? Nevertheless, I present the following brief reflection. What were the conditions that existed in those days over the entire East, when for a space of forty years the wretched nations were ground to pieces by great generals who successively ravaged them? Since each city in the midst of this warfare was inevitably endangered, it was therefore destined to inflame a new enemy by the very means through which it had rid itself of the old and to suffer disaster from what had been used as a temporary remedy. Terror-stricken embassies from different provinces then went to one Roman general after another and to Mithridates, who was even harsher than he was reputed to be, bringing different offers to each according as he was temporarily favored by the fortunes of war, exaggerating the dangers which they were trying to cure. I shall set forth in a few words what Pompey, who indeed was one of the most moderate of the Romans, accomplished after the close of the Mithridatic War throughout most of the regions of the East.

6. SIX hundred and eighty-nine years after the founding of the City and during the consulship of M. Tullius Cicero and C. Antony, Pompey, upon receiving news of the death of Mithridates, invaded Syria Coele and Phoenicia. He first subdued the Ituraei and then the Arabians, also capturing their city, which they call Petra. Next he sent Gabinius with an army against the city of Jerusalem and against the Jews, over whom Aristobulus was reigning in succession to his brother Hyrcanus, who had been driven out. Aristobulus was the first member of the priesthood to become a king. Pompey himself followed closely behind Gabinius and though he was welcomed in the city by the fathers, nevertheless he was driven away by the people from the wall of the Temple; he therefore decided to capture it. The Temple was fortified not only by its natural location but also by a huge wall and a great ditch.

After throwing legion after legion into the fray day and night
without rest, each legion relieving the preceding one, Pompey
barely managed to take the Temple by storm in the third
month.[18] Thirteen thousand Jews, according to report, were
slain there. The rest of the number submitted to the Romans.
Pompey gave orders for the walls of the city to be dismantled
and leveled to the ground. Later he had a considerable number of the leading Jews executed, restored Hyrcanus to his
priestly office, and had Aristobulus led captive to Rome. Appearing in person before an assembly of the Roman people,
Pompey told the story of this war which he had waged against
twenty-two kings.

In the meantime, there arose the conspiracy of Catiline
against his native land. This conspiracy was betrayed in the
City during these same days, but in Etruria it was extinguished
by a civil war. In Rome the accomplices were put to death.
But this story has been made so well known to all by Cicero's
deeds and Sallust's description, that it is enough for me to
present a much abridged account of it. The Marcelli, father
and son, also instigated a rebellion in the country of the
Palignae, but the uprising was betrayed by Vettius. When the
conspiracy of Catiline was detected, it was crushed as if its
very roots had been cut off; punishment was exacted in two
localities, among the Palignae by Bibulus and among the Bruttii by Cicero.

7.   In the six hundred and ninety-third year after the founding of the City and in the consulship of C. Caesar and L.
Bibulus, the three provinces of Gallia Transalpina, Cisalpina,
and Illyricum, with seven legions were awarded by the Lex
Vatinia to Caesar for a period of five years. Gallia Comata
was later added by the Senate.

Suetonius Tranquillus has most fully unfolded this history,
the significant portions of which I myself have epitomized.

By holding out the hope of successfully invading all the
Gallic provinces, a certain Orgetorix, the chief of the Helvetii,

[18] In the year 63 B.C.

stirred up war among his people, the bravest of all the Gallic tribes. The Helvetii won this reputation because they were almost continuously at war with the Germans, who were separated from them by the Rhine. After Orgetorix had been seized and compelled to kill himself, the other nobles could not hold the people in check once their minds had been set on booty. They formed a conspiracy and on the appointed day burned their villages and homes so that no inducement to return would remain. They then began their march. Caesar blocked their passage at the Rhone River and after twice defeating them in great and hard-fought battles [19] forced them to surrender. The whole number of those who had set out in the first place, that is, the number of the Helvetii, Tulingi, Latobrigi, Rauraci, and Boii, counting both sexes, amounted to one hundred and fifty-seven thousand. Of these, forty-seven thousand fell in battle; the rest were sent back to their own lands.

In the territories of the Sequani, Caesar later conquered King Ariovistus,[20] who was inciting warfare and bringing with him an incredible number of German troops. This king boasted that with these troops he had recently subjugated all the Gallic peoples, while Caesar's army, terrified by the vast number and courage of the Germans, had long declined the challenge to battle. After his defeat Ariovistus immediately seized a skiff, crossed the Rhine to Germany, and escaped; his two wives and two daughters, however, were captured. In the army of Ariovistus were the Harudes, Marcomanni, Triboci, Vangiones, Nemetes, Sedusii, and Suebi. The battle fought was especially severe on account of the formation adopted by the Germans. They were drawn up in the form of a phalanx protected on all sides with advance columns in close formation and with shields interlocked above their heads in order to shatter the attack of the Roman battle line. But

---

[19] Near Bibracte, 58 B.C.

[20] The exact location of the battle is in doubt. It was fought in 58 B.C. Consult the discussion in T. Rice Holmes, *Caesar's Conquest of Gaul* (Oxford, 1911), pp. 636–57. The text has Eduses instead of Sedusii.

after some Roman soldiers, noted for their nimbleness and daring, had leaped over the overspreading *testudo* and had torn away the shields one by one as if they were scales, they pierced the exposed shoulders of the enemy who were caught unawares and without adequate covering. In their terror at this new peril threatening their lives, the Germans broke up their awe-inspiring formation and fled. The Romans pursued them over a distance of fifty miles and inflicted upon them a slaughter that never seemed to be satisfied. It is impossible to estimate either the number of the enemy engaged in that battle or the number slain.

After these events, the tribe of the Belgae, who constituted a third of the Gauls, broke out in rebellion against Caesar. The distribution of their forces was as follows: The Bellovaci, who enjoyed the reputation of excelling in numbers and courage, had sixty thousand picked troops, while the Suessiones had fifty thousand from twelve towns. The Nervii likewise had fifty thousand soldiers. Their untamed barbarity was a matter of common knowledge, it being everywhere known that never up to that time had they permitted merchants to bring into their territories wine or other articles of luxury, the enjoyment of which might paralyze their courage. The Atrebates and the Ambiani also had ten thousand; the Morini, twenty-five thousand; the Menapii, nine thousand; the Caleti, ten thousand; the Veliocasses and Viromandui each ten thousand; and the Aduatuci, eighteen thousand. The Condrusi, Eburones, Caeroesi, Paemani, who were grouped under the one name of Germans, had forty thousand. Altogether there were reported to have been two hundred and seventy-two thousand picked soldiers. Caesar's army was thrown into confusion and put to flight by an unexpected attack made by these men, who suddenly burst forth from the forest. After suffering severe losses, the Roman army finally rallied under the encouragement of its leader, attacked the victors, and destroyed them almost to the last man.[21]

[21] The height of Neuf-Mesnil, opposite Hautmont (57 B.C.). Consult T. R. Holmes, *op. cit.*, pp. 671–77.

8. AFTER Caesar had accomplished great deeds in Gaul and had decided to set out for Italy, Galba was dispatched with the twelfth legion against the Veragri and Seduni. Galba took up his quarters for the winter in a village of the Veragri called Octodurus. He assigned to the inhabitants the central part of the town which was separated from the rest by a rapid stream. One day he noticed that they had left during the previous night and were occupying a nearby hill. The Veragri, indeed, holding in contempt the small numbers of the Romans, who had barely half a legion, thought that booty would of its own accord flow into their hands without any effort on their part. They also had invited their neighbors to participate in this carnage and to share in the spoils.

Galba was alarmed by the dangers now surrounding him on all sides, but hesitated to choose any definite plan because the advice so far received had been conflicting. The Gauls then suddenly poured down the slope of the mountain and laid siege to the unfinished camp. With rocks and darts they overwhelmed the defenders stationed at intervals along the rampart. While the camp was being assaulted, all the Romans, acting on the advice of the primipilar Pacuvius and the tribune Volusenus, burst forth from the gates and suddenly attacked the enemy who were off their guard. The Romans first threw them into confusion and then, after putting them to flight, slaughtered them mercilessly. More than thirty thousand barbarians, according to report, fell at this time.

Though Caesar thought that all the Gallic tribes had now been pacified, he was drawn back into a new and exceedingly great war. While P. Crassus, a young man, was wintering with the seventh legion by the Ocean among the Andicavi, the Veneti and other neighbors suddenly formed a conspiracy to wage war, bound the envoys of the Romans in chains, and announced that they would return these envoys to the Romans only when they had received back their own hostages. As allies for that war, they took the Osismi, Lexovii, Namnetes, Ambivariti, Morini, Diablintes, and Menapii, and they summoned assistance even from Britain.

Caesar was then informed by Crassus that the tribes which had previously surrendered were in rebellion. Although he knew how difficult it would be to begin war, he nevertheless realized that a matter of such grave importance could not be disregarded, lest other tribes might be tempted to follow their example. Consequently he advanced to engage the enemy in a land battle, but to no avail, since the enemy had withdrawn through marshes flooded by the Ocean into places difficult of approach and were now protected by the shelter their hiding places afforded. Therefore he ordered warships to be built on the Liger River,[22] and floated them down to the Ocean. As soon as the enemy saw them, they speedily made ready two hundred and twenty ships of their own, equipped with every kind of armament. Leaving the harbor [23] these ships took a position opposite the Romans. Brutus was aware that the naval conflict would be waged on very unequal terms, because the ships of the barbarians had been joined with beams of solid oak, and their mighty hulls, having the strength of rock, weakened the force of blows struck by the beaks of the opposing ships. His first move to help himself was to prepare sharply pointed hooks fastened to poles and attached with cords. With these contrivances, when need should arise, they could catch hold of the rigging from a distance and cut it down by withdrawing the shafts and retrieving the hook by pulling in the cord.

After these contrivances had been speedily made ready, he gave orders to his men to sever the tackle and sail yards of the enemy ships. When these sail yards had been brought down, many of their ships were rendered as motionless as if they had been captured. Some of the enemy, terrified by this danger, unfurled the sails of their ships where there was any wind at all and attempted to flee, but as the wind soon died, the Romans laughed at them. When all the ships had been set on fire and those Gauls engaged in the battle had been killed, all the rest surrendered. Because of the wrong done his ambassadors, and in order to teach a lesson to

[22] The Loire.   [23] The mouth of the Auray River.

a people who were swayed by every new proposal, Caesar imprinted a terrible example upon their memory. He ordered all their chiefs to be tortured and put to death and the rest of the survivors to be sold into slavery.

In these same days Titurius Sabinius made a sortie and destroyed with unbelievable slaughter the Aulerci, Eburovices, and Lexovii,[24] who had put their own chiefs to death because the latter were unwilling to recommend a renewal of the war. When Publius Crassus had come to Aquitania, he encountered armed resistance. The Sontiates attacked the Romans with a large detachment of cavalry and strong infantry forces, and threw them into serious disorder for a long time but were themselves ultimately defeated,[25] driven into the town of the Sontiates,[26] and besieged. When they saw that they would be conquered, they handed over their arms and surrendered.

Alarmed by this disaster, the Aquitani assembled an army from all sides, summoning assistance even from Hither Spain. They appointed as commanders for that war the same leaders who had served with Sertorius. While they were all making preparations to besiege him, Crassus succeeded in overpowering and destroying them in their own camp.[27] Out of fifty thousand of the Aquitani and Cantabri—forty thousand of the latter had come as auxiliaries—thirty-eight thousand, according to report, lost their lives. Caesar then attacked and reduced almost to the last man the Germans [28] who had crossed the Rhine with huge forces and who at that very time were preparing to bring all Gaul under their control. It is said that they numbered four hundred and forty thousand.

9. AFTER constructing a bridge, Caesar then crossed to the country of the Germans and delivered the Sugambri and Ubii from a siege. His arrival brought terror to the entire country and also to the Suebi, the largest and fiercest tribe, who, according to information given by many people, had a hundred

---

[24] On the peninsula of Cotentin, 56 B.C.   [25] Near the source of the Ciron.
[26] The site is now occupied by the town of Sos.   [27] In the year 56 B.C.
[28] The Usipetes and Tencteri. The exact location of the battle is in doubt.

cantons and districts. Caesar then destroyed the bridge and withdrew to Gaul. Thence he came to the territories of the Morini where is to be found the nearest and shortest passage to Britain, to which, after preparing about eighty transports and swift ships, he set sail.[29] In Britain he was first·harassed by a bitter conflict and then overtaken by a disastrous storm; in the end he lost the greater part of the fleet,[30] a considerable number of soldiers, and almost all of his cavalry. Returning to Gaul, he sent the legions into winter quarters and ordered six hundred ships to be built of every kind needed. With these ships, at the beginning of spring, he again sailed to Britain. While he himself was proceeding with his army against the enemy, the ships, which were riding at anchor, were overtaken by a storm and either smashed against one another or were dashed to pieces on the sands and destroyed. Forty ships were lost; the rest were refitted with great difficulty.

Caesar's cavalry was defeated by the Britons in the first battle, in which the tribune Labienus [31] lost his life. In a second battle, though not without risk to his own men, Caesar defeated and routed the Britons. Thence he advanced to the Thames River which, they say, is fordable only at one place. On the further bank, a vast host of the enemy had taken its position and had planted very sharp stakes under the water along almost the entire ford. When the Romans detected and avoided these obstacles, the barbarians, unable to withstand the onset of the legions, hid themselves in the woods, whence they severely harassed the Romans with their frequent sallies. In the meantime, the powerful city of the Trinobantes and their leader Mandubracius surrendered to Caesar, after giving forty hostages. Several other cities followed this example and entered the Roman alliance. Acting according to their advice, Caesar, after a severe struggle, finally captured the stronghold of Cassivellaunus, which was situated between

[29] The main force embarked at Portus Itius (Boulogne) on 25 August 55 B.C.
[30] Probably refers to the fate of the cavalry transports which arrived several days after the main body of troops. [31] Quintus Laberius Durus, not Labienus.

two swamps and fortified by the covering of the wood and
well stocked with supplies of all kinds.

10. AFTER his return to Gaul from Britain, Caesar dispatched his legions to winter quarters. He was then beset and
harassed on all sides by unexpected uprisings and wars. Ambiorix had formed a conspiracy with the Eburones and Aduatuci. Acting upon the plan suggested by the Treveri, Ambiorix
led the legates Cotta and Sabinus into ambush in the territory
of the Eburones, and slew them.[32] Elated by his victory,
Ambiorix hurriedly persuaded the Aduatuci, Nervii, and many
other tribes to take up arms, and marched quickly against
Cicero, the legate at that time commanding the legion in
winter quarters. The number of the enemy can be deduced
from the following incident. They had been taught by Roman
prisoners that when they were besieging a camp, they should
surround it with a rampart. But not having any farming im-
plements with them, they had to dig up the soil with their
swords and carry it away in military cloaks. It took them
barely three hours to complete a rampart ten feet high and
a ditch that was fifteen feet wide and fifteen thousand feet
in circumference. In addition, they erected one hundred and
twenty towers of unusual height.

Just when the enemy, fighting in wedge formation, were
about to break, after a battle lasting seven continuous days
and nights, a strong wind began to blow. They then used
their slings to fling glowing tiles into the camp and also threw
darts which had become red hot and ablaze from the heat
of the fire. The breeze quickly swept through the straw thatch
and fanned the fires which had already begun to spread. But
not even then did the Romans, though overwhelmed on every
side, yield to the hardship caused by wounds, long watches,
hunger, and fire. Finally news came to Caesar that one legion
had been wiped out and that the other was about to be destroyed.

When Caesar arrived on the scene with two legions, the

[32] The disaster of Aduatuca, 54 B.C.

enemy abandoned the siege and, uniting their forces, rushed out to engage him. Caesar, purposely concealing himself in a small camp, sent ahead the cavalry and ordered them to feign flight and thus lure the enemy, now contemptuous of him, to cross the intervening valley, which appeared to him to be fraught with danger. When the enemy drew near, he also ordered the gates to be barricaded. Upon noticing this, the Gauls, thinking that they had already won the battle, wheeled about in order to surround the rampart. From all gates Caesar suddenly let loose his army that was standing ready and after putting the Gauls to flight wrought great disaster upon them. According to report they numbered sixty thousand, of whom only a few escaped through the almost impassable swamps.

Indutiomarus, the chief of the Treveri, who had a large number of troops with him, after being assured of the unanimous accord of all Gaul, decided first to destroy the camp of Labienus and the legion which the latter commanded in the belief that this could be accomplished easily. Next he planned, in conjunction with the Eburones and Nervii, to overwhelm Caesar. Labienus practiced all sorts of wiles to make Indutiomarus believe that he was afraid, then made a sudden sally and crushed him while the barbarian, accompanied by his troops who were offering insults, was rather carelessly wandering in front of the fortification. This victory of Labienus checked any further attempts on the part of the Gauls, and Caesar spent the remaining part of the winter in comparative peace. Caesar, however, knew that greater difficulties still lay ahead of him in war, especially since the larger part of his army was lost and the remainder was incapacitated by wounds, and that he was apparently in no condition even to maintain his own position to say nothing of smashing the attack of the Gauls. Therefore he requested the proconsul Pompey to enroll legions for him and to dispatch them to his assistance. Before the end of the winter, three legions arrived at his camp.

At the beginning of spring Caesar prepared to attack the

enemy, who were still terrified, and to crush them while they
were still scattered far and wide in their own territories. He
planned to do this before their forces could unite in one body.
His first move was to ravage the territory of the Nervii,
whose rich country he permitted his army to plunder. Then
with three columns he made an attack upon the Menapii, who
appeared to be well protected by immense swamps and almost
impassable forests. After he had inflicted great slaughter upon
them everywhere, he received in surrender the remnant who
came to him as suppliants. In another battle, Labienus slew
all the troops of the Treveri. He tricked them into battle
before the approaching Germans could join them, and speedily
captured their city.

Caesar, who wished to avenge the death of his legates
Sabinus and Cotta, whose legion Ambiorix and the Eburones
had destroyed, then learned that they had taken refuge in
the Arduenna Forest. This forest was the largest in all Gaul
and stretched from the banks of the Rhine and the territories
of the Treveri to the lands of the Nervii, extending in length
over fifty miles. He calculated that the undertaking would
seriously endanger his own men, who were unacquainted with
the region. Therefore he sent messengers to all the Gallic
tribes and invited each, according to its pleasure, to seek and
to plunder the booty hidden in the Arduenna Forest. This
was done, and the Gauls, killing one another as their armies
fought, avenged the great injuries that they had inflicted on
the Romans without the loss of a single Roman soldier. By
thus employing a method of conquest which was absolutely
free from danger, Caesar returned to Italy in safety.

11. AFTER Caesar had returned to Italy, the Gauls again
formed a conspiracy to go to war and many tribes straightway
entered into an alliance. Vercingetorix was their leader and
on his advice all the Gauls of their own accord immediately
set fire to their cities. Biturigo was the first city to be burnt
by its own people. The Gauls then made an attack upon
Caesar, who had secretly hurried back by forced marches

through the province of Narbo. Caesar at this time had invested a town named Cenabum.[33] After this town had been under attack for a long time and the Romans had suffered many disasters, it was finally captured and destroyed by towers that had been brought into action on a rainy day. The rain caused the *agmenta* and thongs of the enemy war machines to become slackened. Of the forty thousand men reported to have been in the engagement, barely eighty slipped away in flight and came to the nearest camp of the Gauls.

The Arverni and other neighbors—even the Aedui were induced to join them—also fought many battles against Caesar. When the enemy had retired to a certain fortress, the soldiers, wearied from fighting yet still eager for booty, were determined to storm the town, even after Caesar had pleaded in vain with them, pointing out the unfavorable character of the terrain. On this occasion Caesar was hard pressed by the enemy who were making sorties from above and, after losing a large part of his army, was defeated and took flight.

While these events were taking place at Alesia, Vercingetorix, who had been chosen king by the unanimous consent of all, persuaded everyone throughout entire Gaul capable of bearing arms to make ready to serve in this war. For this was a war which would result in perpetual liberty, eternal slavery, or death for all. Besides that countless multitude which he had brought together earlier, there were assembled about eight thousand cavalry and two hundred and fifty thousand infantry.

The Romans and the Gauls then occupied two hills opposite each other. From these hills they carried on battle by frequent sorties with changing fortunes, until the Romans won a victory, thanks to the splendid courage of the German cavalry whom they had summoned to their aid and who were friends of long standing. On another day Vercingetorix brought together all who had escaped by flight and said that he had in good faith been the prime mover of this war in defense of their freedom, that he had caused the treaty to be broken,

[33] On the present site of Orléans.

and that he now would be ready to await their decision whether
all the Gauls should offer themselves to the Romans to be
killed or whether they should surrender him alone in behalf
of all. The Gauls then brought to the surface the wish which
through shame they had concealed for a long time; pretending that they were acting on the advice of their king, they
asked pardon for themselves and surrendered Vercingetorix
as the sole perpetrator of the great crime.

In the opinion of the Gauls themselves, the Bellovaci were
braver than any other Gallic tribe. Under the leadership of
Correus, these same Bellovaci resumed the war, securing as
their allies for this new war the Ambiani, Aulerci, Caleti,
Veliocasses, and Atrebates. They occupied a certain stretch of
ground that was surrounded and rendered unapproachable by
marshes. In the battle that followed they slew a large band
of the Remi, who were serving as Roman auxiliaries. They
themselves then occupied a favorable position and one well-
suited for ambuscades. When the Romans discovered this,
they advanced, equipped and drawn up in full battle array,
to the place where the ambuscades were set. Battle was joined.
The Romans surrounded the Gauls as they were fleeing from
the fortified places in which they had been enclosed, and slew
them almost to the last man. Correus, disdaining both flight
and surrender, forced the Romans, who wished to capture
him alive, to kill him on the spot.

When Caesar thought that the whole of Gaul was pacified
and would not dare to raise any rebellion, he dispatched the
legions into winter quarters, but he himself ravaged the territories of Ambiorix, who had stirred up so many wars, and
inflicted a horrible slaughter upon the inhabitants. The legate
C. Caninius,[34] however, upon arriving in the territory of the
Pictones, discovered a war raging there. A vast host of the
enemy had surrounded the legion while it was encumbered on
the march, and placed it in greatest peril. But the legate
Fabius received a letter from Caninius and at once set out for
the territory of the Pictones where he was informed by

[34] C. Caninius Rebilus.

prisoners about the local situation. He took the enemy unawares, overwhelmed them after terrific slaughter, and carried off a great amount of booty. When Caninius had been
notified of the legate's arrival, his soldiers suddenly rushed
out from every part of the camp and threw themselves upon
the enemy. Pressed by Fabius on one side and by Caninius on
another, the countless Gallic forces were slaughtered in a
great and long-drawn-out battle. Fabius then set out against
the Carnutes, for he knew that Domnacus, their ancient leader
and the instigator of the whole rebellion, had escaped from
that battle and that if he were to join the Aremorican peoples,
a great rebellion would again be set in motion in Gaul. By
a remarkable display of courage and speed, Fabius subdued
these tribes while they were dumbfounded by the unprecedented character of his tactics.

In the meantime, Drappes and Lucterius, seeing that
Caninius and his legions were present in their territories, collected forces from all sides and seized the town of Uxello-
dunum.[35] This town was situated on the highest peak of a
mountain and was bordered on two sides by precipitous slopes
and a fair-sized river. It was well supplied with water from
an abundant spring situated in the middle of the slope and
also had a large supply of grain stored within; from its secure
position the city looked with contempt upon the ineffectual
maneuvers of the enemy afar off. Caninius accomplished all
that could be done by Roman foresight. He induced both
Gallic generals with the greater part of their troops to come
down into the plain where he overcame them in a great battle.
When one of these generals had been slain, the other took
flight with a very small number of men. No one returned to
the town. But to capture that town they had to call upon
Caesar.

When Caesar had learned through messengers how matters
stood, he hastened to the place and, viewing the situation from
all angles, saw that if he should try to force his way into the
town by an assault, his army would become subject to the

---

[35] A town of the Cadurci.

ridicule of the enemy. One thing alone could assist him, namely, depriving the enemy in any way whatsoever of their supply of water. But Caesar could not accomplish this if the spring which they were using for drinking purposes continued to pour forth its waters from the middle of one of the sloping sides of the mountain. Caesar ordered mantlets to be moved as near as possible to the spring and a tower erected. A great crowd from the town assembled on the spot. Although the Romans fought stubbornly and repeatedly made successful advances, yet many were slain, since the enemy from their position fought without danger to themselves. A rampart was therefore thrown up and a tower sixty feet high constructed, the top of which was on a level with the spring, so that the Romans could hurl missiles from the same level as the enemy without fear that showers of rocks might be thrown down upon them from above.

When the townsfolk saw that not only their flocks but even their aged men were dying of thirst, they filled tubs with grease, pitch, and shingle, and then, having set them afire, sent them hurtling down the slope. They themselves swarmed out from the entire town and followed closely after them. When his machines caught fire, Caesar saw that the battle would have serious consequences and would be very dangerous to his men. Therefore he ordered some cohorts to go secretly and swiftly around the town and suddenly to raise a loud shout from every quarter. When this was done, the towns-folk became alarmed, and wanting to run back to defend the town, gave up the attack on the towers as well as the work of demolishing the rampart. But the soldiers, working under the safe protection of the rampart, continued to extend the passages they were digging underground and were able to reduce the volume of water encountered in hidden channels by leading it off in many different channels, thereby destroying the supply.

When their spring had become dry, the townspeople were filled with despair and surrendered. Caesar cut off the hands of all who had borne arms but spared their lives. He did this so that posterity might more clearly see what penalty awaited those who did evil. For an example of punishment strikingly set forth is of great value in restraining audacity, since the wretched condition of those left alive warns those who know what happened and compels those who do not know to inquire.

12. WHEN the Gauls had become exhausted and were completely subdued, Caesar, accompanied by his legions, returned in safety to Italy. He had no great fear of rebellion from the Gauls left behind, since he well knew that very few remained who would have the courage to rebel, or who if they should rebel were at all to be feared. At this point I should like to set forth the condition of a Gaul that had been drained of blood and worn out after those blazing fevers and internal fires had scorched her very vitals. I should like now to envisage how emaciated and pale she was, how dejected and enervated she lay, how she feared even the activities of necessary business lest these bring back another onset of misfortune! For the Roman army, attacking unexpectedly, fell upon her just as sometimes a plague far stronger than itself besets an extremely healthy body—a plague whose virulence increases the more impatiently the disease is borne. Wretched Gaul panted, when she was forced at the point of the sword to acknowledge an agreement entailing perpetual slavery besides submitting to have hostages torn from her. She panted with thirst, as I have said, for that well-known sweetness of liberty that is so very delightful to all, just as a feverish patient thirsts for a drink of cold water; and the more she realized that she was losing her liberty the more eagerly did she yearn for it. Herein lay the cause of her oft-repeated resistance to restrictive laws; she was seized by an ill-timed and ravening wilfulness to defend her liberty and to regain that freedom which had been wrested from her, and instead of assuaging the pestilence in her system, as it seemed to do, this wilfulness increased it. We see then that the Roman was a more cunning plotter before battle, a more merciless enemy in battle, a more ruthless victor after battle. So far as overcoming the malady was concerned, all conditions, therefore, were grow-

ing worse and for that reason no faith in remedies existed any longer. Thus if I could ask this nation what she thinks about the days when she was suffering these ills, she would in my opinion answer and say: "The present fever has left me so feeble and made me so cold that even the present change, which has affected almost all people, has been unable to warm or to stir me; moreover, the Romans have so severely oppressed me that I am unable to rise against the Goths." But not even Rome herself escaped the disasters which she inflicted. The illegal extension of powers by military leaders had been so exercised and the strength of the legions had for a long time been so increased in every part of the world, that whenever these legions came into conflict, their victory resulted in injury to Rome and their defeat endangered her. For the return of victorious Caesar from Gaul was followed by civil wars and preceded by other great evils, the murder of Crassus and the butchery of his army by the Parthians.

13. IN THE six hundred and ninety-seventh year of the City, Crassus, who shared the consulship with Pompey, obtained by lot the command against the Parthians. He was a man of insatiable cupidity. When he heard of the riches of the Temple at Jerusalem that Pompey had left untouched, he turned aside to Palestine and came to Jerusalem, where he entered the Temple and plundered its treasures. Thence directing his course to Parthia he requisitioned auxiliaries from the allied states, wherever his march led, and exacted tribute. As soon as he had crossed the Euphrates, he met Vageses, who had been sent as an envoy by Orodes, the king of the Parthians. Vageses violently reproached the Roman for being led by avarice to cross the Euphrates contrary to the terms of the treaty of Lucullus and Pompey. He predicted that on account of this he would soon be burdened with Chinese iron instead of with Parthian gold.

When the Romans had arrived in the neighborhood of Carrhae,[36] the Parthians under their prefects Surenas and Silaces suddenly fell upon them and overwhelmed them with

[36] A town of northwest Mesopotamia. 53 B.C.

arrows. Many senators, as well as some men of consular and praetorian rank, lost their lives. Crassus also, the son of Crassus, and a distinguished young man, was killed while fighting in the line of battle. In addition, four cohorts, together with the lieutenant Vargunteius, were surprised in open country and killed. Surenas set out quickly with his cavalry and by a forced march sought to overtake Crassus. Later he surrounded him and, after the latter had pleaded in vain for a conference, killed him; he would have preferred, however, to have taken him alive. A few escaped under cover of the night and took refuge in Carrhae.

When this disaster of the Romans became known, many provinces of the East would have withdrawn from the alliance and protection of the Roman people, had not Cassius, after collecting a few of the soldiers who had fled, exercised exceptional spirit, courage, and moderation, and thus restrained Syria, which was then in revolt. Cassius killed Antiochus and defeated his mighty forces in a battle. He also fought the Parthians who had been dispatched by Orodes into Syria and who had recently entered Antioch. He drove them off and slew their leader, Osages.

14.   THUS Rome's fortune constantly underwent alternating changes and may be compared to the level of the Ocean, which is never the same from day to day. For a space of seven days the level rises by increases that gradually grow less, and then in the same number of days falls as a result of natural loss and internal absorption. To begin with events that now follow next in order, a Roman army perished at the hands of the conquering Cimbri and Tigurini near the Rhone River. Rome felt herself to be in terrible straits, but when the disaster threatened by the Cimbri was quickly warded off she was elated by her great success and forgot her earlier failures. The Italic War and the carnage of Sulla later restrained her boasting about her recent good fortune. Yet after this domestic and internal calamity, by which she was almost disemboweled and consumed to her very marrow, not only was

Rome again restored in about an equal space of time, but her
boundaries were also enlarged. When Lucullus had subdued
Asia, when Pompey had subdued Spain, and when Caesar had
subdued Gaul, the Roman Empire stretched to almost the
extreme boundaries of the earth. This wide movement of expansion was followed by disasters far-reaching in scope. A
Roman consul was killed and his army wiped out in the territory of the Parthians; the seeds of that terrible civil war
between Pompey and Caesar were sown; and in the midst of
all this, the city of Rome herself was suddenly swept by fire
and reduced to ashes.

In the seven hundredth year after her founding, the greater
part of the City was attacked by a fire of uncertain origin.
People say that never before had so great a fire swept and
devastated the City. Tradition tells us that fourteen sections
of the City, together with the Iugarian quarter, were completely destroyed. At this time the Civil War, which had
long been in the course of preparation as a result of grave
dissensions and important movements, now commences.

15.   WHEN returning as a conqueror from Gaul, Caesar requested that a second consulship be voted him even while he
was still absent. This request was denied by the consul Marcellus with the support of Pompey. The Senate then decreed
that Caesar should not come into the City until he had first
disbanded his army. By the authority of the consul Marcellus, Pompey was sent with the imperium to the legions stationed at Luceria. Caesar then betook himself to Ravenna.
M. Antony and Q. Cassius, the tribunes of the plebs, intervened in Caesar's behalf, but upon being barred from the
Curia and Forum by order of the consul Lentulus, they set
out, accompanied by Curio and Caelius, to join Caesar. After
crossing the Rubicon River, Caesar came to Ariminum, where
he at once instructed the five cohorts, the only body of troops
he had with him at that time, what he expected them to do.
With these cohorts, according to Livy, he set out to attack
the whole world.

Bitterly bewailing the injustices done him, Caesar openly declared that the restoration of the tribunes to Rome was the cause of the Civil War. He then received from Lucretius, through Antony, the seven cohorts tarrying at Sulmo; the three legions tarrying at Corfinium with Domitius, he transferred to his own party. Alarmed at the increasing strength of Caesar, Pompey and the entire Senate were driven, so to speak, from Italy, and crossed over to Greece where they selected Dyrrachium as the base from which to carry on the war. Caesar came to Rome, where, after breaking down the doors of the treasury, he seized the money that had been refused him. He took away four thousand one hundred and thirty-five pounds of gold and nearly nine hundred thousand pounds of silver. He then left for Ariminum to join his legions, and, crossing the Alps rapidly, came to Massilia.

Leaving Trebonius there with three legions to storm the city because it had refused to receive him, Caesar hastened to the Spanish provinces that the Pompeian generals L. Afranius, M. Petreius, and M. Varro were holding with their legions. After overcoming Petreius and Afranius in many battles, Caesar concluded a pact with them and let them go. In Further Spain, however, he took over two legions from the hands of M. Varro. Moreover, his own generals were equally successful. Curio drove Cato from Sicily, Valerius drove Cotta from Sardinia, and Varus expelled Tubero from Africa. Upon his return to Massilia, which had been captured after a siege, Caesar thoroughly sacked the city, conceding to the inhabitants only their lives and liberty.

In Illyria, however, Dolabella, a member of Caesar's faction, upon being defeated by Octavius and Libo and deprived of his troops, fled to Antony. Basilus and Sallustius, with the separate legions that they commanded, and Antony and Hortensius, the latter coming with his fleet from the Etruscan Sea, all together set out to do battle with Octavius and Libo, who, however, defeated them. When Antony had surrendered himself and his fifteen cohorts to Octavius, all were led away to Pompey by Libo. Curio, who crossed from Sicily

to Africa with an army, was immediately overtaken by
King Juba and slaughtered with his entire forces. While
he was attempting to storm Salonae, Octavius lost almost
all the troops that he was leading. Caelius revolted from
Caesar and joined Milo in exile. Both were killed when
they were trying, with the help of a band of slaves,
to carry Capua by assault. Bibulus, worn out from lack
of food and long watches, was overwhelmed with shame at
Corcyra, because the enemy had made a laughingstock of the
defenses he had constructed along the sea and before the
town.

Appius Claudius Censorinus, who was guarding Greece at
Pompey's order, wished to test the already discredited credibility of the Pythian oracle. He compelled the prophetess to
descend into the grotto where she is said to have replied to his
query about the war: "O Roman, this war does not concern
you; you will obtain the Coela of Euboea." Now this Coela
people call the Euboic Gulf. So Appius departed, confused by
the perplexing prophecy.

The consulting of the oracle by Appius reminds me to take
up with my critics a point they have raised. They complain
everywhere that through the Christian faith their sacred rites
have been forbidden them and their ceremonies abolished.
They complain especially on the ground that when the con-
sultation of entrails and prophecies was discontinued, future
disasters were not avoided, since they could not be foreseen.
Why, then, long before the reign of Caesar and the birth of
Christ, as their own authorities bear witness, had the credibility of the Pythian oracle vanished? It vanished, indeed,
because it was despised. To carry the argument further, why
was it despised unless it had proven false or groundless, or at
least dubious? Hence, wisely the poet foretold:

Men depart uncounseled and detest the seat of the Sibyl.[37]

And let them not by any chance consider it of little moment
that the oracle was abolished because it fell into contempt and

[37] Vergil *Aeneid* iii. 452.

became out of date, that is, both the divinity and the place. It was that same Pythian Apollo who, they say, appeared after the death of Python as the heir to the seat, to powers of divination, and to the name of that great serpent who was the founder and chief of all prophecy. Moreover, they also say that he chose to render the responses in the place where the power of divination itself, along with its author, apparently originated. His name is forcibly vented throughout other parts of the world by all those who are possessed with madness and pour meaningless words from their foaming mouths. A great number of earthly kings have run to him as if to find the living voice of a divinity who could be consulted. Even the Romans have very often sent the richest of gifts to him. And if this Pythian Apollo, due to the slow infiltration of knowledge, came to be despised, given up, and abandoned, what life can be expected of a dead animal, what truth, indeed, from a mad woman?

When the Tuscan at the altars has blown his pipe of ivory,[38]

what finally, after the intestines of a splendid animal had been laid open, in his greed for gain would the oracle not invent, if, as they themselves admit, Apollo himself leads one astray by speaking either obscurely or falsely? Wherefore, even though in the meantime they are unwilling to follow us, let them tolerate calmly our action in prohibiting by a true judgment that which their own forefathers were led by experience to despise.

Meanwhile, at Dyrrachium many kings of the East joined Pompey with reinforcements. When Caesar arrived there, he besieged him in vain, blockading him on the land side by a ditch fifteen miles long, though the sea remained open to him. Pompey overthrew a certain fortress near the sea, which Marcellinus was guarding, and killed the garrison stationed there by Caesar. Caesar then set out to attack Torquatus and his single legion. When Pompey was informed of the danger threatening his allies, he concentrated all his forces at that

---

[38] Vergil *Georgics* ii. 193.

spot, but Caesar abandoned the siege and moved against him immediately. Torquatus, however, rushed forth instantly and attacked the rear guard of Caesar, whose soldiers became terrified by this twofold peril and took flight, even though Caesar himself tried in vain to stop them. But Pompey, whom Caesar admitted was the victor, recalled his army from the pursuit. Four thousand of Caesar's soldiers, twenty-two centurions, and some of the Roman cavalry fell in that battle.

When Caesar proceeded to Thessaly by a forced march through Epirus, Pompey followed with huge forces and engaged him in battle. The lines of battle were then drawn up on both sides. Pompey stationed eighty-eight cohorts in a triple line. There were forty thousand infantrymen and six hundred cavalry on the left wing, and five hundred on the right, not to speak of many kings, a great many Roman senators and knights, and a large force of light-armed troops. Caesar in like manner drew up his eighty cohorts in a triple line. His troops numbered less than thirty thousand infantry and a thousand horse. One could moan at the sight of the concentrated strength of Rome standing on the Pharsalian fields arrayed for mutual slaughter; had harmony only reigned, no nations or kings could have withstood them.

In the first engagement, the cavalry of Pompey was repulsed and its left flank was exposed. When mutual slaughter had gone on for a long time and while the issue was still in doubt, with Pompey on one side encouraging his soldiers, saying "spare the citizens," but not sparing them, and on the other side, Caesar crying "soldier, hit them in the face," the whole army of Pompey finally took flight and abandoned their camp to plunder. Fifteen thousand of Pompey's troops and thirty-three centurions were slain in this battle. This was the result of the battle fought at Palaeopharsalus.

In his flight Pompey came upon a merchant vessel at the mouth of the Peneus River and crossed into Asia. Thence he reached Egypt by way of Cyprus. As soon as he touched shore, he was killed by order of the youthful Ptolemy, who hoped thereby to win the favor of the victorious Caesar. The wife and children of Pompey took flight and the rest of Pompey's fleet was destroyed and all those on board were slaughtered with the utmost cruelty. Pompey Bithynicus also lost his life there, while Lentulus, a man of consular rank, was killed at Pelusium.

After having arranged his affairs in Thessaly, Caesar went to Alexandria. Upon seeing the head and ring of Pompey that were brought to him, he burst into tears. When he had betaken himself to the royal palace, he was cheated by the keepers, who, to prevent Caesar from getting the spoils, cunningly stripped their own temples in order that they might show that the royal treasures were gone and at the same time inflame the populace against Caesar. Moreover, Achillas, the royal commander, whose hands were stained with Pompey's blood, was also planning to kill Caesar. When he was ordered to dismiss his army consisting of twenty thousand armed troops, he not only scorned the order but even drew up his troops in battle array. During the combat orders were issued to set fire to the royal fleet, which by chance was drawn on shore. The flames spread to part of the city and there burned four hundred thousand books stored in a building which happened to be nearby. So perished that marvelous monument of the literary activity of our ancestors, who had gathered together so many great works of brilliant geniuses. In regard to this, however true it may be that in some of the temples there remain up to the present time book chests, which we ourselves have seen, and that, as we are told, these were emptied by our own men in our own day when these temples were plundered—this statement is true enough—yet it seems fairer to suppose that other collections had later been formed to rival the ancient love of literature, and not that there had once been another library which had books separate from the four hundred thousand volumes mentioned, and for that reason had escaped destruction.

Later Caesar captured the island on which Pharos was situated. Thither Achillas came with the Gabinian soldiers and there fought a great battle in which a great number of

Caesar's troops fell and all the slayers of Pompey were killed. When hard pressed by the force of the enemy's attack, Caesar boarded a skiff. This quickly became heavy from the added weight and sank, but Caesar swam two hundred yards to a ship, holding high the hand that held the charts. Soon afterward he was compelled to engage in a naval encounter and by a great stroke of luck sank or captured the vessels of the royal fleet.

16. IN REPLY to the Alexandrians, who were making entreaties in behalf of their king, Caesar gave warning that the king would do better to cultivate Roman friendship. Nevertheless the king, as soon as he was free, immediately declared war. He and his army were at once destroyed in a battle in which twenty thousand men, according to report, were slain, while twelve thousand men and seventy warships surrendered. Five hundred of the victors are also said to have fallen. The king himself, a minor, entered a boat in order to escape, but so many jumped into the skiff that he was forced under the water and drowned. His body, which was washed ashore, was identified by a golden lorica. After sending this lorica in advance to Alexandria, Caesar forced all the Alexandrians, who were in despair, to surrender, and he bestowed the kingdom of Egypt on Cleopatra. Thence he overran Syria and conquered Pharnaces in Pontus.

When Caesar later came to Rome, he was made dictator and consul. He then crossed to Africa and at Thapsus [39] engaged in battle with Juba and Scipio, a great number of whose men he killed. The camps of both were plundered and sixty elephants were captured. Cato committed suicide at Utica. Juba paid a man to cut his throat and Petreius transfixed himself with the same sword. Scipio, hurriedly taking ship for Spain, was turned back by the wind to Africa, where he cut his own throat. On the same ship, T. Torquatus was likewise slain. Caesar ordered the grandchildren of Pompey the Great to be killed and, at the same time, the daughter of

[39] April, 46 B.C.

Pompey together with Faustus Sulla, Afranius, and his son Petreius. Thereupon Caesar entered the city and was given four triumphs.

Having set in order the affairs of the restored Republic, Caesar immediately set out for the Spains against the Pompeys, that is, against the sons of Pompey. Seventeen days after leaving the City, he arrived at Saguntum and at once engaged the two Pompeys, Labienus, and Attius Varus in many battles with varying success. The last battle was fought at the Munda River.[40] There huge forces contended and the slaughter of the combatants was so great that even Caesar —since his own veterans were not ashamed to yield ground— seeing that his battle line was being cut to pieces and forced back, was beginning to entertain the idea of suicide, anticipating the disgrace of coming defeat, when suddenly the army of the Pompeys broke and turned to flight. Indeed this battle was finished on the very day that Pompey, the father, had fled from the City to wage war, and for four years afterward the thunders of this Civil War reverberated incessantly over the whole earth. T. Labienus and Attius Varus were slain in the line of battle, but Gnaeus Pompey escaped with a hundred horse. His brother Sextus Pompey quickly gathering together a considerable band of Lusitani, engaged in battle with Caesonius, but after being defeated, he was killed in flight.

The city of Munda, after its inhabitants had suffered severe casualties from Caesar's assault, was finally captured with great difficulty.

17. CAESAR returned to Rome. There he attempted to make minor changes in the form of the government of the Republic, which were contrary to the precedents set by the forefathers. While he was in the Senate House, he was stabbed twenty-three times and died. This conspiracy was instigated by Brutus and Cassius, but they also say that the greater part of the Senate knew of it and that there were more than sixty accomplices. The two Brutuses, C. Cassius, and the other con-

[40] 17 March, 45 B.C.

spirators, with drawn daggers withdrew to the Capitol. For a long time the people deliberated whether they should burn the Capitol together with the perpetrators of the murder. In their grief, the people took up Caesar's body and cremated it in the Forum on a pyre erected from pieces broken from the tribunal benches.

Rome spread her own misfortunes over the length and breadth of her realm and, turning to accomplish her own ruin, rendered satisfaction to all the separate nations in the very places where she had conquered them. In Asia, Europe, and Africa—I do not say in the three parts of the world, but in all the corners of the three divisions—Rome exhibited her own sons as gladiators and presented to enemies, who were enjoying the holiday, a spectacle of a vengeance that arouses pity. And yet the matter did not end when causes of war and those responsible for them had been destroyed; the seeds, returning to the soil and germinating in the self-same field, were destined at once to produce a great increase of disasters for those who harvested them with much sweat. Caesar, the victor of the Civil War, was killed by his fellow citizens. Large numbers were implicated as accomplices in the murder of this man. Caesar, done to death so shamefully, would ordinarily have found many avengers. But at this time the greater part of the nobility was linked in a single chain of crime to the end that this great source of evil might rather lead to a great war and not be settled by the prompt infliction of a penalty. We are told in fable that when the famous Medea had once sown the teeth of a dead serpent armed men sprang forth from the earth, as if indeed the crop were appropriate to the seed, and that they soon destroyed one another in combat. Verily poets in their fancies have invented this story. But upon the death of Caesar to how many armies did our Rome give birth from his ashes! How many great wars did his death stir up as a proof of his virulent fertility, not to serve merely as reading matter for youths, but actually to be a spectacle for the people to see! And yet the beginning of all these calamities was pride: from it civil wars blazed forth, from it they again multiplied. Therefore the slaughter of those who unjustly strove after slaughter was justifiable, provided that the punishment for this ambitious rivalry was visited upon the same persons who caused it. This will always be so until those who have declined a partnership in power learn to bear the rule of a master and, when supreme authority has been vested in one man, all men submit to a far different mode of life, that is, to humbly strive to please rather than to offend by an insolent spirit. For such a salutary doctrine of humility a teacher was needed. Therefore, when the affairs of Augustus Caesar had been opportunely arranged, the Lord Christ was born, Who, though in the image of God, humbly took upon Himself the form of a servant, that finally at that time the teaching of humility might become more effective, and that throughout the whole world the punishment for pride might serve as a warning to all.

18.   IN THE seven hundred and tenth year of the City, Octavianus, according to the terms of the will of his uncle Julius Caesar, became his heir and assumed his name. After he had later won control of affairs, he was called Augustus. As soon as he, still a youth, had come to Rome, he dedicated his talents to civil wars. To unfold briefly that mass of evils, he waged five civil wars, that is, those involving Mutina, Philippi, Perusia, Sicily, and Actium. Of these, two (the first and last) he fought against M. Antony, the second against Brutus and Cassius, the third against L. Antony, and the fourth against Sextus Pompey, the son of Cn. Pompey. After Antony had been declared an enemy by the Senate and had besieged D. Brutus at Mutina, the consuls Hirtius and Pansa,[41] together with Caesar, were sent to liberate Brutus and to subdue Antony. Pansa, who arrived first, was trapped in an ambush; while his forces were being slaughtered, he himself was seriously wounded by a javelin and died from the wound some days later. Hirtius, bringing aid to his colleague, destroyed Antony's great army with frightful carnage. Thus far Caesar

[41] A. Hirtius and C. Vibius Pansa.

had guarded his camp. In a second engagement with Antony, both sides suffered severe losses. For at that time and place, the consul Hirtius was killed, Antony fled after being defeated, and Caesar won the victory. To him, D. Brutus confessed his part in the conspiracy that had resulted in the murder of Julius Caesar and poured forth prayers of repentance. At Smyrna, Dolabella killed Trebonius, one of Caesar's assassins. The Senate declared Dolabella an enemy. Both armies of the slain consuls submitted to Caesar, and later D. Brutus was captured and put to death by the Sequani in Gaul. Basilus, likewise one of the assassins, was slain by his own slaves. Through the intercession of Lepidus, Caesar took Antony into his favor and as a pledge of their friendly reconciliation married the latter's daughter.

When they had reached the City, a rumor about a future proscription arose. C. Thoranius, a man of praetorian rank, fearing nothing of that kind, was killed in his own home by an attack of the soldiery. Many others were also slain, and in order that indiscriminate slaughter might not rage on a wider scale and without restraint, the names of one hundred and thirty-two senators were posted on the proscription list. The first list included those ordered and named by Lepidus, the second those by Antony, and the third those by Caesar. On his list Antony had proscribed his enemy Tullius Cicero and also his own uncle L. Caesar and—what made the crime worse—he did this while his mother was still alive. To his list, Lepidus added the name of his own brother, L. Paulus, and later thirty Roman knights were added to the number of proscribed. Over a long period of time many murders took place, the homes of the proscribed were demolished, and everything was stolen.

In Syria, however, Dolabella waged many battles with Cassius, but when he met defeat Dolabella took his own life. After assembling great armies, Brutus and Cassius united their forces at Athens and laid waste all Greece. Cassius forced the Rhodians to surrender after attacking them on land and sea; he left them nothing but their lives. Caesar and Antony then pursued Brutus and Cassius into Macedonia and compelled them to commit suicide. It is very clear, however, that this battle was brought to an end, not by courage on the part of Antony but by the good fortune of Caesar. The latter, feeling ill at the time, decided to confine himself to his camp so that he might rest. However, on the advice and entreaty of his physician, who confessed that he had been warned in a dream to lead Caesar from his camp on that day in order to save his life, Caesar made a great effort and set out with his troops for the field. Forthwith his own camp was captured by the enemy. But the troops of Caesar in turn captured the camp of Cassius. Reduced to desperation, Brutus and Cassius both resolved to commit suicide before the battle [42] came to an end. Cassius offered his head to the executioners whom they had summoned, while Brutus offered his side. At Rome, Fulvia, the wife of Antony and mother-in-law of Caesar, exercised her authority after the manner of a woman. Nobody knows whether in this change from the rank of a consul to that of a king she is to be counted as the last representative of a declining power or the first of a rising power, but certainly she acted in a haughty manner towards those who were placing her in a position to be arrogant. She even assailed Caesar with insults, party strife, and plots after he had returned to Brundisium. When he warded off her attacks, she betook herself to Greece to join Antony.

After Sextus Pompey had found his name among the number of those proscribed, he turned to piracy and laid waste the whole coast of Italy with slaughter and pillage. He quickly seized Sicily and by cutting off the flow of provisions brought famine upon Rome. The triumvirs—not to say tyrants— Lepidus, Caesar, and Antony, speedily made peace with him. But once Pompey, contrary to the terms of agreement, had allowed fugitives to join his forces, he was regarded as an enemy. Mena, the freedman of Pompey, with a fleet of sixty vessels, deserted to the side of Caesar who appointed him commander of the whole fleet. He and Statilius Taurus imme-

[42] Battle of Philippi, 42 B.C.

diately fought a naval engagement against Menecrates, the
Pompeian leader. Caesar himself then fought a very bloody
naval battle against these same Pompeians; but very soon after
he lost almost all his victorious fleet by shipwreck at Scylaceum.
Ventidius in three great battles routed the Persians and
Parthians who had broken into Syria, and killed their king
Pacorus in the battle line on the very day, indeed, on which
Crassus had been slain by the Parthians.

After capturing only one fort, Antony made peace with
Antiochus in order that he himself might appear to have been
the one who had brought so important an affair to a conclusion.
He placed Ventidius in charge of Syria and ordered him to
make war upon Antigonus, who at that time had by chance
vanquished the Jews, and who, after the capture of Jerusalem,
had despoiled the Temple and transferred the rule to Herod.
Ventidius at once defeated Antigonus and accepted his surrender. The freedman Mena, who had returned with six ships
to Pompey and had been kindly received by him, then set fire
to the fleet of Caesar. Incidentally Caesar only a short time
before had lost another fleet by a second shipwreck. This
Mena was later overcome by Agrippa in a naval engagement
and went over to the side of Caesar with six triremes. Caesar
for the third time spared the deserter's life, but he left him
powerless. After that, Agrippa fought a naval engagement
against Demochares and Pompey between Mylae and the
Liparian Islands and was victorious in an encounter in which
he sank or captured thirty vessels and damaged the remainder.
Pompey then took refuge in Messana.

Meanwhile Caesar crossed over to Tauromenium,[43] but
Pompey defeated him by a sudden attack. After many of his
ships had been sunk and a great number of his troops lost,
Caesar fled to Italy and then immediately returned to Sicily,
where he met Lepidus who was coming from Africa. The
latter by terror, threats, and a display of arrogance made good
his claim to the greater part of the troops. Several days later,
at the order of Caesar who had drawn up his battle lines and

[43] A Greek city of Sicily situated between Messana and Catana.

was watching the engagement from the shore, Agrippa fought a terrific naval battle against Pompey and was victorious, sinking or capturing one hundred and sixty-three ships. Pompey with seventeen ships barely managed to slip away and escaped.

Lepidus, who was now much puffed up with pride on account of the fact that he had twenty legions, plundered Messana, which had been turned over to his soldiers. Later he twice spurned Caesar himself who had come in person, and even went so far as to give an order that spears be hurled at him. By wrapping a cloak around his left arm, Caesar managed to ward off the attack and then made his escape. He quickly spurred his horse and riding back to his own men then drew up his forces and marched against Lepidus, the greater part of whose legions went over to Caesar's side as soon as they had suffered a few casualties. When Lepidus finally realized where his pride had led him, he laid aside his military cloak, put on a dark grey garment, and humbly petitioned Caesar. He was granted his life and property, but was condemned to perpetual exile. Taurus, Caesar's prefect, accepted the allegiance of almost all Sicily, which had been sorely tried and greatly terrified by warfare. Forty-four legions were now under the sole command of Caesar. The soldiers, somewhat arrogant on account of their numbers, began agitating for land grants; but Caesar, who had great courage, discharged twenty thousand of them from service and restored thirty thousand slaves to their masters; six thousand slaves who no longer had masters he had crucified. When Caesar entered the City in triumph, the Senate decreed that he should be given the tribunician power for life. At this time from an inn situated on the other side of the Tiber a spring of oil burst out and poured forth a great stream throughout the whole day.

19. AFTER Antony had crossed the Araxes,[44] he was beset on all sides by every kind of misfortune and barely managed in the end to make his way back with a few men to Antioch.

[44] A large river of Armenia on the border of Media.

Though defeated [45] by the great numbers of the cavalry and archers in all of the many battles he attempted, he always managed to escape. But once he was caught in unexplored and unknown parts of the country and compelled by severe hunger to eat unspeakable foods; many of his soldiers surrendered to the enemy. From this region he crossed to Greece and ordered Pompey, who after his defeat at the hands of Caesar was recruiting an army for the renewal of the war, to come to him with a small force. Pompey, fleeing from Antony's generals, Titius [46] and Furnius, after he had repeatedly been defeated in battle on land and sea, was captured and a little while later put to death.

Caesar subdued and conquered Illyria, Pannonia, and part of Italy. Antony, who had captured Artabanes, [47] the king of Armenia, by treachery and fraud, forced the king, whom he had bound with a silver chain, to reveal the location of the royal treasures. He next stormed the city where the king had disclosed that the treasures were hidden and carried off a large amount of gold and silver. He became puffed up with pride over the possession of this money and gave orders for war to be declared against Caesar and for divorce proceedings to be instituted against his own wife, Octavia, who was Caesar's sister. He also bade Cleopatra to leave Alexandria and join him. He himself set out for Actium, [48] where he had stationed his fleet. When he found that almost a third of his rowers had perished from hunger, he said, without any display of emotion, "Let oars only be safe, for as long as Greece has men, we shall not lack for rowers." Caesar then set out from Brundisium for Epirus with two hundred and thirty beaked ships.

Agrippa, whom Caesar had ordered to proceed in advance, captured a large number of merchant vessels loaded with

[45] In reality, according to Plutarch (*Antony.* 50) he won eighteen victories, but lack of cavalry prevented him from completing his pursuit.

[46] Titius, whose life Pompey had once saved, had him murdered at Miletus.

[47] Artavasdes I was invited to visit the camp of Antony who seized him, 34 B.C.

[48] A promontory at the entrance of the Gulf of Arta in Acarnania, the most westerly province of Greece.

grain and arms on their way from Egypt, Syria, and Asia, to
assist Pompey. Agrippa also worked his way into the Peloponnesian Gulf and took by storm the city of Mothona, which
was defended by a very strong garrison of Antony's. Next he
captured Corcyra; he then pursued and routed the fugitives
in a naval battle, and finally, after accomplishing many acts
of the utmost cruelty, came back to Caesar.

Alarmed by the fact that his soldiers were deserting and
were hungry, Antony decided to hasten the beginning of the
battle. After quickly drawing up his troops, he advanced toward Caesar's camp but suffered defeat. On the third day
after the battle, Antony transferred his camp to Actium and
prepared to decide the issue by a naval engagement. There
were two hundred and thirty beaked ships in Caesar's fleet and
thirty without beaks, triremes equal in swiftness to Liburnian
vessels; eight legions, not counting five praetorian cohorts,
were stationed on board the fleet. Antony's fleet had one
hundred and seventy ships, but this smaller number was offset
by their exceptional size, for in height they stood ten feet
above the level of the sea.

This battle at Actium [49] was both famous and great. From
the fifth to the seventh hour, it raged with terrific losses on
both sides and with the issue still undecided; the later hours
of the day and the following night turned the scales of victory
in Caesar's favor. Queen Cleopatra was the first to flee with
sixty of her swift vessels. Antony then pulled down the standard of the commander's ship and followed his wife in flight.
At daybreak Caesar completed his victory. On the side of
the conquered, twelve thousand, according to report, lost
their lives; six thousand were wounded, and of these a thousand died later despite [medical] care.

Antony and Cleopatra decided to send part of the royal
treasure and the children born of their marriage on ahead to
the Red Sea. After stationing garrisons around the two ex-
tremities of Egypt, Pelusium [50] and Paraetonium,[51] they them-

[49] September 2, 31 B.C.
[50] Pelusium, a city of lower Egypt, situated on the easternmost bank of the
Nile, was renowned as a fortress.
[51] Paraetonium, a town of Marmarica, famous for its spacious harbor.

selves prepared a fleet and troops for the renewal of the struggle.

Caesar, who had been named imperator for the sixth time and consul for the fourth time (in this instance with M. Licinius Crassus) went to Brundisium where he assigned different legions to posts throughout the world. From there he set out for Syria and soon drew near Pelusium where Antony's garrison of their own free will welcomed him. In the meantime Cornelius Gallus, whom Caesar had sent in advance, received the allegiance of the four legions that Antony had placed as a garrison about Cyrene. After first defeating Antony, he then captured Paraetonium, the first city of Egypt from the side of Libya, and then without delay again defeated him at Pharos.[52]

Antony contended with Caesar in a cavalry battle but was miserably defeated and took flight. At dawn of the Kalends of August, when Antony was going down to the harbor to draw up his fleet, all his ships suddenly went over to Caesar's side. When he had thus been deprived of his only source of protection, he became alarmed and with a few men hastened to the royal palace. When Caesar was menacing him and the city was in a state of turmoil, Antony stabbed himself with a sword and was carried half dead to the tomb, where Cleopatra, resolved on death, had concealed herself. Cleopatra, realizing that she would be spared to grace the triumphal procession, sought a voluntary death. She was found dead, having been bitten on her left arm, it is believed, by the fangs of a serpent. Caesar at once summoned Psylli, snake charmers who are accustomed to draw off the poison of serpents from the wounds of men by sucking and drinking, but they could not save her.

Caesar, now a conqueror, obtained control over Alexandria, a city by far the richest and greatest of all cities. Its riches so enhanced Rome's wealth that the abundance of money raised the value of property and other salable goods to double what they had been up to this time. Caesar ordered Antony's elder son to be put to death and also P. Canidius, who had always

[52] An island off Alexandria connected by a mole with the mainland.

been one of Caesar's bitterest enemies and who was disloyal to Antony as well. Cassius Palmensis, the last victim to atone for the murder of his father, Caesar, was put to death as was also Q. Ovinius. It was especially charged that he, a senator of the Roman people, had not been ashamed to superintend, most improperly, Cleopatra's spinning and weaving. From Alexandria, Caesar and his infantry went into Syria and thence departed into Asia for winter quarters. Later he came to Brundisium by way of Greece.

20.   In the seven hundred and twenty-fifth year after the founding of the City and during the consulship of the emperor Caesar Augustus who was then consul for the fifth time (in this instance with Sex. Appuleius), Caesar returned from the East as a conqueror. On the sixth of January, he entered the City in triple triumph. It was at this time, when all the civil wars had been lulled to sleep and brought to an end, that he first gave orders for the gates of Janus to be closed. On this day Caesar was first saluted as Augustus. This title, which everyone up to that time had held inviolate and one to which other rulers hitherto had not presumed, signifies that the assumption of the supreme power to rule the world was legitimate. From that time on the highest power of the state reposed in one man and so it remained thereafter. This type of government the Greeks call monarchy.

Furthermore, every believer, or even disbeliever, knows that this is also the same day (namely, the sixth of January) on which we observe the Epiphany, that is, the Feast of the Apparition and Manifestation of the Sacrament of the Lord. There is no reason nor does the occasion now call for a fuller discussion of this sacred rite which we most faithfully keep. Let it appear that we have left it for interested inquirers to look into and that we have not forced it upon those who are indifferent. Yet it was fair to have recorded this event faithfully, so that the empire of Caesar might be proven in every respect to have been prepared for the future advent of Christ.

In the first place, when Augustus was entering the city on

his return from Apollonia after the murder of his uncle C. Caesar, though the sky was clear and cloudless at the time, about the third hour a circle resembling a rainbow suddenly formed around the sun's disk. This phenomenon apparently indicated that Augustus alone was the most powerful man in this world and alone was the most renowned in the universe; it was in his time that Christ would come, He who alone had made and ruled the sun itself and the whole world.

In the second place, when Augustus, after receiving in Sicily the legions from Pompey and Lepidus, had restored thirty thousand slaves to their masters and by his own authority had distributed forty-four legions for the protection of the world, he entered the City with an ovation. He decreed that all the former debts of the Roman people should be remitted and the records of account books should also be destroyed. In those same days an abundant spring of oil, to use my former expression, flowed through the course of a whole day from an inn. What is more evident than that by this sign the coming nativity of Christ was declared in the days when Caesar was ruling the whole world? For Christ is interpreted as meaning anointed, to speak in the language of the people among whom and from whom He was born. Therefore at that time when the tribunician power was decreed to Caesar to be held forever, a spring of oil at Rome flowed throughout the whole day. Under the principate of Caesar and under the Roman Empire throughout a whole day, that is, throughout the entire duration of the Roman Empire, signs in the heavens and prodigies on the earth were very clear to those who did not heed the voices of the prophets. These signs and prodigies revealed that Christ and from Him, Christians, that is, the Anointed One and from Him, the anointed ones, would copiously and incessantly come forth from an inn, that is, from an hospitable and bountiful Church; that all slaves who still acknowledged their master must be restored by Caesar, and the others who were found without a master must be delivered to death and to punishment; and that the penalties due from offenders must be remitted under Caesar's rule in that City in which the oil had spontaneously flowed.

In the third place, after his triumphal entry into the City, no doubt on that very day mentioned above, he, consul for the fifth time, had the gates of Janus closed for the first time after a lapse of two hundred years and assumed the very distinguished name of Augustus. What is there that we can more faithfully and truthfully believe and recognize—when peace, name, and day united together for the purpose of such a manifestation—than that he had been predestined by some hidden order of events for the service of His preparation? Caesar on that day, the same on which the Lord a few years later was to make His appearance, chose the banner of peace and assumed the title of power.

But what happened after Caesar's fourth return to the City, when he had brought the Cantabrian War to an end and had pacified all nations, will be better set forth in its proper place in order to bear witness to the faith we practise.

21. IN THE seven hundred and twenty-sixth year of the City, when the emperor Augustus Caesar was consul for the sixth time and M. Agrippa for the second time, Caesar, realizing how little had been accomplished in Spain in the course of two hundred years, since he permitted the Cantabri and Astures, the two bravest peoples of Spain, to enjoy their own laws, opened the gates of Janus and in person set out with an army for the Spanish provinces. The land of the Cantabri and Astures is part of the province of Gallaecia, where the extended range of the Pyrenees terminates in the north not far from the second ocean. These tribes, who not only were ready to defend their own freedom but also dared to take away the liberty of their neighbors, were ravaging the Vaccaei, Turmogidi, and Autrigones by incessant raids.

Caesar then pitched his camp near Segisama [53] and invested almost all of Cantabria with three armies. After his army had long wearied itself without accomplishing anything and

[53] A town of the province of Tarraco.

had often exposed itself to danger, Caesar finally ordered a fleet to be brought from the Gulf of Aquitania through the Ocean, and the troops to be disembarked while the enemy were off their guard. The Cantabri finally fought a mighty battle under the walls of Attica; when defeated they took refuge on Mount Vinnius,[54] which was a natural fortress. They were there reduced to desperate straits by the hunger brought on by the siege. Next, the town of Racilium [55] was captured and destroyed, though for a long time it offered strong resistance. The legates Antistius and Firmius fought many severe battles and subdued the further parts of Gallaecia, which are wooded and mountainous and which border on the Ocean. By means of a ditch fifteen miles long they also surrounded and besieged Mount Medullius, which towered above the Minius River; [56] on this mountain a large number of the enemy had taken refuge. When this group of men, by nature wild and fierce, realized that they were neither able to withstand a siege nor strong enough to fight it out, they agreed to take their own lives because of their fear of slavery. Almost all unhesitatingly killed themselves by fire, sword, or poison.

The Astures, who had pitched camp near the Astura River, would have overpowered the Romans by the soundness of their strategy and the strength of their forces had they not been betrayed and forestalled. Their sudden attempt to overwhelm the three legates, whose legions were divided into equal columns, became known in time when their own men disclosed the plan. Later when they had withdrawn from the war, they were overcome in battle by Carisius, but not without causing the Romans to suffer heavy losses. Some of the Astures escaped from the battle and fled to Lancia.[57] As the soldiers were preparing to attack the invested city with fire, the general Carisius not only persuaded his own men to desist

---

[54] This mountain formed the boundary between Cantabria and Asturia.

[55] A town of the Cantabri in Hispania Tarraconensis.

[56] A river of Spain, said to derive its name from the vermilion (*minium*) its waters carried.

[57] The chief city of the Lanceati, a tribe of the Astures, in Hispania Tarraconensis.

from using fire but also prevailed upon the barbarians voluntarily to surrender. As a testimonial of his victory, he strove
hard to leave the city intact and uninjured. Caesar carried
away this reward from his Cantabrian victory: he could now
order the gates of war to be barred fast. Thus for a second
time in these days, through Caesar's efforts, Janus was closed;
this was the fourth time that this had happened since the
founding of the City.

Later Claudius Drusus, the stepson of Caesar, after having
been allotted Gaul and Raetia, subdued the largest and bravest
tribes of Germany with his armies. For at that time, just as
if they were hastening toward the day set for peace, all the
tribes were moved like waves toward a trial of war or an
agreement of peace, with the intention of accepting the terms
of peace if they were defeated, or if they should conquer, of
enjoying tranquillity and peace. The Norici, Illyrii, Pannonii,
Dalmatae, Moesi, Thraces, and the Daci Sarmatae, the largest
and strongest peoples of Germany, were either overcome or
subdued by different generals and shut in by the mightiest of
rivers, the Rhine and the Danube. Drusus in Germany conquered first the Usipetes and then the Tencteri and Chatti,
and slaughtered the Marcomanni almost to the last man.
Later, in a single battle, which was severe upon his own men
as well, he overcame the bravest tribes (the Cherusci, Suebi,
and Sugambri) to whom nature gave strength, and practice
experience in the use of their strength. We can judge their
courage and fierceness from the fact that if ever their women
were shut in amid their own carts by an advance of the Romans
and if their arms and everything that in their rage might serve
them as a weapon failed them, they were wont to dash their
small children on the ground and then throw them in the
faces of the enemy, committing murder twice by the separate
slaughters of their children.

At that time also, in Africa, Caesar's general Cossus confined within a limited area the Musolani and Gaetuli, who
were accustomed to range far and wide, and thus forced
them through fear to keep away from the Roman boundaries.

In the meantime, embassies of the Indians and Scythians, after traversing the whole world, at length came upon Caesar at Tarraco, a city of Hither Spain, beyond which they could not have sought him. They poured into his ears an account of the glory of Alexander the Great. Just as the embassy of the Spaniards and Gauls came to Alexander at Babylon in the center of the East to consider peace, so in Spain in the furthest West, eastern India and northern Scythia besought Caesar as suppliants and brought tribute from their countries. After conducting the Cantabrian War for five years, Caesar turned back and restored all Spain to a state of lasting peace. Then, after he had taken some rest to relieve his weariness, he returned to Rome.

In those days Caesar often fought in person, and many wars also were fought by his generals and lieutenant generals. Among others Piso was dispatched against the Vindelici. When he had subdued them, he returned as a victor to greet Caesar at Lugdunum. Tiberius, the stepson of Caesar, who had most cruelly slaughtered and destroyed the Pannonians when they had risen in a new revolt, immediately engaged the Germans in war. As a conqueror he carried off forty thousand of them as captives. This truly was a great and most formidable war waged by fifteen legions over a period of fifteen years; nor had there been, according to the testimony of Suetonius, another conflict equally great since the Punic wars.

In these same days, Quintilius Varus treated the conquered peoples in an exceedingly haughty and avaricious manner; he and the three legions accompanying him were totally destroyed by the Germans who revolted. Caesar Augustus took this disaster suffered by the state so hard that his intense sorrow made him dash his head against a wall, crying out, "O, Quintilius Varus, give me back my legions."

Agrippa, however, overcame the Bosporani and, after recovering in battle the Roman standards formerly carried off under Mithridates, forced the defeated enemy to surrender.

The Parthians acted as if the eyes of the entire world, both conquered and pacified, were focussed upon them, and as if the entire strength of the Roman Empire were to be directed against them alone. They had long been conscious of the fact that the slaughter suffered by Crassus would have to be avenged. Therefore they voluntarily returned to Caesar the standards that they had taken away on the death of Crassus and after giving hostages obtained a lasting treaty by humbly promising to observe good faith.

22. IN THE year of the City seven hundred and fifty-two, when all nations, from the East to the West, from the North to the South, and throughout the entire circuit of the Ocean, were united in the bonds of peace, Caesar Augustus had the gates of Janus closed for the third time. From that time onward they remained bolted in complete stillness for almost twelve years. Rust even gathered upon them and it was not until Augustus was a very old man that they were forced to be opened because of a revolt of the Athenians and the com- motion raised by the Dacians. During this period when the gates of Janus were closed, the emperor strove by the main- tenance of peace to nourish and to enlarge the state which he had acquired by war, establishing many laws to inculcate in men the habit of discipline through a reverence that was will- ingly given. The title "lord" he avoided on the ground that he was only a man. Once, indeed, when he was attending a play, this line was spoken in the farce: "Oh, what a just and gracious lord"; whereupon the entire audience sprang to its feet and applauded violently, as if these words had been spoken of him. He immediately checked their unseemly flat- tery with a look and a gesture, and on the following day re- buked them in a severely worded edict. Thereafter he would not permit even his own children or grandchildren to call him lord either in jest or in earnest.

At that time, that is, in the year when Caesar, by God's ordination, established the firmest and truest peace, Christ was born, Whose coming that peace waited upon and at Whose birth the angels joyfully sang in the hearing of men, "Glory to God in the highest, and on earth peace to men of good will." It was at this time that he who had secured universal supremacy refused to be called Lord of men, or rather dared not, when the true Lord of all mankind was born among men. It was also in this year when God had deigned to assume the appearance and nature of man, that this same Caesar, whom God had predestined for this great mystery, for the first time ordered a census to be taken of each and every province and that all men should be enrolled. In these days, then, Christ was born and His name was entered in the Roman census list immediately after His birth. This is that earliest and most famous acknowledgment which designated Caesar first of all men and the Romans lords of the world; for in the census list all men were entered individually, and in it the very Maker of all men wished to be found and enrolled as a man among men. From the very foundation of the world and the beginning of the human race an honor of this kind had never been granted, not even to Babylon or to Macedonia, not to mention any kingdom of lesser rank. Neither is there any doubt that it is clear to everyone from his own knowledge, faith, and investigation, that it was by the will of our Lord Jesus Christ that this City prospered, was protected, and brought to such heights of power, since to her, in preference to all others, He chose to belong when He came, thereby making it certain that He was entitled to be called a Roman citizen according to the declaration made in the Roman census list.

Now that I have reached the epoch when the Lord Christ first enlightened this world by His coming and granted a very peaceful reign to Caesar, let me conclude this sixth book of mine. The seventh, provided God gives me the requisite strength, will embrace the budding years of Christianity, its growth amid efforts made to suppress it, and its present state of advancement which is so sharply criticized by those whose statements force us to reply in kind. Since I have from the beginning declared both that men are sinners and that they are punished for their sins, so now, apart from the proposition that all men in general are inclined to sin and individually are chastised for their sins, I shall set forth first the various persecutions of the Christians and the retributions that followed.

THE SEVENTH BOOK

1. SUFFICIENT evidence has now been gathered, I think, that these truths may be publicly submitted for the approval of my critics without my making use of any secret known only to a small number of the faithful.[1] The One and true God, whom the Christian religion preaches, made the world and its creatures when He so willed, setting His creation in order through many separate acts, though in many of these acts His agency was not recognized. He established it for one purpose, when He was revealed by one event,[2] and at one time He manifested and proved His power and patience in various ways. In this regard, indeed, I have for some time noticed that people who are narrow-minded and pessimistic resent the fact that great patience is associated with great power. If, indeed, He had the power, they say, to create the world, to establish peace therein, and to make known to it the worship and the knowledge of Himself, what need was there of so great a patience, or, as they themselves regard it, so pernicious a patience, that in the end the sins, disasters, and sufferings of mankind finally brought about conditions which could just as well have been produced in the beginning through the might of the God whom you are preaching? To these persons, indeed, I might truly answer that the human race from the beginning was so created and fashioned that, living according to the precepts of religion, in peace, and without toil, it might gain eternal life as a reward for its obedience. But having abused the goodness of the Creator, who had given it freedom, it turned His gift of liberty into stubborn disobedience and

[1] Orosius is probably referring to the custom prevalent in the earliest ages of the Church by which knowledge of the more intimate mysteries of the Christian religion was kept from the pagans and from those undergoing elementary instruction in the faith.

[2] The Incarnation.

passed from the contempt of God into forgetfulness of God. In view of this, the patience of God is just in either case; for even if He is held in contempt He does not wholly destroy anyone to whom He wishes to be merciful, but by virtue of His power, as long as it is His will, He permits the man who despises Him to suffer trials. Hence it follows that it is always just for Him to guide such people in their ignorance, as He will in time, upon their repentance, mercifully restore to them the riches of their former grace.

These arguments, though advanced with great force and truth, do require, after all, a devout and willing listener. My present audience, however, whether or not they may come to believe at some future time, are certainly unbelievers now. Therefore I shall bring forward rather quickly arguments which, though my opponents may not approve, they certainly cannot disprove. Now, within the limits of our human comprehension, we and our opponents both revere religion and acknowledge and worship a higher power. The difference lies only in the nature of our belief; whereas we acknowledge that all things are from one God and through one God, they think there are as many gods as there are things. If, they say, it was in the power of the God whom you preach to make the Roman Empire so large and exalted, why then did His patience prevent it from reaching that state earlier? I shall answer them in the same vein: If it was in the power of the gods whom you preach to make the Roman Empire so large and exalted, why then did the patience of their gods prevent it from reaching that state earlier? Was it because the gods themselves did not exist? Or because Rome herself did not exist? Were the gods not worshipped at that time? Or did Rome not yet seem ready for power? If the gods were not yet in existence, their argument fails; but why discuss the delay of the gods, when I have not even discovered their nature? If, on the other hand, the gods were in existence, either their power, as my opponents really believe, or their patience was at fault; that is, either they could have acted and failed to do so, or else they wished to act but had not the power to do so. Or, if it seems more plausible to say that there were indeed gods at that time who could have aided the progress of the Romans, but that there were as yet no Romans who could rightly be assisted, I reply that we are looking for a power capable of creating suitable material to work on, not for mere workmanlike skill in shaping material already there. Our concern is with those whom the heathen consider as great gods, not with base artisans whose skill is useless unless their material is at hand. If indeed it was always possible for these gods to foreknow and to ordain—their fore-knowledge should rather be assumed, since, in the case of omnipotence, to foreknow and to will concerning its own works are the same—whatever was foreknown and ordained ought not to have been delayed but to have been put into effect. Especially is this so since the pagans say that their Jove was wont to amuse himself by turning anthills into tribes of men. Nor do I think that we need to consider further the performance of rites, inasmuch as in the midst of continual sacrifices there was no end or relief from incessant disasters, except when Christ, the Saviour of the world, appeared. Although I think that it has already been sufficiently shown that the peace of the Roman Empire was prearranged for His coming, nevertheless I will endeavor to add a few more arguments to the previous ones.

2.   At the beginning of the second book I touched lightly upon the period of the founding of Rome and there I consistently noted many points of similarity between the Assyrian city of Babylon, then first among the nations, and Rome, now holding the same position of primacy. I showed that Babylon was the first, Rome the last empire; that Babylon grew weak little by little, while Rome gradually waxed strong; that Babylon lost her last king at the same time that Rome crowned her first; and that Babylon was attacked and captured by Cyrus and fell dying, just as Rome, rising confidently after the expulsion of the kings, began to enjoy the freedom of ruling herself. Moreover, I pointed out that in those very

days, when Rome was asserting her independence, the Jewish people, who were slaves of the king of Babylon, regained their liberty, returned to holy Jerusalem, and rebuilt the Temple of the Lord, as the prophets had foretold. Furthermore, I have said that there intervened between the Babylonian Empire which was in the East and the Roman Empire which arose in the West and was nourished by the legacy of the East, the Macedonian and African empires. These empires may be regarded as playing the rôle of a guardian and trustee for brief intervals in the North and in the South. To my knowledge no one has ever doubted that the Babylonian and the Roman empires are rightly called that of the East and that of the West. That the Macedonian Empire was in the North is obvious both from its geographical position and the altars of Alexander the Great which stand to this day near the Riphaean Mountains. Carthage, on the other hand, ruled over the whole of Africa and extended the boundaries of her empire not only to Sicily, Sardinia, and other adjacent islands but even to Spain, as is shown by the records of history and by the remains of cities. I have also stated that after each city had stood for the same number of years Babylon was sacked by the Medes and Rome stormed by the Goths.

To these arguments, I now add the following proofs to make it clearer that God is the sole ruler of all the ages, kingdoms, and regions. The Carthaginian Empire, from its founding to her overthrow, lasted a little more than seven hundred years; the Macedonian, from Caranus [3] to Perses, [4] a little less than seven hundred. Both, however, came to an end in the number seven, by which all things are decided. Rome herself endured to the coming of the Lord Jesus Christ with her empire unbroken. Nevertheless she too suffered somewhat when she arrived at that same number.

For in the seven hundredth year after the founding of the

---

[3] According to some legends, Caranus founded the Argive dynasty in Macedonia about the middle of the eighth century before Christ.

[4] Perses, the last king of Macedon and the eldest son of Philip V, fought a series of wars against the Romans from 171 to 168 B.C., and died a captive in Italy.

City a fire of unknown origin consumed fourteen districts. According to Livy, a worse conflagration never visited Rome. So great were its ravages that some years later Caesar Augustus granted a large sum of money from the public treasury for the reconstruction of the burnt areas. If I were not restrained by a consideration of the present state of affairs, I could also show that Babylon had existed for twice that length of time when, more than fourteen hundred years after her founding, she was finally captured by King Cyrus. I should like, however, to add this. Holy Abraham, to whom the promises were renewed and from whose seed Christ would come, was born in the forty-third year of the reign of Ninus. He was the first of all the Babylonian kings, though there is a doubtful report that his father, Belus, was king before him. Later, Christ was born in the time of Augustus Caesar, who was the first of all the [Roman] emperors though his father Caesar had preceded him, but more as a surveyor of the Empire than as emperor. Toward the close of the forty-second year of his imperial rule, I say, Christ was born, Who had been promised to Abraham in the time of Ninus, the first king. Since, however, He was born on the twenty-fifth of December, when all the increase of the coming year begins, the result is that, whereas Abraham was born in the forty-third year, the nativity of Christ fell at the end of the forty-second, and so, instead of His being born in some part of the third year, the third year was born in Him. The greatness, novelty, and extraordinary character of the blessings in which that year abounded must, I think, surely be well enough known without my repeating them. One peace reigned over the whole earth as a result of the fact that wars had not merely ceased but had been totally abolished. After the causes of war had been wholly removed rather than merely checked, the twin gates of Janus were closed. The first and greatest census was then made. The great nations of the whole world took an oath in the one name of Caesar and were joined into one fellowship through their participation in the census.

3. IN THE seven hundred and fifty-second year of the City,
Christ was born and brought the religion that gives salvation
to the world. He is in truth the rock placed in the center of
things.[5] Whosoever strikes against Him shall be dashed to
pieces, and whosoever believeth in Him shall be saved. He is
in truth the glowing fire which illumines those who follow
Him and consumes those who assail Him. He is Christ Himself, the Head of the Christians, the Saviour of the good, the
Punisher of the wicked, the Judge of all. He set a pattern
in word and in deed for those who were to follow Him and,
in order to teach them patience in the persecutions that they
would undergo for the sake of eternal life, He began His
own sufferings as soon as He was brought into the world by
the Virgin's travail. For no sooner had Herod, king of Judea,
learned of His birth than he resolved to slay Him and, while
he was seeking out this one infant, had a great many infants
put to death. Hence we see the wicked suffer a just punishment for their malicious attacks; and hence, when the course
of the world is peaceful, it is so because of those who believe,
and when the world is vexed and disturbed, it is due to the
punishments of blasphemers. Faithful Christians, however,
are safe in any event, since at least they have either the assurance of rest in the life to come or the advantage of peace in
this life. I shall show this more clearly by the facts themselves, as I relate them in order.

After the Lord Jesus Christ, the Redeemer of the world,
had come to earth and had been enrolled in Caesar's census
as a Roman citizen, the gates of war were kept closed twelve
years, as I have said, in the happy serenity of peace. In the
meantime Caesar Augustus sent his grandson Gaius to govern
the provinces of Egypt and Syria. As Gaius was passing by
the borders of Palestine, on his way from Egypt, he disdained,
as Suetonius Tranquillus tells us,[6] to worship at Jerusalem in
the Temple of God, which was at that time venerated and

---

[5] I Corinthians 10: 4.
[6] C. Suetonius Tranquillus, the famous biographer of the Caesars, mentions
this incident in his *Life of Augustus* 93.

much frequented. When he told Augustus about his conduct, the latter had the poor judgment to praise it as wise. Then so dreadful a famine visited the Romans in the forty-eighth year of Caesar's rule that Caesar ordered the gladiatorial bands, all foreigners, and also great numbers of slaves to be expelled from the City. Physicians and teachers were excepted. Thus, when the princeps sinned against the Holy One of God and the people were seized by famine, the greatness of the offense was shown by the nature of the punishment. Let me next quote the words of Cornelius Tacitus: "Janus was opened in the old age of Augustus and remained so until the rule of Vespasian, while new tribes were sought at the ends of the earth, often with gain and sometimes with loss." [7] So much for Cornelius.

After the capture and overthrow of Jerusalem, as the prophets had foretold, and after the total destruction of the Jewish nation, Titus, who had been appointed by the decree of God to avenge the blood of the Lord Jesus Christ, celebrated with his father Vespasian his victory by a triumph and closed the Temple of Janus. Now, although the Temple of Janus was opened in the last days of Caesar, nevertheless there were no alarms of war for long periods thereafter, even though the army was ready for battle. Our Lord Jesus Christ Himself also had these facts in mind in the Gospels; for, when the whole world in those days was enjoying great quiet and all nations were united under the shelter of peace, He was asked by His disciples about the end of the coming times and replied in part as follows:

And you shall hear of wars and rumors of wars: see that you be not troubled: for all these things must come to pass, but the end is not yet. For nation shall rise against nation, and kingdom against kingdom: and there shall be pestilences, famines, and earthquakes, in diverse places. All these are the beginning of sorrows. Then shall they deliver you up to be afflicted, and shall kill you: and you shall be hated of all nations for my name's sake. [8]

[7] This passage is found only in Orosius. It is taken from a lost book of the *Histories* of Tacitus.

[8] Matthew 24: 6–9.

Thus He taught in His divine foresight and not only strengthened the faithful by His warning but also confounded the unbelieving by His prediction.

4. IN THE seven hundred and sixty-seventh year of the City,
after the death of Augustus Caesar,[9] Tiberius Caesar assumed
the sovereignty and held it for twenty-three years.[10] He waged
no wars in person nor did his commanders wage any
important wars, except that uprisings of peoples in some
localities were anticipated and quickly crushed. To be sure,
in the fourth year of his reign, Germanicus, the son of Drusus
and father of Caligula, celebrated a triumph over the Germans, against whom he had been sent by Augustus in the
latter's old age. Tiberius himself, however, during the greater
part of his reign administered the affairs of the state with so
deep a sense of responsibility and so great moderation that
he wrote to some governors who had advised an increase in
the tribute levied upon the provinces to the effect that "it is
the duty of a good shepherd to shear his flock and not to flay
them."

When the Lord Christ had suffered and risen from the dead
and had sent forth His disciples to preach, Pilate, the governor of the province of Palestine, made a report to the emperor
Tiberius and to the Senate concerning the passion and resur-
rection of Christ, and also the subsequent miracles that had
been publicly performed by Him or were being done by His
disciples in His name. Pilate also stated that a rapidly increasing multitude believed Him to be a god. When Tiberius,
amid great approval, proposed to the Senate that Christ
should be considered a god, the Senate became indignant because the matter had not been referred to it earlier in accordance with the usual custom, so that it might be the first to
pass upon the recognition of a new cult. The Senate therefore
refused to deify Christ and issued an edict that the Christians
should be banished from the City. There was also the special

---

[9] 14 August, A.D. 19.
[10] From A.D. 14 to 37.

reason that Sejanus, the prefect of Tiberius, was inflexibly opposed to the recognition of this religion. Nevertheless in an edict Tiberius threatened denouncers of Christians with death.

Now it came about that the emperor little by little abandoned his most praiseworthy policy of moderation in order to take revenge upon the Senate for its opposition; for he took pleasure in doing whatever he wished and from the mildest of princes he became the most savage of wild beasts. He proscribed a great army of senators and drove them to death. Of the twenty noblemen whom he had selected as his counselors, he left scarcely two unharmed and destroyed the others on various pretexts. He put to death his prefect Sejanus who was trying to stir up a revolution. There were clear indications that he poisoned both Drusus, his son by birth, and Germanicus, his son by adoption. He also killed his grandchildren, the sons of Germanicus. To recite his deeds one by one would be too horrible and scandalous. Suffice it to say that his lust and cruel rage grew so violent that those who had scorned to be saved under the rule of Christ were punished under the rule of Caesar.

In the twelfth year of Tiberius, a strange and unbelievable disaster occurred at the city of Fidenae.[11] While the people were watching a gladiatorial performance, the seats of the amphitheater collapsed and killed more than twenty thousand persons. In truth, the ages to come may well heed the lesson of this great catastrophe that befell those who had so eagerly assembled to witness the death of their fellow men. And this at the very time when God had been pleased to become man for the sake of securing man's salvation!

In the seventeenth year of this emperor, the Lord Jesus Christ of His own free will submitted to His passion. Nevertheless, it was through their own impiety that the Jews arrested Him and nailed Him to the cross. At that time a very severe earthquake shook the whole world. The rocks upon the mountains were rent, and many sections of the larg-

[11] An ancient city of Latium, situated on the Via Salaria, about five miles from Rome.

est cities were overthrown by its unusual violence. On that day, too, at the sixth hour, the sun was also entirely obscured and a hideous darkness suddenly overshadowed the earth; in the words of the poet,

a godless age feared eternal night.[12]

It is, however, perfectly plain that the sun's light was not cut off either by the moon or by clouds. For we are told that the moon, being fourteen days old at the time, was in the opposite quarter of the heavens, farthest from the sun, and that the stars were shining throughout the entire sky at that hour of the daytime or rather in that awful night. These facts are attested not only by the authority of the Holy Gospels but also by several books of the Greeks.

From the time of the passion of our Lord to this day, the Jews, who had persecuted Him to the extent of their power, have complained incessantly of an unbroken succession of disasters, until finally their nation, drained of its lifeblood and scattered abroad, disappeared from history. For Tiberius dispatched the youth of the Jewish nation to provinces having an unhealthful climate, using their military obligation as a pretext. He also forced the remainder of the Jews, as well as those who practiced similar rites, to leave Rome, threatening to make them slaves for life if they failed to obey. When the earthquake mentioned above demolished many cities of Asia, he remitted their tribute and made a donation to them from his own purse as well. The circumstances of the death of Tiberius led to suspicions that he had been poisoned.

5. IN THE seven hundred and ninetieth year of the City, Gaius Caligula, the third emperor counting from Augustus, began his reign. He ruled barely four years.[13] He was more wicked than all his predecessors and seemed well worthy to be an instrument of vengeance upon the blaspheming Romans and the persecuting Jews. Let me show in a word the extent of his savagery by quoting the exclamation that is attributed

[12] Vergil *Georgics* i. 468.   [13] From 37 to 41.

to him: "Would that the Roman people had but a single neck!" [14] Furthermore, he often complained bitterly about the state of his times because they had been marked by no public disasters.

O, blessed beginnings of Christianity! So great was your power over the affairs of men that even the cruelty of man could only wish for disaster without finding them. See how hungry savagery loudly complains of the general peace:

> Within, impious rage,
> Sitting on savage arms, his hands
> Bound behind his back with a hundred brazen knots,
> Will send forth horrible roars from bloody lips.[15]

Up to this time mutinous slaves and runaway gladiators terrified Rome, overturned Italy, ruined Sicily, and were dreaded by mankind throughout almost the whole world. But in the days of salvation, that is, in Christian times, not even a hostile Caesar could break the peace. Caligula, after making almost incredible preparations, set out to find an enemy in order to give his idle troops an opportunity to fight. Traversing Germany and Gaul he stopped on the seacoast opposite Britain. There he received the submission of Minocynobelinus who had been banished by his father, the king of the Britons, and who was now wandering about accompanied by a few followers. Lacking a ground for war, Caligula returned to Rome.

At this time the Jews, already harassed by misfortunes everywhere as a retribution for Christ's passion, were crushed in a riot that had broken out in Alexandria. They were driven from the city. Thereupon they commissioned a certain Philo, unquestionably a scholar of the first rank, to go as their representative to the emperor and set forth their grievances. But Caligula, who hated mankind in general, particularly detested the Jews. He therefore treated Philo's mission with contempt and commanded that all the holy places of the Jews, and especially that famous ancient sanctuary in Jerusalem,

---

[14] Suetonius *Gaius Caligula* xxx.　　　　[15] Vergil *Aeneid* i. 294–96.

should be profaned with heathen sacrifices and filled with statues and images. He also gave orders that he himself should be worshipped there as a god. When Pilate, the governor who had pronounced the death sentence upon Christ and who had been the instigator as well as the object of many riots in Jerusalem, received this order, he was so tormented that he stabbed himself with his own hand and so quickly put an end to his miseries.

In addition to his other acts of lust, Gaius Caligula committed the crime of violating his own sisters. He then condemned them to exile and later ordered their execution and that of all other exiles. He himself, however, was murdered by his bodyguard. Among his private papers there were found two notebooks. One of these he had entitled *The Dagger*, the other, *The Sword*.[16] Each contained the names of the most distinguished men of the two orders, senatorial and equestrian, together with marks indicating those who were to be killed. A huge chest of various poisons was also found. Claudius Caesar soon afterward ordered these poisons to be thrown into the sea, whereupon the waters became polluted and killed great numbers of fish, whose dead bodies were cast up by the waves along all the neighboring shores.

A really strong evidence of God's mercy may be seen in his manifestation of grace toward a people of whom only part were destined to become believers, and from the tempering of His wrath against them at that time when they persisted in their unbelief. How great a multitude of human beings escaped the death that had been prepared for them may be surmised and was indeed clear to all from the numbers of fish that had been poisoned. What havoc so great an amount of poison might have caused in the unfortunate city, if it had been skillfully used, is evident, since even its careless disposal polluted the sea.

6. DURING the seven hundred and ninety-fifth year of the City, Tiberius Claudius, the fourth in succession from Augus-

[16] Suetonius *Gaius Caligula* xlix.

tus, came to the throne. He occupied it for fourteen years.[17]
In the beginning of his reign, Peter, the apostle of the Lord
Jesus Christ, came to Rome. There he taught by the true
word the religion that brings salvation to all believers and
attested it by mighty miracles. From that time on there began
to be Christians in Rome. The City felt that this favor had
been bestowed on her because of her faith. After the murder
of Caligula, the Senate and the consuls passed many resolu-
tions with a view to abolishing the empire, restoring the commonwealth to its former status, and wiping out completely
the entire family of the Caesars. Soon after establishing his
rule, Claudius exercised a clemency previously unknown in
Rome. To prevent vengeance from venting its rage, if it
should get a start, upon so many of the nobility, he consigned
to oblivion the memory of those two days during which those
unhappy measures and acts had been passed regarding the
form of government, and decreed that all that had been done
or said during that period should be pardoned and forever
forgotten. This was that renowned and glorious Athenian
amnesty, which the Senate, on the advice of Cicero, had tried
to introduce at Rome after the death of Julius Caesar, but
which at that time had come to naught because of the onslaughts
made by Antony and Octavian in their efforts to avenge
Caesar's murder. Yet Claudius, without being asked by anyone, assented because of his humanity, though he had serious
provocation to execute those who had conspired against him.

Now at this time by the grace of God a great miracle
occurred. Furius Camillus Scribonianus, the governor of Dalmatia, had been plotting a civil war and had persuaded many
of the strongest legions to break their allegiance. But on the
day appointed for their assembling at the side of the new
emperor, they found it impossible either to adorn the eagles
or to pull up and move the standards. This unique miracle
so impressed the soldiers that they gave up their plan, abandoned Scribonianus, killed him four days later, and returned
to their former allegiance. Now it is well known that nothing

[17] From 41 to 54.

has ever brought more sorrow and destruction upon Rome than civil wars. Of a certainty God repressed this rising tyranny and threatening civil war on account of the coming of the apostle Peter and for the sake of the few Christians, who, like tender shoots springing up here and there, were just beginning to profess the holy faith. If anyone would deny this fact, let him produce a similar instance of the suppression of civil war in past ages.

In the fourth year of his reign Claudius looked about everywhere for an opportunity to engage in a successful war, for he wanted to appear as a prince who was of some service to the state. Accordingly he undertook a campaign in Britain, which was in the throes of an insurrection. This insurrection had apparently arisen because certain deserters had been barred from returning home.[18] He crossed over to the island, which no one before had ventured to approach except Julius Caesar. There, to quote the words of Suetonius Tranquillus, "within a very few days he reduced the greater part of the island to submission without fighting or bloodshed."[19] He also added to the Roman Empire the Orcades Islands situated in the Ocean beyond Britain and within six months of the date of his departure he returned to Rome.

Any person of the present day who pleases may make comparisons in regard to this one island, period with period, war with war, Caesar with Caesar. I say nothing of the outcome, since in this case it was the most fortunate of victories, previously the bitterest of disasters. Thus Rome may finally come to see that the God through Whose Providence she formerly enjoyed partial success in her undertakings is the God through Whose recognition she now enjoys success in all its fullness to the extent that she does not become corrupted through the stumbling block of her blasphemies.

In the same year of this emperor's reign, as the prophets had foretold, there was a terrible famine throughout Syria. The needs of the Christians at Jerusalem, however, were bountifully supplied with grain that Helena, the queen of

<hr>

[18] The identity of these deserters is not clear. [19] Suetonius *Claudius* xvii.

Adiabeni and a convert to the faith of Christ, had imported from Egypt.

In the fifth year of the reign of Claudius, an island,[20] extending over a space of thirty stadia, suddenly appeared out of the deep sea between Thera and Therasia.

Two years later, when Cumanus was procurator of Judaea, an insurrection broke out in Jerusalem at the time of the Passover. So great was this riot that the people were crushed while stampeding through the gates. Thirty thousand Jews are said to have been trampled to death or suffocated in the congestion.

In the ninth year of his reign, Claudius expelled the Jews from Rome. Both Josephus and Suetonius record this event, but I prefer, however, the account of the latter, who speaks as follows: "Claudius expelled the Jews from Rome because in their resentment against Christ they were continually creating disturbances."[21] As a matter of fact, however, no one can say whether the emperor ordered the Jews to be restrained and repressed because they were creating disturbances against Christ or whether he wished the Christians to be expelled at the same time on the ground that they were members of an allied religion.

Nevertheless, during the following year there was so great a famine in Rome that the emperor was taunted and insulted by the people in the middle of the Forum and shamefully pelted with pieces of bread. He barely managed to escape the fury of the excited mob by fleeing through a private entrance into the Palace.

Not long afterward, Claudius, acting upon the flimsiest pretext, put to death thirty-five senators and three hundred Roman knights at one time. In the matter of his own death, however, there were clear indications that he had been poisoned.

7.   IN THE eight hundred and eighth year of the City, Nero

[20] The event, which occurred in 46, is mentioned by several writers. The island, called Thia, or Mikra Kamméni, is located in the Aegean Sea about seven hundred stadia from Crete.   [21] Suetonius *Claudius* xxv.

Caesar, the fifth in succession from Augustus, became princeps. He held the office for almost fourteen years.[22] In every
vice and crime he followed his uncle, Gaius Caligula, and
indeed he even surpassed him. There was no form of wickedness that he did not practice—wantonness, lust, extravagance,
avarice, and cruelty. In the first place, his wantonness led
him to visit nearly all the theaters of Italy and Greece, where
he disgraced himself by wearing motley attire. Indeed he often
imagined that he carried away the palm symbolizing victory
from heralds, musicians, actors, and charioteers. Then the
violence of his lusts became so great that he is said to have
respected neither his mother's nor his sister's honor nor any
blood relationship. Also he took a man to wife and was himself received as a wife by a man. His extravagance was so
unbridled that he fished with nets of gold, which were drawn
up by cords of purple, and he bathed in hot and cold per-
fumed waters. It is even said that he never traveled with less
than a thousand carriages. He caused Rome to be burned in
order to enjoy the spectacle and for six days and seven nights
feasted his eyes on the blazing city. The warehouses, built of
square stone, and the huge tenements of a bygone day, which
the spreading flames could not reach, were demolished by
great machines originally designed for use in foreign wars,
and these buildings were then set on fire. The unfortunate
plebeians were driven for shelter to monuments and tombs.
The emperor himself viewed the conflagration from the lofty
Tower of Maecenas.[23] And while enjoying the beauty of the
flames, it is said that he declaimed the Iliad in a tragedian's
costume. The avarice of Nero was likewise so uncontrolled
that, after the burning of the City, which Augustus, according to his boast, had changed from brick into marble, he
would not allow anyone to approach the remains of his own
property, but himself seized everything that had by any chance
escaped the flames. He also ordered the Senate to appropriate

[22] From 54 to 68.
[23] A tower connected with the house and gardens of Maecenas on the Es-
quiline Hill in Rome.

ten million sesterces a year for his expenses. He deprived a great many senators of their property without cause, and in one day wiped out the entire wealth of all the merchants and inflicted torture upon them as well. His insane cruelty made him so savage that he killed the greater part of the Senate and almost annihilated the equestrian order. He did not even refrain from murdering members of his own family and without scruple destroyed his mother, brother, sister, wife, and all the rest of his blood relations and kinsmen.

All this mass of crime was crowned by Nero's daring impiety toward God. He was the first emperor to torture and put to death Christians at Rome and he ordered them to be harassed by a like persecution throughout all the provinces. In his attempt to root out their very name, he put to death Peter and Paul, the most blessed apostles of Christ, one by the cross and the other by the sword. Soon wretched Rome was engulfed by disasters pressing in upon her from every side. The following autumn so great a plague visited the City that thirty thousand funerals were entered in the register of the goddess Libitina. Britain at once suffered a disaster. Two of the principal towns were sacked and a great number of Roman citizens and their allies were slaughtered and destroyed.[24] In the East, moreover, the important Armenian provinces were lost. Roman legions were forced to pass beneath the Parthian yoke, and Syria was retained only with great difficulty. In Asia an earthquake destroyed three cities, Laodicia, Hierapolis, and Colossae. In the meantime, Nero learned that the army in Spain had proclaimed Galba emperor. His courage and his hope utterly collapsed. In the midst of his wicked and unbelievable attempts to ruin and even to destroy the state, the Senate declared him a public enemy. He ignominiously fled and killed himself four miles from the City. With Nero the entire family of the Caesars became extinct.

8.   IN THE eight hundred and twenty-fourth year of the City,

---

[24] The towns were Camulodunum and Verulanium.

Galba assumed the imperial title in Spain. As soon as he learned of Nero's death, he came to Rome.[25] Here he offended everyone by his avarice, cruelty, and indolence. He adopted as his son and successor Piso, a highborn and industrious young man, but both were slain by Otho after a reign of seven months.

Thus Rome atoned for the wrongs done to the Christian religion through the slaughter of her rulers and the breaking out of civil war. When the apostle Peter came to the City, the legionary standards, you will recall, were held fast by the will of Heaven and could not be pulled up by any means whatsoever to set in motion the civil war which Scribonianus had planned. But after Peter had been killed in the City and the Christians had been mangled by every sort of punishment the standards were loosened from the ground throughout the world. Galba now raised the standard of revolt in Spain. Upon his downfall, Otho in Rome, Vitellius in Germany, and Vespasian in Syria, all assumed the imperial title and took up arms at the same time. Here truth compels those who decry the Christian era to acknowledge, even against their own will, both the power and the mercy of God. Let them but consider how suddenly the fires of war flared up and how swiftly they were quenched. Formerly slight causes stirred up great and long lasting disasters. Now the mighty peals of thunder resounding on all sides from great evils are stilled with but slight difficulty. For in spite of persecution, the Church already existed at Rome; and from there she made supplications to Christ, the Judge of all, even in behalf of her enemies and persecutors.

Otho made his way to the throne amid rioting and bloodshed after the murder of Galba and Piso at Rome. He began a civil war as soon as he learned that the legions of Germany had proclaimed as emperor Vitellius, who was in Gaul. At first Otho won three unimportant victories over the generals of Vitellius, one in the Alps, another near Placentia, and the

[25] His reign extended from 9 June 68 to 15 January 69.

third near a place called Castores. But when he saw in a fourth battle fought at Bedriacum [26] that his troops were being worsted, he took his own life. This occurred three months after he had begun his reign.[27]

Vitellius, the victor, came to Rome. There, after much cruelty and vileness, he brought disgrace upon humanity by his unbelievable gluttony. As soon as he learned what Vespasian was doing, he tried to abdicate. Later, encouraged by certain persons, he forced the partisans of Vespasian, including the latter's brother Sabrinus, who had not suspected any trouble, to take refuge in the Capitol. He set the temple on fire and let the flames and falling walls together envelop all in a common death and a common tomb. Later he was abandoned by his army, which went over to the cause of Vespasian. In his fright at the enemy's approach, he hid himself in a small storeroom near the Palace. From this hiding place he was ignominiously dragged forth and, naked as he was, led along the Sacred Way to the Forum, while the bystanders pelted his face with dung. Eight months after he had usurped the throne,[28] he was tortured to death at the Germonian Steps by countless tiny pricks and stabs. He was then dragged away with a hook and flung into the Tiber without even receiving the usual privilege of burial. For a number of days thereafter, amid scenes of general lawlessness, the soldiers of Vespasian vented their fury upon the Senate and people of Rome by an indiscriminate massacre.

9. DURING the eight hundred and twenty-fifth year of the City, after the passing of violent but brief storms in the form of illegal attempts to seize the throne, peace and calm returned under the rule of Vespasian.[29] To go back a little in my story, the Jews, who after Christ's passion first were utterly forsaken by the grace of God and then beset on all sides by every kind of misfortune, were led astray by certain oracular re-

[26] A small town of Cisalpine Gaul, situated between Verona and Cremona.
[27] Otho reigned from 15 January 69 to 25 April 69.
[28] The reign of Vitellius extended from 3 January 69 to 21 December 69.
[29] From 69 to 79.

sponses given on Mount Carmel.[30] These foretold that leaders would come out of Judaea and seize control of the government. Applying this prediction to themselves, the Jews broke out in rebellion. They massacred the Roman garrisons, put to flight the governor of Syria when he came with reinforcements, captured his standard, and cut his forces to pieces.

Vespasian, whom Nero sent against them, took his elder son Titus with him as one of his lieutenants. He also brought with him to Syria a number of strong legions. After taking many of the towns, he blockaded the Jews in Jerusalem, where they had gathered in large numbers because it was a feast day.[31] On learning of Nero's death, he declared himself emperor. He was strongly urged to take this step by numerous kings and generals but most of all by the words of Joseph, a leader of the Jews. This man, when made prisoner and put in chains, had most confidently declared, as Suetonius tells us,[32] that he would be released directly by the same person who had imprisoned him, but that that person would be the emperor. Vespasian, leaving his son Titus in camp to manage the siege of Jerusalem, set out for Rome by way of Alexandria. But when he heard that Vitellius had been killed, he stopped at Alexandria for a short time.

Titus, on his part, wore down the Jews by a long close siege. He finally made a breach in the city walls by using engines and all kinds of military apparatus, though not without the loss of many of his men. But it took more strength and a much longer time to capture the inner fortification of the Temple. A number of the priests and chief men had shut themselves up there and were maintaining its defense. When Titus had finally gained control of it, the construction and antiquity of the Temple aroused his admiration. He was for some time undecided whether he should burn it since its survival would encourage the enemy or whether he should preserve it as a memorial of his victory. But now that the Church

---

[30] A mountain sacred throughout Jewish history as a place of prayer and intercession and, according to Tacitus (*Histories* ii. 78), the site of an oracle.
[31] The day of the Passover. [32] Suetonius *Vespasian* v.

of God had already blossomed forth richly throughout the world, it was His will that this building should be removed as an empty shell that had outlasted its usefulness. Therefore, Titus, after being acclaimed imperator by the army, set on fire and destroyed the Temple at Jerusalem, which, from the day of its founding to its final overthrow, had endured for 1102 years. All the walls of the city were leveled to the ground. According to Cornelius and Suetonius, six hundred thousand Jews were killed in this war. But Joseph the Jew, who was in command of the war at that time and who later found pardon and favor with Vespasian by predicting his accession, writes that eleven hundred thousand perished by the sword and by famine and that the remainder of the Jews were driven off in various conditions of misfortune and scattered throughout the world. These are said to have numbered about ninety thousand.

The emperors Vespasian and Titus celebrated their victory over the Jews by a magnificent triumphal entry into Rome. Of all the three hundred and twenty triumphs that had been held from the founding of the City until that time, so fair and strange a sight had not been seen by man—father and son riding in the same triumphal chariot after their glorious victory over those who had offended the Father and the Son. Now that all wars and uprisings had been put down at home and abroad, these emperors without delay proclaimed universal peace and decreed that double-faced Janus should be confined by the barring of his gates. This was the sixth time that this had occurred since the founding of the City. It was indeed right that the same honor should be paid to the avenging of the Lord's Passion as had been bestowed upon His Nativity. The Roman state then made great progress without suffering any of the tumults of war. Achaia, Lycia, Rhodes, Byzantium, Samos, Thrace, Cilicia,[33] and Commagene were

---

[33] Some manuscripts of Suetonius, copied by Eutropius, from whom Orosius took this list, have the form "Trachiam." By this reading, Cilicia Trachea, the mountainous part of Cilicia, is intended.

for the first time reduced to provinces and obeyed the judges and the laws of Rome.

In the ninth year of this emperor's reign, an earthquake destroyed three cities of Cyprus and at Rome there was a great plague. Vespasian died of dysentery at his country place among the Sabines in the ninth year of his principate.

In the eight hundred and twenty-eighth year of the City, Titus, eighth in the succession from Augustus if we exclude Otho and Vitellius from the list of emperors, succeeded Vespasian. He reigned for two years.[34] His reign was so quiet that it is said that he did not shed the blood of a single person during his administration of the government. At this time, however, a conflagration suddenly broke out at Rome and consumed a great number of public buildings. It is also related that the top of Mount Bebius blew off and poured forth masses of molten lava and that these torrents of fire destroyed the surrounding country with its cities and their inhabitants. Titus succumbed to disease in the same country estate where his father had died. He was deeply mourned by all.

10. IN THE eight hundred and thirtieth year of the City, Domitian, the ninth in succession from Augustus, succeeded his brother Titus on the throne. For fifteen years this ruler progressed through every degree of wickedness. Finally he dared to issue edicts for a general and most cruel persecution to uproot the Christian Church, which was now very firmly established throughout the world. He even fell into such a state of pride that he ordered the people to speak, to write of, and to worship him as Lord and God. Moved by envy and greed, he put to death the noblest men of the Senate; some he killed publicly, others he forced into exile and there butchered them. Whatever uncontrolled lust suggested to him he did. In Rome he erected many buildings upon the ruins of the people's property. Equally harmful to the state was the war which his legates waged against the Germans and the

[34] From 79 to 81.

Dacians. While the Domitian himself at the Capitol was a scourge to the Senate and to the people, his enemies abroad were continually cutting to pieces his badly led armies. I should like to tell in detail of the great battles fought by the Dacian king Diurpaneus [35] against the general Fuscus, [36] as well as of the extent of the Roman losses. But Cornelius Tacitus, who wrote an exhaustive history of these events, has declared that Sallustius Crispus [37] and very many other authors established the practice of keeping silence about the numbers of the slain, and that he himself preferred to do likewise.

Domitian, however, who was puffed up by the lowest form of vanity, held a triumph. Nominally this triumph celebrated his victory over the enemy, but in reality it celebrated the loss of his legions. Crazed by his pride, which made him want to be worshipped as a god, he was the first emperor after Nero to order a persecution of the Christians. Also in these days the most blessed apostle John was banished to the island of Patmos. The Jews, too, were subjected to cruel tortures and to the bloodiest of inquisitions for the purpose of searching out and destroying the race of David. The emperor did this because he both hated and yet believed the holy prophets, and thought that One was still to come from the seed of David who would ascend the throne. Domitian soon was cruelly assassinated in his palace by members of his own household. The public corpse bearers carried out his body on a common bier and buried it most dishonorably.

11. IN THE eight hundred and forty-sixth year of the City—although Eutropius says that it was the eight hundred and fiftieth [38]—Nerva was proclaimed emperor. [39] He was a man advanced in years and was named emperor by the praetorian prefect Petronius and the eunuch Parthenius, the latter the murderer of Domitian. Nerva was the tenth emperor in

---

[35] From 81 to 96. This king is called Decebalus by Dion Cassius.

[36] Cornelius Fuscus was surprised by the Dacians, who destroyed the greater part of his army and captured his baggage and standards.

[37] Sallustius Crispus, the famous historian of the later years of the Republic.

[38] Eutropius *Breviarium historiae Romanae* viii. 1.   [39] From 96 to 98.

succession from Augustus. He adopted Trajan as his own successor, revealing by this choice that a divinely inspired foresight had guided him in taking care of the sorely afflicted state. In his first edict, Nerva recalled all the exiles. This general pardon freed the apostle John who then returned to Ephesus. After a reign of one year Nerva succumbed to a disease and died.

12.   IN THE eight hundred and forty-seventh year of the City, Trajan, a Spaniard by birth, and the eleventh emperor in succession from Augustus, took the helm of state from Nerva. He held it for nineteen years.[40] Trajan assumed the emblems of the imperial office at Agrippina, a city in Gaul. He at once restored Germany beyond the Rhine; he subdued many tribes beyond the Danube; he formed provinces of the districts beyond the Euphrates and the Tigris; and he took possession of Seleucia, Ctesiphon, and Babylon. Trajan erred in judgment, however, in his persecution of the Christians, the third persecution from that of Nero. He ordered that Christians should be compelled, wherever found, to sacrifice to idols or be put to death if they refused. Great numbers of them were executed.

Pliny the Younger, who had been appointed persecutor with other judges, reported that the Christians were doing nothing contrary to the Roman laws apart from their profession of belief in Christ and their inoffensive meetings. Moreover, he said that none of them, sustained by their harmless belief, thought death a matter of grief or of dread. Upon receiving this information, the emperor at once modified his edict by rescripts couched in milder terms. Nevertheless the Golden House at Rome, which Nero had built with a great outlay of both private and public wealth, was suddenly burned to the ground. Thus it was made plain that, though the persecution was set in motion by another, the punishment fell most heavily upon the buildings of that man who first began the persecution and who was the real author of it.

At the same time an earthquake laid low four cities in

[40] From 98 to 117.

Asia, Elaea, Myrina, Pitane, and Cyme, and in Greece, the two cities of the Opuntii and the Oriti. This same earthquake demolished three cities of Galatia. Lightning struck and burned the Pantheon at Rome, while at Antioch an earthquake laid almost the entire city in ruins. Then violent rebellions among the Jews broke out simultaneously in various parts of the world. The Jews acted as if turned into mad savages. Throughout Libya they waged pitiless war against the inhabitants and caused great desolation by killing the tillers of the soil. So merciless were they that if the emperor Hadrian had not afterward colonized the country with people from without, the land would have remained absolutely destitute and entirely without inhabitants. They disturbed all Egypt, Cyrene, and the Thebaid by sedition and bloodshed. In Alexandria, however, the Jews were defeated and crushed in a pitched battle. When they also rebelled in Mesopotamia, the emperor ordered war to be declared against them; many thousands of them were exterminated in a vast carnage. It is true that they did destroy Salamis, a city of Cyprus, after they had killed all the inhabitants. Trajan, according to some authors, died of dysentery at Seleucia, a city of Isauria.

13. IN THE eight hundred and sixty-seventh year of the City, Hadrian, the nephew of Trajan on his mother's side, became the twelfth emperor in succession from Augustus. He ruled for twenty-one years.[41] Hadrian underwent instruction and came to know thoroughly the doctrines of the Christian faith through treatises written by Quadratus,[42] a disciple of the Apostles, by Aristides [43] of Athens, a man full of faith and wisdom, and by Serenus Granius, the legate. He therefore gave orders in a letter to Minicius Fundanus, the proconsul of Asia, that no one should have authority to condemn the Christians without allegation and proof of a crime. In viola-

[41] From 117 to 138.

[42] Quadratus, an author of an apology for the Christians in the time of Hadrian, received this title from Eusebius in his Chronicle.

[43] Aristides of Athens also wrote a well-known apology for the Christians and presented it to the emperor Hadrian.

tion of a precedent, Hadrian soon received in the Senate the
title Father of His Country and his wife the title Augusta.
He governed the state very justly and conducted a successful
war against the Sauromatae. In one final massacre he subdued the Jews who, excited by the disorders caused by their
own crimes, were ravaging the province of Palestine, which
had once been their own. In this way he avenged the Christians, whom the Jews, under the leadership of Cochebas, were
torturing because they would not join them against the
Romans. The emperor gave orders that no Jew should be
permitted to enter Jerusalem and that only Christians should
be permitted to occupy the city. He restored it to great prosperity by rebuilding the walls and named it Aelia, from his
own first name.

14. IN THE eight hundred and eighty-eighth year of the City,
Antoninus, surnamed Pius, was proclaimed the thirteenth emperor in succession from Augustus. Jointly with his sons
Aurelius and Lucius, he governed the state for almost twenty-
three years.[44] So peaceful and so upright was his rule that
he was well named the "Pius" and the "Father of His Country." It was in his time that Valentinus, the heresiarch,[45] and
Cerdo,[46] the teacher of Marcion, came to Rome. The philosopher Justin,[47] however, submitted to Antoninus his book in
defense of the Christian religion and so disposed the emperor
kindly toward the Christians. Antoninus was attacked by disease and died at a place twelve miles from the capital.

15. DURING the nine hundred and eleventh year of the City,
Marcus Antoninus Verus,[48] the fourteenth emperor in suc-

[44] From 138 to 161.

[45] Valentinus, the founder and leader of a Gnostic sect in the time of Hadrian, came to Rome early in the reign of Antoninus Pius.

[46] A Gnostic teacher whose doctrines are little known. He probably came to
Rome about 135. His disciple Marcion was one of the most influential and
famous heretics of the second century.

[47] Justin Martyr wrote two apologies. This reference is probably to the first
which was written about 148.

[48] M. Aurelius Antoninus Augustus, 161 to 180. He ruled jointly with Commodus, from 177 to 180; jointly with L. Verus, from 161 to 169.

cession from Augustus, came to the throne with his brother
Aurelius Commodus.[49] They occupied it jointly for nineteen
years and were the first to govern the state on terms of
equal authority. They waged war against the Parthians
with admirable bravery and success. Vologesus (III), the
king of the Parthians, had invaded Armenia, Cappadocia, and
Syria, and was causing frightful devastation. Annius Antoninus Verus proceeded to the battle front and there, after
performing great exploits with the aid of his energetic generals, captured Seleucia, an Assyrian city of four hundred
thousand inhabitants situated on the Hydaspes River. He
and his brother celebrated the victory over the Parthians by
a joint triumph. Shortly afterward, while sitting with his
brother in a carriage, Verus choked to death during an attack
of a disease that the Greeks call apoplexy.

Upon the demise of Verus, Marcus Antoninus became sole
ruler of the state. During the Parthian War, however, persecutions of the Christians arose for the fourth time since
Nero's reign. These persecutions were carried on by the emperor's order with great severity in Asia and in Gaul, and
many of the saints received the crown of martyrdom. A plague
now spread over many provinces, and a great pestilence devastated all Italy. Everywhere country houses, fields, and towns
were left without a tiller of the land or an inhabitant, and
nothing remained but ruins and forests. It is said that the
Roman troops and all the legions stationed far and near in
winter quarters were so depleted that the war against the
Marcomanni, which broke out immediately, could not be carried on without a new levy of soldiers. At Carnuntium,[50]
Marcus Antoninus held the levy continuously for three years.

This war was undoubtedly directed by the Providence of
God, as is clearly shown by many proofs and especially by a
letter of that very grave and judicious emperor, Antoninus.
Numerous barbarous and savage tribes, that is to say, the

---

[49] Known as Lucius Verus.

[50] An important Celtic town in northern Pannonia, situated on the southern
bank of the Danube.

Marcomanni, the Quadi, the Vandals, the Sarmatians, the
Suebi, in fact the tribes from nearly all of Germany, rose in
rebellion. The Roman army advanced as far as the territories
of the Quadi. There the enemy surrounded it; but on account
of the scarcity of water the army was in more immediate
danger from thirst than from the enemy. Publicly calling
upon the name of Christ, certain of the soldiers with great
constancy of faith poured forth their souls in prayer. Immediately there came so heavy a shower that the Romans were
abundantly refreshed without suffering harm. The barbarians,
however, became terrified by the incessant bolts of lightning,
particularly after the lightning had killed many of them, and
they took to their heels. Attacking from the rear, the Romans
slaughtered them to the last man and thus won a most glorious victory. With a small band of raw recruits but with the
all-powerful aid of Christ, they had outdone nearly all the
achievements of the past. Several authors also state that a
letter of the emperor Antoninus still exists in which he ac-
knowledges that the thirst of the army was relieved and the
victory won because the Christian soldiers had invoked the
name of Christ.

   This emperor associated his son Commodus with him in
the government.[51] He remitted the arrears of tribute in all
the provinces and ordered all the accusing evidence of in-
debtedness to the treasury to be piled up and burned in the
Forum. He also modified the severer laws by new enact-
ments. Finally, while staying in Pannonia, he died of a sudden
illness.

16.   IN THE nine hundred and thirtieth year of the City,
Lucius Antoninus Commodus, the fifteenth in succession from
Augustus, succeeded his father on the throne. During his
reign of thirteen years,[52] he conducted a successful war
against the Germans. However, he became thoroughly depraved as a result of scandalous excesses and obscenities;
frequently he fenced in public exhibitions with the weapons

---

[51] From 177 to 180.   [52] From 180 to 192.

of gladiators, and often he encountered wild beasts in the arena. He also put to death a great many of the senators, especially those who, he noticed, were most prominent by reason of birth and ability. The punishment for his crimes was visited upon the City; lightning struck the Capitol and started a fire which, in its devouring course, burned the library that the fathers had founded in their enthusiasm for learning, and also other buildings adjoining it. Another fire, breaking out later in Rome, leveled to the ground the Temple of Vesta, the Palace, and a large part of the city. Adjudged when alive an enemy of the human race, Commodus, who incommoded [53] everyone, was strangled to death, so it is said, in the house of Vestilianus.

After Commodus, the Senate proclaimed the elderly Helvius Pertinax emperor. He was the sixteenth ruler in succession from Augustus. Six months after his accession [54] he was slain in the Palace at the instigation of the jurist Julianus. The latter thereupon seized the imperium; [55] but in the course of a civil war he was soon defeated by Severus at the Mulvian Bridge and killed seven months after he had begun to rule. Thus Pertinax and Julianus between them occupied the throne for only one year.

17. IN THE nine hundred and forty-fourth year of the City, Severus, an African from the town of Leptis in Tripolis, gained the vacant throne. He wished to be called Pertinax after the emperor whose murder he had avenged. He was the seventeenth emperor in succession from Augustus and held the throne for eighteen years. [56] A cruel man by nature, he was continually harassed by wars, and he had to struggle hard to maintain his strong rule. At Cyzicus [57] he defeated and killed Pescennius Niger, [58] who had set himself up as a usurper in Egypt and Syria. When the Jews and the Samaritans tried

---

[53] *Cunctis incommodus.*   [54] From 1 January to 28 March 193.
[55] From 28 March to 1 June 193.   [56] From 193 to 211.
[57] A city on the Propontis in Mysia.
[58] As pretender, May 193 to November 194. He was not present at this battle but was later captured and put to death.

to rebel, he put them down with the sword. He conquered the Parthians, the Arabians, and the Adiabeni. He harassed the Christians by a severe persecution, the fifth since Nero's reign, and in various provinces many of the saints received the crown of martyrdom. Immediate vengeance from Heaven followed this wicked and presumptuous action of Severus against the Christians and the Church of God. Straightway the emperor was compelled to hasten, or rather was brought back, from Syria to Gaul for a third civil war. He had already fought one war at Rome against Julianus,[59] and another in Syria against Pescennius, and now a third was stirred up by Clodius Albinus, who had made himself Caesar in Gaul.[60] Albinus had been an accomplice of Julianus in the murder of Pertinax. In this war much Roman blood was shed on both sides. Albinus was overthrown at Lugdunum and lost his life.[61] The victorious Severus was drawn to the British provinces by the revolt of almost all of his allies. Having recovered part of the island after a number of stubbornly contested battles, he determined to shut if off by a wall from the other tribes that remained unsubdued. He therefore constructed a large ditch and a very strong rampart extending from sea to sea, a distance of one hundred and thirty-two miles. These works he fortified at frequent intervals by towers. Severus died of a disease at the town of York in Britain. Two sons survived him, Bassianus and Geta. Bassianus, who assumed the name of Antoninus, took possession of the throne.

18. IN THE nine hundred and sixty-second year of the City, Aurelius Antoninus Bassianus, also known as Caracalla, the eighteenth emperor in succession from Augustus, obtained the principate. He held it for almost seven years.[62] In his way of life Caracalla was harsher than his father, and the most uncontrollable of men in his lust, as is evident from his

[59] Didius Julianus purchased the throne by bribing the praetorians.
[60] April 193. Albinus possessed great physical strength and skill as a soldier.
[61] He declared himself Augustus in 196 and died 19 February 197.
[62] From 211 to 217. Co-ruler with Severus, from 198 to 211; with Geta, from 211 to 212.

marriage to his stepmother Julia. In the course of a difficult campaign against the Parthians, he was surrounded by the enemy between Edessa and Carrhae and killed.

Following him as the nineteenth emperor in succession from Augustus, Opelius Macrinus, the praetorian prefect, seized the supreme power with the aid of his son Diadumenus. He was slain, however, a year later in a mutiny of the soldiers at Archelais.[63]

In the nine hundred and seventieth year of the City, Marcus Aurelius Antoninus, the twentieth emperor in succession from Augustus, obtained the supreme power. He held it for four years.[64] This emperor, who was priest of the Temple of Heliogabalus, was remembered for nothing but his notorious profligacy, crimes, and utter vileness. He and his mother were killed at Rome during an uprising of the soldiery.

In the nine hundred and seventy-fourth year of the City, Aurelius Alexander,[65] the twenty-first emperor in succession from Augustus, was proclaimed emperor by the will of the Senate and the soldiers. For thirteen years he ruled with a deserved reputation for fair dealing; incidentally his mother, Mamea, who was Christian, made it her concern to receive instruction from the presbyter Origen.[66] Immediately after his accession Alexander undertook a campaign against the Persians and in a great battle won a decisive victory over Xerxes, their king. He employed Ulpian as his legal adviser and showed the greatest self-restraint in his administration of the state. He was nevertheless killed in a mutiny of the soldiers at Mainz.

19.   IN THE nine hundred and eighty-seventh year of the City, Maximinus, twenty-second in line from Augustus, became emperor.[67] He was elected not by the will of the Senate but by the army, after he had waged war successfully against the

---

[63] From 217 to 218. Archelais is a city of Cappadocia on the Halys River.
[64] From 218 to 222. Better known as Heliogabalus or Elagabalus.
[65] From 222 to 235. He is usually called Severus Alexander.
[66] The famous Christian theologian and teacher of the third century.
[67] From 235 to 238.

Germans. He instituted a persecution against the Christians, the sixth since the time of Nero. But soon, that is, in the third year of his reign, he was killed by Pupienus at Aquileia. His death also brought the persecution to an end. His chief reason for instituting a persecution against the priests and clergy, that is, against the doctors, was the fact that his predecessor, Alexander, and the family of the latter's mother, Mamea, were Christians; another very important motive was his dislike of the presbyter Origen.

In the nine hundred and ninety-first year of the City, Gordian, the twenty-third emperor in succession from Augustus, was proclaimed emperor. He reigned for six years.[68] Pupienus, the slayer of Maximinus, and his brother Balbinus, who with him had usurped the supreme power,[69] were shortly afterward murdered in the Palace. According to Eutropius,[70] Gordian, still a mere boy, opened the gates of Janus before setting out for the Parthian War in the East. I do not remember that any writer has stated whether anyone, after the time of Vespasian and Titus, closed them. Cornelius Tacitus, however, does report that they were opened a year later by Vespasian himself. After winning mighty battles against the Parthians, Gordian was treacherously killed by his own men, not far from Circessus on the Euphrates.

20. In the nine hundred and ninety-seventh year of the City, Philip, the twenty-fourth emperor in succession from Augustus, was proclaimed emperor and shared his throne with his son Philip.[71] He occupied it for seven years, the first of all the emperors who was a Christian. The third year of his reign was the occasion of the thousandth anniversary of the founding of Rome. This anniversary year, more memorable than any that had gone before, the Christian emperor celebrated with magnificent games. There is no doubt that Philip gave this devout thanksgiving and honor to Christ and to

[68] Gordian III, 238 to 244.
[69] The beginning of March to the middle of June 238.
[70] *Breviarium historiae Romanae* ix. 2.
[71] From 244 to 249. Jointly with his son, from 247 to 249.

the Church, since no author mentions any procession up to the Capitol nor any sacrifice of victims according to the usual custom. The father and the son died in different places, one in the course of a mutiny of the soldiers, the other as a result of the treachery of Decius.

21.   IN THE one thousand and fourth year of the City, Decius, who had instigated and quelled a civil war, after the murder of the two Philips seized the supreme power as the twenty-fifth emperor in succession from Augustus. He held it for three years.[72] His motives for murdering Philip soon became obvious when he published merciless edicts authorizing the persecution and slaughter of Christians. He sent a great many of the saints from their crosses to receive their crowns from Christ. This was the seventh persecution since the time of Nero. This emperor appointed his own son Caesar. Both were not long after killed in the midst of the barbarians.

In the one thousand and seventh year of the City, Gallus Hostilianus, the twenty-sixth emperor in succession from Augustus, came to the throne. He and his son Volusianus [73] together occupied it barely two years. A plague, which brought in its train unbelievable diseases and extended to all the regions where the edicts of Decius for the destruction of the churches had been promulgated, now avenged the wrong done to Christianity. Hardly a Roman province, city, or house escaped being smitten and desolated by that widespread pestilence. Gallus and Volusianus, whose reign was distinguished by this calamity alone, were killed while they were undertaking a civil war against the pretender Aemilianus. The latter, however, perished in the third month of his usurpation.[74]

22.   IN THE one thousand and tenth year of the City, the twenty-seventh place in the Augustan succession was filled by two emperors: Valerian, who was hailed as Augustus by the

[72] From 249 to 251.

[73] From 251 to 253. Both his sons, Gallus and Volusianus, assumed a share of the rule a few months after his accession.   [74] From June to September 253.

army in Raetia, and Gallienus, who was proclaimed Caesar
by the Senate at Rome.[75] Gallienus had an unhappy reign
lasting fifteen years. During this time the human race had
little respite from unusually severe and continuous pestilences.
Wickedness, easily forgetful, provokes its own punishment;
for impiety, though it feels the scourge when beaten, is too
callous to perceive the one scourging it. Leaving out of consideration the earlier persecutions of the Christians, the one
inflicted by Decius caused the whole Roman Empire to be
harassed by a great plague. But injustice, cheated by poor
judgment to its own ruin, deceived itself. For the wicked
thought that the plague was a matter of ordinary chance and
that death resulting from disease was a natural end and not
a punishment.

Within a short time, therefore, their wicked actions again
so provoked the anger of God that they received a blow
which they long were forced to remember. As soon as
Valerian had seized the throne, he began the eighth persecution since Nero's time. He ordered that the Christians be
forced by torture into idolatry and that they be killed if they
should refuse to worship the Roman gods. As a result, the
blood of the saints was shed throughout the length and
breadth of the Roman Empire. Immediately, Valerian, the
author of this abominable edict, was captured by Sapor, king
of the Persians. He who had been emperor of the Roman
people grew old among the Persians and suffered the supreme
humiliation of slavery. For he was condemned for the term
of his life to perform the menial service of helping the king
mount his horse, not by giving him his hand, but by bending
to the ground and offering his back.

Gallienus became terrified by such an unmistakable judgment of God and was alarmed by the wretched fate of his
colleague. He therefore made quick amends by restoring peace
to the churches. But, when so many thousands of the saints
had been tortured, the captivity of one impious man, even
though his punishment lasted throughout his life and was of

[75] Valerian, 253 to 260; Gallienus, 253 to 260 with Valerian, to 268 alone.

an exceedingly abhorrent kind, could not atone for the wrong nor satisfy vengeance. The blood of the just cried out to God and demanded to be avenged in the same land where it had been shed. Not only did a righteous judgment exact the penalty upon the one who issued the order, but also upon the agents, informers, accusers, spectators, judges, and finally upon all who had favored the unjust and cruel persecution, even by their silent wish—for God knows all secrets. Most of these men were scattered through the provinces, and the same avenging blow justly smote them all. By God's will the nations stationed on the boundaries of the empire and left there for this purpose were suddenly loosed on every side, and no sooner did the reins of control release them than they invaded all the Roman territories. The Germans made their way through the Alps, Raetia, and the whole of Italy as far west as Ravenna. The Alemanni roamed through the Gallic provinces and even crossed into Italy. An invasion of the Goths ruined Greece, Pontus, and Asia; Dacia beyond the Danube was lost forever. The Quadi and the Sarmatians ravaged the Pannonian provinces. The Further Germans stripped Spain and took possession of it. The Parthians seized Mesopotamia and completely devastated Syria. Throughout the various provinces, there exist today poor and insignificant settlements situated in the ruins of great cities which still bear evidences of their names and tokens of their misfortunes. Our own city Tarraco in Spain is one of these, and we can point to it to console ourselves over our recent misery. Furthermore, lest any part of the Roman body politic should escape being mangled, there were internal conspiracies formed by usurpers. Civil wars arose, and everywhere streams of Roman blood flowed while Romans and barbarians vented their fury. But soon the wrath of God was turned to mercy, and the mere beginning of a punishment rather than an actual penalty was reckoned to be a sufficient satisfaction.

First of all, Ingenuus, who had assumed the imperial purple, was slain at Mursa.[76] Next Postumus[77] usurped the

[76] In Lower Pannonia.

[77] From some time between 10 December 258 and 28 January 259 to 10 December 268.

sovereignty in Gaul, but this usurpation brought good fortune to the state. For in the course of ten years he drove out the enemy and restored the lost provinces to their former condition, conquering by the exercise of great bravery and self-restraint. He was killed, however, in a mutiny of the soldiers. Aelianus, while attempting a revolution, was overcome at Mainz. After the death of Postumus, Marius seized the supreme power at that city, but he was killed immediately afterward. The Gauls, acting on their own initiative, then proclaimed Victorinus [78] emperor. It was not long before Victorinus was murdered, and Tetricus,[79] who at the time held the office of governor of the province of Aquitania, succeeded him. This ruler had to put up with many mutinies. In the East, in the meantime, a certain Odenathus gathered together a band of Syrian peasants. They defeated and drove back the Persians, defended Syria, recovered Mesopotamia, and as a result of conquest advanced with their leader as far as Ctesiphon. Gallienus abandoned the state to its fate and was slain while indulging his lust at Milan.

23. IN THE one thousand and twenty-fifth year of the City, Claudius,[80] the twenty-eighth emperor, assumed the sovereignty by the will of the Senate. He at once attacked the Goths, who for fifteen years had been devastating Illyria and Macedonia, and destroyed them with frightful carnage. The Senate voted that a golden shield be placed in the Senate House in his honor, and ordered that a statue, likewise of gold, be placed in the Capitol. But before he had been two full years in power, a disease overtook him and he died at Sirmium.

After the death of Claudius, his brother Quintillus [81] was chosen emperor by the army. He was a man of singular self-restraint and the only Roman emperor superior to Claudius; he was killed on the seventeenth day of his reign.

During the one thousand and twenty-seventh year of the City, Aurelian, the twenty-ninth emperor, gained the sover-

---

[78] From 268 to 270.   [79] From 270 to 273.
[80] Claudius II, 268 to 270.   [81] He reigned about two months in 270.

eignty which he held for five years and six months.[82] He was
a man of consummate ability in war. In a campaign on the
Danube he crushed the Goths in decisive battles and established the Roman rule within its former boundaries. Then he
turned to the East against Zenobia, who, after her husband
Odenathus had been murdered, was appropriating the recently
recovered province of Syria. Aurelian brought her under his
power more by threat of battle than by actual combat. In
Gaul, Aurelian overcame Tetricus, who was altogether unable
to control the mutinies of his soldiers, and who even wrote
to Aurelian,

> Snatch me, unconquered one, from these woes.[83]

Hence Aurelian won an easy victory over Tetricus who betrayed his own army. Thus, as the reconqueror of the East
and of the North, he celebrated a triumph in great glory.
Aurelian surrounded the city of Rome with stronger walls.
Finally, when he was giving orders for a persecution of the
Christians, the ninth in succession from Nero's, a thunderbolt struck in front of him, causing great terror among the
bystanders. Shortly afterward he was slain while on a journey.

24. In THE one thousand and thirty-second year of the
City, Tacitus, the thirtieth emperor, gained the sovereignty,
but he was slain in Pontus within six months.[84] After him
Florian suffered a similar fate during his reign; within three
months [85] he was killed at Tarsus.

In the one thousand and thirty-third year of the City,
Probus, the thirty-first emperor, secured the throne. He held
it for six years and four months.[86] He finally destroyed the
enemy in a number of bitterly contested battles and completely
freed the Gallic provinces that had so long been occupied by
the barbarians. He then waged two very bloody civil wars;
one in the East where he overthrew and captured the usurper
Saturninus, and the other at Agrippina where he defeated

---

[82] From March 270 to August 275. [83] Vergil *Aeneid* vi. 365.
[84] From autumn, 275 to the beginning of April 276.
[85] From April to July 276. Two months and twenty days. [86] From 276 to 282.

Proculus and Bonosus in a series of great battles and killed them. While in an iron-covered tower at Sirmium, Probus himself was killed by mutinous soldiers.

In the one thousand and thirty-ninth year of the City, Carus of Narbo, the thirty-second emperor, came to the throne. He reigned for two years.[87] After establishing his sons Carinus and Numerian as co-rulers,[88] Carus made war upon the Parthians and captured two of their most famous cities, Coche and Ctesiphon. Afterward, while in his camp on the Tigris, he was struck by lightning and killed. Numerian, who had accompanied his father, was treacherously killed, as he was retreating, by his father-in-law Aper.

25. IN THE one thousand and forty-first year, Diocletian was chosen by the army as the thirty-third emperor. He reigned for twenty years.[89] Upon assuming full command, he at once killed with his own hand Aper, the murderer of Numerian. He next defeated Carinus in a stubbornly contested battle. This man had been leading a dissolute life in Dalmatia, where Carus had left him as Caesar. Later Amandus and Aelianus in Gaul gathered together a band of farmers, who were called Bacaudae, and stirred up destructive insurrections. Diocletian appointed Maximianus, surnamed Herculius, Caesar and sent him into the Gallic provinces. Here, by his military prowess, he easily put down the inexperienced and disorderly company of peasants.

At this time a certain Carausius, a man of lowly birth to be sure, but quick in thought and action, was in charge of the defense of the coasts of the Ocean, which were infested by the Franks and Saxons. He did more to injure than to help the government, for he did not restore to its true owners any of the booty recovered from the pirates but claimed it for himself alone. In this way he aroused the suspicion that it was his deliberate neglect that had allowed the enemy to make raids. For this reason Maximianus ordered his execution.

[87] From 282 to 283. [88] Carinus, from 283 to 285; Numerian, from 283 to 284.
[89] From 284 to 305.

Carausius at once assumed the purple and seized control of the British provinces.

Thus the thunders of strife suddenly reverberated throughout the territories of the Roman Empire. Carausius was leading a rebellion in Britain, and Achilleus one in Egypt; the Quinquegentiani were attacking Africa, and Narseus, king of the Persians, was waging destructive wars in the East. In view of this dangerous situation, Diocletian advanced Maximianus Herculius from the rank of Caesar to that of Augustus [90] and appointed Constantius and Galerius Maximianus Caesars.[91]   Constantius now married Theodora, the stepdaughter of Herculius Maximianus, and by her had six sons, the brothers of Constantine. Carausius, after laying claim to Britain, held it firmly in his grasp for seven years.[92] Finally, however, he was treacherously killed by his comrade Allectus. The latter held for three years the island that he had taken away from his friend.[93] The praetorian prefect Asclepiodotus then overthrew him and regained Britain, ten years after it had been lost. In Gaul, in the first encounter, the Alemanni routed Constantius Caesar's army. He himself barely managed to escape. In the second battle, however, he won a complete victory. It is said that sixty thousand of the Alemanni were slain in the course of a few hours. Maximianus Augustus subdued the Quinquegentiani in Africa. Then Diocletian besieged Achilleus at Alexandria for eight months. He finally captured and killed him; but, far from showing moderation in his victory, he gave Alexandria over to pillage, and made life in all Egypt hideous with proscriptions and massacres.

Galerius Maximianus fought two battles against Narseus. In a third engagement, which took place somewhere between the cities of Callinicus and Carrhae, Narseus defeated him. After losing his troops, Galerius took refuge with Diocletian, who received him with extreme arrogance. The story goes that though clad in scarlet robes he was forced to run before the emperor's carriage for several miles. Nevertheless Gale-

---

[90] In the year 286.   [91] In the year 293.   [92] From 286 to 293.
[93] From 293 to 296.

rius made this insult serve as a whetstone to his valor. Spurred on by this treatment, when the rust of kingly pride was rubbed off, he was able to sharpen his mind to a keen edge. He at once made a general levy of troops throughout Illyricum and Moesia, and hurriedly returning to meet the enemy, he overwhelmed Narseus by skillful strategy and superior forces. After annihilating the Persian army and putting Narseus himself to flight, he seized the latter's camp, made prisoners of his wives, sisters, and children, appropriated an immense amount of Persian treasure, and led away many of the Persian nobles into captivity. On his return to Mesopotamia he was welcomed by Diocletian and given the highest honors. Later these same generals fought vigorously against the Carpi and the Basternae. They then conquered the Sarmatians and distributed a great number of captives from this people among the garrisons of the Roman frontiers.

In the meantime Diocletian in the East and Maximianus Herculius in the West ordered the churches to be destroyed and the Christians persecuted and put to death. This persecution, the tenth in succession from Nero's, was longer and more cruel than any other that had preceded it. For ten years it was carried on without interruption; churches were burned, the innocent were proscribed, and martyrs were slaughtered. Then followed an earthquake in Syria. Thousands of people throughout Tyre and Sidon were crushed by falling buildings. In the second year of the persecution, Diocletian suggested to the unwilling Maximianus that both of them should at the same time lay aside the purple and the imperial power and, after substituting younger men for themselves in the government, pass their declining years in the leisure of private life. Accordingly on the day agreed they laid aside the power and trappings of empire—Diocletian at Nicomedia, and Maximianus at Milan.[94]

The Augusti, Galerius and Constantius, were the first to divide the Roman Empire in two: the former took Illyricum,

[94] The date was 1 May 305.

Asia, and the East; the latter took Italy, Africa, and the Gallic provinces. Constantius, however, who was of an extremely mild disposition, was satisfied with Gaul [and Spain] alone and permitted Galerius to take the other districts. Galerius chose two Caesars: Maximinus,[95] whom he stationed in the East, and Severus, to whom he entrusted Italy. He himself established his government in Illyricum. Constantius Augustus, a mild-tempered man and one skilled in the conduct of government, died in Britain, leaving Constantine, a son by his concubine Helena, emperor of the Gallic provinces.

26.   IN THE one thousand and sixty-first year of the City, Constantine, the thirty-fourth emperor, received the helm of state from his father Constantius. He held it for thirty-one years to the good fortune of everyone.[96]

At this point somebody suddenly runs up to me and dancing with joy taunts me, saying: "Aha! we have long waited for you and at last you have fallen into our trap. Here we were lying in wait for you to overrun your mark, here we caught you when you fell down, here we held you fast then you became confused. Until now we have borne with you while with a certain skill and ingenuity you fitted together the accidental vicissitudes of history with the vengeances exacted in behalf of the Christians. At times, indeed, we men, in our ignorance of the secrets of Heaven, were disturbed by the apparent truth of the parallel. We turned pale with fear. But now our Maximianus has cleared away the entire stage setting of your play and has himself become conspicuous as the unshakable pillar and prop of our ancient religion. For ten years your churches were overthrown, as you yourself admit; the Christians throughout the world were racked with torture and their ranks depleted by slaughter. We have your plain testimony that no previous persecution was either so severe or so long continued. Yet see, amid the quiet and prosperity of those days, the unusual good fortune of the very emperors who accomplished the deeds. At home there was no famine, no pes-

[95] Maximinus Daia and Flavius Severus.   [96] From 306 to 337.

tilence; abroad there was no war except by their own choice, and that only to exercise their strength and not to endanger their forces. There was also a condition of affairs previously unknown to mankind—the lasting association of a number of rulers at the same time, their remarkable harmony, and a joint sovereignty directed to the common good, now as never before. Finally—and this was an act never known before the time of these great emperors—these very persecutors laid aside their office and found rest as private citizens, a lot that men consider the greatest blessing and highest good of a life well lived. And this came, as it were, as a reward to the authors of the persecution at the very time when its fires were still raging in the middle of their course throughout the world. Or do you maintain that even this happiness which befell that generation was a punishment, and do you try to frighten us on this ground also?"

To these persons I reply in all humility that in my extreme regard for piety I am reminding them of the truth and not frightening them with falsehoods. Ten persecutions, from Nero to Maximianus, were suffered by the Church of Christ. Nine vengeances, as I have called them, or calamities, as my opponents themselves do not deny them to be, immediately ensued. I do not insist upon the form of expression. It makes little difference whether these vengeances be regarded as merited or as vicissitudes of chance, since at any rate they were disasters according to the admission of both sides. These poor blind people indeed think there was some difficulty with regard to the tenth vengeance; they do not see that it was all the more severe the less it was perceived. For the impious man is beaten and does not feel it. After my explanation the convincing nature of the facts will compel them to admit, even though unwillingly, that it was as a supreme punishment for Maximian's persecution that these blows have come which still cause them pain. Indeed they even cry out and provoke us to cry out in turn, so that we are now becoming anxious about the way to silence them.

27.   As WE set forth in the first book, according to the in-
complete references of Pompeius Trogus and Cornelius Tacitus and according to the trustworthy and adequate account of
our own Moses, who even my critics admit was a reliable
authority, the Egyptians and their king were vexed by ten grievous plagues. In order to restrain the devotion of God's people, who were ready and eager to serve Him, the Egyptians
called the Jews back to the clay and straw. Severe misfortunes later crushed the Egyptians. Then they not only urged
the Jews to go in haste but even loaded them down with gold
and silver vessels. Afterward they forgot the lesson of the
plagues. Led by greed for property which did not belong to
them and by hatred for a foreign religion, they eagerly pursued the innocent exiles but were finally overwhelmed in the
Red Sea and were all destroyed. This event can be confirmed
by its result even if we do not accept it on faith. I recall and
mention it at this moment because these events came to pass
as an example to us. In each case a people served the same
God and struggled for the same cause. The synagogue of
the Israelites was subject to the Egyptians; the Church of the
Christians was subject to the Romans. The Egyptians inflicted
persecutions; so also did the Romans. In the one case the Egyptians sent ten refusals to Moses; in the other, the Romans
directed ten edicts against Christ. In the one case the Egyptians
suffered various plagues; in the other, the Romans suffered
various calamities.

In order to draw a parallel between these two series of
plagues, so far as their different appearance admits comparison, let me point out the following. In Egypt the first visitation caused quantities of blood to rise from the wells and to
flow in the rivers. In the Empire the first slaughter in the
reign of Nero filled the whole land with the blood of the dying, whether flowing from the diseased in Rome or shed in
war throughout the world. In Egypt, during the second
plague, frogs that croaked and hopped in the temples caused
the inhabitants to starve and to go into exile. Rome likewise suffered a similar punishment. During the reign of

Domitian, his retainers and soldiers, executing the orders of their bloodthirsty prince, reduced nearly all of the citizens to want and scattered them in exile. In Egypt the third affliction consisted of sciniphes, that is, very small and troublesome flies, which often in midsummer gather in dense swarms about filthy places and as they buzz around settle down and lodge in men's hair and on the hides of cattle, stinging their victims and causing acute pain. At Rome the third plague, in the reign of Trajan, stirred up the Jews, who in their general dispersion had until then been as quiet as if they had not existed, but who suddenly became enraged and vented their fury upon their fellow inhabitants everywhere. I say nothing of the great destruction numerous cities suffered when they were overthrown during these same days by the frequent earthquakes. In Egypt, during the fourth plague, there were dog flies, truly the offspring of putrefaction and breeders of worms. In the Empire, during the fourth plague, under the rule of Marcus Antoninus, a pestilence spread over a great many provinces, and the whole of Italy, including the City of Rome; it also attacked the Roman army which was scattered along the distant frontiers in its various winter camps and made its dying members at once a prey to decay and worms. In Egypt the fifth visitation came as a sudden destruction of the flocks and beasts of burden. In Rome, similarly, a fifth vengeance, under the persecutor Severus, caused the very vitals and support of the state—I mean the people of the provinces and the military legions—to be wasted by incessant civil wars. In Egypt the sixth affliction brought running sores and festering ulcers. Rome, in like manner, suffered her sixth punishment as a result of the persecution of Maximianus. He had ordered the slaughter of the bishops and priests especially, that is, the chief men of the churches, and had spared the common people. Thereupon this sacrilege was revenged by repeated outbreaks of rage and hatred—not by the slaughter of the masses, but by the wounding and death of the princes and powerful men. In Egypt the seventh plague was a shower of hail caused by condensation of the air that brought destruction to men, beasts, and crops. In Rome, similarly, during the reign of Gallus and Volusianus, who had succeeded the short-lived persecutor Decius, the seventh plague came from the poisoning of the air. This caused a pestilence which, spreading through all the regions of the Roman Empire from east to west, not only killed off almost all mankind and cattle, but also poisoned the lakes and tainted the grass.[97] The eighth affliction in Egypt was caused by locusts that swarmed everywhere, occupying, devouring, and covering everything. The eighth in Rome, in like manner, was inflicted by nations that swarmed on every side seeking to lay waste whole provinces with fire and sword and to overthrow the Roman world. There the ninth disturbance brought a long-continued darkness so thick that it could almost be grasped with the hand; it threatened more harm than it actually inflicted. Here, in like manner, the ninth visitation occurred when, during a fearful gale, a thunderbolt, terrible and distressing in its consequences, struck at the very feet of Aurelian, who was ordering a persecution, and showed, when such a vengeance was exacted, what so great an avenger could do, were He not at the same time both merciful and patient. Even so, within six months from that time, three emperors in succession, Aurelian, Tacitus, and Florian, were killed for one reason or another. In Egypt, finally, the tenth plague, the last of all, was the slaughter of every first-born son. In Rome herself the tenth and last punishment was the destruction of all the idols, which were the first and foremost love of the Romans.

The Egyptian king experienced, tested, and learned to fear the power of God, and therefore he allowed the people of God to go free. At Rome the king experienced, tested, and learned to believe in the power of God, and therefore he also allowed the people of God to be free. In Egypt the people of God were never afterward dragged back into slavery. In Rome the people of God were never afterward forced into idolatry. There, the precious vessels of the Egyptians were

97 Vergil *Georgics* iii. 481,

handed over to the Hebrews; here, the principal pagan temples were turned into Christian churches. It is certainly my duty to indicate, as I have said, that everlasting ruin overwhelmed the Egyptians beneath the waves when, having allowed the Hebrews to leave after the ten plagues, they undertook to pursue them. So alas a persecution by the Gentiles at some future time awaits us while we are journeying in freedom, until we cross the Red Sea, that is, the fire of the judgment, with our Lord Jesus Christ Himself as our leader and judge. Those, however, who assume the rôle of the Egyptians, the power having temporarily been given them by the permission of God, will show their fury and persecute the Christians with the most grievous tortures. But all those enemies of Christ, together with their king, Antichrist, will be caught in the lake of eternal fire, which, because of the thick darkness, is entered upon without being seen; and they will receive the lot of everlasting damnation, being doomed to burn in eternal torment.

28. Now, as I have said, after the death of Constantius in Britain, Constantine was proclaimed emperor. He was the first Christian emperor with the exception of Philip, whose Christian reign of a very few years was, in my opinion, established only to the end that the thousandth anniversary of Rome should be dedicated to Christ rather than to idols. From the time of Constantine, however, all the emperors have been Christians up to the present day, with the exception of Julian, whose pernicious life, it is said, was cut off while he was plotting shameful deeds. This is the slow but inevitable punishment of pagans. This is why they rave, though in their right mind. This is why they are goaded by the stings of conscience, though they have not been hurt. This is why they groan, though they laugh. This is why they begin to fail, though they are still in sound health. This is why they are tortured in secret, though no one persecutes them. Finally, this is why there are now but few left, though they have never been punished by any persecutor. Now I shall show the sort of end that awaited those persecutors who tried to

make their immunity from punishment a ground not only for boasting but even for insults.

While Constantine was most vigorously carrying out the policies of the government in Gaul, the praetorian soldiers at Rome named as Augustus, Maxentius,[98] the son of Herculius, who was at that time living in retirement in Lucania. This Maximianus Herculius remained a public persecutor of the Christians. He was tempted by his son's opportunity and seized the tyranny.[99] Galerius Augustus then sent Severus Caesar with an army to Rome against Maxentius, but soldiers of Severus treacherously abandoned and betrayed him while he was besieging the city. He took to flight but was killed at Ravenna. The persecutor Maximianus Herculius, once an Augustus and now a usurper, attempted to seize the garb and royal authority from his son, who held the imperial office. However, he was terrified by the open insults and rioting of the soldiery. He then proceeded to Gaul, in order to effect a union, equally treacherous, with his son-in-law Constantine, intending later to supplant him as emperor. When detected and betrayed by his daughter, he fled, but was seized and killed at Marseilles.[100]

After the murder of Severus, Galerius made Licinius emperor.[101] Galerius himself issued harsher edicts and thus intensified the persecution started by Diocletian and Maximian, and for ten years he drained the provinces of their population. Finally an inward rotting of the chest and a decay of vital organs attacked him so that, in addition to the ordinary hideousness of human disease, he even vomited worms. While his physicians, who were unable any longer to endure the stench, were being put to death one after another by his orders, one of them rebuked him with the courage of despair, saying that his punishment was the vengeance of God, and that he could not be cured by physicians. The emperor then sent edicts far and wide recalling the Christians from their places of exile, but still finding his torment unendurable, he took his own life.

[98] From 307 to 312.   [99] February, 307.   [100] In the year 310.
[101] In the year 308.

Thus the state at that time came to be ruled by four new princes, Constantine and Maxentius, the sons of the Augusti, and Licinius and Maximianus, self-made men. When Constantine gave the churches peace after they had been harassed by persecution for ten years, a civil war broke out between him and Maxentius. The latter, exhausted by a long series of battles, was finally defeated and slain at the Mulvian Bridge. Maximianus, who had instigated and carried on the persecution of the Christians with the greatest bitterness, died at Tarsus while preparing for civil war against Licinius, who, stirred by sudden madness, had ordered all Christians to be expelled from his palace. Soon a violent war raged between this Licinius and Constantine. The latter first defeated Licinius—who was his sister's husband—in Pannonia, and then crushed him at Cibalae.[102] After gaining possession of all Greece and thwarting the attempts of Licinius by land and sea in numerous battles, Constantine finally forced him to surrender. Being warned by the example of his own father-in-law, Maximianus Herculius, he ordered Licinius, who was now deprived of office, also to be put to death, so that he might not again assume the purple and bring ruin upon the state. Thus, although all the agents of that detestable persecution had already been destroyed, this man, who persecuted as much as he could, was overtaken by the punishment he deserved. Crispus and Constantine, the sons of Constantine, and the youthful Licinius, the son of Licinius Augustus and, on his mother's side, a nephew of Constantine, were proclaimed Caesars.

At this time Arius, a priest of the city of Alexandria, turned from the truth of the Catholic faith and set forth a dogma that was fatal to many. As soon as he became famous, or rather infamous, at Alexandria among his universally confused adherents and his opponents, he was expelled from the Church by Alexander, who at that time was bishop of that city. When Arius also incited to riot those whom he had led into error, an assembly of three hundred and eighteen bishops was convened at Nicaea, a city of Bithynia. These bishops,

---

[102] A town of considerable importance in Lower Pannonia.

clearly perceiving the vile and pernicious nature of the Arian doctrine, publicly exposed and condemned it.

The emperor Constantine, without apparent cause, now turned the sword of vengeance and the punishment appointed for the impious against even his nearest and dearest. He put to death his own son Crispus and his sister's son Licinius. He also subdued many tribes in different campaigns, and was either the first or the only Roman ruler to found a city named after himself. As the only city free from idols, Constantinople was raised up within a very short time after her founding by a Christian emperor to be, in splendor and power, the only worthy rival of Rome, which had been advanced to her supremacy after many centuries and much suffering. Then for the first time Constantine reversed the situation by a just and pious order. He issued an edict that the pagan temples should be closed without the killing of a single man. Soon afterward he destroyed the valiant and populous Gothic tribes in the very heart of the barbarian territory, that is, in the region of the Sarmatians. In Cyprus he crushed a certain Calocaerus, who was plotting a revolution; and, on the thirtieth anniversary of his accession, he appointed Dalmatius Caesar. Constantine died in his official residence near Nicomedia, while he was preparing for war against the Persians. He left the state in good order for his sons.

29. IN THE one thousand and ninety-second year of the City, Constantius, the thirty-fifth emperor, ascended the throne.[103] He shared it with his brothers Constantine and Constans [104] and held it for twenty-four years. Among the successors of Constantine was Dalmatius Caesar, the son of his brother; this Caesar, however, was soon entrapped by a faction of the army.

The ever-malignant opposition of the devil to the true God from the beginning of the world until now has been confusing the minds of men with the mists of error and leading their uncertain steps astray from the undefiled path

[103] Constantius II, 337–361.   [104] Constantine II, 337–340; Constans, 337–350.

of religious faith. But it ceased to persecute the Church of Christ with the zeal of idolatry after the Christian emperors had applied the sovereign power to better ends. The devil then devised another scheme to harass the Church of Christ through these same Christian emperors. Arius, the author of the new heresy, and his disciples found ready access and an easy road to the friendship of Constantius. Arius induced the emperor to believe that there are certain gradations in God, and thus, after leaving the error of idolatry by the main door, he was led back into it through a side entrance, as it were, while seeking to find gods in God. His authority, when ridiculed, became armed with a perverted zeal, and a violent persecution was started in the name of religious devotion. An argument arose about the choice of a new name, and it was urged that the churches should belong to the Arians rather than to the Catholics. Then followed a fearful earthquake that leveled to the ground many cities of the East.

Constantine [II], while making war upon his brother Constans, exposed himself to danger in a foolhardy fashion and was slain by his brother's generals. Constans fought nine unsuccessful campaigns against the Persians and Sapor, who had been ravaging Mesopotamia. Finally his soldiers, now out of control, mutinied and compelled him to make a night attack, and he not only lost the victory that had been almost won but was actually defeated himself. Later, when he had given himself up to excessive license and was gaining the favor of the soldiers by oppressing the provincials, he was treacherously killed by Magnentius at a town called Helena on the border of Spain.

This Magnentius assumed the imperial title at Augustodunum and immediately extended his authority over Gaul, Africa, and Italy.[105] In Illyria the soldiers proclaimed as their emperor the aged Vetranio, a man of simplicity and kindly disposed toward all, but one who had never received even the rudiments of an education. While the aged emperor against his will was studying the alphabet and the syllables of words,

---

[105] From 350 to 353.

he was ordered to abdicate by Constantius, who, burning to avenge his brother, was preparing war against Magnentius. Vetranio laid aside the purple along with his studies and gave up palace and school at the same time, content to lead a life of leisure as a private citizen.

Nepotian, the son of Constantine's sister, aided by a band of gladiators, then seized the imperial power at Rome. His wickedness, however, made him universally hated. He was defeated by the generals of Magnentius. Then followed that fearful battle between Constantius and Magnentius at the city of Mursa. The great losses of the Roman forces in this battle brought harm even to posterity. Magnentius, however, escaped after his defeat and not long afterward killed himself with his own hand at Lugdunum. His brother Decentius, whom he had appointed Caesar over the Gauls, hanged himself at Senones. Constantius at once chose his cousin Gallus as Caesar, but since the latter behaved in a cruel and tyrannical manner, he had him put to death soon after his appointment. The emperor also took care that Silvanus, who was eager to see a revolution in Gaul, was speedily surrounded and overcome. He then killed Silvanus, appointed his cousin Julian, the brother of Gallus, Caesar, and sent him to the Gallic provinces, which the enemy had overrun and devastated. With a great display of energy, Julian restored the provinces to their former condition, routed a vast multitude of the Alemanni with but a small force, and again pushed back the Germans beyond the Rhine. Elated by these successes, Julian usurped the dignity of Augustus. Soon afterward he made his way through Italy and Illyria, and deprived Constantius, who was occupied with the Parthian War, of a great part of his realm. When he learned of Julian's treachery, Constantius abandoned the Parthian campaign and turned back to engage in civil war, but he died on the road between Cilicia and Cappadocia. Thus the man who had rent asunder the peace and unity of the Catholic faith and had, so to speak, dismembered the Church by civil war, arming Christians against Christians, used, passed, and expended the entire period of his troubled reign and his wretched span of life in civil wars which his own kinsmen and blood relations stirred up.

30. IN THE one thousand one hundred and sixteenth year of the City, Julian, who had previously been Caesar, then established himself as the thirty-sixth emperor in succession from Augustus. He reigned alone for a year and eight months.[106] Attacking the Christian religion by cunning instead of by force he sought to make men deny the faith of Christ and adopt the worship of idols by the temptation of honors rather than by the infliction of tortures. Our elders tell us that when he issued a public edict forbidding any Christian to be a professor of the liberal branches of learning, almost all Christians everywhere, in compliance with the terms of the ordinance, preferred to abandon their positions rather than their faith.

When Julian was preparing war against the Parthians and was taking Roman forces recruited from all quarters with him to certain destruction, he vowed the blood of the Christians to his Gods, intending to persecute the churches openly if he should be victorious. In fact, he ordered an amphitheater to be constructed at Jerusalem in which upon his return from Parthia he could expose bishops, monks, and all the saints of the locality to the fury of wild beasts that had been deliberately enraged and then could watch the martyrs being torn to pieces. After he had moved his camp away from Ctesiphon, he was treacherously led into the desert by a traitor. When his army was perishing from thirst, the heat of the sun, and the fatigue of marching through the sands, the emperor, becoming anxious at so dangerous a situation, rashly ventured to wander through the desert. There he encountered one of the enemy's cavalrymen and met his death from a blow of the other's lance. Thus God in his mercy brought these evil designs to naught through the death of their evil author.

31. IN THE one thousand one hundred and seventeenth year

[106] From 3 November 361 to 26 June 363.

of the City, when her affairs were in a most critical state, Jovian became the thirty-seventh emperor. He was proclaimed emperor by the army which had been caught in an unfavorable situation and hemmed in by the enemy without chance of escape. In these circumstances Jovian made a treaty with Sapor, king of the Persians, which, though considered quite dishonorable, was unavoidable. Sapor agreed to leave the Roman army safe and unharmed either from attack or from the dangers of the locality, provided the Romans surrendered to the Persians the town of Nisibis and a part of Upper Mesopotamia. While marching through Galatia on his way to Illyria, Jovian withdrew to sleep in a newly built bedchamber. There he was overpowered and suffocated by the fumes arising from the action of the heat of the burning coals on the dampness of the newly plastered walls. His life came to an end in the eighth month of his reign.[107]

32. IN THE one thousand one hundred and eighteenth year of the City, Valentinian, the thirty-eighth emperor, was proclaimed emperor at Nicaea by agreement of the soldiers. He held office for eleven years.[108] Though a Christian, Valentinian without violating his faith had performed military duty under the emperor Julian as tribune of the *scutarii*. But when he was ordered by that sacrilegious emperor either to sacrifice to idols or to leave the service, he withdrew voluntarily, knowing as a faithful man that God's judgments are severer and His promises more to be desired.

Thus it happened that soon after the killing of Julian and directly after the death of Jovian, this man, who had lost his tribuneship in defense of Christ's name, became emperor in his own persecutor's stead as his reward from Christ. Later he made his brother Valens joint emperor [109] and subsequently killed the usurper Procopius and many of the latter's followers. At this time an earthquake occurred throughout the

---

[107] From 27 June 363 to 16 February 364.

[108] From 364 to 375. Part of the time he shared the sovereignty with Valens and Gratian. [109] In the year 364. Valens was emperor until 378.

world and so greatly agitated the sea, that, according to report, the plains along the coast were inundated, and many cities, situated on islands, were struck, collapsed, and perished. Valens was baptized and converted by the bishop Eudoxius, a supporter of the Arian views, and thus he fell into most terrible heresy. For a long time Valens concealed his wicked intention to persecute and did not use his power to further his desire because the authority of his brother, so long as the latter lived, restrained him; for he well knew what force Valentinian as emperor could exert in avenging the faith, when he had possessed such firmness in keeping it as a soldier.

In the third year of the reign of these brothers, Gratian, the son of Valentinian, was made emperor.[110] In the same year, in the territory of the Atrebates, real wool, mixed with rain, fell from the clouds.

Moreover, Athanaric, king of the Goths, with the greatest cruelty persecuted the Christians living among his own people and raised many of the barbarians to the crown of martyrdom by putting them to death for their faith. There were many who, because they acknowledged Christ, had to flee to the territory of the Romans. They went, not apprehensively as if going to enemies, but with assurances as to brethren.

The Saxons, a tribe living on the shores of the Ocean in inaccessible swamps and dreaded for their bravery and rapidity of movement, undertook a dangerous raid in full force against the Roman possessions, but they were crushed by Valentinian in the land of the Franks. The Burgundians, a new enemy with a new name, numbering, it is said, more than eighty thousand armed men, settled on the bank of the Rhine. In earlier times, when the interior of Germany had been subjugated by Drusus and Tiberius, the adopted sons of Caesar, the Burgundians were stationed at different frontier posts. Later they united to form a great people. They took their name from their stations, for the dwelling places at frequent intervals along the frontier are commonly called *burgi*. The power and destructiveness of their tribes is manifest even

---

[110] In the year 367. Gratian ruled until 383.

today from the condition of the Gallic provinces where they have now settled, their right to do so being undisputed. Nevertheless, through the providence of God they have all recently become Christians, embracing the Catholic faith and acknowledging obedience to our clergy, so that they live mild, gentle, and harmless lives, regarding the Gauls not as their subjects but in truth as their Christian brethren.

In the eleventh year of his reign, Valentinian started to make war upon the Sarmatians who had overrun and were ravaging the Pannonian provinces. But at the town of Brigitio [111] he was choked to death by the sudden hemorrhage that the Greeks call apoplexy.

Valentinian was succeeded as emperor of the West by his son Gratian, while Valens, the latter's uncle, ruled in the East. The new emperor shared his throne with his brother Valentinian, who was a mere child.[112]

33. FROM the one thousand one hundred and twenty-eighth year of the City, Valens, the thirty-ninth emperor, ruled for four years after the death of Valentinian, who alone had been able to make him blush for his impious deeds. Immediately, as if his shameless boldness knew no bounds, he made a law requiring military service of the monks. These men were Christians who had given up the transaction of secular business in its various forms and were devoting themselves solely to the work of the Faith. The vast solitudes of Egypt and its stretches of sand, which were unfit for human use because of their aridity, barrenness, and the extreme danger from numerous serpents, were then filled and inhabited by great numbers of monks. Thither officers and soldiers were sent on a new type of persecution to drag away to other places the saintly and true soldiers of God. Many companies of saints suffered death there. As for the measures taken against the Catholic churches and orthodox believers throughout the various provinces under these and similar orders, let my decision to remain silent be sufficient indication of their nature.

[111] A Roman *municipium* in Lower Pannonia.   [112] In the year 375.

Meanwhile, in certain parts of Africa Firmus stirred up the Moorish tribes, made himself king, and laid waste Africa and Mauretania. Caesarea, the most important city of Mauretania, was captured by treachery, filled with fire and carnage, and given over to the barbarians for pillage. Thereupon Count Theodosius, the father of the Theodosius who afterwards became emperor, acting under Valentinian's orders, broke the strength of the roaming Moorish tribes in a number of engagements and compelled the discouraged and vanquished Firmus to take his own life. Later, acting with well-trained foresight, he more than restored Africa and Mauretania to their former condition, but without realizing it he aroused so much envy that he was condemned to death. Before his execution at Carthage, he resolved to be baptized in order to obtain the remission of his sins; having received the sacrament of Christ which he had desired, he offered his throat to the blow of the executioner with the assurance of eternal life to come after his glorious life in this world.

Meanwhile the emperor Gratian, who was still a youth, saw a countless multitude of enemies invade the Roman domain. Relying on the power of Christ, he met them with far inferior forces and, in a battle at the Gallic town of Argentaria, straightway by a wonderful stroke of good fortune brought to an end a most formidable war. More than thirty thousand of the Alemanni, according to report, were killed there with but slight loss on the Roman side.

In the thirteenth year of the reign of Valens, that is, in the short interval of time that followed the wrecking of the churches by Valens and his slaughtering of the saints throughout the East, that root of our miseries simultaneously sent up a very great number of shoots. The race of Huns, long shut off by inaccessible mountains, broke out in sudden rage against the Goths and drove them in widespread confusion from their old homes. The Goths fled across the Danube and were received by Valens without negotiating any treaty. They did not even surrender their arms to the Romans, an act which might have made it safer to trust the barbarians. But the general Maximus

by his unbearable avarice brought famine and injuries upon the
Goths and drove them to arms and rebellion. After defeating
an army of Valens, they overran Thrace and swept the whole
country with fire, murder, and rapine. When Valens had left
Antioch and was going to his doom in that ill-fated war, he
was pricked with a tardy remorse for his heinous sin and gave
orders for the recall of the bishops and other dignitaries from
exile.

In the fifteenth year of his reign, Valens fought that lamentable battle in Thrace against the Goths, who by that time
were well prepared in the matter of military training, and who
had an abundance of resources. The very first attack threw
the squadrons of Roman cavalry into confusion and left the
infantry forces without protection. The infantry legions were
at once encircled by the enemy's cavalry. They were first
overwhelmed by showers of arrows, then, mad with fear, were
forced to scatter by devious paths, and finally were cut to
pieces by the swords and lances of their pursuers. The emperor himself, wounded by an arrow, turned to flight and was
with difficulty brought to a cottage on a small farm. While
he was hiding there, the pursuing enemy came upon him.
They set fire to the building, and Valens perished in the flames.
In order that the punishment visited upon him—this manifestation of divine wrath—might serve all the more as a
dreadful example to posterity, he was not even given a common burial.

The wretched and obstinate heathen may find comfort in
this one fact alone: these great disasters in Christian times and
under Christian rulers (the ruin of the provinces, the destruction of the army, and the burning of the emperor) occurred
all at once and bowed down the neck of the state already
sore oppressed. This indeed grieves us much and is all the
more lamentable for being so unprecedented. But how does
it serve to comfort the pagans who can plainly perceive that in
this case a persecutor of the churches was also punished? The
one God revealed one faith and spread one Church over all
the world. It is She whom He beholds, whom He loves, whom
He defends; and, whatever the name by which a man shields

himself, he is an alien if he is not associated with Her, and an enemy if he attacks Her. Let the heathen take what comfort they may in the suffering of the Jews and the heretics, but only let them confess that there is one God and that He is no respecter of persons as is most conclusively proven by the destruction of Valens. The Goths had petitioned through ambassadors that bishops be sent to them from whom they might learn the rule of the Christian faith. In fatal perverseness the emperor Valens sent teachers of the Arian doctrine, and the Goth continued to believe what they first learned concerning the basic principles of the faith. Therefore, by the just judgment of God Himself, Valens was burned alive by the very men who, through his action, will burn hereafter for their heresy.

34. IN THE one thousand one hundred and thirty-second year of the City, Gratian, the fortieth emperor in succession from Augustus, became emperor. He reigned for six years following the death of Valens,[113] although he had already reigned for some time in conjunction with his uncle Valens and his brother Valentinian. Seeing the distressed and almost ruined condition of the state, he exercised the same foresight which led Nerva, in a former time, to choose the Spaniard Trajan, who restored the state. Gratian in his turn chose Theodosius, likewise a Spaniard, invested him with the purple at Sirmium for the necessary work of reëstablishing the government, and made him ruler of the East and of Thrace as well.[114] In one respect Gratian's judgment was the better; for Theodosius, who was Trajan's equal in all the virtues of our mortal life, surpassed him beyond all comparison in his devotion to the faith and in his reverence for religion, inasmuch as the earlier emperor was a persecutor, and the latter a propagator, of the Church. Trajan was not blessed with even a single son of his own to succeed him, whereas the glorious descendants of Theodosius have ruled over the East and the West alike through successive generations to this very day.

Theodosius believed that the state, which had been brought

---

[113] To 25 August 383.   [114] In the year 379.

low by the wrath of God, would be restored by His mercy. Putting all his trust in the help of Christ, he attacked without hesitation those mighty Scythian tribes, which had been the dread of all the earlier ages and had been avoided even by Alexander the Great, as Pompeius and Cornelius declare. These same tribes were equipped with Roman horses and arms, though the Roman army no longer existed. Yet he defeated these tribes, that is, the Alans, Huns, and Goths, in a series of great battles. He entered the city of Constantinople as a victor, and made a treaty with Athanaric, the king of the Goths, so that he might not exhaust the small body of Roman troops by continual campaigning. Athanaric, however, died immediately after reaching Constantinople. Upon the death of their king, all the Gothic tribes, on seeing the bravery and kindness of Theodosius, submitted to Roman rule. At the same time the Persians voluntarily sent ambassadors to Theodosius at Constantinople and humbly begged for peace. These Persians previously had killed Julian and frequently defeated other emperors. Recently they had put Valens to flight and were now venting their satisfaction over this latest victory by offering foul insults. A treaty was then made, the fruits of which the entire East has enjoyed in great tranquillity until the present day.

In the meantime, by subjugating the barbarian tribes in the East, Theodosius finally freed the Thracian provinces from the enemy. He made his son Arcadius associate emperor. The army in Britain proclaimed Maximus emperor against his will.[115] Maximus was an energetic and able man and one worthy of the throne had he not risen to it by usurpation, contrary to his oath of allegiance. He crossed into Gaul where he treacherously killed the emperor Gratian, who, in his fright at the sudden invasion, was planning to go to Italy. He drove Gratian's brother, the emperor Valentinian, from Italy. The latter took refuge in the East with Theodosius, who received him with a father's affection and soon even restored him to his imperial dignity.

[115] In the year 383.

35. IN THE one thousand one hundred and thirty-eighth year of the City, after Gratian had been killed by Maximus, Theodosius, the forty-first emperor, became ruler of the Roman world. He remained in office for eleven years.[116] He had already reigned in the East for six years during Gratian's lifetime. The demands of justice and necessity persuaded him to engage in civil war, since, of the two imperial brothers, the blood of the one slain demanded vengeance and the misery of the other in exile pleaded for restoration to his former position. Theodosius therefore put his trust in God and hurled himself against the usurper Maximus with no advantage but that of faith, for he was inferior in every point of military equipment. Maximus at that time had established himself at Aquileia, to be a spectator of his own victory. Andragathius, his count, who was in charge of the general direction of the war, greatly strengthened all the approaches through the Alps and along the rivers, placing there large bodies of soldiers and employing skillful strategy that counted for even more than strength of numbers. But by the inscrutable judgment of God he abandoned of his own accord the very passes that he had closed up, intending to catch the enemy off their guard and destroy them by a naval expedition. Thus Theodosius crossed the undefended Alps without being noticed, much less opposed, by anyone, and arrived unexpectedly before Aquileia. His mighty enemy Maximus, a stern ruler who exacted taxes even from the savage German tribes by the mere terror of his name, was surrounded, captured, and put to death without recourse to treachery and without a contest. Valentinian, after receiving the imperium, attempted to gain control over Italy. On learning of the death of Maximus, Count Andragathius threw himself headlong from his ship into the sea and was drowned. Thus under God's guidance Theodosius gained a bloodless victory.

Observe how, under Christian rulers and in Christian times, civil wars are settled when they cannot be avoided. The victory was won, the city was stormed, the usurper was seized.

[116] Until 395.

And this is not half the story. Look elsewhere and see a hostile army vanquished, a count in the service of that usurper—he was more violent than the usurper himself—forced to take his own life, many ambuscades broken up or evaded, countless preparations rendered useless. Yet no one planned stratagems, no one drew up a line of battle, and, lastly, no one, if I may use the expression, even unsheathed his sword. A most formidable war was brought to a victorous conclusion without bloodshed and with the death of but two persons on the occasion of the victory itself. Now, to prevent anyone from regarding this as the result of chance, let me produce testimony to God's power, which orders and judges the universe, so that its revelation may either confound the objectors or force them to believe. I mention, therefore, a circumstance unknown to all and yet known to all. After this war in which Maximus was slain, many wars, both domestic and foreign, have indeed been the lot of Theodosius and his son Honorius up to the present day, as we all recollect, and yet almost all have ended either without bloodshed or, at least, with very little, as a result of a decisive victory due to divine influence.

After the destruction of Maximus and of his son Victor,[117] whom Maximus had left among the Gauls as their emperor, Valentinian the Younger, now restored to his realm, passed over into Gaul. While living there peacefully in a country then tranquil, so the story goes, he was treacherously strangled to death at Vienne by his count Arbogastes. Valentinian was hanged by a rope so that it might appear he had taken his own life.

Soon after the death of the Augustus Valentinian, Arbogastes ventured to set up the usurper Eugenius,[118] choosing him as a figurehead on whom to bestow the imperial title, but intending to manage the government himself. Arbogastes was a barbarian who excelled in spirit, counsel, bravery, boldness, and power. He gathered together from all quarters enormous forces as yet unconquered, intending to seize the sovereignty. He drew partly on the Roman garrisons and partly on the

[117] Flavius Victor, 384–388.   [118] From May 392 to 6 September 394.

barbarian auxiliaries, in the one case by virtue of his power and in the other on account of his kinship. It is not necessary to dilate in words upon events that many have seen with their own eyes and of which they as spectators have a better knowledge. In every respect the career of Arbogastes clearly shows that Theodosius was always victorious through the power of God. At the time when he was loyal to Theodosius, Arbogastes, in spite of his own slender resources, captured the strongly supported Maximus. But when he clashed with Theodosius, though aided by the united strength of the Gauls and Franks and though also relying upon his devoted worship of idols, he was nevertheless defeated with great ease. Eugenius and Arbogastes had drawn up their army in battle array in the plains and, having very craftily sent ahead ambushing parties, had occupied the narrow slopes of the Alps and the passes which had to be used, so as to win victory by strategy alone, even though they were inferior in numbers and in strength.

Theodosius took up a position on the heights of the Alps and remained there without food or sleep. Knowing that he was abandoned by his men, but unaware that he was surrounded by enemies, he prayed alone to his one and all-sufficient help, the Lord Christ, while he lay with his body stretched upon the ground but with his mind fixed upon Heaven. After passing a sleepless night in continual prayer and leaving as evidence pools of tears that he had shed as the price of Heavenly aid, he confidently took arms alone, knowing that he was truly not alone. Then with the sign of the cross he gave the signal for battle and plunged into the fight as if destined to conquer even though none should follow him. The first step to deliverance appeared in the person of Arbitio, a count of the opposing army. The latter had caught the unsuspecting emperor in an ambush laid for him, but moved to reverence in the presence of his Augustus, he not only freed him from danger but even provided him with aid.

The moment that the forces came within fighting distance, an indescribably great windstorm suddenly began to blow

violently into the faces of the enemy. The darts of our men
flew through the air and were carried over a great distance,
farther than any man could throw, and they fell scarcely anywhere without striking their mark. Furthermore, the force
of the unabating gale now dashed the shields of the enemy so
heavily against their own faces and breasts as to strike them
repeatedly, now pressed their shields so close as to take away
their breath, now tore away their shields so violently as to
leave them unprotected, now held their shields so steadily
against them as to force them backward. Even the weapons
that they had hurled with all their might were caught by the
wind and driven back to transfix the unfortunate throwers.
The terrified consciences of the men drove them to seek safety,
for as soon as a small detachment of the enemy had been routed
their army surrendered to the victorious Theodosius. Eugenius was captured and killed, and Arbogastes destroyed himself by his own hand. Thus in this case too, the fires of civil
war were quenched by the blood of two men, leaving out of
account the ten thousand Goths, who, it is said, were sent
ahead by Theodosius and destroyed to a man by Arbogastes;
for the loss of these was certainly a gain and their defeat a
victory. I do not taunt those who disparage us. Let them
point out a single war in the history of Rome undertaken
from such conscientious and compelling motives, carried out
with such divine good fortune, stilled with such merciful
kindness, one in which the battle did not entail heavy losses
nor the victory a bloody revenge. Then perhaps I may admit
that these blessed victories were not the rewards of the faith
of a Christian general. Yet I am not anxious about this testimony of theirs, since one of their own number, a distinguished
poet but a most obstinate pagan, has borne witness both to
God and to man in these verses:

> O thou much beloved of God! for whom the sky does battle,
> For whom the winds in concert heed the trumpet's call.[119]

Thus Heaven gave judgment between the side that humbly

[119] Claudian *Panegyric on the Third Consulship of the Emperor Honorius*
96–98.

placed its hope in God alone even without the aid of man and
the side that arrogantly trusted in its own strength and in
idols. After reducing the state to order and tranquillity Theodosius died at Milan.

36.   IN THE one thousand one hundred and forty-ninth year
of the City, Arcadius Augustus, whose son Theodosius now
rules the East, and Honorius Augustus, his brother, by whom
our state is now completely supported, occupied the forty-
second place in the imperial line and began to exercise a joint
sovereignty, but in different capitals.[120] Arcadius lived for
twelve years after his father's death, and, when he died, left
the supreme power to his son Theodosius, who was still very
young.

Meanwhile Count Gildo, who was in charge of Africa at
the beginning of his brother's reign, revolted as soon as he
learned that Theodosius had died. Induced by some sort of
envy, according to some, he planned to add Africa to the
districts of the Eastern Empire; according to another view,
he was influenced by the belief that there would be little hope
for the young rulers, since, except for them, hardly any young
boy who inherited the throne had ever before reached full
manhood. This, indeed, was almost an unparalleled instance
in which youths, separated and forsaken, prospered under the
guardianship of Christ on account of their own and their
father's remarkable faith. Gildo, then, dared to claim for
himself Africa, which had been detached from its allegiance
to the state. He did this more because he found satisfaction
in his heathen life of licentiousness than because he was inspired by any ambition or royal pretensions. His brother
Mascezel, thoroughly detesting Gildo's revolutionary undertakings, left his two sons with the troops in Africa and went
back to Italy. Gildo, becoming suspicious both of his brother's
absence and of his nephews' presence, treacherously seized the
youths and put them to death. When it was decided to make
war upon Gildo as a public enemy, Mascezel was given the

---

[120] Honorius in the West, 395–423; Arcadius in the East, 395–408.

command. His fitness for the service of the state was assured by the fresh grief of his own bereavement. Recognizing, like Theodosius, how much in a desperate situation the prayer of man can gain from the mercy of God through faith in Christ, Mascezel visited the island of Capraria and took with him from that place some holy servants of God who were moved by his entreaties. He continued in prayer, fasting, and psalmody with them day and night, and was thus enabled to gain victory without war and vengeance without bloodshed.

The Ardalio is the name of a river that flows between the cities of Theveste and Ammedera. Here Mascezel encamped with a small force of five thousand soldiers, as it is said, against seventy thousand of the enemy. After some delay he laid plans to leave his position and march through the narrow passes of the valley that lay ahead. When darkness came, he dreamt that he saw the blessed Ambrose, the lately deceased bishop of Milan, making a sign with his hand, striking his staff thrice upon the ground, and saying these words, "Here, here, here." He wisely inferred that this vision indicated assurance of victory from the trustworthiness of his prophet, the place from the word spoken, and the day from the number. He therefore held his ground, and on the third day, after keeping vigil through the night with prayers and hymns, went forth from the very mysteries of the Heavenly sacraments to meet the enemy who had surrounded him.

While he was speaking pious words of peace to those whom he first encountered, one of their standard-bearers insolently withstood his entreaties and kept urging his side to begin the battle that was imminent. Thereupon Mascezel struck his arm with a sword, disabled his hand, and thus compelled him to lower the banner to the ground by the force of the blow. At this sight, the other cohorts, thinking that the front ranks were already surrendering, reversed their standards and hastened to give themselves up to Mascezel. The barbarians, of whom Gildo had brought a great number to the war, fled in all directions, after they had been left entirely alone by the desertion of the regular troops. Gildo himself tried to escape by seizing a ship and putting out to sea, but was driven back to Africa where some days later he was strangled to death.

In telling of such miracles we would run the risk of appearing deliberate and shameless liars, if the testimony of those who were eyewitnesses did not outstrip our words. Yet all this was done without the concocting of plots and the practice of corruption. Seventy thousand of the enemy were overcome almost without a battle. The vanquished rebel fled for the time being, lest the angry conqueror dare a greater deed. Gildo was carried away to a different place so that his brother might not know of the slaying whereby he himself was avenged. This Mascezel, it is true, became puffed up with the haughtiness that comes of success and neglected the society of the holy men through whom he had won the victory as a champion of God. He even dared to violate a church, not hesitating to drag from it some refugees. This sacrilege met with its due reward, for some time afterward, while the very men whom he had dragged from the church in order to punish them were still alive, he himself was punished amid their rejoicing. By his own fate he showed that the judgment of God ever watches with a double purpose, since when he trusted in it, he received help, and when he despised it, he was put to death.

37. MEANWHILE the emperor Theodosius the Elder had entrusted the care of his children and the direction of his two courts, respectively, to his two most powerful subjects, Rufinus in the East and Stilicho in the West. What each man did and what he attempted to do, the fates of each made plain. Rufinus, aspiring to the royal dignity for himself, brought in the barbarians; Stilicho, desiring it for his son, gave them support so that the needs of the state in the sudden crisis might veil his wicked aim. I say nothing of King Alaric and his Goths, often defeated, often surrounded, but always allowed to escape. I say nothing of those unhappy doings at Pollentia when the chief command was entrusted to the barbarian and pagan general Saul who wickedly profaned the most solemn days and holy Eastertide and who compelled the enemy, then

withdrawing on account of religious scruples, to fight. The judgment of God soon disclosed not only the power of His favor but also the demands of His vengeance, for although we [121] conquered in fighting we were defeated in conquering. I say nothing of the many internecine conflicts between the barbarians themselves, when two divisions of the Goths, and then the Alans and Huns, destroyed one another in mutual slaughter.

Radagaisus, by far the most savage of all our enemies, past or present, inundated all Italy by a sudden invasion with an army reported to number more than two hundred thousand Goths. Aside from the fact of his own dauntless courage and the support of the vast multitude, he was a pagan and a Scythian, who, according to the custom of the barbarous tribes, had vowed the blood of the entire Roman race as an offering to his gods. Consequently, when he threatened the defenses of Rome, all the pagans in the City flocked together, saying that the enemy was powerful, not merely because of the size of his forces, but especially because of the aid of his gods. They also said that the City was forsaken and would soon perish because it had completely abandoned its gods and its sacred rites. Great complaints were raised everywhere. The restoration and celebration of sacrifices were at once discussed. Blasphemies were rife throughout the City, and the name of Christ was publicly loaded with reproaches as if it were a curse upon the times.

Since in a mixed people the pious deserve grace and the impious punishment, according to God's inscrutable judgment, it was deemed just to allow such enemies to chastise the altogether stubborn and refractory City with a scourge of unusual severity, but not to permit them to destroy everything indiscriminately. At that time there were roaming wildly through the Roman provinces two Gothic peoples, led by two powerful kings. One of these kings was a Christian and more like a Roman, a man, who, through the fear of God, as the event showed, inclined to spare men's lives. The other was a pagan,

[121] That is, the Romans.

barbarian, and true Scythian, who in his insatiable cruelty loved not so much the fame or the rewards of butchery as he did slaughter itself. And this man had already reached the heart of Italy and was causing nearby Rome to shake with fright. If, then, he had been the chosen instrument of vengeance—the Romans feared him especially because he courted the favor of the gods with sacrifices—the slaughter would have been more unrestrained without effecting any reform. Thus the last error would have been worse than the first; for had they indeed fallen into the hands of a pagan and an idolator, not only would the remaining pagans have been firmly persuaded to restore idolatry, but the Christians would to their peril have become confused—the latter terrified by the warning, the former encouraged by this precedent. Hence God, the just steward of the human race, willed that the pagan enemy should perish and allowed the Christian enemy to prevail, in order that the pagan and blaspheming Romans might be thrown into confusion by the death of the one and punished by the invasion of the other. In particular, the holy faith and continence of the emperor Honorius, remarkable in a ruler, merited no small measure of divine mercy.

Against Radagaisus, our most savage enemy, God granted that the minds of our other enemies should be disposed to help us with their forces. Uldin and Sarus, leaders of the Huns and of the Goths, came to the aid of the Romans. But God did not allow the workings of His power to appear as the valor of men, particularly when they were our enemies. He smote Radagaisus with supernatural terror, drove him into the mountains of Fiesole, bottled up his two hundred thousand men—this number is the lowest estimate cited—without food or resource on a rough and arid ridge. Weighted down with apprehension, the band that had but lately found Italy too small was crowded upon one small summit, where it hoped to lie concealed. Why delay the tale? No army was arrayed for battle; no fury or fear prolonged the uncertainties of the fight; no killings were done; no blood was shed; nor finally was there that which is usually considered a reason for con-

gratulations, namely, a loss in battle compensated by the fruits
of victory. While our men were eating, drinking, and making
merry, the enemy, so numerous and so savage, were worn out
by hunger, thirst, and exhaustion. All this would matter little
if the Romans did not know that the man whom they feared
had been captured and subdued and if they did not see that
idol worshipper, whose sacrifices they pretended to dread more
than his arms, defeated without a battle, sent under the yoke,
and exposed to their contempt as a prisoner in chains. So King
Radagaisus secretly deserted his men, hoping to escape by
himself, but he fell into the hands of our soldiers. He was
captured by them, held for a while, and then put to death.
The Gothic captives are said to have been so numerous that
droves of them were sold everywhere like the cheapest cattle
for an *aureus* apiece.

But God did not allow anything to be left of this people;
for immediately all those who had been bought died, and what
the hard bargainers had shamefully saved in price was mercifully spent on their burial. Thus ungrateful Rome, which now
felt the indirect mercy of her God and Judge, not for the
pardoning but for the checking of her bold idolatry, was also
soon to suffer the wrath of God, although not in full measure
on account of the pious remembrance of the saints, both living
and dead. If by some chance she should repent in her bewild-
erment and learn faith through experience, she would be spared
for a short space of time from the invasion of Alaric, a hostile
but a Christian king.

38. MEANWHILE Count Stilicho, who was sprung from the
Vandals, that unwarlike, greedy, treacherous, and crafty race,
thought it insufficient that he had imperial power under the
nominal emperor, and tried by every possible means to place
upon the throne his own son Eucherius. According to common
report, the latter had been planning the persecution of the
Christians from the time when he was a boy and still a private
citizen. Hence, when Alaric and the whole Gothic nation begged
humbly and straightforwardly for peace on very favorable

terms and also for some place to settle, Stilicho supported them
by a secret alliance, but in the name of the state refused them the
opportunity of either making war or peace, reserving them
to wear down and to intimidate the state. Moreover, other
nations irresistible in numbers and might who are now oppressing the provinces of Gaul and Spain (namely, the
Alans, Suebi, and Vandals, as well as the Burgundians who
were driven on by the same movement) were induced by
Stilicho to take arms on their own initiative and were aroused
when once their fear of Rome was removed. Stilicho's plan
was to batter the Rhine frontier and strike against the two
Gauls. This wretched man hoped that in this dangerous situation he could thereby wrest the imperial dignity from his son-
in-law and give it to his son, and that it would be as easy to
repress the barbarian nations as it was to arouse them. When
the character of these crimes was openly revealed to the
emperor Honorius and to the Roman army, the soldiers very
properly mutinied and killed Stilicho, who, in order to clothe
one boy with the royal purple, had imperiled the blood of the
whole human race. Eucherius was also slain, who for the sake
of gaining the favor of the pagans had threatened that he
would celebrate the beginning of his reign by the restoration
of the temples and by the overthrow of the churches. Several
accomplices also were punished for their wicked plots. Thus
the churches of Christ and the devout emperor were freed
as well as avenged with very little trouble and with the punishment of but a few persons. Therefore, after this great increase
of blasphemies without any evidence of repentance, the final,
long-impending doom overtook the City.

39.   ALARIC appeared before trembling Rome, laid siege,
spread confusion, and broke into the City.[122] He first, however, gave orders that all those who had taken refuge in sacred
places, especially in the basilicas of the holy Apostles Peter and
Paul, should be permitted to remain inviolate and unmolested;

---

[122] The chapter in the Latin text begins with the previous sentence, but this
seems a more logical division.

he allowed his men to devote themselves to plunder as much as they wished, but he gave orders that they should refrain from bloodshed. A further proof that the storming of the City was due to the wrath of God rather than to the bravery of the enemy is shown by the fact that the blessed Innocent, the bishop of Rome, who at that time was at Ravenna, through the hidden providence of God, even as Lot the Just was withdrawn from the Sodomites, did not witness the destruction of the sinful populace.

While the barbarians were roaming through the City, one of the Goths, a powerful man and a Christian, chanced to find in a church building a virgin advanced in years who had dedicated herself to God. When he respectfully asked her for gold and silver, she declared with the firmness of her faith that she had a large amount in her possession and that she would bring it forth at once. She did so. Observing that the barbarian was astonished at the size, weight, and beauty of the riches displayed, even though he did not know the nature of the vessels, the virgin of Christ then said to him: "These are the sacred plate of the Apostle Peter. Presume, if you dare! You will have to answer for the deed. As for me, since I cannot protect them, I dare not keep them." The barbarian, stirred to religious awe through the fear of God and by the virgin's faith, sent word of the incident to Alaric. He ordered that all the vessels, just as they were, should be brought back immediately to the basilica of the Apostle, and that the virgin also, together with all Christians who might join the procession, should be conducted thither under escort. The building, it is said, was at a considerable distance from the sacred places, with half the city lying between. Consequently the gold and silver vessels were distributed, each to a different person; they were carried high above the head in plain sight, to the wonder of all beholders. The pious procession was guarded by a double line of drawn swords; Romans and barbarians in concert raised a hymn to God in public. In the sacking of the City the trumpet of salvation sounded far and wide and smote the ears of all with its invitation, even those lying in hiding. From every quarter the vessels of Christ mingled with the vessels of Peter, and many pagans even joined the Christians in making profession, though not in true faith. In this way they escaped, but only for a time, that their confusion might afterward be the greater. The more densely the Roman refugees flocked together, the more eagerly their barbarian protectors surrounded them. O sacred and inscrutable discernment of the divine judgment! O holy and saving river, which begins its course at a small house and, as it flows in its blessed channel to the abode of the saints, bears wandering and imperiled souls to the harbor of salvation by its pious power of drawing them to it! O glorious trumpet of Christian warfare which, inviting by its sweet notes all without distinction to life, leaves those who, for want of obedience, cannot be roused to salvation, to meet their death for want of excuse! The celebration of this mystery with its transferring of the vessels, its singing of hymns, and its escorting of the people, resembled, in my opinion, a huge sieve, through which the congregation of the Roman people was sifted like a great pile of grain; for through all the apertures of the hiding places in the entire circuit of the City the living kernels flowed forth. It was a question whether it was the occasion or the truth that stirred them. All, however, that believed in the present salvation were received as if from the granary of the Lord's preparation, but the rest, like dung and straw, were left to be destroyed and burned, since either their unbelief or disobedience had already been judged. Who can ponder these things with sufficient wonder; who can proclaim them with befitting praise?

The third day after they had entered the City, the barbarians departed of their own accord. They had, it is true, burned a certain number of buildings, but even this fire was not so great as that which had been caused by accident in the seven hundredth year of Rome. Indeed, if I review the conflagration produced during the spectacles of Nero, her own emperor, this later fire, brought on by the anger of the conqueror, will surely bear no comparison with the former, which was kindled by the wantonness of the prince. Nor do I need

in a comparison of this sort to mention the Gauls, who, after
burning and sacking the City, camped upon her ashes for
almost an entire year. Moreover, to remove all doubt that the
enemy were permitted to act in this manner in order to chastise
the proud, wanton, and blasphemous City, it may be pointed
out that her most magnificent sites, which the Goths were
unable to set on fire, were destroyed at this time by lightning.

40.   IT WAS in the one thousand one hundred and sixty-fourth
year of the City that Alaric stormed Rome. Although the
memory of the event is still fresh, anyone who saw the numbers of the Romans themselves and listened to their talk would
think that "nothing had happened," as they themselves admit,
unless perhaps he were to notice some charred ruins still remaining. When the City was stormed, Placidia, the daughter
of the princely Theodosius and sister of the emperors Arcadius and Honorius, was captured and taken to wife by Alaric's
kinsman, as if she had been a hostage given by Rome as a
special pledge, according to divine decree; thus, through her
alliance with the powerful barbarian king, Placidia did much
to benefit the state.

Meanwhile, two years before the taking of Rome, the nations that had been stirred up by Stilicho, as I have said, that
is, the Alans, Suebi, Vandals as well as many others with them,
overwhelmed the Franks, crossed the Rhine, invaded Gaul, and
advanced in their onward rush as far as the Pyrenees. Checked
for the time being by this barrier, they poured back over
the neighboring provinces. While they were roaming wildly
through Gaul, Gratian, a townsman of Britain, was set up in
that island as a usurper. He was later slain and in his place
Constantine, a man from the lowest ranks of the soldiery, was
chosen simply from confidence inspired by his name and without any other qualifications to recommend him. As soon as he
had seized the imperial dignity,[123] he crossed over into Gaul
where, repeatedly tricked by the deceptive alliances of the
barbarians, he did much harm to the state. He sent magis-

[123] Constantine III, from 407 to September 411.

trates into Spain where they were obediently received by the provinces. Thereupon two brothers named Didymus and Verinianus, who were young, noble, and wealthy, undertook not only to seize the power of the usurper, but to protect themselves and their country for the lawful emperor against both the usurper and the barbarians. The order of events made this clear; for every usurper swiftly matures his plans for power before he secretly seizes and publicly establishes it. Success lies in being seen with the diadem and the purple before being found out. These men, on the contrary, spent a long time merely in gathering the slaves from their own estates and in supporting them out of their private incomes. Taking no pains to conceal their purpose, they proceeded to the passes of the Pyrenees without alarming anyone.

To oppose them, Constantine sent into Spain his son Constans, who, shameful to say, had been transformed from a monk into a Caesar. With him Constantine sent certain barbarians, who had at one time been received as allies and drawn into military service, and who were called *Honoriaci*. They were the cause of the first misfortune that befell Spain. After killing the brothers who were trying to defend the Pyrenean Alps with their private forces, these barbarians received permission to plunder the plains of Pallantia as a reward for their victory. Later, after the removal of the faithful and efficient peasant guard, they were entrusted with the defense of the mountains just mentioned and their passes. These *Honoriaci,* having had a taste of plunder and being allured by its abundance, planned to secure both freedom from punishment for their crimes and a wider scope for their wickedness. Therefore they betrayed their watch over the Pyrenees, left the passes open, and so loosed upon the provinces of Spain all the nations that were wandering through Gaul. They themselves even joined the latter. After engaging for some time in bloody raids and inflicting serious damage upon people and property (for which they themselves are now sorry) they cast lots, divided their holdings, and settled down where they are in possession to this day.

41. THERE would be ample opportunity now for me to speak about these things if it were not that, according to all men, the secret voice of conscience speaks in the soul of each and every man. Spain has been invaded and has suffered slaughter and devastation, but this is nothing new. During the last two years, while the sword of the enemy raged, she endured no harsher treatment from the barbarians than that which she had formerly suffered under the Romans for two hundred years, or than that which she experienced when ravaged for almost twelve years by the Germans in the reign of the emperor Gallienus. Nevertheless, if a man knows himself, his acts, and his own thoughts, and fears the judgments of God, would he not admit that all his sufferings are just and even insignificant? Or, if he does not know himself and does not fear God, how can he maintain that his sufferings are not just and insignificant? In the light of these truths, God's mercy brought about the result with the same compassion with which it had formerly made the prediction, for in accordance with His incessant warning in His Gospel, "When they shall persecute you in one city, flee into another," whoever wished to go out and depart, found mercenaries, helpers, and defenders in the barbarians themselves. At that time they were voluntarily offering this help; and though after killing everybody they could have carried off everything, they demanded only a trifling payment as a fee for their services and for the transportation of loads. Many persons indeed did take this course. But those who did not believe the Gospel of God, being obstinate, doubly obstinate if they had not even listened to it, did not flee the coming wrath and were justly overtaken and overwhelmed by a sudden attack of God's anger. Nevertheless, soon afterward, the barbarians came to detest their swords, betook themselves to the plough, and are affectionately treating the rest of the Romans as comrades and friends, so that now among them there may be found some Romans who, living with the barbarians, prefer freedom with poverty to tribute-paying with anxiety among their own people.

Yet if the barbarians had been let loose upon the Roman

lands simply because the churches of Christ throughout the East and the West were filled with Huns, Suebi, Vandals, and Burgundians, and with believers belonging to various and innumerable races, it would seem that the mercy of God ought to be praised and glorified, in that so many nations would be receiving, even at the cost of our own weakening, a knowledge of the truth which they could never have had but for this opportunity. For how does it harm a Christian who is longing for eternal life to be withdrawn from this world at any time or by any means? On the other hand, what gain is it to a pagan who, though living among Christians, is hardened against faith, if he drag out his days a little longer, since he whose conversion is hopeless is destined at last to die?

Because the judgments of God are inscrutable and we can neither know them all nor explain those we know, let me state briefly that the rebuke of our Judge and God, in whatever form it may take, is justly undergone by those who know and likewise by those who know not.

42. IN THE one thousand one hundred and sixty-fifth year of the City, the emperor Honorius, seeing that nothing could be done against the barbarians when so many usurpers were opposed to him, ordered that the usurpers themselves should first be destroyed. Count Constantius was entrusted with the command of this campaign. The state then finally realized what benefit it derived from having a Roman general at last and what ruinous oppression it had been enduring for years from its subjection to barbarian counts. Count Constantius then advanced with his army into Gaul and at the city of Arles besieged, captured, and slew the emperor Constantine.

To take up at this point the succession of usurpers as briefly as possible, Constans, the son of Constantine, was killed at Vienne by Gerontius, his count, a worthless rather than an upright man, who replaced Constans by a certain Maximus. Gerontius himself, however, was killed by his own soldiers. Maximus, stripped of the purple and abandoned by the troops of Gaul, which were transferred to Africa and then recalled to Italy, is now a needy exile living among the barbarians in Spain. Later the tyranny set up by Jovinus, a man of high rank in Gaul, fell as soon as it had been established. His brother Sebastian elected to die as a usurper, for he was slain as he took office. What shall I say of the unlucky Attalus, for whom it was an honor to be slain among the usurpers, and a blessing to die? Alaric, who made, unmade, remade, and again unmade [124] his emperor, doing all this in almost less time than it takes to tell, laughed at the farce and looked on at the comedy of the imperium. Nor is it strange that this pomp was rightly used to mock the wretched man, when his shadowy consul Tertullus dared to say in the Senate House: "I shall speak to you, conscript fathers, as consul and pontifex, holding one of these offices and hoping for the other." But he put his hope in one who had no hope, and in any case he was surely accursed because he had placed his hope in man. Attalus, merely a figurehead of sovereignty, was taken by the Goths into Spain; and, having departed thence in a ship for some unknown destination, he was captured on the sea, brought to Count Constantius, and displayed before the emperor Honorius. His hand was cut off, but he was allowed to live.

Meanwhile Heraclian, who had been appointed count of Africa while Attalus was exercising his shadowy rule [125] and who had vigorously defended Africa against the magistrates sent by the latter, obtained the consulship. Puffed up with pride at this honor, he married his daughter to Sabinus, his chamberlain, a man of keen intelligence and skillful enterprise, who might have been called wise if only he had devoted his mental powers to quiet pursuits. Heraclian sided with him when Sabinus was suspected of dangerous designs. After withholding the African grain supply for some time contrary to law, Heraclian set sail in person for Rome, accompanied by a huge fleet, the size of which was unheard of, at least in our times. He is said to have had thirty-seven hundred ships, a number that was not possessed, according to the histories, even by Xerxes, the famous king of the Persians or by Alex-

---

[124] "facto, infecto, refecto, ac defecto." [125] Priscus Attalus, 409–15.

ander the Great, or by any other ruler. No sooner had he
disembarked with his troops on his way to the capital than he
became terrified in an encounter with Count Marinus and took
to flight. Seizing a ship, he returned alone to Carthage and
was immediately killed by a band of soldiers. His son-in-law
Sabinus fled to Constantinople, but was brought back some
time afterward and condemned to exile.

This entire series of open usurpers or disobedient generals
was, as I have said, overcome by the exceptional piety and
good fortune of the emperor Honorius and by the great diligence and quickness of Constantius. Their success was deserved because in those days, by the order of Honorius and
the aid of Constantius, peace and unity were restored to the
Catholic Church throughout Africa, and the Body of Christ,
which we ourselves constitute, was healed by the closing of the
schism. The execution of the blessed command was entrusted
to the tribune Marcellinus, a man of exceptional common
sense and diligence and an eager follower of all good studies.
He was, however, put to death at Carthage by Count Marinus,
the latter being incited by jealousy or bribed with gold, it is
uncertain which. Marinus was at once recalled from Africa,
reduced to the status of a private citizen, and turned over to
punishment or to the penitence of his own conscience.

43. IN THE one thousand one hundred and sixty-eighth year
of the City, Count Constantius, who was occupying the city of
Arles in Gaul, drove the Goths from Narbonne, and by his
vigorous actions forced them into Spain, especially by forbidding and completely cutting off the passage of ships and the
importation of foreign merchandise. The Gothic peoples at
that time were under the rule of King Athaulf, who, after the
capture of Rome and the death of Alaric, had succeeded him
on the throne and had taken to wife, as I said, Placidia, the
captive sister of the Emperor. This ruler, an earnest seeker
after peace, as was often claimed and finally shown by his
death, preferred to fight loyally for the emperor Honorius
and to employ the forces of the Goths for the defense of the

Roman state. For I have myself, while at the town of Bethlehem in Palestine, heard a certain man of Narbo, who had
served with distinction under Theodosius and who also was a
pious, sensible, and serious person, tell the most blessed priest
Jerome that he himself had been a very intimate friend of
Athaulf at Narbo, and that he had often heard what the
latter, when in good spirits, health, and temper, was accustomed to answer in reply to questions. It seems that at first
he ardently desired to blot out the Roman name and to make
all the Roman territory a Gothic empire in fact as well as in
name, so that, to use the popular expressions, *Gothia* should
take the place of *Romania,* and he, Athaulf, should become all
that Caesar Augustus once had been. Having discovered from
long experience that the Goths, because of their unbridled
barbarism, were utterly incapable of obeying laws, and yet
believing that the state ought not to be deprived of laws without which a state is not a state, he chose to seek for himself at
least the glory of restoring and increasing the renown of the
Roman name by the power of the Goths, wishing to be looked
upon by posterity as the restorer of the Roman Empire, since
he could not be its transformer. On this account he strove to
refrain from war and to promote peace. He was helped especially by his wife, Placidia, who was a woman of the keenest
intelligence and of exceptional piety; by her persuasion and
advice he was guided in all measures leading to good government. While he was thus eagerly occupied in seeking and
offering peace, he was slain at the city of Barcelona in Spain by
the treachery, it is said, of his own men.

After him Segeric was proclaimed king by the Goths, and,
although he likewise was inclined towards peace by the will of
God, he too was nevertheless killed by his own men.

Thereupon Wallia succeeded to the kingdom, having been
chosen by the Goths to break the peace, but appointed by God
to establish it. He was especially terrified by God's judgment,
because a large band of Goths, provided with arms and ships,
had tried to cross into Africa a year before but had been
caught in a storm within twelve miles of the Strait of Gades

and had perished miserably. He also remembered that disaster suffered under Alaric when the Goths had attempted to
cross into Sicily but were shipwrecked and drowned within
sight of their comrades. These fears caused him to conclude
a very favorable peace with the emperor Honorius giving
hostages of the highest rank; he restored Placidia, whom he
had treated with decency and respect, to her imperial brother.
To insure the security of Rome he risked his own life by taking over the warfare against the other tribes that had settled
in Spain and subduing them for the Romans. However, the
other kings, those of the Alans, the Vandals, and the Suebi,
had made a bargain with us on the same terms, sending this
message to the emperor Honorius: "Do you be at peace with
us all and receive hostages of all; we struggle with one another, we perish to our own loss, but we conquer for you, indeed with permanent gain to your state, if we should both
perish." Who would believe these things if they were not
proven by the facts? Thus it is that we are informed by frequent and trustworthy messages that warfare among the barbarian nations is now being carried on daily in Spain and that
much blood is being shed on both sides; especially is it reported
that Wallia, the king of the Goths, is intent upon bringing
about peace. In view of these things I am ready to allow
Christian times to be blamed as much as you please, if you
can only point to any equally fortunate period from the foundation of the world to the present day. My description, I
think, has shown not more by words than by my guiding finger,
that countless wars have been stilled, many usurpers destroyed,
and the most savage tribes checked, confined, incorporated, or
annihilated with little bloodshed, no real struggle, and almost
without loss. It remains for our detractors to repent of their
endeavors, to blush on seeing the truth, and to believe, to fear,
to love, and to follow the one true God, Who can do all things
and all of Whose acts (even those that they have thought
evil) they have found to be good.

I have set forth with the help of Christ and according to
your bidding, most blessed father Augustine, the passions and

the punishments of sinful men, the tribulations of the world, and the judgments of God, from the Creation to the present day, a period of five thousand six hundred and eighteen years, as briefly and as simply as I could, but separating Christian times from the former confusion of unbelief because of the more present grace of Christ. Thus I now enjoy the sure reward of my obedience, the only one that I have a right to enjoy; for the quality of my little books, you who asked for this record will be responsible. If you publish them, they must be regarded favorably by you; if you destroy them, they must be regarded unfavorably.

BIBLIOGRAPHY

Amann, E., "Orose," in Dictionnaire de théologie catholique (Paris, 1931), Vol. XI.

Angus, S., Sources of the first ten Books of Augustine's De civitate Dei (Princeton, 1906).

Bardenhewer, O., Geschichte der altkirchlichen Literatur (Freiburg im Breisgau, 1913-24), 4 vols.

Barnes, H. E., "History, Its Rise and Development," in Encyclopaedia Americana (New York, 1919), XIV, 205-64.

Beck, G. F. H., Dissertatio de Orosii historici fontibus et auctoritate (Gotha, 1834).

Boissier, G., La Fin du paganisme (septième edition: Paris, 1913).

Bosworth, J., King Alfred's Anglo-Saxon Version of the Compendious History of the World by Orosius (London, 1859).

Büdinger, M., "Ueber Darstellungen der allgemeinen Geschichte, insbesondere des Mittelalters," in Historische Zeitschrift (Munich, 1862), VII, 108-32.

Bury, J. B., History of the Later Roman Empire (London, 1923), 2 vols.

Cavallera, F., "Saint Jérôme; sa vie et son œuvre," in Spicilegium sacrum Lovaniense, études et documents (Paris, 1922), fascicle 1.

Cross, S. H., "Notes on King Alfred's North: Osti Este," in Speculum (1931), VI, 296-99.

Dalmasses y Roz, P. J. de, Dissertacion historica por la patria de Paulo Orosio (Barcelona, 1702).

Davids, J. A., De Orosio et Sancto Augustino Priscillianistarum adversariis, commentatio historica et philologica (Rotterdam, 1930).

Dill, S., Roman Society in the Last Century of the Western Empire (London, 1899).

Ebert, A., Allgemeine Geschichte der Literatur des Mittelalters (Leipzig, 1889), Vol. I, Pt. 2, pp. 337-44.

Engelmann, W., Bibliotheca scriptorum classicorum, scriptores Latini (Leipzig, 1882), II, 441-42.

Figgis, J. N., The Political Aspects of S. Augustine's "City of God" (London, 1921).

Gamble, W. T., "Orosius," in Church Historians (Foreword and Index by P. Guilday: New York, 1926), pp. 30-70.

Gams, P. B., Die Kirchengeschichte von Spanien (Regensburg, 1864), Vol. II, Pt. 1, pp. 398-411.

Goldbacher, A., in *Zeitschrift für die oesterreichischen Gymnasien* (1883) XXIV, 104. (Unedited letter of Orosius to Augustine.)

Humphrey, E. F., Politics and Religion in the Days of Augustine (New York, 1912).

Kirsch, J. P., "Orosius," in Catholic Encyclopaedia (New York, 1911), Vol. XI.

Klotz, A., Beiträge zur Analyse des geographischen Kapitels im Geschichtswerk des Orosius. C. Rzach Mélanges. (Reichenberg, 1930.)

Klussmann, R., Bibliotheca scriptorum classicorum et Graecorum et Latinorum, scriptores Latini (Leipzig, 1913), Vol. II, Pt. 2. (Literature appearing from 1878 to 1896.)

Köhler, Ulrich, "Zu Orosius," in *Philologus*, XVII, Jahr 9 (1861), pp. 552-55.

Krüger, G., "Orosius," in Geschichte der römischen Litteratur (ed. M. Schanz: Munich, 1920), Vol. VIII, Pt. 4, Sec. 2, pp. 483-91.

Labriolle, P., History and Literature of Christianity from Tertullian to Boethius (New York, 1925).

Laistner, M. L. W., Thought and Letters in Western Europe, A. D. 500-900 (New York, 1931).

Lot, F., The End of the Ancient World and the Beginnings of the Middle Ages (English translation: New York, 1931).

Malone, Kemp, "King Alfred's North: a Study in Medieval Geography," in *Speculum,* (1930), V, 139-67.
"On King Alfred's Geographical Treatise," in *Speculum* (1933), VIII, 67-78.

Manutius, M., Geschichte der lateinischen Literatur des Mittelalters (second edition: Munich, 1914).

Marouzeau, J., L'Année philologique (Paris, 1927-35). References to studies on special aspects of Orosius's writings.

Mejean, E., Paul Orose et son apologetique contre les paiens (Strassburg, 1862).

Migne, J. P., Patrologiae cursus completus, Series Latina. Text with notes of Havercampus and Bivarius (Paris, 1846), XXXI, pref. 635, 663-1174.

Miller, K., Die ältesten Weltkarten. Mappaemundi VI, rekonstruierte Karten (Stuttgart, 1898).

Moller, D. G., Dissertatio de Paulo Orosio (Altorfii, 1689).

Mörner, T., De Orosii vitae eiusque historiarum libris septem adversus paganos (Berlin, 1844).

Paucker, C., "Die Latinität des Orosius" in Vorarbeiten zur lateinischen Sprachgeschichte, Kleine Studien, III (Berlin, 1883).

Petsch, K., "Zu Orosius" in *Neue Jahrbuch,* Philo-pedag. (1892), CXLV, 219-24.

Pichon, R., Histoire de la litterature latine (Paris, 1903).

Potthast, A., Wegweiser durch die Geschichtswerke des europäischen Mittelalters bis 1500 (Berlin, 1896), 2 vols.

Ritter, M., "Studien über die Entwicklung der Geschichtswissenschaft: die christlich-mittelalterliche Geschichtschreibung" in *Historische Zeitschrift* (Berlin, 1911), CVII, 237-305.

Salvian, On the Government of God (translated by E. M. Sanford: New York, 1930).

Sauvage, H., De Orosio (Paris 1874).

Schilling, H., König Aelfred's angelsächsische Bearbeitung der Weltchronik des Orosius (Halle, 1886).

Shotwell, J. T., Introduction to the History of History (New York, 1922).

Smith, W., and Wace, H., Dictionary of Christian Biography (London, 1887), IV, 157-59.

Svennung, J., Orosiana: syntaktische, semasiologische, und kritische Studien zu Orosius. Inauguraldissertation Uppsala Universitets Årsskrift 1922. Filosofi Sprakvetenskap och Historika Vetenskaper, Vol. V, (Uppsala, 1922).

Teuffel, W. S., Geschichte der römischen Literatur (5th edition, Leipzig, 1890), pp. 1165, 1168.

Wattenbach, W., Deutschlands Geschichtsquellen im Mittelalter (6th edition, Berlin, 1893), I, 80.

Wetzer, H. J., and Welte, B., Kirchenlexikon (Freiburg im Breisgau, 1895), Vol. IX.

Zangemeister, C., "Die Chorographie des Orosius," in Commentationes philologae in honorem Theod. Mommseni (Berlin, 1877).

    Die Periochae des Livius (Carlsruhe, 1882).

    Pauli Orosii historiarum adversum paganos libri VII; accedit euisdem, Liber apologeticus (Vienna, 1882). This is Volume V of Corpus scriptorum ecclesiasticorum Latinorum.

    Pauli Orosii historiarum adversum paganos libri VII (Bibliotheca Teubneriana: Leipzig, 1889).

INDEX

On account of the length of the *Seven Books against the Pagans*, the index is purposely confined to names and events. Zangemeister's edition, published in 1882, contains complete analytical indices.

RECORDS OF CIVILIZATION

SOURCES AND STUDIES

Edited under the auspices of the

DEPARTMENT OF HISTORY, COLUMBIA UNIVERSITY

FORTHCOMING VOLUMES

COLUMBIA UNIVERSITY PRESS
COLUMBIA UNIVERSITY
NEW YORK

Due Due